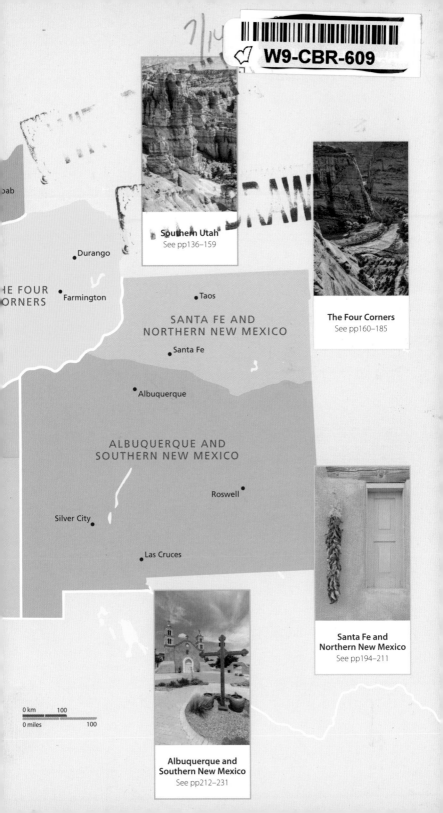

W9-CBR-609

Southern Utah
See pp136–159

The Four Corners
See pp160–185

Durango

THE FOUR
CORNERS

Farmington

• Taos

SANTA FE AND
NORTHERN NEW MEXICO

• Santa Fe

• Albuquerque

ALBUQUERQUE AND
SOUTHERN NEW MEXICO

Roswell •

Silver City •

• Las Cruces

**Santa Fe and
Northern New Mexico**
See pp194–211

0 km   100

0 miles   100

**Albuquerque and
Southern New Mexico**
See pp212–231

ab

EYEWITNESS TRAVEL

SOUTHWEST USA & LAS VEGAS

EYEWITNESS TRAVEL

SOUTHWEST USA & LAS VEGAS

LONDON, NEW YORK,
MELBOURNE, MUNICH AND DELHI
www.dk.com

Produced by Duncan Baird Publishers, London, England
Managing Editors Michelle de Larrabeiti, Rebecca Miles
Managing Art Editor Vanessa Sayers
Editors Liz Atherton, Georgina Harris, Judith Ledger
Designer Dawn Davies-Cook
Design and Editorial Assistance Kelly Cody, Jessica Hughes
Visualizer Gary Cross
Picture Research Ellen Root
DTP Designer Sarah Williams

Contributors Randa Bishop, Donna Dailey, Paul Franklin, Michelle de Larrabeiti, Philip Lee

Photographers Demetrio Carrasco, Alan Keohane, Francesca Yorke

Illustrators Gary Cross, Eugene Fleurey, Claire Littlejohn, Chris Orr & Associates, Mel Pickering,
Robbie Polley, John Woodcock

Printed and bound in China by L. Rex Printing Co. Ltd
First American Edition, 2001
14 15 16 17 10 9 8 7 6 5 4 3 2 1
Published in the United States by DK Publishing, 345 Hudson Street,
New York, New York 10014

Reprinted with revisions 2002, 2003, 2004, 2006, 2008, 2010, 2012, 2014

ISSN 1542-1554

ISBN 978 1 46541 194 5

Floors are referred to throughout in accordance with American usage; ie the "first floor"
is at ground level.

MIX
Paper from
responsible sources
FSC
www.fsc.org   FSC™ C018179

The information in this DK Eyewitness Travel Guide is checked regularly.
Every effort has been made to ensure that this book is as up-to-date as possible at
the time of going to press. Some details, however, such as telephone numbers,
opening hours, prices, gallery hanging arrangements and travel information are
liable to change. The publishers cannot accept responsibility for any consequences
arising from the use of this book, nor for any material on third party websites, and
cannot guarantee that any website address in this book will be a suitable source of
travel information. We value the views and suggestions of our readers very highly.
Please write to: Publisher, DK Eyewitness Travel Guides, Dorling Kindersley,
80 Strand, London WC2R 0RL, UK, or email travelguides@dk.com

Front cover main image: Wind-sculpted Navajo Sandstone at Vermilion Cliffs National
Monument in the Colorado Plateau, Arizona

◀ The Colorado River at Horeshoe Bend, near Page in Northern Arizona

Contents

Introducing the Southwest

View over Grand Canyon's North Rim in
northern Arizona

Arizona

Flute players petroglyph from Walnut
Canyon, Arizona

Mesa Arch overlooking Canyonlands National Park in southern Utah

Half-size replica of the Eiffel Tower at Paris Hotel, Las Vegas

Hispanic pottery

Visitors enjoying a trail ride at a dude ranch in southern Arizona

San Xavier del Bac Mission in Tucson, southern Arizona *(see pp92–3)*

HOW TO USE THIS GUIDE

This travel guide helps you to get the most from your visit to the Southwest US. *Introducing the Southwest* maps the region, and sets it in its historical and cultural context. The region includes the two states of New Mexico and Arizona, the city of Las Vegas, and sizeable chunks of Colorado and Utah. Each chapter describes important sights, using maps, photographs, and illustrations. Recommended restaurants and hotels are listed in *Travelers' Needs*, as is advice on accommodations and food. The *Survival Guide* has tips on such issues as transportation and tipping.

The Southwest Region by Region

The Southwest has been divided into five regions, each of which has its own chapter. Two of these regions are further divided into areas. All major towns and attractions have been numbered on an Area Map at the start of each chapter.

A locator map shows where you are in relation to the rest of the region.

Sights at a Glance lists the chapter's sights by category: Historic Towns and Cities, Areas of Natural Beauty, etc.

2 Area Map
An overview of the landscape and history is followed by a map that numbers and locates all sights.

1 Regional Map
This gives an illustrated overview of the whole region, detailing the main places of interest. It shows the road and rail network and also provides useful hints on getting around the area both by car and by public transportation.

Each area of the Southwest can be identified by its color coding.

3 Detailed Information
All the important towns, important buildings in towns and cities, and other places to visit are described individually. They are listed in order, following the numbering on the Area Map. A map reference refers the reader to the road map inside the back cover.

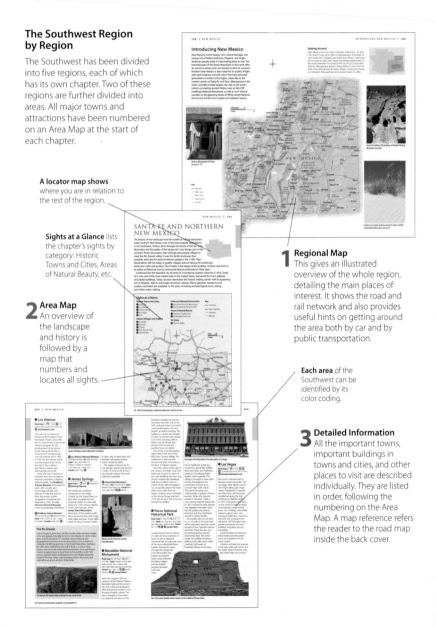

Las Vegas

This unique city has its own chapter, which is introduced by a historical feature. The main sights are numbered and plotted on the *City Map*, as are points of interest in the Greater Las Vegas area. The information for all the sights is easy to locate within the chapter as it follows the numerical order on the map. The city has its own *Practical Information* section, which offers useful advice on shopping, entertainment, and gambling.

1 Introduction
The landscape, history, and character of Las Vegas are described here, showing how the city was developed and what it offers the visitor today.

2 City Map
For easy reference, sights are numbered and located on a map.

3 Street-by-Street Map
This provides a bird's-eye view of the heart of a sightseeing area.

Stars indicate the sights that no visitor should miss.

A suggested route for a walk is shown in red.

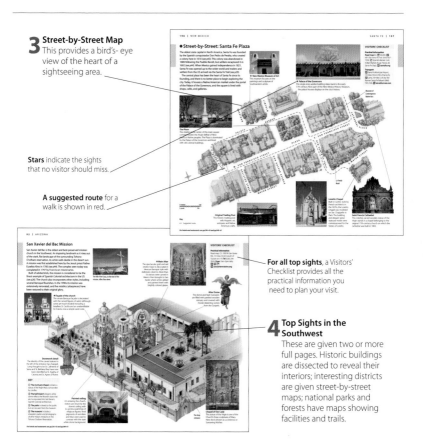

For all top sights, a Visitors' Checklist provides all the practical information you need to plan your visit.

4 Top Sights in the Southwest
These are given two or more full pages. Historic buildings are dissected to reveal their interiors; interesting districts are given street-by-street maps; national parks and forests have maps showing facilities and trails.

INTRODUCING
THE
SOUTHWEST

DISCOVERING THE SOUTHWEST

The following itineraries have been designed to include as many highlights of the American Southwest as possible. All, apart from the two-day tour of Las Vegas, are road trips involving plenty of driving. The first week-long tour sets off from Albuquerque for art-infused Santa Fe and Taos, and then heads west to explore deserts and Indian reservations. The tour of Arizona leads through the cactus-studded hills to the south of Phoenix, before doubling back to reach Sedona and Grand Canyon. The two-week tour follows a huge loop around Grand Canyon, taking in spectacular national parks, the Rocky Mountains, and Monument Valley. Follow your favorite tours, or dip in and out picking those experiences that most inspire.

Las Vegas
The dazzling lights of the casinos and mega-resorts illuminate this 24-hour city.

One Week in Arizona

- Learn about Arizona's past in Phoenix's Heard Museum and visit Frank Lloyd Wright's studio in Scottsdale.

- Head up the Apache Trail into the Superstition Mountains and breathe the rarefied air inside Biosphere 2.

- Hike among the giant cacti in Saguaro National Park.

- Visit the Spanish Colonial mission church, San Xavier del Bac, then dodge a bullet or two in Tombstone.

- Experience the New Age amid the red rocks and flowing streams of Sedona.

- Gaze into the depths of the Grand Canyon from the overlooks along Desert View Drive.

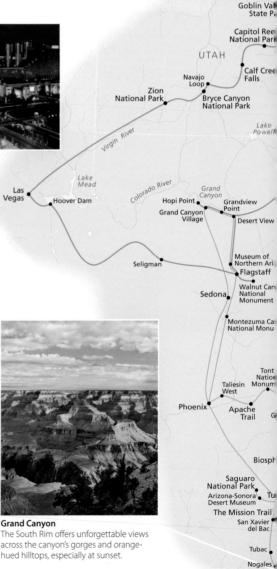

Grand Canyon
The South Rim offers unforgettable views across the canyon's gorges and orange-hued hilltops, especially at sunset.

◀ *The Southwest* (oil on canvas) by Walter Ufer (1876–1936)

Two Weeks in the Southwest

- Taste the high life in Las Vegas, then make a bee-line for the "Beehive State" of Utah.
- Take a riverside stroll in ravishing Zion Canyon, and get lost among the spiked rock formations of Bryce Canyon.
- Hike to the hidden oasis of Calf Creek Falls and wander among the mushroom-shaped hoodoos in Goblin Valley State Park.
- Get adventurous in Moab, then head up to the rocky spans of Arches National Park and the hundred-mile vistas of Canyonlands.
- Thread through the Rockies on the San Juan Skyway, then clamber through the Cliff Palace Ancestral Puebloan cliff dwelling in Mesa Verde.
- Channel your inner cowboy beneath the mighty buttes of Monument Valley.
- Abandon yourself to the abyss at Grand Canyon's South Rim.
- Motor back to Las Vegas on legendary Route 66.

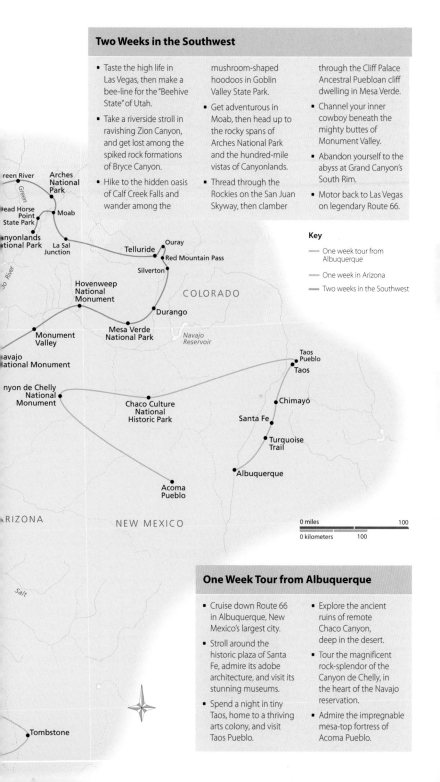

Key

==== One week tour from Albuquerque

==== One week in Arizona

==== Two weeks in the Southwest

Green River

Arches National Park

Dead Horse Point State Park

Moab

Canyonlands National Park

La Sal Junction

Telluride

Ouray

Red Mountain Pass

Silverton

COLORADO

Hovenweep National Monument

Durango

Monument Valley

Mesa Verde National Park

Navajo Reservoir

Navajo National Monument

Canyon de Chelly National Monument

Taos Pueblo

Taos

Chaco Culture National Historic Park

Chimayó

Santa Fe

Turquoise Trail

Albuquerque

Acoma Pueblo

ARIZONA

NEW MEXICO

Salt

Tombstone

0 miles 100
0 kilometers 100

One Week Tour from Albuquerque

- Cruise down Route 66 in Albuquerque, New Mexico's largest city.
- Stroll around the historic plaza of Santa Fe, admire its adobe architecture, and visit its stunning museums.
- Spend a night in tiny Taos, home to a thriving arts colony, and visit Taos Pueblo.
- Explore the ancient ruins of remote Chaco Canyon, deep in the desert.
- Tour the magnificent rock-splendor of the Canyon de Chelly, in the heart of the Navajo reservation.
- Admire the impregnable mesa-top fortress of Acoma Pueblo.

Two Days in Las Vegas

The ultimate 24-hour city, Las Vegas is a neon playground filled with eye-popping architecture and entertainment of all kinds, centering on its unmatched array of vast casino hotels.

- **Arriving** McCarran International Airport is within a mile of the south end of the Strip; taxis and shuttle buses connect with all hotels.

- **Booking ahead** For blockbuster shows (Cirque du Soleil in particular), book months ahead.

Day 1

Morning Start your day exploring the central Strip by visiting the elegant **Bellagio** *(p114)* casino, and the eccentric floral displays in its showpiece Conservatory. Then catch the futuristic **CityCenter** *(p112)* monorail to see the contemporary sculptures in **Aria** *(p113)*, and the stylish **Crystals** *(p112)* shopping mall. Now head north across the Strip to **Paris** *(p114)*, and enjoy a panoramic view from atop the "Eiffel Tower". Eat lunch outdoors beside the Strip, or in one of the city's legendary all-you-can-eat buffets.

Afternoon Spend an hour or two in **Caesars Palace** *(p115)*, admiring its version of Michelangelo's David and browsing beneath the artificial sky of the **Forum Shops** *(p128)*, then move on to the rival **Venetian** *(p118)* and cruise along the Grand Canal in a gondola. Later on, as well as dining in a gourmet restaurant and taking in a **Cirque du Soleil** show *(p130)*, join the after-dark crowds on the Strip sidewalk to see free attractions such as the erupting volcano outside **Mirage** *(p119)* and the dancing fountains of Bellagio.

Day 2

Morning Start by touring the mega-casinos at the southern end of the Strip. Enter the **Luxor** *(p110)* pyramid between the

CityCenter's striking architecture, including Crystals mall and Veer condo towers, Las Vegas

paws of the giant Sphinx, and visit its exhibitions of artifacts from the sunken *Titanic* and "plastinated" human bodies. Then walk through **Excalibur** castle *(p111)* to reach **New York New York** *(p111)*; to see its Manhattan skyline close-up, take a swooping ride on its roller coaster. Now head north to the other end of the Strip, where the **Stratosphere** *(p121)* tower offers amazing views and more thrill rides.

Afternoon Continue to the city's original downtown core, where the **Mob Museum** *(p122)* tells the bloody saga of Las Vegas's crime-ridden history in entertaining detail. Venture into a casino or two along **Fremont Street** *(p122)*, then, once the sun goes down, turn your gaze skywards to watch the amazing sound and light shows on the over-arching canopy. Head back to the Strip for the evening, to

Strolling along the Strip, Las Vegas's main thoroughfare

get a taste of old-style Las Vegas glamor in the long-running show **Jubilee!** *(p130)*, and party into the night in one of the city's nightclubs.

One Week Tour from Albuquerque

- **Airports** Land at and take off from Albuquerque's International Sunport.

- **Transport** The Rail Runner *(p289)* connects Santa Fe and Albuquerque; otherwise renting a car is essential.

- **Booking ahead** Taos Pueblo closes for some ceremonies and for up to 10 weeks in early spring. You must book in advance for a tour to visit Acoma Pueblo.

Day 1: Albuquerque

As well as strolling through Albuquerque's original Hispanic core, centered on **Old Town Plaza** *(pp214–15)*, be sure to visit the city's fine crop of museums including the **Indian Pueblo Cultural Center** *(p218)*.

Day 2: Up the Turquoise Trail to Santa Fe

Head east from the city to follow the time-forgotten **Turquoise Trail** *(pp220–21)* along the eastern flanks of the Sandía Mountains, passing through the quaint former mining towns of Madrid and Cerrillos, then continue north to historic **Santa Fe** *(pp196–203)*, with its superb hotels and restaurants.

For practical information on traveling around the Southwest, see pp286–91

Day 3: Santa Fe

Spend a full day in Santa Fe visiting the **Palace of the Governors** (p198) and **Georgia O'Keeffe Museum** (p198) downtown, and the **Museum of International Folk Art** (p200).

Day 4: Chimayó and Taos

Head into the hills to the pilgrim chapel at **Chimayó** (p207), then continue to picturesque **Taos** (p208), where the twin adobe "houses" at **Taos Pueblo** (p210) date back centuries.

Day 5: Chaco Culture National Historic Park

Head west to **Chaco Culture National Historic Park** (pp178–9) where the vast pre-Columbian settlement held "great houses" such as 650-room Pueblo Bonito. Camp in the park or continue northwest and stay overnight at **Farmington** (p177).

Day 6: Canyon de Chelly National Monument

Continue west over the Arizona border to **Canyon de Chelly** (pp172–5), where ancient ruins nestle into sheer red-rock cliffs, and Navajo shepherds graze their flocks below monolithic Spider Rock.

Day 7: Acoma Pueblo

En route back to Albuquerque, detour south to **Acoma Pueblo** (p221), whose inhabitants defied Coronado's *conquistadores*.

One Week in Arizona

- **Airports** Arrive at and depart from Sky Harbor International Airport in Phoenix.
- **Transport** Renting a car is essential.
- **Booking ahead** Contact Taliesen West beforehand if you plan to take a tour.

Day 1: Phoenix

Visit the **Heard Museum** (pp82–3) in downtown for an introduction to Arizona's Native peoples, then drive into the hills north of Scottsdale to see Frank Lloyd Wright's purpose-built architectural studio, **Taliesin West** (p85).

Day 2: The Apache Trail and Biosphere 2

Drive up the **Apache Trail** (p86), east of Phoenix, into the Superstition Mountains, and explore the ancient cliff dwellings in **Tonto National Monument** (p86). Then go south through the silver-mining town of Globe (p87), and take a tour of the futuristic **Biosphere 2 Center** (p91), en route to Tucson.

Day 3: Tucson and Saguaro National Park

Once you've strolled around Tucson's historic, Hispanic downtown (pp88–9), drive west to hike in the cactus-studded hills of **Saguaro National Park** (p90), and see desert wildlife in the **Arizona-Sonora Desert Museum** (p90).

Day 4: The Mission Trail and Tombstone

Follow the Mission Trail south towards Mexico, stopping to swoon at the Southwest's finest Spanish mission church, **San Xavier del Bac** (pp92–3). Indulge in a little shopping in the arts colony of Tubac (pp94–5), before heading east from the border town of **Nogales** (p95) to catch a staged shootout in the fabled Wild-West town of **Tombstone** (p96).

Day 5: Sedona

Turning your attentions to northern Arizona, head back up I-10, beyond Phoenix, to reach the red-rock paradise (and New-Age rendezvous) of **Sedona** (p77).

The ruins of the five-story Montezuma Castle, a 12th-century cliff dwelling

Day 6: The Grand Canyon and Flagstaff

Set off early for a full day at the South Rim of the **Grand Canyon** (pp62–7). Begin with the views from Grand Canyon Village, then tour the overlooks along Desert View Drive. Once the sun goes down, head for the lively college town of **Flagstaff** (pp70–71).

> **To extend your trip...**
> Take a day to explore the Navajo Nation east, staying overnight at **Monument Valley** (see pp168–9) or **Canyon de Chelly** (pp172–5).

Day 7: Flagstaff to Phoenix

Spend the morning exploring Flagstaff, with a visit to the **Museum of Northern Arizona** (p72). Then drive back to Phoenix, pausing to see the pink-tinged ruins in **Montezuma Castle National Monument** (p76).

Giant saguaros, iconic cacti of the Southwest in the Saguaro National Park

Two Weeks in the Southwest

- **Airports** Fly in and out of McCarran International Airport in Las Vegas.
- **Transport** A rental car is essential.
- **Booking ahead** The in-park lodges in Zion, Bryce Canyon, and Grand Canyon tend to get booked up as much as a year in advance.

The orange and red sandstone spires of Bryce Canyon National Park

Day 1 and 2: Las Vegas
See the city itinerary on p12.

Day 3: Zion National Park
Head northeast from Las Vegas in the morning to reach your lodgings in or near beautiful **Zion Canyon** *(pp158–9)* by lunchtime. Ride the park shuttle buses the full length of the canyon, then follow the short River Walk to see the Virgin River emerge from the mouth of the Narrows.

> **To extend your trip…**
> Spend a day on the **North Rim of the Grand Canyon** *(p67)*, spotting inner-canyon landmarks from Cape Royal Drive.

Day 4: Bryce Canyon National Park
Tunnel your way east out of Zion via the extraordinary **Zion–Mt. Carmel Highway** *(p159)*, then head north to spend the night near the fiery red-rock hoodoos of **Bryce Canyon**

(pp156–7). Hiking the Navajo Loop takes you into the heart of this labyrinth of towering pinnacles, while Sunset Point offers an evening vista of the vast desert ahead.

Day 5: Calf Creek Falls and Capitol Reef National Park
Continue east along Hwy 12, a stunning route through the wilderness of **Grand Staircase–Escalante National Monument** *(p152)*. Hike to the iridescent waters of **Calf Creek Falls** *(p151)*; then, back on the road, cross the knife-edge **Hogsback** *(p151)* to reach Torrey *(see p240)*, the next night's stopover, just west of the forbidding 100-mile (160-km) wall of rock at **Capitol Reef National Park** *(p150)*.

Day 6: Goblin Valley and Arches National Park
Beyond the clay badlands that lie east of Capitol Reef, the bizarre rock formations of little-known **Goblin Valley State Park** *(p147)* resemble fairy-tale monsters. Farther north, visit the museum dedicated to pioneer river-rafter John Wesley Powell in the town of **Green River** *(p147)*. Southeast of there, **Arches National Park** *(pp144–5)* holds the world's largest array of naturally formed stone arches, while nearby **Moab** *(p145)* makes a lively overnight base.

Day 7: Canyonlands National Park
Stay another night in Moab, and visit the Island in the Sky District of **Canyonlands National Park**

(p146), hike the short trail to Mesa Arch, and take in sweeping views over the mighty canyons carved by the Green and Colorado rivers. Stop off on your way back to admire the similarly dramatic viewpoints at **Dead Horse Point State Park** *(p147)*.

> **To extend your trip…**
> Tour the remoter areas of the park – **Horseshoe Canyon** and the **Needles District** *(p146)*; each takes a day to reach and explore.

Day 8: Telluride and the San Juan Skyway
Drive east into Colorado from La Sal Junction, south of Moab, to the Rocky Mountains. After lunch in the rugged-chic resort of **Telluride** *(p183)*, follow the **San Juan Skyway** *(p182)* up amid the snow-crested peaks, to the former mining town of **Ouray** *(p183)*, then cross the 11,000-foot Red Mountain Pass and drop back down to the Wild-West outpost of **Silverton** *(p183)*.

> **To extend your trip…**
> Stay an extra night to ride a steam train through the scenic high-mountain Rockies on the **Durango & Silverton Narrow Gauge Railroad** *(p183)*.

Day 9: Mesa Verde National Park via Durango
Head west from **Durango** *(p183)*, a Victorian frontier town that is now the mountain-bike

Delicate Arch, one of the most spectacular of the 80 arches in Arches National Park, Utah

The ruins of Cliff Palace, huddled beneath an overhang at Mesa Verde National Park

capital of the West, then climb into the forested tablelands above the Montezuma Valley to reach **Mesa Verde National Park** *(pp184–5)*. In cliff-top alcoves here, almost 1,000 years ago, the Ancestral Puebloans constructed dwellings such as Balcony House and the beautiful Cliff Palace.

Day 10: Hovenweep and Monument Valley

Accessed via remote backroads in Utah's southeastern corner, **Hovenweep National Monument** *(p176)* preserves a collection of mysterious masonry towers, perched on the rims of sandy gullies. Southwest from here, and familiar from a thousand movies, **Monument Valley** *(pp168–9)* represents the Wild West at its most majestic; spending a night there may be the highlight of your entire trip.

> **To extend your trip…**
> Head southeast to **Canyon de Chelly National Monument** *(pp172–5)*, where two canyons are lined with stunning Ancestral Puebloan ruins.

Day 11: Navajo National Monument and Grand Canyon South Rim

As you continue west, take a tiny detour to see **Navajo National Monument** *(p170)*,

where the ancient pueblo of Betatakin can be visited on guided hikes. Then press on to the South Rim of the **Grand Canyon** *(p64)*, where you'll enter the national park at **Desert View** *(p67)*. Visit sites along Desert View Drive, including **Tusayan Ruin** *(p65)* and the South Rim's highest overlook, **Grandview Point** *(p67)*, then spend the night in **Grand Canyon Village** *(p66)*.

Day 12: Grand Canyon South Rim

To make the most of a full day on the South Rim, and minimize exposure to the desert sun, set off early to hike the **Bright Angel Trail** *(p67)* down into the canyon; don't try to reach the Colorado River, and turn back well before you're tired. Spend the afternoon touring the

canyon along **Hermit Road** *(p66)*, and try to catch the sunset at **Hopi Point** *(p63)*.

Day 13: Flagstaff

Head southeast to the buzzing pioneer town of **Flagstaff** *(pp70–71)*, and enjoy its many **Route 66** relics. Allow a couple of hours to visit the stimulating **Museum of Northern Arizona** *(p72)*, and venture a few miles east to see the ancient ruins in **Walnut Canyon National Monument** *(p73)*.

Day 14: Las Vegas

Take time on the long route back to Las Vegas to drive the final remaining segment of **Route 66** *(pp54–5)*, stopping in Seligman, and to plumb the depths of the colossal **Hoover Dam** *(p124)*, on the Arizona/ Nevada border.

View from the South Rim of the Colorado River winding through Grand Canyon

Putting the Southwest on the Map

For the purposes of this guide the Southwest includes Arizona, New Mexico, the Four Corners area, which takes in southwestern Colorado and southern Utah, and the city of Las Vegas. The region is contained by borders with Mexico in the south, California in the west, and Texas in the east, and covers around 326,000 sq miles (835,000 sq km). The region is sparsely populated since 60 percent of its population of around 14 million lives in the cities.

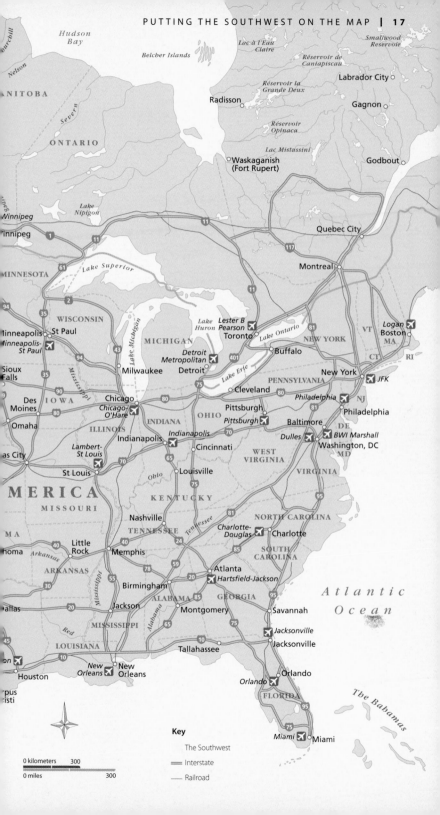

Key

The Southwest

Interstate

Railroad

0 kilometers 300

0 miles 300

A PORTRAIT OF THE SOUTHWEST

Distinguished by its dramatic landscape, the Southwest is a land of twisting canyons, cactus-studded desert, and rugged mountains. For more than 15,000 years, the region was inhabited exclusively by Native Americans, but by the 20th century Anglo-American traditions had mingled with those of the Hispanic and Native populations to create the Southwest's multicultural heritage.

America's Southwest includes the states of Arizona and New Mexico, southwestern Colorado and southern Utah, and the city of Las Vegas, Nevada. Perceptions of this region are influenced by the landscape: the red sandstone mesas of Monument Valley, the tall saguaro cacti in Arizona's Sonoran Desert, the staggering scale of Grand Canyon, and the adobe architecture of New Mexico. At the heart of the region is its defining geological feature – the Colorado Plateau – a rock tableland rising more than 12,000 ft (3,660 m) above sea level and covering a vast area of around 130,000 sq miles (336,700 sq km). The plateau was created by the same geological upheavals that formed the Rocky Mountains. Subsequent erosion by wind, water, and sand molded both hard and soft rock to form the plateau's canyons, mesas, and mountains.

Many of these natural wonders are now protected by national parks, such as the Grand Canyon and Zion. The region's underground attractions are no less beautiful, with the cave formations of Carlsbad Caverns in New Mexico and the Kartchner Caverns in southern Arizona.

Cacti and dried chiles adorn this flower shop in Tucson's historic El Presidio district

◀ Navajo woman spinning wool, Monument Valley

Society

The Southwest is a crossroads of the three great cultures that shaped America: Native American, Hispanic, and Anglo-American. The Spanish language is prominent, and everyday English is peppered with a range of Spanish phrases, reflecting a heritage stretching back to the 16th century: Spanish explorers were in the Southwest in 1540, 80 years before the Pilgrims landed at Plymouth Rock.

A host of Native American languages are also spoken across the Southwest, reflecting the history of the region's native inhabitants. The Hopi and other Pueblo peoples trace their ancestry back to the ancient peoples who built the cliff dwellings at Mesa Verde, Canyon de Chelly, and Chaco Canyon. The Navajo occupy the largest reservation in the US, stretching across the northern ends of both Arizona and New Mexico. The Apache and several other tribes also occupy land here. Today's Native populations have a hand in the government of their own lands and use a variety of ways to supplement their traditional economies – through casinos, tourism, the production of coal, and crafts such as pottery, baskets, and Hopi *kachina* dolls. Some Native festivals and dances are open to visitors, although, for spiritual reasons, some are private affairs.

Hopi *kachina* doll

A trinity of religions is dominant in the Southwest. Native American spiritual beliefs are complex, as each tribe has different practices often tied to ancestors and the land. The Roman Catholicism brought here by the conquering Spanish is the main religion in much of the region, although some Protestant denominations are also prominent. Utah's residents, however, are predominantly Mormon.

Politics

When Arizona and New Mexico gained statehood in 1912, they became part of the democratic republic of the United States of America. Today, they are the nation's fifth- and sixth-largest states. Although Phoenix is the sixth most populated city in the US, the region still remains one of the least populated.

The cities of Phoenix, Tucson, Santa Fe, Albuquerque, and Las Vegas account for

Looking out from Mummy Cave Overlook in Canyon de Chelly's Canyon de Muerto

Mountains rise behind the towering walls of Hoover Dam across the Colorado River bordering Nevada and Arizona

International star performers visit such cities as Phoenix and Las Vegas, which is world-renowned for its dazzling casinos.

One of the region's most famous attributes is the quality of light found in the hills of northern New Mexico. Georgia O'Keeffe's paintings of the local landscape from 1929 onwards helped to make the area around Santa Fe a mecca for all kinds of artists. Today, the city has the second-largest art trade in the US. Native artisans also produce fine artifacts: the pottery of Maria Martínez (1881–1980) of San Idelfonso Pueblo is highly regarded, as are the paintings of Navajo R. C. Gorman (1931–2005), and the work of Pueblo potter Nancy Youngblood Lugo. The Southwest is as much a state of mind as it is a geographical region. The attractions of the landscape and a romantic sense of the past combine to conjure up the idealized legends of the "Wild West." For many visitors, the Southwest offers the opportunity to indulge that bit of cowboy in their souls.

around 60 percent of the Southwest's population. Such intense urbanization has put pressure on the region's resources, particularly water. In the 1930s, dam-building projects were initiated in the western states, starting with the Hoover Dam. By the 1960s, however, it was clear that in order to generate electricity, irrigate farms, and supply cities, more dams were needed. The controversial Glen Canyon Dam, opened in 1963, flooded a vast area of natural beauty, as well as Native ruins and sacred sites. Today, many local tribes have asserted ownership of the water on their lands.

Culture and the Arts

Vast wilderness and a warm climate make outdoor leisure popular in the Southwest. There are miles of hiking trails, rivers for white-water rafting, lakes for watersports, ski resorts, and some of the US's finest golf courses. One of the best ways to experience the landscape is on a trail ride, while armchair cowboys can attend that great Southwestern event – the rodeo.

Phoenix, Tucson, Santa Fe, and Albuquerque are home to symphony orchestras, theater, opera, and dance companies. A flourishing Hispanic music scene and Native American traditional dances meet in the fusion sound of Carlos R. Nakai, a Navajo flautist who performs classical music and jazz.

Hikers on the Bright Angel Trail in Grand Canyon

Landscapes of the Southwest

The colorful, beautiful, and varied landscape of the Southwest has been shaped by volcanic eruption, uplift, and wind and water erosion. For much of the Paleozoic Era (between about 570 to 225 million years ago) the region was mostly covered by a vast inland sea that deposited over 10,000 ft (3,048 m) of sediment, which eventually hardened into rock. Following the formation of the Rocky Mountains, some 80 million years ago, rivers and rainfall eroded the rock layers and formed the deep canyons and arches that distinguish the landscape of the Southwest.

Coral Pink Sand Dunes State Park's shimmering pink sand dunes cover more than 50 percent of this 3,700-acre (1,497-ha) park *(see p153)*.

The central geological feature of the region is the Colorado Plateau, which covers some 130,000 sq miles (336,700 sq km). The plateau is cut through by many canyons, including Grand Canyon *(see pp62–7)*.

The butte formations of Monument Valley *(see pp168–9)* are the result of erosion and their tops mark the level of an ancient plain.

The mountains of the Southwest are part of the Rockies and were formed during volcanic activity and continental plate movement some 65 million years ago. Snow-covered peaks, forests of pine and juniper, spruce and fir, streams and small lakes fed by snow melt, as well as alpine meadows are all found in this area.

Geographical Regions

Despite the great variations in the landscape, more than 70 percent of the land is classified as desert, with four distinct areas: the Great Basin, Chihuahuan, Sonoran, and Mojave deserts *(see pp24–5)*. Each area supports flora and fauna uniquely adapted to their harsh environment.

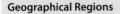

Colorado Plateau

Foothills of the Rocky Mountains

Grasslands

Key

☐ Great Basin Desert

☐ Chihuahuan Desert

☐ Sonoran Desert

☐ Mojave Desert

Large areas of grassland once covered the broad river basins of New Mexico and Arizona. However, little of this landscape remains as it was largely turned to desert through overgrazing by Anglo-American ranchers in the 1880s.

Canyons such as this one at Zion National Park *(see pp158–9)* started life when a stream began to cut a relentless path into the rock. As the cut grew deeper, erosion by wind, rain, and ice began widening it, and the stream carried away the debris.

The orange sand of Monument Valley's desert floor is dotted with sagebrush.

Mesas, Buttes, and Spires

Like canyons, mesas come in many sizes. Some very large ones measure over 100 miles (161 km) across and are often the result of land being forced up by geological forces. Other mesas, buttes, and spires are hard-rock remains left behind as a large plain cracked, and then eroded away.

The Colorado Plateau is crossed by river-forged canyons. Elevations here range from 2,000 ft (600 m) above sea level to around 13,000 ft (3,900 m). Dramatic variations in the landscape include desert, verdant river valleys, thickly forested peaks, and eroded bizarre sandstone formations.

Desert Flora and Fauna

Despite the fact that around 70 percent of the Southwest region is occupied by desert, it is not an arid, lifeless wasteland. There are four distinct deserts: the Sonoran, the Chihuahuan, the Great Basin, and the Mojave. The Sonoran Desert has one of the richest arrays of flora and fauna in the country. The Chihuahuan Desert supports hardy yuccas and agaves, and its hills and plains are covered with a dry, wheat-colored grass. The Great Basin is a cooler desert and home to a variety of grasses and desert animals. Spring rains and run-off from the mountains can transform even the driest deserts. At such times some 250 species of flower bloom in the Mojave.

Bighorn sheep are shy, elusive creatures and are not easily spotted. Now a protected species, they are being gradually reintroduced throughout the desert areas.

   All living things in these southwestern desert regions adapt remarkably well to their harsh environment; the plants in particular are capable of storing water when it is available and using it sparingly during dry periods.

The Sonoran
Found in southern Arizona, the Sonoran's summer "monsoons" and winter storms make it the greenest of the deserts. It is famous for the tall saguaro cactus *(see p90)*, some of which attain heights of 50 ft (15 m) and provide a home for such desert animals as the Gila woodpecker and the elf owl.

The Chihuahuan
Mainly found in Mexico, the Chihuahuan also reaches north to Albuquerque, New Mexico, and into parts of southeastern Arizona. Cacti, agaves, and yuccas, and lizards, rattlesnakes, and coyotes survive in conditions that include snowfall in winter and high temperatures and thunderstorms in summer.

The desert tortoise can live for more than 50 years. It is now a protected species and is increasingly difficult to spot.

The javelina is a strange piglike mammal that wanders the Chihuahuan and Sonoran deserts in small packs.

Prickly pear cacti flower in spring and are among the largest of the many types of cacti that flourish in the Sonoran Desert.

Yucca plants have been gathered for centuries and have many uses: their fruit can be eaten, and the roots make shampoo.

Dangers in the Desert

The danger of poisonous desert creatures has often been exaggerated. Although some desert creatures do, on rare occasions, bite or sting people, the bites are seldom fatal unless the victims are small children or have serious health problems. To avoid being hurt, never reach into dark spaces or up onto overhead ledges where you can't see. Watch where you place your feet, and shake out clothes and shoes before putting them on. Never harass or handle a poisonous creature. If you are bitten, stay calm and seek medical help immediately.

The Gila monster is the only venomous lizard in the US. It is a slow-moving but rarely seen inhabitant of the desert regions, and will only bite if it feels threatened.

The desert scorpion is golden in color. Its bite is venomous so anyone who has been bitten should go to a hospital for an antidote.

The Great Basin

With its canyons, cliffs, mesas, and buttes, the landscape of the Great Basin Desert appears most characteristic of the region. It extends from the far northwest corner of Arizona into eastern Utah and Oregon, and its scattering of cacti, sage, and mesquite is home to the bighorn sheep and various types of rattlesnake.

The Mojave

This vast desert extends into central and northern Arizona. The Mojave is dry for most of the year, but a small amount of winter rain results in a display of wildflowers in spring. Other flora and fauna found here include creosote bush, cacti, yucca, jackrabbits, desert tortoises, and bighorn sheep.

Sagebrush is a pervasive subshrub that covers vast areas of the cooler Great Basin Desert. It smells of sage.

The blacktailed jackrabbit is born with a full coat of muted fur to camouflage it from predators such as the coyote.

Golden eagles can be seen high in the sky in daytime as they hunt for prey across the Great Basin Desert.

The Joshua tree was named by Mormons who pictured the upraised arms of Joshua in its branches.

Architecture of the Southwest

The history of architecture in the Southwest reaches back to the Ancestral Puebloan or Anasazi builders of the pueblos of Chaco Canyon *(see pp178–9)*, demonstrating skilled craftsmanship. Across the region, historic architecture can be seen in many towns and cities, with the adobes of their old-town districts arranged around a central plaza. But there are also other architectural styles, from the Spanish Colonial of the 18th century to those of the 19th and early 20th century. Wooden storefronts, Victorian mansions, and miners' cottages all lend a rustic charm to many mountain towns, and one of the 20th century's most famous architects, Frank Lloyd Wright, set up an architectural school in Scottsdale *(see p85)*.

San Felipe de Neri Church, Albuquerque Old Town

Traditional Adobe

Adobe ovens *(hornos)* at El Rancho de las Golondrinas

The traditional building material of the southwestern desert is adobe, a mixture of mud or clay and sand, with straw or grass as a binder. This is formed into bricks, which harden in the sun, then built into walls, cemented with a similar material, and plastered over with more mud. Adobe deteriorates quickly and must be replastered every few years. Modern adobe-style buildings are often made of cement and covered with lime cement stucco painted to look like adobe. Original dwellings had dirt floors and wooden beams *(vigas)* as ceiling supports. Roofs were flat, with pipes *(canales)* for water run-off.

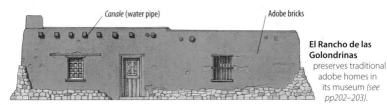

Canale (water pipe) Adobe bricks

El Rancho de las Golondrinas preserves traditional adobe homes in its museum *(see pp202–203)*.

Spanish Colonial

In the 17th and 18th centuries, Spanish Colonial missions combined the Baroque style of Mexican and European religious architecture with native design, using local materials and craftsmen. This style underwent a resurgence in the 20th century as Spanish Colonial Revival, from 1915 to the 1930s, being incorporated into private homes and public buildings. Red-tiled roofs, ornamental terra-cotta, and stone or iron grille work were combined with white stucco walls. A fine example is Tucson's Pima County Courthouse *(see p88)*, with its dome adorned with colored tiles.

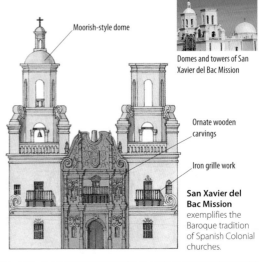

Moorish-style dome

Domes and towers of San Xavier del Bac Mission

Ornate wooden carvings

Iron grille work

San Xavier del Bac Mission exemplifies the Baroque tradition of Spanish Colonial churches.

Mission Revival

Similar in spirit to Spanish Colonial trends, the early 20th-century Mission Revival style is characterized by stucco walls made of white lime cement, often with graceful arches, flat roofs, and courtyards, but with less ornamentation. A fine example of a Mission Revival-style bungalow is the J. Knox Corbett House in Tucson's Historic District (see p88). Built of brick but plastered over in white to simulate adobe, it has a red-tile roof and a big screen porch at the back.

Façade of the J. Knox Corbett House

Red-tiled roof

White plaster

J. Knox Corbett House in Tuscon was designed in the popular Mission Revival style by the Chicago architect David Holmes in 1906.

Pueblo Revival

Santa Fe Museum of Fine Arts

Pueblo Revival was another southwestern style that became particularly fashionable in the first three decades of the 20th century. It featured adobe or simulated adobe walls, with projecting *vigas*, and flat roofs with *canales*. The second and third stories were usually set back to resemble multistory pueblo dwellings, such as Taos Pueblo (see p210), hence the name. Features include rounded parapets, framed portal windows, and wood columns. This style has been used frequently in public buildings; the Museum of Fine Arts in Santa Fe (see p198) is an outstanding example.

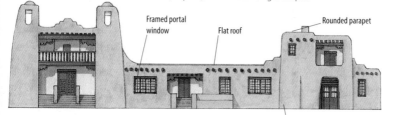

Framed portal window

Flat roof

Rounded parapet

Adobe wall

The Museum of Fine Arts in Santa Fe was built in 1917 and was the first building in Pueblo Revival style in the city. A central courtyard providing shade from the sun is one of its features.

Contemporary Architecture

Two of America's most prominent architects, Frank Lloyd Wright (1867–1959) and Paolo Soleri (1919–2013), practiced in the Southwest. Wright's "organic architecture" advocated the use of local materials and the importance of the setting. His architectural complex at Taliesin West (see p85) included a school, offices, and his home. It was built from desert stones and sand, and the expansive proportions reflect the Arizona desert. In the 1940s, Italian Soleri studied at Taliesin. In 1956 he established the Cosanti Foundation (see p85) devoted to "arcology," a synthesis of architecture and ecology that minimizes the waste of energy endemic in modern towns.

Interior of Taliesin West, designed by Frank Lloyd Wright

Colonizers of the Southwest

The remote wilderness areas of the Southwest were among the last regions of the US to be settled by Anglo-Americans, in the mid- to late 19th century. The Spanish were the first Europeans to reach this area in the 1500s, led by soldier and explorer Francisco Vasquez de Coronado (1510–54), and Santa Fe was established in 1610. In 1752, the Spanish established the first European settlement in what is now Arizona at Tubac. Kit Carson and fellow fur trappers explored east–west routes in the mid-19th century, while the Mormons founded Salt Lake City in the 1840s. In the later 19th century, explorers and prospectors, most notably US national hero John Wesley Powell, traveled across the region.

Inscription Rock rises over a natural spring in New Mexico *(see p221)*, and was a resting place for travelers over centuries. The rock features Zuni petroglyphs and graffiti, including Oñate's carved name.

The Butterfield Stage route was established in 1858. Sanctioned by Congress to provide a twice-weekly service for isolated Westerners, it aided the establishing of settlements in remote areas.

Routes of The Colonizers

The promise of gold brought the first Spanish travelers to the Southwest in the 1500s. Various groups of colonizers and traders soon followed, forging many new routes across this rugged region.

Key

- ▬ Coronado Trail
- ▬ Oñate Trail
- ▬ Santa Fe Trail
- ▬ Butterfield Stage route
- ▬ Old Spanish Trail
- ▬ Powell Expedition
- ▬ Anza Trail
- ▬ Camino Real
- --- State boundary

UTAH

NEVADA

CALIFORNIA

ARIZONA

Los Angeles

Fort McDowell

San Diego

Colorado River

Fort Yuma

Tucson

MEXICO

Juan Bautista de Anza, Spanish commander of the Tubac settlement *(see p94)*, explored the Anza Trail from 1774 to 1776. Reaching the Pacific Coast, Anza went on to found San Francisco.

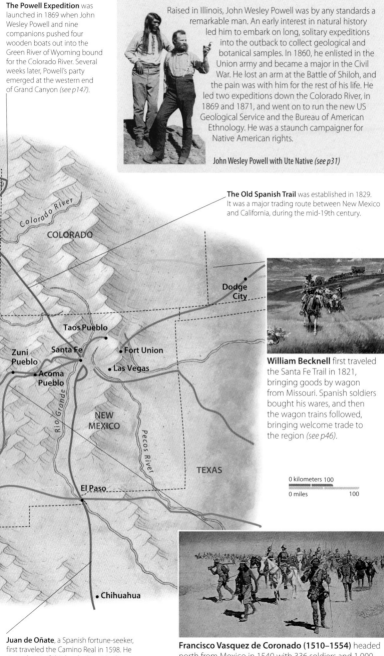

John Wesley Powell (1834–1902)

Raised in Illinois, John Wesley Powell was by any standards a remarkable man. An early interest in natural history led him to embark on long, solitary expeditions into the outback to collect geological and botanical samples. In 1860, he enlisted in the Union army and became a major in the Civil War. He lost an arm at the Battle of Shiloh, and the pain was with him for the rest of his life. He led two expeditions down the Colorado River, in 1869 and 1871, and went on to run the new US Geological Service and the Bureau of American Ethnology. He was a staunch campaigner for Native American rights.

John Wesley Powell with Ute Native *(see p31)*

The Powell Expedition was launched in 1869 when John Wesley Powell and nine companions pushed four wooden boats out into the Green River of Wyoming bound for the Colorado River. Several weeks later, Powell's party emerged at the western end of Grand Canyon *(see p147)*.

The Old Spanish Trail was established in 1829. It was a major trading route between New Mexico and California, during the mid-19th century.

William Becknell first traveled the Santa Fe Trail in 1821, bringing goods by wagon from Missouri. Spanish soldiers bought his wares, and then the wagon trains followed, bringing welcome trade to the region *(see p46)*.

0 kilometers 100

0 miles 100

Juan de Oñate, a Spanish fortune-seeker, first traveled the Camino Real in 1598. He named part of this harsh, desert path "Journey of the Dead" but safely reached the Rio Grande *(see p43)*.

Francisco Vasquez de Coronado (1510–1554) headed north from Mexico in 1540 with 336 soldiers and 1,000 Native Americans to spend two years exploring the region. His route became the Coronado Trail.

Native Cultures of the Southwest

The Native peoples of the Southwest have maintained many of their distinct ways of life, in spite of more than 400 years of hardship since the arrival of the Spanish in 1539. Disease, armed conflict, and brutal attempts at cultural assimilation have forged the determination of Native groups to retain their cultural identity. Since the late 19th century they have campaigned for the restoration of homelands and compensation for past losses.

Today, there are more than 50 Native reservations in the Southwest, the Navajo Reservation being the largest. Native peoples are found across the region, working in cities and running modern farms. In most tribes, a growing economy based on tourism and gambling has brought much-needed revenue, but battles over land rights and environmental issues are ongoing.

Rodeo at the Mescalero Apache reservation near Ruidoso, New Mexico

The Apache

Despite their reputation as fierce warriors, reinforced by their legendary leaders Cochise and Geronimo (see p46), the Apache were mainly hunter-gatherers thought to have roamed south, along with the Navajo, from their Athabaskan-speaking homelands in northern Canada during the 15th century. Just as, historically, the Apache lived in bands, so today they are divided into three main groups: the Jicarilla, Mescalero-Chiricahua, and Western Apaches.

Successful management of their natural resources has ensured a degree of economic stability. The Jicarilla Reservation in northern New Mexico is noted for its excellent hunting and fishing programs, and the Mescalero Reservation in southern New Mexico, near the town of Ruidoso (see p228) boasts a ski area and a casino.

Visitors are welcome at the Apache reservations, to watch rituals such as the Nah'ih'es or Sunrise Ceremony which marks a girl's transition to woman-hood. Dances, festivals, and rodeos are also held on reservations (see pp36–9).

The Navajo

With a population of more than 200,000, the Navajo Nation is the largest reservation in the Southwest, covering more than 25,000 square miles (64,750 sq km) in Arizona, New Mexico, and southern Utah. The spiritual center of the Navajo Nation is Canyon de Chelly (see pp172–5), where Navajo farmers still live, tending the sheep that were introduced by the Spanish and using their wool to make rugs.

The Navajo are generally welcoming to visitors and act as guides in Monument Valley and other sites on their land (see pp168–9). Until 2008 when they opened Fire Rock Casino in New Mexico, they resisted building casinos to raise money, basing their economy on tourism and the sale of natural resources such as oil, coal, and uranium. Another casino opened near Flagstaff in 2013, reducing their dependence on industrial practices such as strip-mining.

While many Navajo now live off the reservation in cities and towns, the traditional dwelling, the hogan, remains an important focus of their cultural life. Today's hogan is an octagonal wood cabin, often fitted with electricity and other modern amenities, where family gatherings take place.

Navajo religious beliefs are still bound up with daily life, with farmers singing corn-growing songs and weavers incorporating a spirit thread into their rugs. Colorful sand paintings play a part in healing ceremonies, which aim to restore hozho, or harmony, to ill or troubled individuals.

Navajo Indian woman shearing the wool from a sheep

The Pueblo People

Comprising 20 tribes in New Mexico, including the Zuni, and the Hopi in Arizona, the Pueblo people share religious and cultural beliefs. However, there are linguistic differences, with five languages spoken

Hopi Spirituality

Religion is a fundamental element of the Hopi lifestyle. Their religious ceremonies focus on *kachina* (or *katsina*), spirit figures which symbolize nature in all its forms. Familiar to visitors as the painted, carved wooden dolls available in many gift stores, the *kachina* lie at the heart of Hopi spirituality. During the growing season (December to July), these spirit figures are represented by *kachina* dancers who visit Hopi villages. During the rest of the year, the spirits are believed to reside in a shrine in the high San Francisco Peaks, north of Flagstaff. Hopi religious ceremonies are often held in the *kiva*, a round underground chamber, usually closed to visitors *(see p165)*. Other Pueblo tribes also use kivas for ceremonial events, a practice thought to date from the days of the Ancestral Puebloans.

Young Hopi Rainbow Dancer

in different pueblos. Most Pueblo tribes trace their ancestry to the Ancestral Puebloan people *(see pp164–5)*, who spread across the area from around 300–200 BC. Acoma Pueblo, also known as "Sky City" because of its high position on a sandstone mesa, is thought to be among the oldest inhabited pueblos in the country. Nineteen of the pueblos are strung out along the fertile valley of the Rio Grande River Valley. Their history and varied culture is traced at Albuquerque's impressive Indian Pueblo Cultural Center *(see pp218–19)*.

Today, most pueblos produce distinctive arts and crafts, such as the artistic pottery of the Hopi or the fine silver jewelry of Zuni. The highly colorful ceremonies of the Rio Grande Pueblos vary from village to village, with the Corn Dance being the most common. Held on various dates from late spring to summer *(see p37)*, the dance is meant to insure a successful harvest. Visitors should behave respectfully, remembering that despite the festive atmosphere, these dances are religious rituals. Much Pueblo ceremony is carried out in private, away from the eyes of tourists.

Tohono O'odham painters restore frescoes at San Xavier del Bac

The Tohono O'odham

Along with their close relatives, the Pima people, the Tohono O'odham live in southern Arizona's Sonoran Desert. Due to the harsh nature of the environment here, neither tribe has ever been moved off its ancestral lands. However, both tribes are among the most anglicized in the region. The Pima were guides to the US Army during the Indian Wars of the 1860s. Today's Tohono O'odham are mainly Christian, the mission church of San Xavier del Bac is on Tohono O'odham land south of Tucson *(see pp92–3)*, but still hold some of their traditional ceremonies, such as the Nawait or Saguaro Wine Festival and the Tcirkwena Dance. They are also known for their fine basketwork.

The Ute

This tribe once dominated a vast territory. As late as the 1850s their lands covered 85 percent of Colorado. Steady encroachment by settlers and mining interests eventually forced them to resettle. Today, the Ute welcome visitors to their two reservations along the southern Colorado border. The Ute Mountain Reservation is home to the little known but spectacular Ancestral Puebloan ruins of Ute Mountain Tribal Park *(see p176–7)*, and the southern Ute Reservation attracts thousands of visitors each year to the popular Sky Ute Casino, Lodge, and Museum. The southern Utes also hold a colorful Bear Dance on Memorial Day weekend that is open to the public.

Ute woman sewing moccasins with Mount Ute in the background

Native Art of the Southwest

The Native peoples of the American Southwest have a proud artistic heritage. They produced painted pottery, basketwork, and jewelry of distinction for centuries, often using stylized images of animals and plants to express their spiritual relationship with nature. As the region's tourist trade developed, in the 19th century, such products became sought after by visitors. In the 20th century a Native fine art movement began with watercolors, which initially depicted Native ceremonies. Such works proved popular with collectors and marked the beginning of an interest in and market for southwestern Native art. Today, artists work in all media, including sculpture, video, and installations, and in all styles such as abstract expressionism or realism.

Basketwork is a tradition associated with all Native peoples of the Southwest. Braided, twined, or coiled from willow or yucca leaves, the baskets are decorated differently according to the tribe.

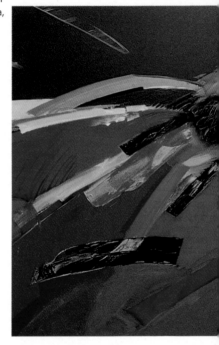

Rugmaking traditions in the Southwest belong to the Navajo and Pueblo, with Puebloan examples dating from prehistoric times. Navajo weaving is best known; these rugs were sought after by tourists as early as the mid-1800s, and by the late 19th century colorful regional distinctions emerged.

Native American Painting

The Apache developed the art of animal-skin painting in which warriors celebrated their deeds in pictographs. Designs, often scenes of men and horses in battle or hunting, were scratched on the surface and color added with bone or brush. After 1900 a fine art movement developed, including fine impressionistic and abstract works such as Red Tailed Hawk *(1986) by Hopi/Tewa artist Dan Namingha.*

Pottery originated around 200 BC with the coiled pots of the Mimbres people. These mid-20th-century pots are a polished blackware jar from San Ildefonso Pueblo *(left)* and a patterned jar from Acoma *(above).*

Contemporary sculpture by Native American artists can be seen in galleries across the Southwest. They include this piece called *Dineh* (1981) by famous American sculptor Allan Houser. Dineh is the word the Navajo use to describe themselves. This is a modernist work, cast in bronze, whose smooth planes and clean lines appear to represent the dignity and strength of this couple.

Early Native American Art

Outstanding examples of early Southwestern pottery, basketwork, and hide paintings have been marvelously preserved because of the area's dry climate, in spite of the fact that they are made from perishable organic materials such as clay, yucca fiber, and painted animal skins. As a result, more is known about early indigenous art here than in any other part of North America. The earliest pieces date back to around 200 BC, with textiles a later development. By AD 600, the styles of the three main groups: the Hohokam, Mogollon, and Ancestral Puebloan peoples had begun to merge and to absorb outside influences, seen in the Mexican designs on some ancient pots.

Mimbres pottery bowl

Silverwork has been produced by the Navajo, Zuni, and Hopi peoples for centuries. Since the mid-19th century, Navajo jewelers have incorporated Spanish styles. Zuni and Hopi silver is made in a different way. They adopted an intricate overlay process in the 1930s, distinguished by raised silver patterns against a dark background.

Carving focuses mainly on wooden dolls, or *kachinas*, whittled mostly from pine or cottonwood. The Pueblo peoples, especially the Hopi, are noted for their masked figurines, which depict *kachina* spirits.

The Southwest: Backdrop for the Movies

The panoramic desert landscape of the Southwest is familiar the world over thanks to the countless movies that have been filmed here. As legendary actor John Wayne once said: "TV you can do on the back lot; for the real outdoor dramas, you have to do them where God put the West." Monument Valley *(see pp168–9)* is famous for its association with John Ford's Westerns, while the stark beauty of southern Utah, particularly around the Moab and Kanab areas, has appeared in several films. The popular idea of the "Wild West" *(see pp58–9)* has been formed more through film than by any other medium, and visitors to the Southwest may find much of its scenery strangely familiar. Many TV series and commercials have also been shot here.

Old Tucson Studio was built for the 1940 motion picture *Arizona*. The studio is still a popular movie location and is now also home to a family-oriented, Wild West theme park *(see pp90–91)*.

Johnson Canyon, near Kanab *(see p152)*, was the location of the 1962 film *How the West was Won*. It is a western town set that was built for the 1952 movie *Westward the Women*.

John Ford and Monument Valley

John Ford was not the first director to shoot a movie using Monument Valley's spectacular buttes as a backdrop. That honor goes to George B. Seitz, who filmed *The Vanishing American* there in 1924. But it was John Ford's genius that captured the spectacle of the West as people had never seen it before. His first movie there, *Stagecoach* (1939), so enthralled audiences that it brought the Western back into vogue and made the young John Wayne into a star. Ford set a new standard for movies, bringing the grandeur of the West to the big screen, and setting off a "studio stampede" of directors wanting to utilize the beauty of the region. In all, over 60 movies and countless TV shows, commercials, and videos have used Monument Valley as a spectacular panoramic backdrop.

Moab's snow-capped mountains, red rock formations, and deep river canyons *(see p145)* have been the backdrop for over 100 major motion pictures, including *Thelma and Louise* in 1991.

Director John Ford on the set of *Stagecoach*

Robert Zemeckis used Monument Valley in 1990 as the backdrop for the third installment of his *Back to the Future* series of films, starring Michael J. Fox and Christopher Lloyd.

The Sundance Film Festival

Actor and director Robert Redford owns the Sundance Resort, which combines an environmentally responsible mountain vacation development with an institute for the promotion of the cinematic arts. Founded by Redford in 1981, the Sundance Film Festival takes place annually in the second half of January. The majority of screenings, which showcase independent film- and documentary-makers, are not held at the Sundance Resort (about 75 miles (121 km) northwest of Moab), but in Park City and at the Tower Theater in Salt Lake City. The festival has become America's foremost venue for innovative cinema and attracts the big Hollywood names. Tickets sell out quickly, so make ticket and lodging reservations ahead.

Robert Redford at the Sundance Film Festival in 1998

Monument Valley was favored by John Ford, who directed nine movies using the area dubbed "Ford Country" and other southern Utah sites as backdrops. Many, like the 1956 epic *The Searchers*, are considered classics.

Dead Horse Point State Park *(see p147)* has long been used by directors who want a spectacular setting. It was seen in the 1991 film *Thelma and Louise* and, in 2000, actor Tom Cruise free-climbed up the sheer cliff-face in the thrilling opening sequence of *Mission Impossible: 2.*

Tombstone was the setting for the 1993 film of the same name *(see p96)*. Starring Val Kilmer, Sam Elliott, Bill Paxton, and Kurt Russell, it is a modern interpretation of the Western genre.

Lake Powell is the most spectacular artificial lake in the US *(see pp154–5)*. Its stark and otherworldly beauty has been used as a set for such diverse movies as the 1967 Dean Martin Western *Rough Night in Jericho*, the 1965 biblical epic *The Greatest Story Ever Told* (pictured here), with Charlton Heston, and the 1968 science fiction classic *Planet of the Apes*.

THE SOUTHWEST THROUGH THE YEAR

The weather in the Southwest is well known for its extremes, ranging from the heat of the desert to the ice and snow of the mountains – temperatures vary according to altitude, so the higher the elevation of the land, the cooler the area will be. Because the climate can be unbearably hot during the summer, particularly in Arizona, southern Utah, and New Mexico, many people prefer to travel to the Southwest during spring and fall. This part of the world is particularly beautiful in fall, with its astounding array of golds, reds, and yellows in the forests and national parks. The area's diverse mix of Native, Hispanic, and European (Anglo) cultures gives visitors the opportunity to experience many different kinds of festivals and celebrations.

Spring

Although the weather can be unpredictable in the spring, many festivals and celebrations are held at this time throughout the Southwest. Around Easter, prayers for a good harvest inspire several of the festivals and rituals held in the pueblos.

March
Guild Indian Fair and Market *(first weekend)* Phoenix. Held at the Heard Museum, the fair features Indian dancing, arts, crafts, and Native American food.
Rio Grande Arts and Crafts Festival *(mid-Mar)* Albuquerque. This popular festival features handcrafted items from more than 200 artists and crafts people.

April
American Indian Week *(mid-Apr)* Albuquerque. Arts and dancing at the Indian Pueblo Cultural Center.

Hispanic musicians or *mariachis* play at a Cinco de Mayo celebration

Tucson International Mariachi Conference *(late Apr)* Tucson. Annual celebration of Mexican *mariachi* music and dancing.
Gathering of Nations Pow Wow *(late Apr)* Albuquerque. Native American performers and traders from 300 tribes.

Summer

The warm summer weather is the time for many open-air events, from boat racing and rodeos to cultural events as diverse as country music and opera. The weather in July and August, however, can be extreme, especially in southern Arizona, which sees very high temperatures and violent summer storms.

May
El Cinco de Mayo *(May 5)* Celebrated across many southwestern towns. Festivities to mark the 1862 Mexican victory over the French include parades, dancing, and Mexican food.
Santa Cruz Feast Day *(early May)* Taos Pueblo. Celebrations include blessing the fields and a colorful corn dance.
Tucson Folk Festival *(early May)* Tucson. A wide selection of folk music at various venues in Tucson.
T or C Fiesta *(early May)* Truth or Consequences. A rodeo and old-time fiddlers' competition.
Santa Fe Film Festival *(early May)* Santa Fe. Screening of world films, including the best in contemporary cinema and tributes to veteran stars.
Taste of Durango *(mid-May)* Durango. Food, music, and family fun fill the streets as the town's restaurants stage a cook-off contest.
Helldorado Days and Rodeo *(mid-May)* Las Vegas, NV. A four-day festival of rodeo events and concerts.

Native dancer at the Guild Indian Fair and Market, Phoenix

An exhibit at Roswell's UFO Encounter event

Phippen Western Art Show & Sale *(Memorial Day weekend)* Prescott. Western art and sculpture buyers, sellers, and admirers come for the juried fine art show.
Wyatt Earp Days *(Memorial Day weekend)* Tombstone. Mock gunfights, street entertainment, and barbecue.

June
Utah Summer Games *(Jun)* Cedar City. The games include a marathon, cycling, tennis, and swimming.
San Antonio Feast Day *(Jun 13)* Sandia, San Idelfonso, Ohkay Owingeh, and Taos pueblos. This festival welcomes visitors and features tribal dancing.
Albuquerque Pride *(mid-Jun)* Albuquerque. A three-day celebration of music and comedy hosted by the gay and lesbian community.
Telluride Bluegrass *(mid-Jun)* Telluride. Often coinciding with the solstice, this four-day roots-music festival is one of the West's biggest music events.
New Mexico Arts and Crafts Fair *(late Jun)* Albuquerque. Traditional arts and crafts, plus food and entertainments.

Utah Shakespeare Festival *(late Jun–Oct)* Cedar City. Plays are produced in two of the town's theaters.
Taos Summer Chamber Music Festival *(Jun–Aug)* Taos and Angel Fire. This festival involves a series of outdoor concerts.
Santa Fe Opera *(late Jun–Aug)* Santa Fe. A variety of operas are performed in an open-air arena.

July
UFO Encounter *(early Jul)* Roswell. A series of lectures on UFOs, also featuring concerts and entertainment.
Fourth of July *(Jul 4)* Most Southwestern towns. Celebrations include parades, fireworks, rodeos, music festivals, and ceremonial Indian dances.
Nambe Falls Celebration *(early Jul)* Nambe Pueblo. Traditional dancing, food, and arts and crafts in a beautiful hillside setting.
Hopi Festival of Arts and Culture *(early Jul)* Flagstaff. Music, dance, and over 70 award-winning Hopi carvers, painters, jewelers, potters, quilters, and weavers.
Frontier Days *(first week)* Prescott. The oldest professional rodeo in the world, featuring events such as calf roping and wild horse racing.
Chamber Music Festival *(mid-Jul–Aug)* Santa Fe. One of the finest chamber music festivals in America is held at venues throughout the city.
Taos Pueblo Pow Wow *(second week)* Taos Pueblo. Traditional ceremonies and dances at the Taos Pueblo.

Rainbow Dancers at Nambe Falls Celebration

Bat-Flight Breakfast *(late Jul)* Carlsbad Caverns. Participants can enjoy an outdoor breakfast while watching thousands of bats as they return to the caves.
Arizona Cardinals Training Camp *(late Jul–mid-Aug)* Flagstaff. Most practice sessions of this NFL team are open to the public.
Spanish Market *(last weekend)* Santa Fe. A lively celebration featuring arts and crafts by contemporary Hispanic artists.

August
Old Lincoln Days *(first weekend)* Lincoln. A festival featuring a re-enactment of the death of Billy the Kid, including the *Last Escape of Billy the Kid* pageant.
Inter-Tribal Indian Ceremonial *(mid-Aug)* Red Rock State Park, near Gallup. Fifty tribes take part in dances, pow wows, parades, rodeos, and races. Includes arts and crafts.
Indian Market *(third weekend)* Santa Fe. Held since 1922, this is a chance to buy a wide selection of high-quality Native arts and crafts.
Payson Rodeo *(third weekend)* Payson. Part of the August "Do'ins" and authorized by the Professional Rodeo Cowboys Association (PRCA); the best of the best compete for sizeable prize money.
Great American Duck Race *(fourth weekend)* Deming. Includes live duck racing, a tortilla toss, a best dressed duck contest, concerts, food, and Deming's biggest parade.

Acoustic duo entertain at Bluegrass festival in Telluride

Fall

The autumnal forests and mountains of the Southwest are striking, ablaze with brilliant yellows, reds, and golds. Fall is one of the best seasons for touring and sightseeing because the temperatures become cooler and more comfortable.

September
Navajo Nation Fair and Rodeo *(early Sep)* Window Rock. The largest Indian fair in the US features a parade, a rodeo, traditional song and dance, and arts and crafts.
Hatch Chile Festival *(early Sep/ Labor Day weekend)* Hatch. Cooking, music, and arts and crafts in the center of the chile-growing industry.
Rendezvous of the Gunfighters *(Labor Day weekend)* Tombstone. Includes a parade, stagecoach rides, chili cook-offs, and mock shootouts.
The All-American Futurity *(early Sep/Labor Day)* Ruidoso

Downs Racetrack. Quarter horse race with prize money in excess of $2 million.
Grand Canyon Music Festival *(early & mid-Sep)* Grand Canyon Village. Fine chamber music, from baroque to classical, jazz, fusion, and crossover.
New Mexico State Fair *(mid-Sep)* Albuquerque. One of the largest state fairs in the nation, with rodeos, carnivals, exhibits, and music.
Flagstaff Festival of Science *(late Sep)* Flagstaff. Ten days of events, including field trips and interactive exhibits, at museums and observatories.
The Whole Enchilada Festival *(late Sep)* Las Cruces. Featuring the world's largest *enchilada (see p246)*, as well as arts and crafts.

October
Albuquerque International Balloon Fiesta *(early Oct)* Albuquerque. More than 850 balloons take part in this stunning event *(see p272)*, which is the largest of its kind in the world.

Lincoln County Cowboy Symposium *(second weekend)* Ruidoso. A celebration of life in the Old West, with cowboy poets, storytellers, and musicians as well as country dancing.
Helldorado Days *(third weekend)* Tombstone. The festival features re-enactments, parades, a carnival, music, and street entertainment.
Moab Ho-Down Bike Festival *(last week)* Moab. Mountain bike guided tours, workshops, and a hill climb.

Calf roping at Lincoln County Cowboy Symposium

Climate
The climate varies across the region. Phoenix and the southern areas have hot and dry summers and mild, sunny winters, whereas such areas as Southern Utah, Northern Arizona, and Northern New Mexico have snowy winters that are colder due to their higher elevation.

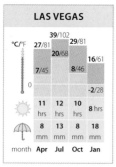
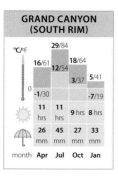
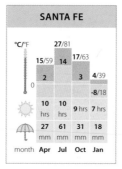
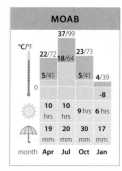

Winter

Christmas in the Southwest is celebrated in traditional American style, with lights decorating almost every building and tree. The ski season stretches from mid-November to early April in the region's many resorts. Skiing, snow-boarding, and ice-skating are all popular.

November

Festival of the Cranes (*mid-Nov*) Socorro. Festival held during the November migration of whooping cranes to the Bosque del Apache Wildlife Refuge (*see p222*).

December

La Fiesta de Tumacácori (*first weekend*) Tumacácori. Festival held on mission grounds to celebrate the Native American heritage of the upper Santa Cruz Valley.

Old Town Stroll (*first Friday*) Albuquerque. The town's Christmas festivities begin in the Old Town with a parade, lighting of the tree, live music, and food stalls.

Parade of Lights (*early Dec*) Lake Mead Marina. Fifty boats show off their special light decorations to thousands of spectators, a tradition that has been going since 1975.

Shalako Ceremony (*early Dec*) Zuni Pueblo. Starting with a symbolic crossing of the river,

A skier descending the Ridge in Taos Ski Valley

this all-night ritual snakes through the pueblo's streets.

Canyon Road Farolito Walk (*Dec 24*) Santa Fe. Candle-lit tour of Canyon Road with carol singing and bonfires.

Fiesta Bowl Festival and Parade (*late Dec or early Jan*) Phoenix. College football at ASU Sun Devil Stadium.

January

Ice Festival (*early Jan*) Ouray. The world's largest ice climbing event (half competition, half party), high in the Colorado Rockies.

Tucson Area Square Dance Festival (*mid-Jan*) Tucson. The festival attracts thousands of dancers.

San Ildefonso Pueblo Feast Day (*late Jan*) San Ildefonso Pueblo. Ceremonial dances commemorate this feast day.

Public Holidays

New Year (Jan 1)

Martin Luther King Jr Day (third Mon in Jan)

Presidents' Day (third Mon in Feb)

Easter Sunday (variable)

El Cinco de Mayo (May 5)

Memorial Day (last Mon in May)

Independence Day (Jul 4)

Pioneer Day (Jul 24 – Utah)

Labor Day (first Mon in Sep)

Columbus Day (secnd Mon in Oct)

Veterans Day (Nov 11)

Thanksgiving (fourth Thu in Nov)

Christmas Day (Dec 25)

Saguaro Cactus illuminated by Christmas lights

February

Tubac Festival of the Arts (*early Feb*) Tubac. A highlight of the town's calendar, and one of the most important arts and crafts festivals in southern Arizona.

PGA Phoenix Golf WM Open (*early Feb*) Phoenix. The PGA's largest annual tournament takes place in Phoenix.

Silver Spur Rodeo (*mid-Feb*) Yuma. Along with the rodeo, this festival features arts and crafts and Yuma's biggest parade.

Tucson Gem and Mineral Show (*mid-Feb*) Tucson. Open to visitors, this is one of the biggest gem and mineral shows in the US.

La Fiesta de los Vaqueros (*late Feb*) Tucson. A rodeo and assorted cowboy events, plus the country's largest non-motorized parade.

Player at PGA/WM Open golf championship in Phoenix

THE HISTORY OF THE SOUTHWEST

The Southwest is known for its landscape, dominated by desert, deep canyons, and high mesas. Despite the arid conditions native civilizations have lived here for thousands of years, adjusting to the arrival of other cultures – the Hispanic colonizers of the 17th and 18th centuries and the Anglo-Americans of the 19th and 20th. Its rich history has created a fascinating multicultural heritage.

Long before the appearance of the first Spanish explorers in the 1500s, the Southwest was inhabited by a variety of native populations. Groups of hunters walked here across the Bering Straits over a land bridge that once joined Asia with North America; estimates of when that occurred range from 15,000 to 35,000 years ago. Descendants of these primitive hunter-gatherers, sometimes called Paleo-Indians, gradually fanned out across the American continent as far south as present-day Argentina. The early inhabitants of the Southwest endured centuries of hardship and adaptation to develop the technology and skills required to survive the rigors of life in this arid landscape.

The First Inhabitants

The first Native American peoples in the Southwest region have been called the Clovis, named for the site in New Mexico where stone spearheads were found embedded in mammoth bones. This hunter society roamed the area in small groups between 10,000 and 8,000 BC. Gradually, however, their prey of large Pleistocene mammals died out, and tribal people turned to roots and berries to supplement their diets. Anthropologists believe settled farming societies appeared gradually as the population grew, and that new crops and farming techniques were introduced by migrants and traders from Mexico in around 800 BC, when corn first began to be cultivated in the region.

Among the early farmers of the Southwest were the Basketmakers, named for their finely wrought baskets. Part of the Early Ancestral Puebloan, or Anasazi, culture, these people are thought to have lived in extended family groups, in pithouse dwellings. These were holes dug out of the earth up to 6 ft (2 m) deep, with roofs above ground. The Basketmakers were efficient hunters, using spears and domesticated dogs. They kept turkeys, whose feathers were highly valued as decoration.

By around AD 500, agrarian society was well established in the Southwest and large villages, or pueblos, began to develop. These usually centered around a large pithouse that was used for communal or religious use – the forerunner of the ceremonial *kiva*, which is still very much in use today *(see p165)*.

Stone spear point

	10,000–8,000 BC Nomadic Clovis culture hunted in New Mexico. They made tools out of mammoth ivory and stone	**800 BC** Corn brought to the Southwest from Mexico. Start of agriculture, although the semi-nomadic quest for food still predominates
30,000 BC	**20,000 BC**	**10,000 BC**
30,000–25,000 BC First nomadic people cross Bering Strait land bridge from Asia to North America	**10,000 BC** Man reaches the tip of South America	**5,000–500 BC** Cochise people arrive in southeastern Arizona. Also known as people of the "Desert Culture"

◀ Papago Indian woman from Pima County, Arizona, 1903

Ancient Cultures

By AD 700 there were three main cultures in the Southwest: the Hohokam, the Mogollon, and the Ancestral Puebloan. They had slowly developed, from around 200 and 300 BC, into societies based on settled communities and cultivated crops. Ancestral Puebloan people began to build more elaborate dwellings that grew into settlements such as Chaco Canyon *(see pp178–9)* in AD 800 and Mesa Verde *(see pp184–5)* in AD 1000. These settlements were abandoned in the 12th and 13th centuries

Hohokam pot

(see p165). It is thought the people migrated to the Pueblo Indian settlements along the Rio Grande valley and northwest New Mexico, and to the Hopi mesas and Acoma, where their descendants live today.

The Hohokam farmed the deserts of central and southern Arizona between 300 BC and AD 1350. Their irrigation systems enabled them to grow two crops a year. It is thought that today's Tohono O'odham (Papago) and the Pima Indians of southern Arizona are descendants of the Hohokam *(see pp30–31)*.

The Mogollon were known for their pottery and adjusted to an agrarian lifestyle when agricultural crops arrived from Mexico. They are thought to have become assimilated into Ancestral Puebloan groups and their descendants living in the north of the region.

The Navajo and the Apache

The Navajo and Apache peoples originated in the Athabascan culture of the north of the American continent, in Canada and Alaska. The Navajo moved south between 1200 and 1400, while the Apache are thought to have arrived in the Southwest some time in the late 15th century.

The Navajo were hunters who took to herding sheep brought by the Spanish. There were four Apache groups: the Jicarilla, the Mescalero, the Chiricahua, and the Western Apache, who continued their nomadic lifestyle. The Apache were known as skillful warriors, especially the Chiricahua Apache of southern Arizona, whose leaders Cochise and Geronimo fought Hispanic and Anglo settlers in an attempt to deter them from colonizing the area in the late 19th century.

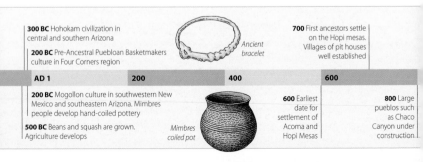

Navajo cornfield near Holbrook, Arizona, in 1889

The Arrival of the Spanish

In 1539, the Franciscan priest, Fray Marcos de Niza, led the first Spanish expedition into the Southwest region. He was inspired by hopes of finding wealthy Indian cities, such as those the Spanish had conquered in South America, and the desire to convert native populations to Christianity. His expedition sent an advance party into Zuni

300 BC Hohokam civilization in central and southern Arizona

200 BC Pre-Ancestral Puebloan Basketmakers culture in Four Corners region

Ancient bracelet

700 First ancestors settle on the Hopi mesas. Villages of pit houses well established

AD 1	200	400	600

200 BC Mogollon culture in southwestern New Mexico and southeastern Arizona. Mimbres people develop hand-coiled pottery

500 BC Beans and squash are grown. Agriculture develops

Mimbres coiled pot

600 Earliest date for settlement of Acoma and Hopi Mesas

800 Large pueblos such as Chaco Canyon under construction

Hopi Mesas and Acoma Pueblo

The Hopi villages of Old Oraibi and Walpi, and the Acoma Pueblo perch on high mesas in northeastern Arizona and northern New Mexico. Dated to AD 1150, they are believed to be America's oldest continually occupied settlements. The Ancestral Puebloan forebears of the Hopi and Acoma peoples arrived between AD 1100 and 1300, a period known as the "Gathering of the Clans." The first to arrive was the Bear Clan, from Mesa Verde. Others came from Canyon de Chelly, Chaco Canyon, the cliff dwellings of Keet Seel, and Betatakin in the Navajo National Monument.

Acoma pueblo, New Mexico *(see p221)*

tribal lands. Messages came back describing villages that Marcos identified as the fabled kingdom of gold, or Cibola. The priest never got there, but the myth of riches persisted.

A year later, Francisco Vasquez de Coronado *(see p220)* returned with 330 soldiers, 1,000 Indian allies, and more than 1,000 head of livestock. He overwhelmed the trading center of Zuni Pueblo and spent two years traversing Arizona, New Mexico, Texas, and Kansas in search of Cibola. Coronado's brutal treatment of the Pueblo people, sacking homes and burning villages, sowed the seeds for the Pueblo Revolt 140 years later.

The Colony of New Mexico

Without gold, the Spanish lost interest until Juan de Oñate's 1598 expedition. Oñate established the city of Santa Fe and the colony of New Mexico, which included the present-day states of New Mexico and Arizona and parts of Colorado, Utah, Nevada, and California.

Spanish attempts to conquer the Indian pueblos led to bloody battles. Governor Oñate's cruelty, the harsh conditions, and bad harvests caused many settlers to flee

Engraving by Norman Price of Coronado setting out to discover a legendary kingdom of gold in 1540

1100–1300 "Gathering of the Clans" on the Hopi mesas

1400 The Navajo and Apache migrate from Canada to the Southwest

1300 Mesa Verde deserted

1540–42 Francisco Vasquez de Coronado leads a search for gold in New Mexico

1610 Don Pedro de Peralta founds the capital of Santa Fe

1000   **1200**   **1400**   **1600**

1020 Chaco Canyon is at its height as a trading and cultural center

c.1250 Ancient sites are mysteriously abandoned; new pueblos established along Rio Grande

Juan de Oñate

1539 Fray Marcos de Niza heads first Spanish expedition to Southwest

1598 Juan de Oñate founds permanent colony in New Mexico

1680 The Pueblo Revolt

Illustration of the 1680 Pueblo Indian Revolt

the colony. A new governor, Don Pedro de Peralta, was instated in 1610, and Santa Fe became the capital.

Despite the harsh conditions, more settlers, priests, and soldiers began to return to the area, determined to subdue the native people and to suppress their religious practices.

The Pueblo Revolt

As the colonists spread out, they seized Pueblo farmlands and created huge ranches for themselves. The Pueblo people refused to work for them and continued to resist the new religion. When, in 1675, three native religious leaders were hanged in Santa Fe and more than 40 others publicly whipped, Popé, a Pueblo leader, started a resistance movement. The uprising on August 9, 1680, resulted in the deaths of 375 colonists and 21 priests, with the remaining 2,000 settlers driven south across the Rio Grande.

The Pueblo people did not manage to rid the region of the Spanish. In 1692, Don Diego de Vargas reclaimed Santa Fe. There were signs, however, of a relatively more tolerant relationship between Indian and colonizer.

The End of the Spanish Era

By the late 18th century, the Spanish wanted to extend their power to California and secure the Pacific coast against the English and the Russians. Their first Arizona settlement was at Tubac, near Tucson in 1752. In 1775, Juan Bautista de Anza reached the Pacific Coast and founded San Francisco in Alta California *(see p28)*. As the Southwest opened up, Anglo-Americans were presented with new trading opportunities. In the Louisiana Purchase of 1803, Napoleon sold Louisiana, an enormous area of about 828,000 sq miles (2.2 million sq km) of land, to the

The Missions

In the late 17th century, Jesuit missionary Father Eusebio Kino lived alongside and established a rapport with the Pima people of southern Arizona. He initiated the Jesuit practice of bringing gifts of livestock and seeds for new crops, including wheat. Those natives involved in the missionary program escaped forced labor. Kino inspired the natives living south of Tucson, at a place called Bac, to begin work on what was to become the Southwest's most beautiful mission church, San Xavier del Bac *(see pp92–3)*. When Kino died in 1711, there were around 20 missions across the area.

Father Eusebio Kino

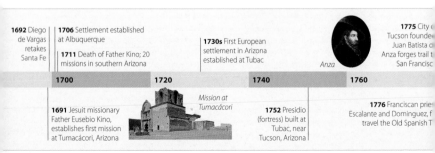

1692 Diego de Vargas retakes Santa Fe	1706 Settlement established at Albuquerque		1730s First European settlement in Arizona established at Tubac		1775 City of Tucson founded; Juan Batista de Anza forges trail to San Francisco
	1711 Death of Father Kino; 20 missions in southern Arizona			Anza	
	1700	**1720**	**1740**	**1760**	
1691 Jesuit missionary Father Eusebio Kino, establishes first mission at Tumacácori, Arizona		*Mission at Tumacácori*	1752 Presidio (fortress) built at Tubac, near Tucson, Arizona		1776 Franciscan priests Escalante and Dominguez, travel the Old Spanish Trail

recently formed United States. The US and New Mexico now shared a border, but the Anglos proved the stronger power.

The fight for Mexico's indepen- dence from Spain began on September 16, 1810, but it was not until 1821 that independence was finally declared. The Republic of Mexico was founded in 1824. Newly independent Mexicans were glad to do business with their Anglo-American neighbors, who brought much-needed trade after the Spanish block on goods going west.

Anglo-American Settlement

Conflicts over land rights marked the period following the 1803 Louisiana Purchase. While the Hispanic and Native inhabitants of the region were happy to trade with the Anglos, they were angered by the new settlers who built ranches and even towns on lands to which they had no legal right. By the 1840s the United States had embarked on a vigorous expansion westward, with settlers accompanied by United States' soldiers. In 1845 the US acquired Texas and, when Mexico resisted further moves, the president sent an army to take control of New Mexico, starting the Mexican War. The Treaty of Guadalupe-Hidalgo ended the conflict in 1848, and gave the US the Mexican Cesion (comprising California, Utah, including Nevada and parts of Wyoming and Colorado, and New Mexico, which included northern Arizona) for $18.25 million. In 1854 the United States bought southern Arizona through the Gadsden Purchase for $10 million. While each

region had its own territorial capital for administering law, they were not able to elect national representatives to Congress.

The Impact of the American Civil War

When the Civil War broke out in 1861, many Southwesterners had Confederate sympathies, siding with the southern states against the north, or Union. They tried to declare Arizona a Confederate territory but in 1862, Union forces repelled Confederates at Glorieta Pass, near Santa Fe. In 1863, the federal government recognized Arizona as a separate territory, and drew the state line that exists between it and New Mexico today.

After the Civil War, reports of land and mineral wealth in the West filtered back east, and Anglo settlement of the West rapidly increased. Rich lodes of gold, silver, and copper were discovered in Arizona, and mining camps such as Tombstone, Jerome, and Bisbee in Arizona *(see pp96–7)*, and Silver City in New Mexico became boomtowns. In Colorado, Silverton, Ouray, and Telluride *(see pp182–3)* also grew up around the mining industry in the late 19th century.

Engraving depicting an Apache attack on Anglo settlers (c.1886)

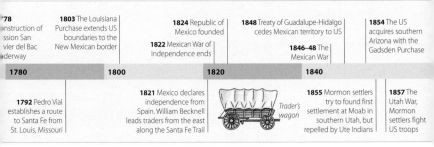

'78 onstruction of ssion San vier del Bac derway	**1803** The Louisiana Purchase extends US boundaries to the New Mexican border	**1824** Republic of Mexico founded **1822** Mexican War of Independence ends	**1848** Treaty of Guadalupe-Hidalgo cedes Mexican territory to US **1846–48** The Mexican War	**1854** The US acquires southern Arizona with the Gadsden Purchase	
1780	**1800**	**1820**	**1840**		
1792 Pedro Vial establishes a route to Santa Fe from St. Louis, Missouri		**1821** Mexico declares independence from Spain. William Becknell leads traders from the east along the Santa Fe Trail	*Trader's wagon*	**1855** Mormon settlers try to found first settlement at Moab in southern Utah, but repelled by Ute Indians	**1857** The Utah War, Mormon settlers fight US troops

The Arrival of the Anglo-Americans

The first non-Spanish people of European descent, or Anglo-Americans, to arrive in the Southwest were "mountain men" or fur trappers in the early 1800s. They learned survival skills from Native tribes, married Native women, and usually spoke more than one Native language, and Spanish.

The opening of the Old Spanish Trail in 1776, and the forerunner to the Santa Fe Trail from St. Louis in the East in 1792, made the region accessible to traders and settlers *(see pp28–9)*. Yet it was only after Mexican independence was declared in 1821 that the territory opened up to Anglo traders who brought luxury goods such as oranges, silk handkerchiefs, and whisky. American soldiers arrived in 1846, and by the 1850s the US government had taken the region from the Mexicans. The Anglos, determined to subdue both Native and Hispanic populations, wrested away their lands to make way for vast ranches and towns such as Tombstone, which grew around the discovery of silver in 1877.

Mountain Man
Jim Bridger was one of many rugged individuals to open up trade routes to the west in the 1820s.

The Mexican War
This lithograph shows a battle in the 1846–8 war between the US and Mexico. After capturing Mexico City, the Americans agreed to pay $18.25 million in exchange for possession of New Mexico and California.

Apache Warriors

The nomadic Apache lived in small communities in southeastern Arizona, and southern and northwestern New Mexico. Seeing the Apache as a threat to the settlement of these territories, the US military was determined to wipe them out. The hanging of one of Chief Cochise's relatives in 1861 instigated a war which lasted more than a decade until Apache reservations were established in 1872. In 1877, a new leader, Victorio, launched a three-year guerrilla war against settlers that ended only with his death. The most famous Apache leader, Geronimo, led a campaign against the Mexicans and Anglos from 1851 until he surrendered in 1886 and was sent to a reservation in Florida.

Apache leader Geronimo, in a fierce pose in this picture from 1886

Mining Boom Prospector
In the second half of the 1800s, the region was a magnet for miners seeking their fortune. In reality, few individuals profited as large companies swiftly gained control of the mining areas.

The Coming of the Railroad
In 1869, the transcontinental railroad brought an influx of miners, adventurers, and tourists to the Southwest, and saw new industries emerge.

The Long Walk
Portrait of Navajo leader, Manuelito (1818–94) taken after the Long Walk. More than 8,000 Navajo were sent to New Mexico in 1864. Many died on the way.

Wagon Trains on the Santa Fe Trail

Charles Ferdinand's The Attack on the Emigrant Train *(1856) depicts the conflicts between the Apache and traders and settlers who poured into the Southwest after the establishment of the Santa Fe Trail* (see pp28–9).

Apache were often depicted attacking wagon trains. The Apache, who had a fierce reputation, felt justifiably threatened by Anglo settlers.

Anglo-American Influence
John Gast's *American Progress* (1872) shows Indians pursued by a woman in a white robe – a symbol of American culture. The schoolbook represents education; trains, ships, and settlers are all signs of "civilization."

A group of cowboys roping a steer, painted by C. M. Russell (1897)

Land Disputes

After the Civil War, the US government set about clearing more land for settlers. In 1864, more than 8,000 Navajo people were forced from their lands and made to march "The Long Walk" of 400 miles (644 km) east to a reservation at Bosque Redondo in New Mexico. Some died en route as a result of the harsh weather and many more from disease at the reservation. In 1868, the Navajo were given 20,000 square miles (51,800 sq km) of land across Arizona, New Mexico, and southern Utah. The Chiricahua Apache continued to fight against forced settlement for most of the 19th century until their defeat and the surrender of their leader, Geronimo, in 1886.

In the 1870s, vast areas of the Southwest became huge cattle and sheep ranches. Battles between farmers, smallholders, and ranchers were common. Frequent "Range Wars"

Engraving showing Billy the Kid shooting a man in a bar

included the Lincoln County War, known for its famous protagonist, Billy the Kid *(see p58)*. As Anglo ranchers seized land, the New Mexicans' tradition of communal land use was overturned and many indigenous farmers lost their livelihoods.

By the 1880s four major railroads crossed the region bringing new Anglo settlers in search of prosperity. They came fully believing in their right to exploit the resources of this new land, and the railroad became a catalyst for new industries in the region, such as lumberjacking, cattle farming, and mineral mining. Luxury goods brought from the East by rail also made life a little easier.

New Mexico and Arizona were granted statehood in 1912. In the years leading up to and following World War I, Arizona, in particular, experienced an economic boom because of its rich mineral resources.

1877 Copper found at Bisbee, Arizona. Silver discovered at Tombstone, Arizona

Geronimo (1829–1909)

1886 Indian Wars end with the surrender of Geronimo

1912 New Mexico and Arizona become 47th and 48th states of the Union

1917 The US enters World War I

1931–36 Hoover Dam constructed in Arizona

| 1860 | 1880 | 1900 | 1920 |

1868 Navajo Reservation established in the Four Corners region

1878 The Lincoln County War begins in Lincoln, New Mexico

1881 Gunfight at OK Corral. Billy the Kid shot in New Mexico

1889 Phoenix becomes the territorial capital of Arizona

1901 Grand Canyon railroad opens, bringing tourists to the region

Grand Canyon steam train

The Demand for Water

As the region's population expanded, water supply became a pressing issue, and a series of enormous, federally funded dams were built to channel precious water for the burgeoning population of such cities as Phoenix. Dam- and road-building projects aided the region's economy and attracted even more settlers.

Patriot missile test at White Sands, New Mexico

The Hoover Dam was constructed between 1931 and 1936, but by the 1960s even that proved inadequate. Glen Canyon Dam was completed in 1963, flooding forever an area of great beauty. The dam created the huge reservoir of Lake Powell, destroying a number of ancient Native ruins.

The issue of water continues to be a serious problem in the Southwest as the population keeps on rising. Projects to harness water from any available source are under debate.

World War II

The legacy of the war years changed the economic course of the Southwest. New Mexico's sparsely populated and remote desert areas provided secret research, development, and testing sites for the first atomic bomb, starting with Los Alamos and the Manhattan Project from 1943 onwards (see p190). Military installations such as the Titan Missile Base in southern Arizona and New Mexico's White Sands Missile Range were of national importance during the Cold War period of the 1950s.

Military research, computer technology, and other industrial off-shoots led to urbanization and a post-war population boom. Phoenix and Albuquerque subsequently ranked among the fastest-growing cities in the US. The Southwest continues to be a major center for national defense research and development, as well as for research into space travel.

The Southwest Today

The Southwest's economy continues to prosper, and its population is still growing, augmented by numbers of winter residents or "snowbirds." Ever-increasing numbers of tourists visit the region's scenic and historic wonders, preserved in the area's national parks. Established in the early 20th century, the parks have encouraged a heightened awareness of both Native cultures and their legacies and conservation issues, all of which will help guard the Southwest's precious heritage for generations to come.

Return of an early 19th-century Ancestral Puebloan artifact

1945 First atomic bomb tested at the Trinity site in southern New Mexico

1958 Joint Use Area established in Arizona to settle Hopi and Navajo land disputes

1974 Start of the Central Arizona Project to extract water from the Colorado River

1996 Bill Clinton signs Navajo-Hopi Land Dispute Settlement Act

2011 Spaceport America constructed near Las Cruces, New Mexico: to be the base for the first commercial space flights

1960 **1980** **2000** **2020**

1943 Scientists begin the top-secret Manhattan Project to build an atomic bomb at Los Alamos, New Mexico

1963 Opening of the Glen Canyon Dam

Fat Man atomic bomb

1982 Space Shuttle Columbia lands at White Sands Space Harbor

Columbia

Flowering cactus in the Sonoran Desert, Saguaro National Park ▶

ARIZONA

Introducing Arizona

This large expanse of land is a region of stunning natural beauty. In Arizona's southwest corner lies the hostile, but eerily beautiful, Sonoran desert. Its boundaries are occupied by the cities of Tucson and Phoenix, the state's biggest city and its economic center. To the north, the landscape changes, rising through high desert plateaus toward forests, canyons, and mountains. Here, the city of Flagstaff and the picturesque mountain towns of Sedona and Jerome attract thousands of visitors. The state's most famous sight is Grand Canyon (*see pp62–7*), which draws millions of tourists to Arizona every year.

The distinctive buttes of Cathedral Rock overlooking a fishing lake at Red Rock crossing near Sedona

Getting Around

Phoenix is a major hub for international and domestic flights. Driving, however, is the preferred option and Arizona has a good network of well-maintained highways. Northern Arizona is bisected by I-40 and I-10 cuts across the south; I-17 is the main north-south artery. Amtrak operates two train services that cross Arizona, and Greyhound buses run regular services to Arizona from major cities across the US.

Skyscrapers dominate the skyline of
Downtown Phoenix

Key

— Highway
— Major road
⋯ Minor road
— Main railroad
▮▮▮ International border
— State border
△ Summit

For additional map symbols *see back flap*

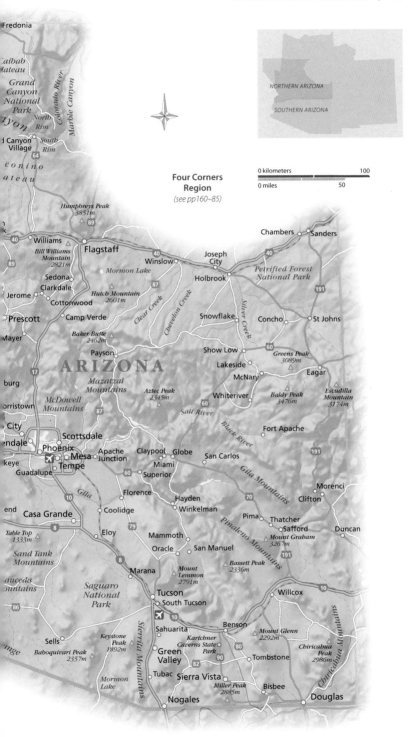

NORTHERN ARIZONA

SOUTHERN ARIZONA

Four Corners Region
(see pp160–85)

0 kilometers — 100
0 miles — 50

Fredonia

Kaibab Plateau

Grand Canyon National Park

Colorado River

Marble Canyon

North Rim

Canyon

South Rim

Canyon Village

64

Coconino Plateau

Williams

Bill Williams Mountain 2821m

Flagstaff

40

Sedona

Clarkdale

Jerome

Cottonwood

Prescott

Camp Verde

Mayer

Baker Butte 2462m

Payson

ARIZONA

Mazatzal Mountains

Aztec Peak 2345m

Salt River

McDowell Mountains

orriston

City

ndale

Scottsdale

Phoenix

Mesa

Tempe

Apache Junction

keye

Guadalupe

10

Gila

Florence

Coolidge

Casa Grande

end

Table Top 1333m

8

Eloy

Sand Tank Mountains

auceda untains

86

Sells

Baboquivari Peak 2357m

Keystone Peak 1892m

Marana

8

Saguaro National Park

Sierrita Mountains

Humphreys Peak 3851m

89

Winslow

Joseph City

40

Mormon Lake

Holbrook

Hutch Mountain 2601m

Clear Creek

Chevelon Creek

Snowflake

Chambers

Sanders

Petrified Forest National Park

191

Concho

St Johns

Silver Creek

Show Low

60

Greens Peak 3089m

Lakeside

Eagar

McNary

Whiteriver

Baldy Peak 3476m

Escudilla Mountain 3174m

Fort Apache

Claypool

Globe

San Carlos

Miami

Superior

Black River

Gila Mountains

191

Morenci

Clifton

Hayden

Winkelman

70

Pima

Thatcher

Safford

Duncan

Mount Graham 3267m

Mammoth

Oracle

San Manuel

Pinaleno Mountains

Bassett Peak 2336m

191

Mount Lemmon 2791m

Tucson

South Tucson

10

Sahuarita

Benson

Mount Glenn 2292m

Willcox

10

Chiricahua Mountains

Kartchner Caverns State Park

80

Chiricahua Peak 2986m

Green Valley

90

Tombstone

Tubac

82

Sierra Vista

Miller Peak 2885m

Bisbee

Douglas

Nogales

Mormon Lake

Route 66 in Arizona

Route 66 is America's most famous road. Stretching for 2,448 miles (3,941 km), from Chicago to Los Angeles, it is part of the country's folklore, symbolizing the freedom of the open road and inextricably linked to the growth of automobile travel. Known also as "The Mother Road" and "America's Main Street," Route 66 was officially opened in 1926 after a 12-year construction process linked the main streets of hundreds of small towns that had been previously isolated. In the 1930s, a prolonged drought in Oklahoma deprived more than 200,000 farmers of their livelihoods and prompted their trek to California along Route 66. This was movingly depicted in John Steinbeck's novel *The Grapes of Wrath* (1939).

Seligman features several Route 66 stores and diners. Set among Arizona's Upland mountains, the road here passes through scenery that evokes the days of the westward pioneers.

Route 66 in Arizona passes through long stretches of wilderness bearing none of the trappings of the modern world. The state has the longest remaining stretch of the original road.

Key

▬ Route 66

═ Other road

--- State line

0 kilometers 40

0 miles 40

Nelson

Hackberry Valentine

•Bullhead City

Kingman

Oatman is a former gold-mining boomtown. Today, its historic main street is lined with 19th-century buildings and boardwalks. Gunfights are regularly staged here.

The Grand Canyon Caverns, discovered in 1927, are around 0.75 miles (1.2 km) below ground level. On a 45-minute guided tour visitors are led through football field-sized caverns adorned with stalagmites and seams of sparkling crystals.

Route 66 in Popular Culture

In the 1940s and 1950s, as America's love affair with the car grew and more people moved west than ever before, hundreds of motels, restaurants, and tourist attractions appeared along Route 66, sporting a vibrant new style of architecture. The road's end as a major thoroughfare came in the 1970s with the building of a national network of multilane highways. Today, the road is a popular tourist destination in itself, and along the Arizona section, enthusiasts and conservationists have helped to ensure the preservation of many of its most evocative buildings and signs.

Locator Map
— Route 66
▨ Map area

Holbrook was founded in 1882 and is another Route 66 landmark. It is famous for Wigwam Village, a restored 1950s motel, where visitors can stay in rooms that are designed to resemble Indian teepees.

Bobby Troup, composer of the popular song, *Route 66*, in a 1948 Buick convertible

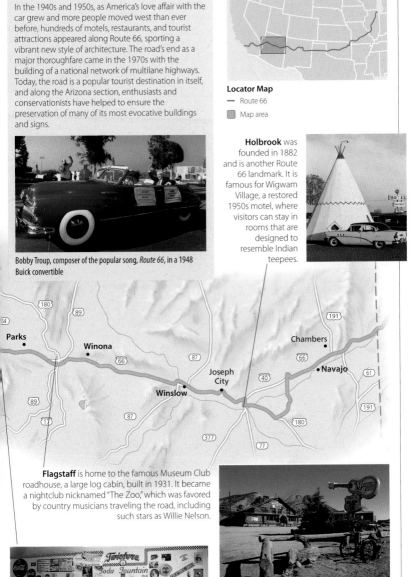

Flagstaff is home to the famous Museum Club roadhouse, a large log cabin, built in 1931. It became a nightclub nicknamed "The Zoo," which was favored by country musicians traveling the road, including such stars as Willie Nelson.

Williams is known for its many nostalgic diners and motels. Twisters café *(see p249),* also known as the Route 66 Place, is crammed with road memorabilia, including the original 1950s soda fountain and bar stools.

The Geology of Grand Canyon

Grand Canyon's multicolored layers of rock provide the best record of the Earth's formation of anywhere in the world. Each stratum of rock reveals a different period in the Earth's geological history beginning with the earliest, the Precambrian Era, which covers geological time up to 570 million years ago. Almost two billion years of history have been recorded in the canyon, although the most dramatic changes took place relatively recently, five to six million years ago, when the Colorado River began to carve its path through the canyon walls. The sloping nature of the Kaibab Plateau has led to increased erosion in some parts of the canyon.

A view of Grand Canyon's plateau and South Rim

View of the North Rim
The canyon's size and beauty are what make it one of the most visited sights in the US *(see pp62–67)*.

Canyon rim

KAIBAB FORMATION
TOROWEAP FORMATION
COCONINO SANDSTONE
HERMIT FORMATION

SUPAI GROUP

REDWALL LIMESTONE

TEMPLE BUTTE FORMATION

MUAV LIMESTONE

BRIGHT ANGEL SHALE

TAPEATS SANDSTONE

SUPERGROUP

Record of Life
The fossils found in each layer tell the story of the development of life on Earth. One of the oldest layers in the canyon, the Vishnu Schist, was formed in the Proterozoic era, when the first bacteria and algae were just emerging. Many of the layers were created by billions of small marine creatures whose hard shells eventually built up into thick layers of limestone.

The Asymmetrical Canyon
The North Rim of Grand Canyon is more eroded than the South Rim. The entire Kaibab Plateau slopes to the south, so rain falling at the North Rim flows toward the canyon and over the rim, creating deep side canyons and a wide space between the rim and the river.

The Surprise Canyon Formation
Classified by geologists in 1985, this new strata can be seen only in remote parts of the canyon. It was formed 320 million years ago.

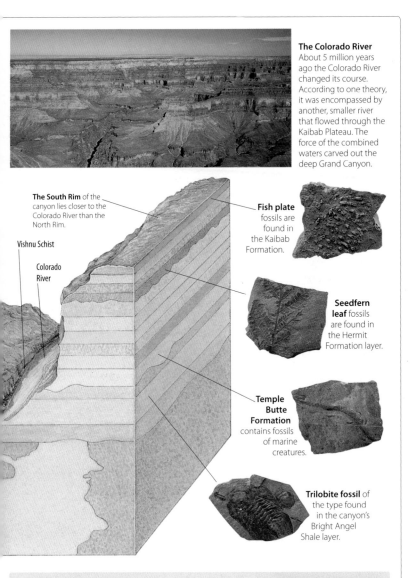

The Colorado River
About 5 million years ago the Colorado River changed its course. According to one theory, it was encompassed by another, smaller river that flowed through the Kaibab Plateau. The force of the combined waters carved out the deep Grand Canyon.

The South Rim of the canyon lies closer to the Colorado River than the North Rim.

Vishnu Schist

Colorado River

Fish plate fossils are found in the Kaibab Formation.

Seedfern leaf fossils are found in the Hermit Formation layer.

Temple Butte Formation contains fossils of marine creatures.

Trilobite fossil of the type found in the canyon's Bright Angel Shale layer.

How the Canyon Was Formed

While the Colorado River accounts for the canyon's depth, its width and formations are the work of even greater forces. Wind rushing through the canyon erodes the limestone and sandstone a few grains at a time. Rain pouring over the canyon rim cuts deep side canyons through the softer rock. Perhaps the greatest canyon-building force is ice. Water from rain and snowmelt works into cracks in the rock. When frozen, it expands, forcing the rock away from the canyon walls. The layers vary in hardness. Soft layers erode quickly into sloped faces. Harder rock resists erosion, leaving sheer vertical faces.

The Colorado River winding through the canyon

The Wild West

Romanticized in a thousand cowboy movies, the "Wild West" conjures up images of tough men herding cattle across the country before living it up in a saloon. But frontier life was far from romantic. Settlers arriving in this wilderness were caught up in a first-come-first-serve battle for land and wealth, fighting Native Americans and each other for land.

The rugged life of the mining prospectors and ranch cowboys helped to create the idea of the American West. Today, visitors can still see mining ghost towns such as Jerome *(see p76)* or enjoy re-enacted gunfights on the streets of Tombstone. In the late 19th century, however, such survival skills as good shooting often co-existed with a kill-or-be-killed ethos.

Old mining cottages, such as this one, may be seen in the Southwest's many former mining towns. The region's mining past can be traced in towns such as Oatman *(see p74)* and Bisbee *(see p96)*.

A reward poster for William Bonney (better known as Billy the Kid), who was one of the Wild West's most notorious outlaws. He was eventually tracked and killed by Sheriff Pat Garrett at Fort Sumner on July 14, 1881 *(see p229)*.

Deadwood Dick was the nickname of cowboy Nat Love – earned because of his cattle-roping skills. Although there were around 5,000 black cowboys, there are no sights or museums commemorating them in the Southwest today.

Cowboys were famous for their horsemanship and sense of camaraderie. The painting shows two friends attempting to save another.

The Questionable Companionship (1902) by Frederic Remington highlights the tensions between Native Americans and the US army, who had played a central role in removing tribes from their ancestral lands.

all over the west they wear

LEVI STRAUSS & CO'S
COPPER RIVETED
Overalls.

Cowboy fashion began to appear in advertisements in around 1900. The ever popular Levi Strauss denim clothing can be bought across the region *(see p264)*.

Guided trail rides are a great way to explore the Wild West and are part of the package of activities available at dude ranches *(see p271)*. These ranches offer visitors the opportunity to experience the contemporary cowboy lifestyle.

Horses were vividly depicted in Remington's dramatic action scenes. They were painted with astonishing realism, revealing a profound knowledge of their behavior and physique.

Southwestern Cowboys

New York-born artist Frederic Sackrider Remington (1861–1909) became well known for his epic portraits of cowboys, horses, soldiers, and Native Americans in the late 19th century. One such example of his work is the oil painting Aiding a Comrade (1890), *which celebrates the bravery and loyalty of the cowboy, at a time when they and small-scale ranchers were being superceded by powerful mining companies and ranching corporations. Remington lamented the passing of these heroes: "Cowboys! There are no cowboys anymore!"*

The Gunfight at the OK Corral

One of the most famous tales of the Wild West is the Gunfight at the OK Corral, in Tombstone, Arizona *(see p96)*. This struggle pitted two clans against each other, the Clantons and the Earps. The usual, often disputed, version features the Clantons as no-good outlaws and the Earps as the forces of law and order. In 1881 Virgil Earp was the town marshal, and his brothers Morgan and Wyatt were temporary deputies. The showdown on October 26 had the Earps and their ally Doc Holliday on one side and Billy Clanton and the McLaury brothers, Tom and Frank, on the other. Of the seven combatants, only Wyatt Earp emerged untouched by a bullet. Billy, Tom and Frank were all killed. Wyatt Earp moved to Los Angeles, where he died in 1929.

Scene from the 1957 film, *Gunfight at the OK Corral*, with Burt Lancaster and Kirk Douglas

GRAND CANYON AND NORTHERN ARIZONA

For most people, northern Arizona is famous as the location of Grand Canyon, a gorge of breathtaking proportions carved out of rock by the Colorado River as it flows southwest across the state towards the Gulf of Mexico. Northern Arizona's other attractions include the high desert landscape of the Colorado Plateau, with its sagebrush and yucca, punctuated by the forested foothills of the San Francisco Peaks. The Kaibab, Prescott, and Coconino National Forests cover large areas and provide the setting for the lively city of Flagstaff as well as for the charming towns of Sedona and Jerome. This region is also dotted with fascinating mining ghost towns such as Chloride and Oatman, a reminder that Arizona won its nickname, the Copper State, from the mineral mining boom that took place in the first half of the 20th century.

More than 25 percent of Arizona is Native American reservation land. The state is also home to several centuries-old Puebloan ruins, most notably the hilltop village of Tuzigoot and the hillside remains of Montezuma Castle.

Sights at a Glance

Historic Towns and Cities
- ❷ Flagstaff
- ❼ Williams
- ❽ Grand Canyon Skywalk/ Grand Canyon West
- ❾ Oatman
- ❿ Lake Havasu City
- ⓬ Camp Verde
- ⓮ Jerome
- ⓰ Sedona

National Parks and Monuments
- ❶ Grand Canyon
- ❸ Wupatki National Monument
- ❹ Sunset Crater National Monument
- ❺ Walnut Canyon National Monument
- ⓭ Montezuma Castle National Monument
- ⓯ Tuzigoot National Monument
- ⓲ Petrified Forest National Park

Areas of Natural Beauty
- ❻ Oak Creek Canyon
- ⓫ Heart of Arizona Tour
- ⓱ Meteor Crater

Key
- Interstate
- Major highway
- Highway
- Railroad

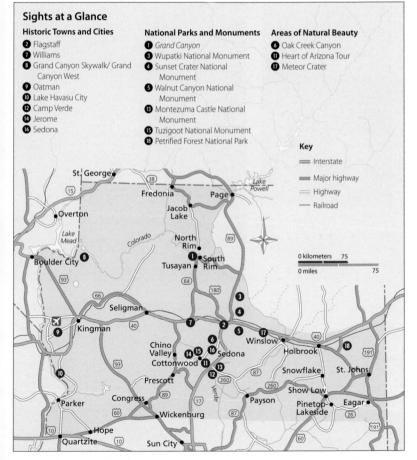

◀ Cathedral Rock reflected in Oak Creek, Red Rock State Park *(see p77)*　　**For additional map symbols** *see back flap*

❶ Grand Canyon

Grand Canyon is one of the world's great natural wonders and an instantly recognizable symbol of the Southwest. The canyon runs through Grand Canyon National Park *(see pp64–7)*, and is 277 miles (446 km) long, an average of 10 miles (16 km) wide, and around 5,000 ft (1,500 m) deep. It was formed over a period of six million years by the Colorado River, whose fast-flowing waters sliced their way through the Colorado Plateau *(see pp22–3)* which includes the gorge and most of northern Arizona and the Four Corners region. The plateau's geological vagaries have defined the river's twisted course and exposed vast cliffs and pinnacles that are ringed by rocks of different color, variegated hues of limestone, sandstone, and shale *(see pp56–7)*. By any standard, the canyon is spectacular, but its special beauty is in the ever-shifting patterns of light and shadow and the colors of the rock, bleached white at midday, but bathed in red and ocher at sunset.

Mule trip convoy
Mule rides, which must be booked in advance for the South Rim, are a popular way to explore the canyon's narrow trails.

Havasu Canyon
Since 1300 Havasu Canyon has been home to the Havasupai Indians. Now a population of around 500 Indians lives on the Havasupai Reservation, making a living from the tourist trade.

Grandview Point
At 7,400 ft (2,250 m), Grandview Point is one of the highest places on the South Rim, the canyon's southern edge. It is one of the stops along Desert View Drive *(see p65)*. The point is thought to be the spot from where the Spanish had their first glimpse of the canyon in 1540.

North Rim

The North Rim receives roughly one tenth the number of visitors of the South Rim. While less accessible, it is a more peaceful destination offering a sense of unexplored wilderness. It has a range of hikes, such as the North Kaibab Trail, a steep descent down to Phantom Ranch on the canyon floor *(see p64)*.

View from Hopi Point

Projecting far into the canyon, the tip of Hopi Point offers one of the best sunset-watching spots along Hermit Road. As the sun sets, it highlights the canyon's beautiful sculpted peaks.

Yavapai Point at the South Rim

Situated 5 miles (8 km) north of the canyon's South Entrance, along a stretch of the Rim Trail, is Yavapai Point. Its observation station offers spectacular views of the canyon, and a viewing panel identifies several of the central canyon's landmarks.

Bright Angel Trail

Used by both Native Americans and early settlers, the Bright Angel Trail follows a natural route along one of the canyon's enormous fault lines. It is an appealing option for day-hikers because unlike some other trails in the area, it offers some shade and several seasonal water sources.

Grand Canyon National Park

Grand Canyon National Park is a World Heritage Site located entirely within the state of Arizona. The park covers 1,904 sq miles (4,930 sq km), and is made up of the canyon itself, which starts where the Paria river empties into the Colorado, and stretches from Lees Ferry to Lake Mead *(see p124)*, and adjoining lands. The area won protective status as a National Monument in 1908 after Theodore Roosevelt visited in 1903, observing that it should be kept intact for future generations as "… the one great sight which every American … should see." The National Park was created in 1919.

The park has two main entrances, on the North and South rims of the canyon, However, the southern section of the park receives the most visitors and can become very congested during the summer season *(see pp66–7)*.

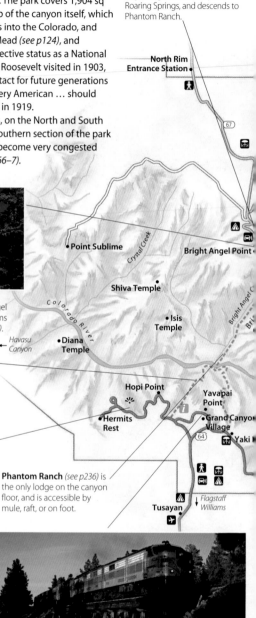

North Kaibab Trail follows Bright Angel Creek bed, past Roaring Springs, and descends to Phantom Ranch.

North Rim Entrance Station

Point Sublime

Crystal Creek

Bright Angel Point

Shiva Temple

Colorado River

Isis Temple

Havasu Canyon →

Diana Temple

Hopi Point

Yavapai Point

Hermits Rest

Grand Canyon Village

Yaki

Phantom Ranch *(see p236)* is the only lodge on the canyon floor, and is accessible by mule, raft, or on foot.

Tusayan

Flagstaff Williams ↓

Grand Canyon Lodge
Perched above the canyon at Bright Angel Point, the Grand Canyon Lodge has rooms and a number of dining options *(see p67)*.

Bright Angel Trail starts from the South Rim. It is well maintained but demanding. It descends into the canyon, where it meets the corresponding North Kaibab Trail from the North Rim.

Hermit Road
A free shuttle bus runs along this route to the Hermits Rest view-point during the summer. It is closed to private vehicles March to November.

Grand Canyon Railway
Restored steam trains make the 64-mile (103-km) trip from the town of Williams to Grand Canyon Village.

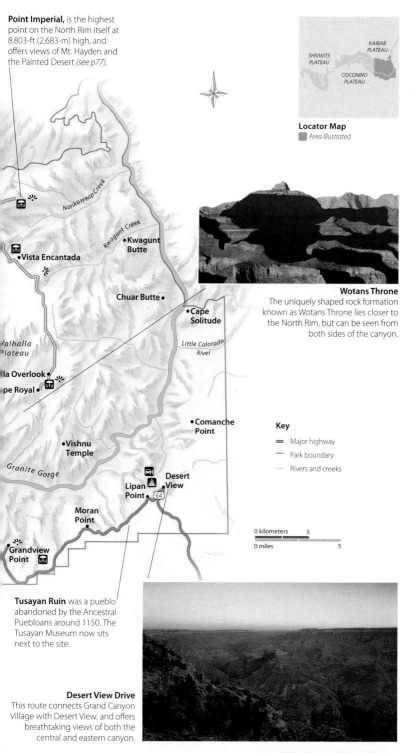

Point Imperial, is the highest point on the North Rim itself at 8,803-ft (2,683-m) high, and offers views of Mt. Hayden and the Painted Desert *(see p77).*

Locator Map
▓ *Area Illustrated*

SHIVWITS PLATEAU

KAIBAB PLATEAU

COCONINO PLATEAU

Nankoweap Creek

Kwagunt Creek

● **Kwagunt Butte**

▓ ● **Vista Encantada**

Chuar Butte ●

● **Cape Solitude**

Little Colorado River

Wotans Throne
The uniquely shaped rock formation known as Wotans Throne lies closer to the North Rim, but can be seen from both sides of the canyon.

Valhalla Plateau

la Overlook ●
pe Royal ● ▓

● **Comanche Point**

● **Vishnu Temple**

Granite Gorge

▓ **Desert View**
Lipan Point ● (64)

Moran Point

Grandview Point ▓

Key
▬ Major highway
┈ Park boundary
── Rivers and creeks

0 kilometers   5
0 miles   5

Tusayan Ruin was a pueblo abandoned by the Ancestral Puebloans around 1150. The Tusayan Museum now sits next to the site.

Desert View Drive
This route connects Grand Canyon Village with Desert View, and offers breathtaking views of both the central and eastern canyon.

For additional map symbols *see back flap*

Exploring Grand Canyon National Park

Grand Canyon offers awe-inspiring beauty on a vast scale. The magnificent rock formations with towers, cliffs, steep walls, and buttes recede as far as the eye can see, their bands of colored rock varying in shade as light changes through the day. The park's main roads, Hermit Road and Desert View Drive, both accessible from the south entrance, overlook the canyon. Grand Canyon Village is located on the South Rim and offers a full range of facilities. Visitors can also enter the park from the north, although this route (Hwy 67) is closed during winter. Walking trails along the North and South rims offer staggering views, but to experience the canyon at its most fascinating the trails that head down toward the canyon floor should be explored. The Bright Angel Trail on the South Rim, and the North Kaibab Trail on the North Rim, descend to the canyon floor, and are tough hikes involving an overnight stop.

Adobe, Pueblo-style architecture of Hopi House, Grand Canyon Village

🏠 Grand Canyon Village

Grand Canyon National Park. **Tel** (928) 638-7888. ♿ partial.

Grand Canyon Village has its roots in the late 19th century. The extensive building of visitor accommodations started after the Santa Fe Railroad opened a branch line here from Williams in 1901, though some hotels had been built in the late 1890s. The Fred Harvey Company constructed a clutch of well-designed, attractive buildings. The most prominent is El Tovar Hotel *(see p236)*. Opened in 1905, it is named after Spanish explorers who reached the gorge in 1540. The Hopi House also opened in 1905 – a rendition of a traditional Hopi dwelling, where locals could sell their craftwork as souvenirs. It was built by Hopi craftsmen and designed by Mary E. J. Colter. An ex-schoolteacher and trained architect, Colter drew on Southwestern influences, mixing both Native American and Hispanic styles *(see pp26–7)*. She is responsible for many of the historic structures that now grace the South Rim, including the 1914 Lookout Studio and Hermits Rest, and the rustic 1922 Phantom Ranch on the canyon floor.

Today, Grand Canyon Village has a wide range of hotels, restaurants, and stores. It can be surprisingly easy to get lost here since the buildings are spread out and discreetly placed among wooded areas. The Village is not only the starting point for most of the mule trips through the canyon, but also the terminus for the Grand Canyon Railway.

The South Rim

Most of the Grand Canyon's 4.4 million annual visitors come to the South Rim, since, unlike the North Rim, it is open year-round and is easily accessible along Highway 180/64 from Flagstaff or Williams. **Hermit Road** is closed to private vehicles from March to November each year, but there are free shuttle buses. **Desert View Drive** (Hwy 64) is open all year, winter snows permitting. Both roads start at Grand Canyon Village and encompass a selection of the choicest views of the gorge. From Grand Canyon Village, Hermit Road extends 8 miles (13 km) to Hermits Rest and, in the opposite direction, Desert View Drive takes 26 miles (42 km) to reach the stunning Desert View overlook, and then continues another 34 miles (54 km) west to Cameron.

Beginning at Grand Canyon Village, Hermit Road meanders along the South Rim, its first viewpoint being **Trailview Overlook**, which provides an overview of the canyon and the winding course of the Bright Angel Trail. Moving on, **Maricopa Point** offers especially panoramic views of the canyon but not of the Colorado River, which is more apparent from nearby **Hopi Point**. At the end of Hermit Road lies **Hermits Rest**, where a gift shop, decorated in rustic style, is located in yet another Mary Colter-designed building. Just east of Grand Canyon Village is **Yavapai**

The interior of the Hermits Rest gift store with crafts for sale lining the walls

Desert View's stone watchtower on Desert View Drive

California Condors

The California Condor is America's largest bird, with a wingspan of over 9 ft (2.7 m). The species was almost extinct in the 1980s, when the last 22 condors were captured for breeding in captivity. In 1996 the first captive-bred birds were released in Northern Arizona. Today, over 70 condors fly the skies over Northern Arizona. They are frequent visitors to the South Rim, though visitors should not approach or feed them.

A pair of California condors

Point from where it is possible to see Phantom Ranch *(see p236)*. This is the only roofed accommodation available on the canyon floor, across the Colorado River.

The longer Desert View Drive winds for 12 miles (20 km) to **Grandview Point**, where the Spaniards may have had their first glimpse of the canyon in 1540. Ten miles (16 km) farther on lie the pueblo remains of Tusayan Ruin, where there is a small museum featuring exhibits on Ancestral Puebloan life. After a few miles, the road leads to **Desert View** where the Watchtower was Colter's most fanciful creation, its upper floor decorated with early 20th-century Hopi murals.

The North Rim

Standing at about 8,000 ft (2,400 m), the North Rim is higher, cooler, and greener than the South Rim, with dense forests of ponderosa pine, aspen, and Douglas fir. Visitors are likely to spot wildlife on the North Rim. Mule deer, Kaibab squirrel, and wild turkey are among the most common sights. The North Rim is reached via Highway 67, off Highway 89A, ending at **Grand Canyon Lodge** *(see pp236 and 248)* where there are visitor services, a campground, gas station, restaurant, and a general store. Nearby, the North Rim Visitor Center offers maps of the area. Facilities on the North Rim are closed mid-October–mid-May, while the road access

is blocked by snow for most of the winter. The North Rim is twice as far from the river as the South Rim, and the canyon really stretches out from the overlooks giving a sense of its 10-mile (16-km) width. There are about 30 miles (45 km) of scenic roads along the North Rim as well as hiking trails to high viewpoints or down to the canyon floor (particularly the North Kaibab Trail that links to the South Rim's Bright Angel Trail.) The picturesque **Cape Royal Drive** starts north of Grand Canyon Lodge and travels 23 miles (37 km) to Cape Royal on the Walhalla Plateau.

From here, several famous buttes and peaks can be seen, including Wotans Throne and Vishnu Temple. There are also several short, easy walking trails around Cape Royal, both along the top. A 3-mile (5-km) detour leads to **Point Imperial**, the highest point on the canyon rim, while along the way the **Vista Encanta** has delightful views and picnic tables overlooking the gorge.

Mule deer on the canyon's North Rim

The Bright Angel Trail

This is the most popular of all Grand Canyon hiking trails. The Bright Angel trailhead is at Grand Canyon Village on the South Rim. The trail begins near the Kolb Studio at the western end of Grand Canyon Village. It then switches dramatically down the side of the canyon for 9 miles (13 km). The trail crosses the river over a suspension bridge, ending a little further on at Phantom Ranch. There are two resthouses and a fully equipped campground along the way. Do not attempt to walk all the way to the river and back in one day. Many walk from the South Rim to one of the rest stops and then return up to the rim. Temperatures at the bottom of the canyon can reach 110°F (43°C) or higher during the summer. It is essential for day hikers to carry a quart (just over a liter) of water per person per hour for summer hiking, as well as plenty of salty snacks. Carrying a first-aid kit is also recommended.

Visitors at the trailhead of the Bright Angel Trail

The sheer cliffs of Grand Canyon and the Colorado River far below ▶

❷ Flagstaff

Nestling among the pine forests of Northern Arizona's San Francisco Peaks, Flagstaff is one of the region's most attractive towns. It is a lively, easy-going place with a good selection of bars and restaurants among the maze of old red-brick buildings that make up its compact downtown. Flagstaff's first Anglo settlers were sheep ranchers who arrived in 1876. The railroad came in 1882, and the town developed as a lumber center.

Flagstaff is the home of Northern Arizona University, which has two appealing art galleries, and is a good base for visiting Grand Canyon's South Rim, which is just under two hours' drive away. The surrounding mountains attract hikers in summer and skiers in winter.

The town of Flagstaff with the San Francisco Peaks as a backdrop

Exploring Flagstaff

Flagstaff's center is narrow and slender, channeling north toward the Museum of Northern Arizona and south to the University. At its heart is a pocket-sized historic district, an attractive ensemble of red-brick buildings, which houses the best restaurants and bars. Lowell Observatory is located on Mars Hill, a short distance from downtown, and the popular Arizona Snowbowl ski resort is an enjoyable ten-minute drive to the north of the town.

🏛 The Lowell Observatory

1400 West Mars Hill Rd. **Tel** (928) 233-3212. **Open** Jun–Aug: 9am–10pm daily; Sep–May: times vary; call for details. **Closed** public hols. 🅿 ♿ 📷
🌐 **lowell.edu**

Tucked away on a hill about a mile northwest of the town center, the Lowell Observatory was founded in 1894 and named for its benefactor,

Percival Lowell, a member of one of Boston's wealthiest families. He financed the observatory to look for life on Mars and chose the town because of its high altitude and clear mountain air.

The Lowell Observatory went on to establish an international reputation with its documented evidence of an expanding universe, data that was disclosed

1930 Pluto dome at Flagstaff's Lowell Observatory

to the public in 1912. One of the observatory's famous astronomers, Clyde Tombaugh, discovered the dwarf planet Pluto on February 18, 1930. The Observatory continues to build upon this legacy today.

Visitors have access to the main rotunda, exhibition halls, and the John Vickers McAllister Space Theater, which shows presentations on the night sky and current research at Lowell. Tours are available daily, and telescope viewings nightly.

🖼 Historic Downtown

Just ten minutes' walk from end to end, Flagstaff's historic downtown dates mainly from the 1890s. Many buildings sport decorative stone and stucco friezes and are now occupied by cafés, bars, and stores. Architecturally, several buildings stand out, particularly the restored Babbitt Building and the 1926 train station that today houses the visitor center. Perhaps the most attractive building is the Weatherford Hotel, which was opened on January 1, 1900. It was named after its owner, Texan entrepreneur John W. Weatherford, and was much admired for its grand two-story wraparound veranda and its sunroom.

🏛 Northern Arizona University

624 S. Knoles Dr. Flagstaff. **Tel** (928) 523-9011. **Open** times vary, so call in advance. 🌐 **nau.edu**

Flagstaff's lively café society owes much to the 18,000 students of Northern Arizona University (NAU). The main entrance point to the campus is located on Knoles Drive. Green lawns, stately trees, and several historic buildings make for a pleasant visit.

Of particular note are two campus art galleries: the Beasley Gallery in the Fine Art Building, which features temporary exhibitions and student work, and the Old Main Art Museum and Gallery housed in Old Main Building – the university's oldest. This features the permanent Weiss collection, which includes works by the famous Mexican artist Diego Rivera.

Arts and Crafts swinging settee at Riordan Mansion

🏛 **Riordan Mansion State Historic Park**

409 Riordan Rd. **Tel** (928) 779-4395.
Open May–Oct: 9:30am–5pm Thu–Mon; Nov–Apr: 10:30am–5pm Thu–Mon. **Closed** Dec 25. 🈳 &
W azstateparks.com

In the mid-1880s, Michael and Timothy Riordan established a lumber company that quickly made them a fortune. The brothers then built a house of grandiose proportions, a 40-room log mansion with two wings, one for each of them. Completed in 1904 and now preserved as a State Historic Park, the house has a rustic, timber-clad exterior, and Arts and Crafts furniture inside.

🏛 **Pioneer Museum**

2340 N. Fort Valley Rd. **Tel** (928) 774-6272. **Open** 9am–5pm Mon–Sat. **Closed** Sun, public hols. 🈳
W arizonahistoricalsociety.org

Flagstaff's Pioneer Museum occupies an elegant stone building that was originally built as a hospital in 1908. The museum opened in 1960 and incorporates the Ben Doney homestead cabin. On display in the grounds are a steam locomotive of 1929 and a Santa Fe Railroad caboose. Inside, a particular highlight is a selection of Grand Canyon photographs taken in the early 1900s by photographers Ellsworth and Emery Kolb.

Arizona Snowbowl

Snowbowl Rd, off Hwy 180. **Tel** (928) 779-1951. **Tel** Flagstaff Snow Report: (928) 779-4577. **Open** Dec–mid-Apr.
W arizonasnowbowl.com

Downhill skiing is available at the Arizona Snowbowl just 7 miles (11 km) north of town. The mountains here are the San Francisco Peaks, which receive an average of 260 in (660 cm) of snow every year, enough to supply the various ski runs that pattern

the lower slopes of the 12,356-ft-(3,707-m-) high Agassiz Peak. Facilities include four chairlifts, and a ski school for beginners.

In summer, there is a hiking trail up to the peak, while for those less inclined to walk the Arizona Scenic Chairlift offers spectacular views of the scenery.

🏛 **Museum of Northern Arizona**

See p72.

See p72.

VISITORS' CHECKLIST

Practical Information
Road map C3. 🚗 66,000. ℹ
Flagstaff Visitor Center, at Amtrak depot, 1 East Route 66, Flagstaff (928) 774-9541. **Open** 8am–5pm Mon–Sat, 9am–4pm Sun. **Closed** public hols. 🎿 Hopi Festival of the Arts (early July).
W flagstaffarizona.org

Transport
✈ Pulliam Airport, 4 miles (6 km) south of town. 🚉 Amtrak Flagstaff Station, 1 East Route 66. 🚌 Flagstaff bus station, 800 E. Butler Ave.

Flagstaff

① The Lowell Observatory
② Historic Downtown District
③ Northern Arizona University
④ Riordan Mansion State Historic Park

For keys to symbols *see back flap*

Museum of Northern Arizona, Flagstaff

The Museum of Northern Arizona holds one of the Southwest's most comprehensive collections of Southwestern archaeological artifacts, as well as fine art and natural science exhibits. The collections are arranged in a series of galleries around a central courtyard. Beside the main entrance is the Archaeology Gallery, with a fine introduction to the region's historic cultures. The Ethnology Gallery documents 12,000 years of Hopi, Zuni, Navajo, and Pai tribal cultures on the Colorado Plateau. The museum shop sells contemporary native fine arts and the bookstore specializes in native arts and crafts.

VISITORS' CHECKLIST

Practical Information
3101 North Fort Valley Rd.
Tel (928) 774-5213. **Open** 9am–
5pm daily. **Closed** public hols.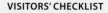
musnaz.org

The inner courtyard has exhibits that focus on the variety of plants and animals found on the Colorado Plateau through the ages.

★ Ethnology Gallery
This gallery highlights the living cultures of the region; that of the Hopi, Navajo, Pai, and Zuni people.

The Kiva Gallery replicates the inside of a *kiva (see p165).*

Babbitt gallery

Geology Gallery
A lifesize skeletal model of a Dilophosaurus is ringed by dioramas of ancient Arizona desert scenes.

Key

- Archaeology Gallery
- Ethnology Gallery
- Babbitt Gallery
- Geology Gallery
- Historic courtyard
- Exhibition Gallery
- Non-exhibition space

Entrance

Archaeology Gallery

Museum Façade
Built in 1935, the museum has a stone façade and is listed on the National Register of Historic Places.

❸ Wupatki National Monument

Road map C3. Forest Service Rd 545, Sunset Crater/Wupatki Loop Rd. **Tel** (928) 679-2365. 🚋 Flagstaff. 🚌 Flagstaff. **Open** 9am–5pm daily. **Closed** Dec 25. 🅿️ 🚻 partial. 📷 🌐 nps.gov/wupa

Covering over 56 sq miles (142 sq km) of sun-scorched wilderness to the north of Flagstaff, the Wupatki National Monument incorporates about 2,700 historic sites once inhabited by the ancestors of the Hopi people. The area was first settled after the eruption of Sunset Crater in 1064. The Sinagua people and their Ancestral Puebloan cousins realized that the volcanic ash had made the soil more fertile and consequently favourable for farming. The power of the volcanic eruption may also have appealed to their spirituality. They left the region in the early 13th century, but no one really knows why *(see pp164–5)*.

The largest site here is the Wupatki Pueblo, built in the 12th century and once a four-story pueblo complex of 100 rooms, housing more than 100 Sinagua. The structures rise from their rocky outcrop overlooking the desert. A trail explores the remains, the most unusual feature of which is a Central American-style ballcourt. Here the Sinagua may have played at dropping a ball through a stone ring without using hands or feet.

❹ Sunset Crater Volcano National Monument

Road map C3. Hwy 545 off Hwy 89, Sunset Crater/Wupatki Loop Rd. **Tel** (928) 526-0502. 🚋 Flagstaff. 🚌 Flagstaff. **Open** daily. **Closed** Dec 25. 🅿️ 🚻 🌐 nps.gov/sucr

In 1064, a mighty volcanic eruption formed the 400-ft- (120-m-) deep Sunset Crater, leaving a cinder cone that rises 1,000 ft (300 m) above the surrounding lava field. Aptly named, the cone is black at the base and tinged with reds and oranges farther up. The one-mile (1.6-km) self-guided Lava Trail offers an easy stroll around the ashy landscape with its lava tubes, bubbles, and vents.

❺ Walnut Canyon National Monument

Road map C3. Hwy 40 exit 204. **Tel** (928) 526-3367. 🚋 Flagstaff. 🚌 Flagstaff. **Open** 9am–5pm daily (8am–5pm May–Oct). **Closed** Dec 25. 🅿️ 🚻 partial. 📷 🌐 nps.gov/waca

Located about 10 miles (16 km) east of Flagstaff, off Interstate Hwy 40, Walnut Canyon houses an intriguing collection of cliff dwellings. These were inhabited by the Sinagua, ancestors of the Hopi, in the 12th and 13th centuries. The

Sinagua were attracted to the canyon by its fertile soil and plentiful water from nearby Walnut Creek.

Today, visitors can tour 25 cliff dwellings huddled underneath the natural overhangs of the canyon's eroded sandstone and limestone walls. The Sinagua left the canyon abruptly around the middle of the 13th century, possibly as a result of war, drought, or disease *(see pp164–5)*. Sinagua artifacts are on display in the Walnut Canyon Visitor Center.

Petroglyph from Walnut Canyon

❻ Oak Creek Canyon

Road map C3. ℹ️ (800) 288-7336.

Just south of Flagstaff, Highway 89A weaves a charming route which makes for a very pleasant drive through Oak Creek Canyon on the way to the town of Sedona *(see p77)*. In the canyon, dense woods shadow the road, and the steep cliffs are colored in bands of red and yellow sandstone, pale limestone, and black basalt. This is a popular summer vacation area with many day-hiking trails, such as the East Pocket Trail, a steep wooded climb to the canyon rim. At nearby Slide Rock State Park, swimmers enjoy sliding over the rocks that form a natural water chute.

The Wupatki National Monument with ruins of a 12th-century pueblo building and San Francisco Peaks behind

❼ Williams

Road map B3. 🏠 3,000. 🚉
ℹ️ 200 W. Railroad Ave. (928) 635-
1418. 🌐 experiencewilliams.com

This distinctive little town was
named in 1851 for Bill Williams
(1787–1849), a legendary
mountain man and trapper who
lived for a time with the Osage
Indians in Missouri. The town
grew up around the railroad
that arrived in the 1880s, and
when this was followed by a
spur track to Grand Canyon's
South Rim in 1901, Williams
became established as a tourist
center. By the late 1920s, it was
also a popular rest stop on
Route 66 (see pp54–5).

Today, the town retains its
frontier atmosphere, complete
with Stetson-wearing locals.
Most of its hotels and diners are
arranged around a loop that
follows Route 66 on one side
and its replacement, Interstate
Highway 40, on the other.
Diners evoke the 1950s and
are filled with Route 66
memorabilia, including original
soda fountains and posters.

Twisters, a retro-style diner off Route 66 in
Williams (see p249)

❽ Grand Canyon Skywalk/Grand Canyon West

Road map B3. ℹ️ Grand Canyon
West: reservations (928) 769 2636. 🚌
🌐 grandcanyonwest.com

The Grand Canyon Skywalk –
a dramatic 70-ft (21-m) glass
walkway cantilevered beyond
the rim and 4,000 ft (1220 m)
above the floor of the Grand
Canyon – is a project of the
Hualapai tribe. Located near
their modest resort, the
Hualapai Ranch, the Skywalk
and Grand Canyon West are
situated much closer to Las
Vegas than to the famous
South Rim of the canyon

The Skywalk, overlooking the Colorado River

which is nearly 250 miles
(402 km) away by road. All-
inclusive package tours can
be booked from Las Vegas –
most visitors fly – and on site.

These include demonstrations
of cowboy skills, horseback
riding, and helicopter or boat
rides, in addition to the Skywalk
itself. An Indian Village features
recreated dwellings of the
Hualapai tribe and three other
Arizona tribes. Native American
cultural performances and
presentations are put on daily in
the village's amphitheater.

A shuttle bus operates
within the Grand Canyon West
area as no private vehicles
are permitted.

❾ Oatman

Road map A3. 🏠 100. ℹ️ P.O. Box
423, Oatman (928) 768-6222.
🌐 oatmangoldroad.org

In 1904, prospectors struck gold
in the Black Mountains and
Oatman became their main
supply center. Today, it is
popular with visitors wanting a
taste of its boomtown past,
such as the 1920s hotel where

Carole Lombard and Clark Gable
honeymooned in 1939.
Gunfights are staged daily.

❿ Lake Havasu City

Road map A4. 🏠 53,000. ✈️ 🚌 ℹ️
314 London Bridge Road (928) 453-
3444. 🌐 golakehavasu.com

California businessman Robert
McCulloch founded Lake Havasu
City in 1964. The resort city he
built on the Colorado River was
popular with the landlocked
citizens of Arizona. His real
brainwave came four years later
when he bought London Bridge
and transported it from England
to Lake Havasu. Some mocked
McCulloch, suggesting that he
had thought he was buying
London's Gothic Tower Bridge,
not this much more ordinary
one. There was more hilarity
when it appeared that there was
nothing in Havasu City for the
bridge to span. Undaunted,
McCulloch simply created the
waterway he needed. Today this
is one of Arizona's most popular
areas for outdoor recreation,
with visitors enjoying the
shops and restaurants here.

London Bridge spans a man-made waterway in Lake Havasu City

⓫ Heart of Arizona Tour

The Verde River passes through the wooded hills and fertile meadows of central Arizona, before opening into a wide, green valley between Flagstaff and Phoenix. The heart of Arizona is full of charming towns such as Sedona, hidden away among stunning scenery, and the former mining town of Jerome. Over the hills lies Prescott, once state capital and now a busy, likable little town with a center full of dignified Victorian buildings. The area's ancient history can be seen in its two beautiful pueblo ruins, Montezuma Castle and Tuzigoot.

Tips for Drivers

Recommended route: From Sedona, take Hwy 89A to Tuzigoot, Jerome, and Prescott. Hwy 69 runs east from Prescott to the Interstate Highway 17, which connects to Camp Verde, Fort Verde, and Montezuma Castle. **Tour length:** 85 miles (137 km). **When to go:** Spring and fall are delightful; summer is very hot.

① Sedona
Set among dramatic red rock hills, Sedona is a popular resort, known for its New Age stores and galleries as well as for its friendly ambience.

② Tuzigoot National Monument
Stunning views of the Verde River Valley are seen at this ruined hilltop pueblo, occupied until 1425.

Key

▨ Tour route

═ Other road

↑ *Flagstaff*

Sedona

Cottonwood •

Verde River

Prescott Valley •

• Prescott

③ Jerome
A popular relic of Arizona's mining boom, Jerome is known for its 1900s brick buildings that cling to the slopes of Cleopatra Hill.

↓ *Phoenix*

0 km   10
0 miles   10

⑥ Montezuma Castle National Monument
The Ancestral Puebloan ruins here date from the 1100s and occupy one of the loveliest sites in the Southwest.

④ Prescott
This charming historic town is set among the rugged peaks and lush woods of Prescott National Forest, making it a popular center for many outdoor activities.

Camp Verde ⑤
A highlight of this little town is Fort Verde. Built by the US Army in 1865, this stone fort is manned by costumed guides.

For additional map symbols *see back flap*

Pueblo remains of Montezuma Castle, built into limestone cliffs

⑫ Camp Verde

Road map B4. 🏔 6,000. ℹ️ 385 South Main St. (928) 567-9294. 🔺 🌐 **visitcampverde.com**

Farmers founded the small settlement of Camp Verde in the heart of the Verde River Valley in the 1860s. It was a risky enterprise as the Apache lived nearby, but the US Army quickly moved in to protect the settlers, building **Fort Verde** in 1865.

Today, Camp Verde remains at the center of a large and prosperous farming and ranching community. It was from Fort Verde that the army orchestrated a series of brutal campaigns against the Apache, which ended with the Battle of the Big Dry Wash in 1882.

Once the Apache had been sent to reservations, Fort Verde was no longer needed and was decommissioned in 1891. Four of its original buildings have survived. The former army administration building has a collection of exhibits on army life. The interiors of the other three houses, on Officers' Row, have been restored. On weekends from spring to fall, volunteers in period costume act as guides and re-enact scenes from the fort's daily life.

🏛 **Fort Verde State Historic Park** Off Hwy I-17. **Tel** (928) 567-3275. **Open** 9am–5pm Thu–Mon. 🌐

Costumed guides at Fort Verde State Historic Park

⑬ Montezuma Castle National Monument

Road map C4. Hwy I-17 exit 289. **Tel** (928) 567-3322. **Open** 8am–5pm daily. 🌐 **nps.gov/moca**

Dating from the 1100s, the pueblo remains that make up Montezuma Castle occupy an idyllic location, built into the limestone cliffs high above Beaver Creek, a couple of miles to the east of Interstate Highway 17. Once home to the Sinagua people, this cliff dwelling originally contained 20 rooms spread over five floors. Montezuma Castle was declared a National Monument in 1906 to preserve its excellent condition. The visitor center has a display on Sinaguan life and is found at the start of an easy trail along Beaver Creek, with its views of the ruins.

The National Monument also incorporates Montezuma Well, situated about 11 miles (18 km) away to the northeast. This natural sinkhole, 50 ft (15 m) deep and 470 ft (140 m) in diameter, had religious significance for Native Americans, with several tribes believing it was the site of the Creation. Over 1,000 gallons (3,790 liters) of water flow through the sinkhole every minute, an inexhaustible supply that has long been used to irrigate the surrounding land. A narrow trail leads around the rim before twisting its way down to the water's edge.

⑭ Jerome

Road map B4. 🏔 500. ℹ️ Box K, Jerome (928) 634-2900. ♿ partial. 🌐 **jerome chamber.com**

Approached from the east along Highway 89A, Jerome is easy to spot in the distance, its tangle of old brick buildings perched high above the valley, clinging to the steep slopes of Cleopatra Hill. Silver mining began here in the 1870s, but the town's big break came in 1912 when prospectors hit a vein of copper no less than 5 ft (1.5 m) thick. Just two years later, World War I sent the price of copper sky high and Jerome boomed. In the Wall Street Crash of 1929, however, copper prices tumbled and, although the mines survived until 1953, the boom times were over. To make matters worse, underground dynamiting had made Cleopatra Hill unstable, and the town began to slide downhill at a rate of 4 in (10 cm) a year. By the early 1960s, Jerome was virtually a ghost town, but its fortunes were revived by an influx of artists and artisans, whose galleries and stores attracted tourists. Today Jerome is often busy with day-trippers who come to see the late 19th- and early 20th-century brick buildings that make up the town's historic center.

Façade of an early 20th-century store on Jerome's historic Main Street

For hotels and restaurants see pp236–43 and pp248–61

The ford across picturesque Oak Creek at Red Rock Crossing, Sedona

⓲ Meteor Crater

Road map C3. Off Hwy 40 exit 233. **Tel** (800) 289-5898. **Open** Jun–Aug: 7am–7pm daily; Sep–May: 8am–5pm daily. **Closed** Dec 25. 🖼 **w** meteorcrater.com

The Barringer Meteor Crater, a meteorite impact crater, was formed nearly 50,000 years ago. The crater is 550 ft (167 m) deep and 2.4 miles (4 km) in circumference, and so closely resembles a moon crater that NASA astronauts trained here in the 1960s. Guided rim tours are available and the visitor center tells the story of the crater through exhibits and a film.

⓳ Petrified Forest National Park

Road map D3. Off Hwy I-40. **Tel** (928) 524-6228. **Open** hours vary (about 7am–8pm in mid-summer and 8am–5pm in mid-winter). **Closed** Dec 25. 🖼 **w** nps.gov/pefo

This national park is one of Arizona's most unusual attractions. Millions of years ago rivers swept trees downstream into a vast swamp that once covered this area. Ground-water transported silica dioxide into downed timber, eventually turning it into the quartz stone logs seen today, with colored crystals preserving the trees' shape and structure.

Running the length of the forest is the Painted Desert, an area of colored bands of sand and rock changing from blues to reds as light catches mineral deposits.

From the Painted Desert Visitor Center, a scenic road travels the length of the park. There are nine overlooks on the route, including Kachina Point, where the Painted Desert Wilderness trailhead is located. Near the south end of the road is the **Rainbow Forest Museum**.

Ⅲ Rainbow Forest Museum
Off Hwy 180 (south entrance). **Tel** (928) 524-6228. **Open** hours vary. **Closed** Dec 25. 🖼

⓯ Tuzigoot National Monument

Road map B4. Follow signs from Hwy 89A. **Tel** (928) 634-5564. **Open** 8am–5pm daily. **Closed** Dec 25. 🖼 **w** nps.gov/tuzi

On a solitary, slender limestone ridge, the Tuzigoot National Monument ruins offer splendid views of the Verde River Valley. The pueblo was built by the Sinagua people between the 12th and 15th centuries and, at its peak, had a population of around 300. It was abandoned in the early 15th century, when it is believed the Sinagua migrated north to join the Ancestral Puebloans.

Tuzigoot was partly rebuilt by a local and federally funded program during the Depression in the 1930s. This emphasized one of the most unusual features of pueblo building, the lack of doorways. The normal pueblo room was entered by ladder through a hatchway in the roof. Sinaguan artifacts and art are on display at the visitor center.

⓰ Sedona

Road map C3. 🖼 16,000. 🚗 🚌 **i** 331 Forest Rd. (800) 288-7336. **w** visitsedona.com

The town of Sedona sits amid the magnificent red-rock cliffs and canyons south of Flagstaff. In 1981, the psychic and writer Page Bryant identified seven vortexes in the area, which she believed emanated electromagnetic energies that invigorated the soul. The subsequent influx of "New Agers" was followed by a burgeoning tourist industry that is reflected in the range of restaurants, hotels, stores, and art galleries here.

Sedona is a good base from which to explore the area. Accessed from Red Rock Loop Road, Crescent Moon Ranch is a US Forest Service Recreation Area with a ford across Oak Creek. Farther along Red Rock Loop Road is Red Rock State Park, where a gentle, wooded stretch of Oak Creek offers hikes and lovely picnic spots.

Cross section of petrified log

PHOENIX AND SOUTHERN ARIZONA

Mountain ranges and sun-bleached plateaus ripple the wide landscapes of southern Arizona, a staggeringly beautiful region dominated by pristine tracts of desert, parts of which are protected within the Saguaro National Park and the Organ Pipe Cactus National Monument. This land was first farmed around 400 BC by the Hohokam people *(see p42)* who carefully used the meager water supplies to irrigate their crops. When the Spanish settled here in the 18th century, they built fortified outposts throughout the region. This Hispanic heritage is recalled by the beautiful mission churches of San Xavier del Bac and Tumacacori and in the popular historic city of Tucson that grew up around the 1776 Spanish fort. When silver was discovered nearby in the 1870s, the scene was set for a decade of rowdy frontier life. Today, towns such as Tombstone, famous for the "Gunfight at the OK Corral", recreate this wild west era. The influx of miners also spurred the growth of Phoenix, a farming town established on the banks of the Salt River in the 1860s. Phoenix is now the largest city in the Southwest, known for its warm winter climate and recreational facilities.

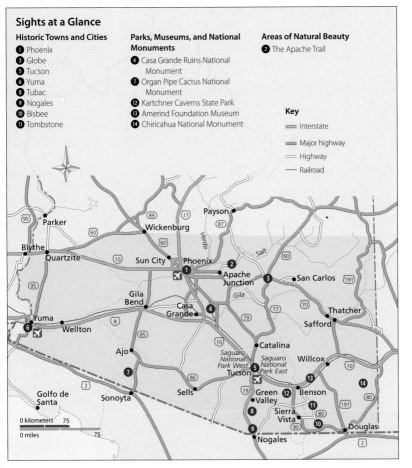

Sights at a Glance

Historic Towns and Cities
1. Phoenix
3. Globe
5. Tucson
6. Yuma
8. Tubac
9. Nogales
10. Bisbee
11. Tombstone

Parks, Museums, and National Monuments
4. Casa Grande Ruins National Monument
7. Organ Pipe Cactus National Monument
12. Kartchner Caverns State Park
13. Amerind Foundation Museum
14. Chiricahua National Monument

Areas of Natural Beauty
2. The Apache Trail

Key
━━━ Interstate
━━━ Major highway
═══ Highway
──── Railroad

◀ The Baroque church at San Xavier del Bac Mission, Tucson

For additional map symbols *see back flap*

❶ Phoenix

Phoenix is a huge metropolis, stretching across the Salt River Valley. Farmers and ranchers settled here in the 1860s. By 1912, the city had developed into the political and economic focus of Arizona and was the state capital. As it grew, it absorbed surrounding towns, although each district still maintains its identity. Downtown Phoenix is home to many historic attractions, including restored Victorian houses in Heritage Square, the Phoenix Art Museum, and the Heard Museum *(see pp82–3)* with its excellent collection of Native American artifacts.

Noodle Forest at the Children's Museum of Phoenix

Exploring Downtown Phoenix

Downtown Phoenix, where the city began in the 19th century, is centered on Washington and Jefferson Streets, running east to west between 7th Street and 19th Avenue. Central Avenue is the main north-south axis: to its east, parallel roads are "Streets," while roads to the west are "Avenues." City sights are mostly too far apart to see on foot, but the Metro Light Rail system connects Downtown sights along its 20-mile (32-km) run from Camelback Road to the towns of Tempe and Mesa in the Phoenix Metropolitan Area.

🏛 Arizona Capitol Museum

1700 West Washington St. **Tel** (602) 926-3620. **Open** 9am–4pm Mon–Fri; Sep–May also 10am–2pm Sat. **Closed** public hols. 🚻 **W** lib.az.us/museum

Completed in 1900, the Arizona Capitol houses the legislative and executive branches of the state government, as well as

the museum. The handsome copper cladding of the dome, originally added in 1975, was replaced in 2012 for the statehood centennial.

The museum covers Arizona government past and present using high-tech as well as traditional displays. Spread over four stories, the exhibits illustrate topics such as Arizona's transition from territory to state and the development of tourism in the Grand Canyon.

🏛 Children's Museum of Phoenix

215 N. 7th St. **Tel** (602) 253-0501. **Open** May–Jul: 9am–4pm daily; Aug–Apr: 9am–4pm Tue–Sun. 🚻 🚾 **W** childrensmuseumof phoenix.org

This is not so much a museum as a very popular indoor play-ground where kids can run freely in a safe environment. Highlights include a giant

indoor tree house, a room just for fort-building, and a forest made of bright-green and orange noodles. There is a special area for under-3s.

🏛 Arizona Science Center

600 E. Washington St. **Tel** (602) 716-2000. **Open** 10am–5pm daily. **Closed** Thanksgiving, Dec 25. 🚻 🚾 **W** azscience.org

This ultra-modern facility has over 300 interactive science exhibits, covering everything from physics and energy to the human body, spread over three levels. The popular "All About Me" gallery on Level One focuses on human biology. Here, visitors can take a virtual reality trip through the body. Level Three has "The World Around You," where visitors explore a 90-ft- (27-m-) long rock wall, as well as testing the surface temperature of different substances. There is a large-screen cinema that is popular with children, but there is something here for everyone.

🏛 Heritage Square

115 N. 6th St. 🚻 partial.
Phoenix is a thoroughly modern city, which grew rapidly after World War II. Many of its older buildings did not survive this expansion.

❶ Arizona Capitol Museum

The 1900 façade of the Arizona Capitol Building

For hotels and restaurants see pp236–43 and pp248–61

However, a few late 19th- and early 20th-century buildings remain, and the most interesting of these are found on tree-lined Heritage Square, which has numerous cafés and restaurants as well, and makes

for a pleasant stroll. Rosson House is a handsome wooden mansion on Monroe Street dating from 1895. It has a wrap-around veranda and distinctive hexagonal turret. Visitors may tour the house, which is furnished in period style (call 602 262-5070).

Next door is the Burgess Carriage House, constructed in an expansive colonial style rare in the Southwest. The 1900 Silva House features exhibits detailing Arizona's history.

VISITORS' CHECKLIST

Practical Information
Road map B4. 1,470,000 (city only). Visit Phoenix, 125 North 2nd St. (877) 225-5749. PGA Phoenix Golf Waste Management Phoenix Open, Feb, yearly.
W visitphoenix.com

Transport
Sky Harbor International Airport, 3 miles (1.5 km) E. of downtown. Greyhound Bus, 2115 E. Buckeye Rd.

Phoenix Art Museum

1625 N. Central Ave. **Tel** (602) 257-1222. **Open** 10am–9pm Wed, 10am–5pm Thu–Sat, noon–5pm Sun. **Closed** Mon, Thanksgiving, Dec 25. W phxart.org

Housed in an austere modern building, the highly acclaimed Phoenix Art Museum has an enviable reputation for the quality of its temporary exhibitions. These usually share the lower of the museum's two floors with a permanent collection of contemporary European and US art. The second floor features 18th- and 19th- century American artists, with a focus on painters connected to the Southwest. The exhibit here includes first-rate work from the Taos art colony of the 1900s and Georgia O'Keeffe (1887–1986) *(see p207)*, the most distinguished member of the group, as well as works by Frederic Remington and Ernest Blumenschein.

0 meters 500
0 yards 500

Main entrance of the Phoenix Art Museum

Sights at a Glance

1 Arizona Capitol Museum
2 Children's Museum of Phoenix
3 Arizona Science Center
4 Heritage Square
5 Phoenix Art Museum
6 Heard Museum

Heard Museum

The Heard Museum was founded in 1929 by Dwight Heard, a wealthy rancher and businessman who, with his wife, Maie, assembled an extraordinary collection of Native Southwestern American art in the 1920s. Several benefactors later added to the collection, including Senator Barry Goldwater of Arizona and the Fred Harvey Company, who donated their *kachina* dolls. The museum's wide-ranging collection contains more than 40,000 works, but the star attraction is its display of more than 500 dolls. Additionally, the museum showcases baskets, pottery, textiles, and fine art, as well as sumptuous silverwork by the Navajo, Zuni, and Hopi peoples.

Entrance to the Heard Museum, which occupies a Spanish Colonial Revival-style building

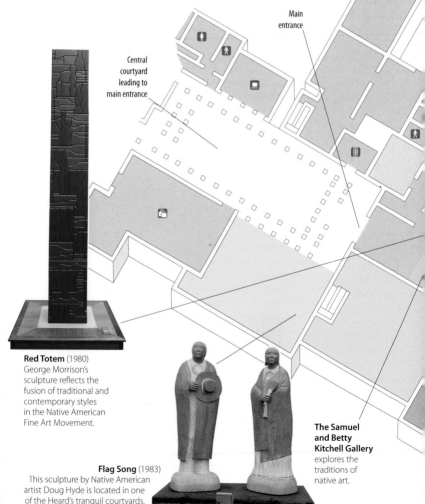

Main entrance

Central courtyard leading to main entrance

Red Totem (1980)
George Morrison's sculpture reflects the fusion of traditional and contemporary styles in the Native American Fine Art Movement.

Flag Song (1983)
This sculpture by Native American artist Doug Hyde is located in one of the Heard's tranquil courtyards.

The Samuel and Betty Kitchell Gallery explores the traditions of native art.

Red Tailed Hawk
Painted in 1986 by Dan Namingha, this is an impressionistic view of a Hopi *kachina* in hawk form. It is displayed as part of the Heard's fine art collection.

Navajo Child's Blanket
Woven in the 1870s, this richly colored, traditional blanket is one of the highlights of the Sandra Day O'Connor Gallery, which documents the history of the Museum, and showcases the Heard family's early collection of Native American artifacts.

Key

- ☐ Samuel and Betty Kitchell Gallery
- ☐ Crossroads Gallery
- ☐ Sandra Day O'Connor Gallery
- ☐ Ullman Learning Center
- ☐ Freeman Gallery
- ☐ Home: Native People in the Southwest Gallery
- ☐ Lincoln Hall
- ☐ Pritzlaff Courtyard
- ☐ Edward Jacobson Gallery of Indian Art
- ☐ Maureen and Dean Nichols Garden
- ☐ Temporary exhibition space
- ☐ Non-exhibition space

Ullman Learning Center features interactive exhibits related to Native American life in Arizona.

Every Picture Tells a Story
An interactive hands-on display shows how artists interpret their environments through art.

The South Courtyard offers additional space for the museum's fine sculptures.

★ Home: Native Peoples in the Southwest
This award-winning gallery spans 14 centuries, encompassing a superb collection of *kachina* dolls as well as jewelry, pottery, basketry, and textiles.

Exploring Metropolitan Phoenix

Phoenix is one of North America's largest cities. In addition to its city population of almost 1.5 million, Phoenix has a burgeoning number of residents in its metropolitan area, totaling more than 4 million. The city fills the Salt River Valley, occupying more than 2,000 sq miles (5,200 sq km) of the Sonoran Desert. It is famous for its winter temperatures of 60–70°F (16–21°C) and around 300 days of sunshine a year. This makes Phoenix a popular destination with both tourists and "snow birds," visitors who spend their winters here.

Metropolitan Phoenix includes the separate incorporated city of Scottsdale, 12 miles (19 km) northeast of Downtown. Replete with air-conditioned malls, designer stores, hotels, and restaurants, it is also a good base for visiting Taliesin West and Papago Park and is famous for its world-class golf courses (see p268). Tempe, 6 miles (10 km) east of Downtown, is home to Arizona State University, while finally Mesa has the Arizona Temple, a large Mormon church built in 1927.

Sights at a Glance

① Taliesin West
② Scottsdale
③ Cosanti Foundation
④ Camelback Mountain
⑤ Pueblo Grande Museum and Archaeological Park
⑥ Papago Park
⑦ Mystery Castle

Key

- ▨ Downtown Phoenix
- ▨ Metropolitan Phoenix
- ▬ Interstate
- ▬ Major highway
- ═ Highway
- — Railroad

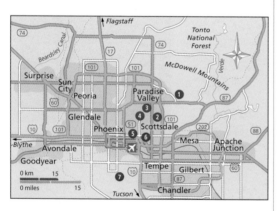

many of the city's most fashionable restaurants as well as bars, antique stores, and art galleries. In addition to the Renaissance-style Borgata shopping mall, there is the El Pedregal Festival Marketplace, and Scottsdale Downtown with its arts shopping district around Main Street, Marshall Way, Old Town, and Fifth Avenue. Scottsdale is also the location for Phoenix's most popular shopping mall – Fashion Square – offering an array of designer stores and excellent restaurants (see p264–5).

Scottsdale's elegant Fashion Square shopping mall

🖾 Camelback Mountain

Scottsdale.
Named for its humped shape, Camelback Mountain rises high above its suburban surroundings just 7 miles (11 km) northeast of Downtown Phoenix. One of the city's most distinctive landmarks, the mountain is a granite and sandstone out-crop formed by prehistoric volcanic forces. Camelback Mountain is best approached from the north via the marked turn off McDonald Drive near the junction of Tatum Boulevard. From the parking lot, a well-marked path leads to the summit, a steep climb that covers 1,300 ft (390 m) in the space of a mile.

Camelback Mountain adjoins the Echo Canyon Recreation Area, a lovely enclave with a choice of shady picnic sites.

Scottsdale

Founded in the late 19th century, Scottsdale was named after its developer, army chaplain Winfield Scott (1837–1910), whose religious scruples helped keep the early settlement free from saloons and gambling. Scottsdale's quiet, tree-lined streets and desert setting attracted the famous architect Frank Lloyd Wright, who established Taliesin West here in 1937. The area still attracts artists and designers, but it is best known for its many golf courses – there are 175 in and around Scottsdale.

At the center of the district, to either side of Scottsdale Road between 2nd Street and Indian School Road, the streets are lined with low, brightly painted adobe buildings, which house

Innovative design of the Cosanti Foundation gift shop

🏛 The Cosanti Foundation

6433 Doubletree Ranch Rd., Paradise Valley. **Tel** (480) 948-6145. **Open** 9am–5pm Mon–Sat, 11am–5pm Sun. **Closed** public hols. 🖼 donation requested. ♿ 🌐 arcosanti.org

In 1947, Italian architect Paolo Soleri (1919–2013) came to study at Taliesin West. Nine years later, he set up the Cosanti Foundation in Scottsdale to further his investigations into what he termed "arcology": a combination of architecture and ecology to create new urban habitats (see p27).

Today, the Cosanti site consists of simple, low structures housing studios, a gallery, and workshops. This is where Soleri and his workers make and sell their trademark windbells. Guided tours can be arranged with advance notice.

Visitors can also tour Soleri's main project, which lies 60 miles (100 km) north of Phoenix on Interstate Highway 17. Arcosanti is an educational housing project that began in 1970 to test the "arcology concept" as a way to reduce human impact on the environment while improving quality of life. Residents live and work in structures that combine work and leisure space. Workshops, tours, and accommodations are available.

🏛 Taliesin West

Cactus Rd. at Frank Lloyd Wright Blvd., Scottsdale. **Tel** (480) 627-5340. **Open** 9am–4pm daily. **Closed** Easter, Thanksgiving, Dec 25. 🖼 ♿ 🎥 🌐 franklloydwright.org

Generally regarded as the greatest American architect of all time, Frank Lloyd Wright (1869–1959) established the 600-acre (240-ha) Taliesin West complex as a winter school for his students in 1937. Wright had come to prominence in Chicago during the 1890s with a series of strikingly original houses that featured an elegant open-plan style. Although noted for his use of local materials such as desert rocks and earth, he also pioneered the use of pre-cast concrete (see p27).

Today, Taliesin West is home to the Frank Lloyd Wright School of Architecture, where students live and work. There are a variety of tours, from one to three hours. One-hour tours begin every half hour from 9am to 4pm.

Taliesin West is approached along a winding desert road. The muted tones of the low-lying buildings reflect Wright's enthusiasm for the desert setting. He was careful to enhance, rather than dominate, the landscape.

🏛 Pueblo Grande Museum and Archaeological Park

4619 E. Washington St. **Tel** (602) 495-0901. **Open** 9:30am–4:45pm Mon–Sat, 1–4:45pm Sun. **Closed** public hols. 🖼 ♿ 🌐 pueblogrande.com

Located 5 miles (8 km) east of Downtown Phoenix, this museum displays an ancient Hohokam ruin, as well as many artifacts, including cooking utensils and pottery. Many pieces come from the adjacent Archaeological Park, the site of a Hohokam settlement from the 8th to the 14th centuries. The site, originally excavated in 1887, has a path through the ruins and signs indicating the many irrigation canals once used by the Hohokam to water crops.

Taliesin West façade, designed to blend with the desert landscape

Cacti in the Desert Botanical Garden at Papago Park

🌵 Papago Park

Galvin Parkway & Van Buren Street.
Tel (602) 261-8318. **W** phoenix.gov/
parks/trails/locations/papago

Papago Park is located 6 miles (10 km) east of Phoenix's Downtown and is a popular place to unwind, with several hiking and cycling trails, picnic areas, and fishing lakes. Within the park, the **Desert Botanical Garden** is a 145-acre (59-ha) area devoted to more than 20,000 cacti and protected desert flora from around the world. The gardens are prettiest in spring. Guided tours explain the extraordinary life cycles of the desert plants.

Trail's End sign at Phoenix Zoo

The rolling hills and lakes of the **Phoenix Zoo** also occupy a large area of the park. The zoo reproduces a series of habitats including the Arizona-Sonora Desert and a tropical rainforest. Each zone provides a home for more than 1,300 animals, their movement controlled by banks and canals rather than fences. A Safari Train provides a narrated tour of the zoo.

🌵 Desert Botanical Garden

1201 N. Galvin Parkway. **Tel** (480) 941-1225. **Open** May–Sep: 7am–8pm daily; Oct–Apr: 8am–8pm daily. **Closed** major public holidays. 🔲🔲 🔲 **W** dbg.org

🦁 Phoenix Zoo

455 N. Galvin Parkway. **Tel** (602) 273-1341. **Open** early Jan–May & Sep–early Nov: 9am–5pm daily; Jun–Aug: 7am–2pm daily; early Nov–early Jan: 9am–4pm daily. **Closed** Dec 25. 🔲 🔲 **W** phoenixzoo.org

🏰 Mystery Castle

800 East Mineral Road. **Tel** (602) 268-1581. **Open** Oct–Jun: 11am–4pm Thu–Sun. 🔲 🔲

Mystery Castle is possibly Phoenix's most eccentric attraction. In 1927, Boyce Luther Gulley came to Phoenix hoping that the warm climate would improve his ailing health. His daughter had loved building sandcastles on the beach, and since Phoenix was so far away from the ocean, Gulley created a real-life fairy-tale sandcastle for her. He started work in 1930 and continued until his death in 1945. Discarded bricks and an assortment of scrapyard junk, including old car parts, have been used to build the structure. The 18-room interior can be seen on a guided tour, which explores the quirky building and its eclectic collection of antiques and furniture from around the world.

❷ The Apache Trail

Road map C4. 🚌 ℹ️ Globe Chamber of Commerce, 1360 N. Broad St., Globe (928) 425-4495 or Visit Phoenix, 125 N. 2nd St. (877) 225-5749. **W** visitphoenix.com

Heading east from Phoenix, Hwy 60 cuts straight across the desert to the suburb of Apache Junction at the start of Hwy 88. This road then begins its winding trail up into the Superstition Mountains. It is called the Apache Trail after the Native Americans who once lived here. The road is a wonderfully scenic mountain route that runs for 45 miles (72 km) up to Theodore Roosevelt Lake, which was created by the damming of the Salt River in 1911. Hwy 88 begins by climbing up into the hills and after 5 miles (8 km) reaches the Lost Dutchman State Park, named after the gold mine quarried here by Jacob Waltz and Jacob Weiser in the 1870s. These two miners cashed in a series of huge gold nuggets but kept the location of the mine to themselves. After their deaths, hundreds of prospectors worked these mountains in search of the famed gold mine but without success.

Beyond the state park, the highway passes by several camp sites and through rugged terrain before reaching the tiny hamlet of Tortilla Flat, 17 miles (27 km) farther on, where there is an excellent café. This settlement is at the east end of slender Canyon Lake, the first of several Salt River reservoirs created to provide Phoenix with water. The lake has a marina, and 90-minute cruises are offered on *Dolly's Steamboat*. As the road climbs higher into the Superstition Mountains it becomes more difficult to negotiate, before it reaches the 280-ft- (84-m-) high Theodore Roosevelt Dam, where there is good fishing and a variety of water sports.

Three miles (5 km) east of the dam lies the **Tonto National Monument**, which comprises two large sets of ruined cliff dwellings. The Salado people,

Façade of Phoenix's unusual Mystery Castle

View of a section of the winding Apache Trail from Fish Creek Hill

who were fine craftsmen and created some of the superb pottery on display at the Heard Museum *(see pp82–3)*, built these pueblos of rock and mud in the early 14th century. A steep, short trail leads up to the 19-room Lower Cliff Dwelling, but the 40-room Upper Cliff Dwelling can be visited only with a ranger.

Mining artifacts at the Gila County Historical Museum

Tonto National Monument

Hwy 188. **Tel** (928) 467-2241. **Open** 8am–5pm daily. **Closed** Dec 25. ♿ **W** nps.gov/tont

❸ Globe

Road map C4. 🏔 6,000. 🚌 **i** Globe Chamber of Commerce, 1360 N. Broad St. (928) 425 4495. ⚠ **W** globemiamichamber.com

The mining town of Globe lies about 100 miles (160 km) east of Phoenix in the wooded Dripping Spring and Pinal Mountains. In 1875, prospectors struck silver near here in what was then part of an Apache Reservation. The reservation was divested of its silver-bearing hills, and Globe was founded as a mining town and supply center. It was named for a massive nugget of silver, shaped like a globe, unearthed in the

hills nearby. The silver was quickly exhausted, but copper mining thrived until 1931. Today, Globe has an attractive historic district with several notable late 19th- and early 20th-century buildings. The **Gila County Historical Museum** outlines its history, with displays of a wide range of mining paraphernalia. On the south side of town are the Besh-Ba-Gowah Ruins, home of the Salado people in the 13th and 14th centuries.

Gila County Historical Museum

1330 N. Broad St. **Tel** (928) 425-7385. **Open** 10am–4pm Mon–Fri, 11am–3pm Sat. **Closed** Jan 1, Dec 25. 🎟 donation requested.

❹ Casa Grande Ruins National Monument

Road map C4. **Tel** (520) 723-3172. **Open** 9am–5pm daily. **Closed** Thanksgiving, Dec 25. ♿ ♿ **W** nps.gov/cagr

From around 200 BC until the middle of the 15th century, the Hohokam people farmed the Gila River Valley to the southeast of Phoenix. Among the few Hohokam sites that remain, the fortress-like

structure that makes up the Casa Grande National Monument is one of the most distinctive. Built in the early decades of the 14th century and named the "Big House" by a passing Jesuit missionary in 1694, this sturdy four-story structure has walls up to 4-ft (1.2-m) thick and is made from locally quarried caliche, a hard-setting subsoil. Experts believe that the holes cut in three of the walls were used for astronomical observations, but this is conjecture. The interior is out of bounds, but visitors can stroll round the exterior. The visitor center has some interesting exhibits on Hohokam history and culture.

Casa Grande is located 15 miles (24 km) east of Interstate Highway 10 (I-10) on the outskirts of the town of Coolidge. It should not be confused with the town of Casa Grande found to the west of I-10.

The fortress-like Casa Grande Ruins National Monument

❺ Tucson

Arizona's second-largest city after Phoenix, Tucson has a friendly, welcoming atmosphere and a variety of interesting attractions to entertain the increasing number of visitors it receives each year. The city is located on the northern boundary of the Sonoran Desert in Southern Arizona, in a basin surrounded by five mountain ranges.

When the Spanish colonizers arrived in the early 18th century they were determined to seize land from the local Tohono O'odham and Pima native tribes, who put up strong resistance *(see p44)*. This led the Spanish to move their regional fortress, or presidio, from Tubac to Tucson in the 1770s. The city was officially founded by Irish explorer Hugh O'Connor in 1775. Tucson's pride in its history is reflected in the careful preservation of 19th-century downtown buildings in the Barrio Historic District.

Contemporary glass skyscrapers in downtown Tucson

Exploring Tucson
Tucson's major art galleries and museums are clustered around two central areas: the University of Arizona campus (lying between Speedway Blvd., E. Sixth Street, Park, and Campbell Avenues) and the downtown area, which includes the Barrio and El Presidio historic districts. The latter contains many of the city's oldest buildings and is best explored on foot, as is the Barrio Historic District, south of Cushing Street.

🏛 Tucson Museum of Art and Historic Block
140 N. Main Ave. **Tel** (520) 624-2333.
Open 10am–5pm Wed, Fri & Sat, 10am–8pm Thu, noon–5pm Sun.
🏃 (free first Sun of month). 🚻 🅿
W tucsonmuseumofart.org

The Tucson Museum of Art opened in 1975 and is located on the Historic Block, which also contains five of the Presidio's oldest dwellings – all of which are at least a hundred years old. These historic buildings form part of the art museum and house parts of its extensive collection. The Museum's sculpture gardens and courtyards also form part of the Historic Block complex.

The art museum itself displays contemporary and 20th-century European and American works. In the adobe Stevens House (1866), the museum has its collection of Pre-Columbian artifacts, some of which are 2,000 years old. There is the Spanish Colonial collection with some stunning pieces of religious art. The 1850s Casa Cordova houses *El Nacimiento*, a Nativity scene with more than 300 earthenware figurines, on display from December to March. The J. Knox Corbett House, built in 1907, has Arts and Crafts Movement pieces such as a Morris chair.

Both guided and self-guided walking tours of this district are available from the Tucson Museum of Art.

🏛 Pima County Courthouse
115 N. Church Ave.
The Courthouse's pretty tiled dome is a downtown landmark. It was built in 1927, replacing its predecessor, a one-story adobe building dating from 1869. The position of the original presidio wall is marked out in the courtyard, and a section of the wall, 3-ft- (1-m-) thick and 12-ft- (4-m-) high, can still be seen inside the building.

🏛 El Presidio Historic District
The El Presidio Historic District occupies the area where the original Spanish fortress (presidio), San Agustín del Tucson, was built in 1775. More than 70 of the houses here were constructed during the Territorial period, before Arizona became a state in 1912. Today, these historic buildings are largely occupied by shops, restaurants, and offices, although archaeological excavations in the area have found artifacts from much earlier residents, the Hohokam people.

⛪ St. Augustine Cathedral
192 S. Stone Ave. **Tel** (520) 623-6351.
Open services only; call for times.
W augustinecathedral.org

St. Augustine Cathedral was begun in 1896 and modeled after the Spanish Colonial style of the Cathedral of Querétaro in central Mexico. This gleaming white building features an imposing sandstone façade with intricate carvings of the yucca, the saguaro, and the horned toad – three symbols of the Sonoran Desert – while a bronze statue of St. Augustine, the city's patron saint, stands above the main door.

Stained-glass window in the cathedral

One of many 19th-century adobe houses in the Barrio Historic District

VISITORS' CHECKLIST

Practical Information
Road map C5. ⚠ 524,300. 🛈 Metropolitan Tucson Convention & Visitors Bureau, 110 S. Church Ave. (520) 624-1817; (800) 638-8350. 🎭 La Fiesta de los Vaqueros (late Feb). 🔲 visittucson.org

Transport
✈ Tucson International, 10 miles (16 km) south of downtown. 🚉 Amtrak Station, 400 E. Toole Ave. 🚌 Greyhound Lines, 471 W. Congress.

🏠 Barrio Historic District

This area was Tucson's business district in the late 19th century. Today, its streets are quiet and lined with original adobe houses painted in bright colors. On nearby Main Street is the "wishing shrine" of **El Tiradito**, which marks the spot where a young man was killed as a result of a lovers' triangle. Local people lit candles here for his soul and still believe that if their candles burn for a whole night, their wishes will come true.

🏛 The University of Arizona

Visitors' Center, 811 N. Euclid Ave. **Tel** (520) 621-5130. **Open** 9am–5pm Mon–Fri. 🔲 arizona.edu

Several museums are located on or near the UA campus, about a mile (1.6 km) east of downtown. The **Arizona History Museum** traces Arizona's history from the arrival of the Spanish in 1540, to modern times. The **University of Arizona Museum of Art** focuses on European and American fine art from the Renaissance to the 20th century. Opposite the Museum of Art is the **Center for Creative Photography**, which contains the work of many of the 20th century's greatest American photographers. Visitors can view the extensive archives by advance reservations. The **Flandrau Science Center** features a range of child-friendly interactive exhibits.

One of the most renowned collections of artifacts, covering 2,000 years of native history, is displayed by the **Arizona State Museum**, which was founded in 1893.

Downtown Tucson

① Tucson Museum of Art and Historic Block
② Pima County Courthouse
③ El Presidio Historic District
④ St. Augustine Cathedral
⑤ Barrio Historic District

0 meters 100
0 yards 100

Tucson Museum of Art and Historic Block
Casa Cordova
① ALAMEDA STREET
② Pima County Courthouse
El Presidio Historic District ③ PENNINGTON STREET
FRANKLIN STREET
COUNCIL STREET
SIXTH STREET
SEVENTH STREET
University of Arizona
EIGHTH STREET
CONGRESS STREET
Amtrak station
BROADWAY BOULEVARD
JACKSON STREET
Greyhound station
OCHOA STREET
④ St. Augustine Cathedral
Armory Park
El Tiradito CUSHING STREET
⑤ Barrio Historic District
SIMPSON ST
KENNEDY STREET
13TH STREET
14TH STREET
15TH STREET
↓ Tucson International Airport 13 km (8 miles)

Exploring Around Tucson

Beyond the city center, metropolitan Tucson extends north to the Santa Catalina Mountains, the foothills of which are the start of a scenic drive to the top of Mount Lemmon. To the west are the Tucson Mountains, which frame the western portion of Saguaro National Park, the other half of which lies east of the city. To the south lies the beautiful mission church of San Xavier del Bac *(see pp92–3)*, which stands out from the flat, desert landscape of the Tohono O'odham Indian Reservation.

Sights at a Glance

① Saguaro National Park (East and West)
② Arizona-Sonora Desert Museum
③ Old Tucson Studios
④ Mission San Xavier del Bac
   See pp92–3
⑤ Pima Air and Space Museum
⑥ Mount Lemmon

Key

▨ Downtown Tucson
▨ Greater Tucson
▬ Interstate
▬ Major highway
═ Highway
— Railroad

Vistas of tall saguaro cacti in Saguaro National Park

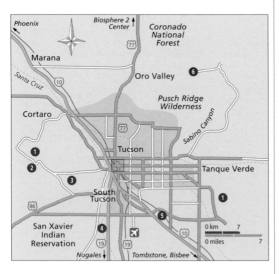

🌵 Saguaro National Park

3693 S. Old Spanish Trail. **Tel** (520) 733-5153. **Open** 24 hrs; visitor center: 9am–5pm daily. **Closed** Dec 25. 🅿 (Loop Drive only). 🅰 🆆 nps.gov/sagu

Perhaps the most famous symbol of the American Southwest, the saguaro (pronounced sa-wah-ro) cactus is unique to the Sonoran desert. The largest species of cactus in the United States, the saguaro has a life span of up to 200 years. Those that survive into old age may reach heights of up to 50 ft (16.5 m) and weigh more than 8 tons (7.3 kg).

Set up in 1994, the park comprises two tracts of land on the eastern and western flanks of Tucson, which together cover more than 142 sq miles (368 sq km). In the western section, the 9-mile (14.5-km) Bajada Loop Drive runs deep into the park on a dirt road, past hiking trails and picnic areas. One of these trails leads to ancient Hohokam petroglyphs carved into the volcanic rock. The eastern park has the oldest saguaros, which can be seen along the 8-mile (13-km) Cactus Forest Drive. There are also more

than 100 miles (160 km) of hiking trails here. Both sections of the park offer ranger-guided walks during the winter season.

🏛 Arizona-Sonora Desert Museum

2021 N. Kinney Rd. **Tel** (520) 883-2702. **Open** Mar–Sep: 7:30am–5pm daily (Jun–Aug: to 10pm Sat); Oct–Feb: 8:30am–5pm daily. 🅿 🅰 🆆 desertmuseum.org

This natural history park covers over 21 desert acres (8.5 ha), and includes a botanical garden, zoo, and natural history museum. At the museum, displays show the history, geology, and flora and fauna of the Sonoran Desert region. Outside, a 2-mile (3-km) walkway passes more than 1,200 varieties of plants, the setting for hummingbirds, wildcats, and Mexican wolves.

One of many flowering cacti from the Arizona-Sonora Desert Museum

🎬 Old Tucson Studios

201 S. Kinney Rd. **Tel** (520) 883-0100. **Open** Jan: 10am–5pm daily: Feb–Apr: 10am–6pm daily; May, Nov & Dec: 10am–5pm Fri–Sun. **Closed** Jun–Oct, Thanksgiving, Dec 24 & 25. 🅿 🅰 🆆 oldtucson.com

Modeled on an old Western town of the 1860s, this Wild West theme park was built as a

---

Map labels:

Phoenix ← | Biosphere 2 Center ↑ | Coronado National Forest
Marana | 77 | Oro Valley ⑥
Santa Cruz | 10 | Pusch Ridge Wilderness
Cortaro | 77 | Sabino Canyon
① | Tucson |
② | | Tanque Verde
③ | South Tucson | ①
86 | | ⑤
San Xavier Indian Reservation | ④ ✈ | 10
19 | 19 | 0 km 7 / 0 miles 7
Nogales ↓ | Tombstone, Bisbee ↘

set for a Western movie, *Arizona*, in 1939. Since then, Old Tucson Studios has formed the backdrop for some of Hollywood's most famous Westerns, such as *Gunfight at the OK Corral* (1957) starring Burt Lancaster and Kirk Douglas, and *Rio Bravo* (1958) starring John Wayne. The popular 1970s TV series *Little House on the Prairie* was also filmed here. *The Three Amigos* (1986) and *Tombstone* (1993) were also partly shot here.

Main Street's 1860s frontier atmosphere provides an authentic setting for performers in period costume, who entertain visitors with stunt shows, gunfights, and stagecoach rides. Visitors can also try panning for gold.

Gunfight staged outside the mission at Old Tucson Studios

🏠 San Xavier del Bac Mission
See pp92–3.

🏛 Pima Air and Space Museum
6000 E. Valencia Rd. **Tel** (520) 574-0462. **Open** 9am–5pm daily. **Closed** Thanksgiving, Dec 25. 🅿 ♿ 🎥 call for times. **W** pimaair.org

Some 9 miles (14.5 km) southeast of downtown Tucson, the Pima Air and Space Museum contains one of the largest collections of aircraft in the world. Visitors are met with the astonishing sight of more than 275 vintage aircraft set out in ranks across the desert.

Three presidential aircraft are displayed here – Kennedy's, Nixon's, and Johnson's – as well as a replica of the Wright brothers' famous 1903 aircraft, and some advanced jet fighters. Exhibits in four aircraft hangars show military and aviation memorabilia, including a replica World War II barracks. The adjacent **Davis-Monthan Air Force Base** displays more than 2,000 planes, including B-29s and supersonic bombers.

Birdwatching in the Canyons of Southern Arizona

The landscape of southern Arizona may seem dry at first glance, but this high desert environment gets about 11 in (280 mm) of rain annually. This enables a surprising range of vegetation to flourish, from cacti to brightly colored wildflowers in spring. In turn, this attracts an amazing variety of birds, and the area is one of the top five birdwatching locations in the US.

The verdant canyons between Tucson and the Mexican border offer the best birdwatching. Just off I-19, near Green Valley, Madera Canyon plays host to some 400 bird species. As well as more common varieties of hummingbirds, flycatchers, and warblers, many rare species such as the brown-crested flycatcher and the black-and-white warbler are often sighted here. Further afield, Ramsey Canyon in the Huachuca Mountains is the country's hummingbird capital with 14 varieties of these tiny delicate creatures.

Broad-billed hummingbird

The museum also runs the **Titan Missile Museum** (open daily all year) located 20 minutes south of the city at Sahuarita, which is a ballistic missile silo.

🏔 Mount Lemmon
ℹ (520) 749-8700.

Mount Lemmon is the highest peak in the Santa Catalina Mountains, standing at 9,157 ft (2,790 m). During the hot summers the cooler air of the mountains' higher elevations attracts many visitors. A one-hour scenic drive, beginning in the Tucson city limits and connecting to the Mount Lemmon Highway, takes you to the summit. There are around 150 miles (240 km) of hiking trails here, while a side road leads to the quaint resort village of Summerhaven, with shops and restaurants. At the top, the Sky Valley lift operates for a small fee most of the year.

🏛 Biosphere 2 Center
5 miles (8 km) NE. of jct. of Hwys 77 & 79. **Tel** (520) 838-6200. **Open** 9am–4pm daily. **Closed** Thanksgiving, Dec 25. 🅿 ♿ 🎥 **W** b2science.org

Biosphere 2 is a unique research facility that was set up in 1991. Eight people were sealed within a futuristic structure of glass and white steel furnished with five of the Earth's habitats: rainforest, desert, savanna, marsh, and an ocean with a living coral reef. Over a period of two years the effect of the people on the environment as well as the effect on them of isolation in this "world," were studied, with varying results.

Today, there are no people living in the Biosphere, which is currently being used to study the effect of increased carbon dioxide in the atmosphere. Visitors can take a 90-minute guided tour of the facility, exploring both inside and outside the Biosphere.

Space-age buildings of the Biosphere 2 Center, north of Tucson

For hotels and restaurants see pp236–43 and pp248–61

San Xavier del Bac Mission

San Xavier del Bac is the oldest and best-preserved mission church in the Southwest. An imposing landmark as it rises out of the stark, flat landscape of the surrounding Tohono O'odham reservation, its white walls dazzle in the desert sun. A mission was first established here by the Jesuit priest Father Eusebio Kino in 1700 *(see p44)*. The complex seen today was completed in 1797 by Franciscan missionaries.

Built of adobe brick, the mission is considered to be the finest example of Spanish Colonial architecture in the US *(see p26)*. The church also incorporates other styles, including several Baroque flourishes. In the 1990s its interior was extensively renovated, and five *retablos* (altarpieces) have been restored to their original glory.

The Hill of the Cross, to the east of the mission, offers fine views

★ **Façade of the church**
The ornate Baroque façade is decorated with the carved figures of saints (although some are much eroded) including a headless St. Cecilia and an unidentifiable St. Francis, now a simple sand cone.

Stonework detail
The identity of the carved statues to the left of the entrance has changed. Long thought to be St. Catherine of Siena and St. Barbara, they have now been identified as St. Agatha of Catania and St. Agnes of Rome.

KEY

① **The mortuary chapel** contains a statue of the Virgin Mary, surrounded by candles.

② **The bell tower's** elegant, white dome reflects the Moorish styles that are incorporated into San Xavier's Spanish Colonial architecture.

③ **The patio** is closed to the public but can be seen from the museum.

④ **The museum** includes a sheepskin psalter and photographs of other historic missions on the Tohono O'odham Reservation.

Painted ceiling
On entering the church, visitors are struck by the dome's ceiling with its glorious paintings of religious figures. Vivid pigments of vermilion and blue were used to contrast with the stark white stone background.

★ Main Altar
The spectacular gold and red *retablo mayor* is decorated in Mexican Baroque style with elaborate columns. More than 50 statues were carved in Mexico then brought to San Xavier where artists gilded and painted them with brightly colored glazes.

VISITORS' CHECKLIST

Practical Information
Road map: C5. 1950 W. San Xavier Rd., 10 miles (16 km) south of Tucson on I-19. **Tel** (520) 294-2624. **Open** 7am–5pm daily.

w sanxaviermission.org

Altar Dome
The dome and high transepts are filled with painted wooden statuary and covered with murals depicting scenes from the Gospels.

③

④

The shop entrance

Chapel of Our Lady
This statue of the Virgin is one of the Church's three sculptures of Mary. Here she is shown as *La Dolorosa* or Sorrowing Mother.

Boats and watersports in the picturesque setting of Lake Yuma

❻ Yuma

Road map A4. 🚇 65,000. 🚆 Amtrak, 281 S. Gila St. 🚌 Greyhound, 1245 Castle Dome Ave. 🛈 Yuma Convention and Visitors' Bureau, 201 N. 4th Ave. (800) 293-0071. 🏔 🌐 visityuma.com

Yuma occupies a strategic position at the confluence of the Colorado and Gila rivers. Though noted by Spanish explorers in the 16th century, it was not until the 1850s that the town rose to prominence, when the river crossing became the gateway to California for tens of thousands of gold seekers. Fort Yuma, built in 1849, also boosted steamboat traffic along the Colorado River.

Today, Yuma's hot and sunny winter climate makes it a popular winter destination for travelers or "snowbirds," escaping colder climes. Two state historic parks highlight its rich history: Yuma Crossing, covering 20 acres (8 ha) along the Colorado, looks at river transportation and army life in the later 1800s, while Yuma Territorial Prison re-creates conditions at the state's main prison facility from 1876–1909.

❼ Organ Pipe Cactus National Monument

Road map B5. **Tel** (520) 387-6849. **Open** daily; visitor center 8:30am– 4:30pm. **Closed** Thanksgiving, Dec 25. 🏕 🚻 🍽 🏔 🌐 nps.gov/orpi

The organ pipe is a Sonoran desert species of cactus, which is a cousin to the saguaro (see p90) but with multiple arms branching up from the base, as its name suggests. The organ

pipe is rare in the United States, growing almost exclusively in this large and remote area of land along the Mexican border in southwest Arizona. Many other plant and animal species flourish in this un-spoiled desert wilderness, although a lot of animals, such as snakes, jackrabbits, and kangaroo rats, emerge only in the cool of the night. Other cacti such as the saguaro, the Engelmann prickly pear, and the teddybear cholla are best seen in early summer for their glorious displays of floral color.

There are two scenic drives through the park: the 21-mile (34-km) Ajo Mountain Drive and the shorter 5-mile (8-km) Puerto Blanco Drive. The Ajo Mountain Drive takes two hours and winds through startling desert landscapes in the foothills of the mountains. The Puerto Blanco Drive leads to a half-hour trail into Red Tanks Tinaja, a natural water pocket, and the picnic

area near Pinkley Peak. A variety of hiking trails in the park range in difficulty from paved, wheelchair-accessible paths to wilderness walks. A visitor center offers exhibits on the park's flora and fauna, as well as maps and camping permits, and there are guided walks available in winter.

Be aware that the park is a good two-and-a-half- to three-hour drive from Tucson one way. If you want to explore this environment in any detail, plan to camp overnight. Ajo, 34 miles (55 km) to the north, has motels and services.

❽ Tubac

Road map C5. 🚇 150. 🛈 Tubac Chamber of Commerce, 2 Tubac Rd (520) 398-2704. **Open** 10am–4pm Mon–Fri (to 1pm summer). 🌐 tubacaz.com

The Royal Presidio (fortress) of San Ignacio de Tubac was built in 1752 to protect the local Spanish-owned ranches and mines, as well as the nearby missions of Tumacacori and San Xavier, from attacks by local Pima natives. Tubac was also the first stopover on the famous overland expedition to colonize the San Francisco Bay area in 1776. The trek was led by the fort's captain, Juan Bautista de Anza (see p44). Following his return, the garrison moved north to Tucson and for the next

Rare cacti at the Organ Pipe Cactus National Monument

Mission church at Tumacácori National Historical Park

celebrates the cultural heritage of the upper Santa Cruz Valley, is held on the mission grounds.

🏛 Tubac Presidio State Historic Park
1 Burruel St. **Tel** (520) 398-2252. **Open** 9am–5pm daily. **Closed** Dec 25. 🅿 ♿ 📷 🌐 tubacpresidiopark. com

🏛 Tumacácori National Historical Park
Tel (520) 398-2341. **Open** 9am–5pm daily. **Closed** Thanksgiving, Dec 25. 🅿 ♿ 📷 🌐 nps.gov/tuma

❾ Nogales
Road map C5. ⚂ 19,500. 🚌 🚌 ℹ 123 W. Kino Park (520) 287-3685. **Open** 9am–5pm Mon–Fri. 🌐 thenogaleschamber.com

Nogales is really two towns that straddle the US border with Mexico, at the end of Mexico's Pacific Highway. This is a busy port of entry, handling huge amounts of freight, including 75 percent of all winter fruit and vegetables sold in North America. The town attracts large numbers of visitors in search of bargains –

decorative blankets, furniture, and crafts are good value. People used to shop on both sides of the border, but the US government has issued warnings over crossing into Mexico, as ongoing drug wars have made border towns potentially dangerous, and visitors are at risk of theft.

If you must cross over into Mexico, you are advised to leave your car on the US side, where attendants mind the parking lots, and to walk across the border. Not only is parking extremely difficult, but cars with US license plates are likely targets for thieves. It can also take 2–3 hours to go through customs by car. Visas are required only for those traveling farther south than the town and for stays of more than 72 hours. US and Canadian citizens should carry a passport for identification, as drivers' licenses are not sufficient proof of citizenship. Foreign nationals should make sure their visa status enables them to re-enter the US; those on the Visa Waiver Program (see p276) should have no problem.

Mexican pottery found in Nogales

hundred years, Tubac declined. Today, the town is a small but thriving art colony, with attractive shops, galleries, and restaurants lining the streets around the plaza.

Tubac's historical remains are displayed at the **Tubac Presidio State Historic Park**, which encompasses the foundations of the original presidio in an underground display, as well as several historic buildings. Also here, the Presidio Museum contains artifacts covering over one hundred years of Tubac's history, including painted altarpieces and colonial furniture.

Environs
Just 3 miles (5 km) south of town lies **Tumacácori National Historical Park** with the beautiful ruined mission. The present church was built in around 1800 upon the ruins of the original 1691 mission established by Jesuit priest, Father Eusebio Kino (see p44). The Mission was abandoned in 1848, and today its weather-beaten ochre façade together with its brick columns, arched entry, and carved wooden door is an evocative reminder of former times. The cavernous interior is wonderfully atmospheric, with patches of exposed adobe brick and faded murals on the sanctuary walls. A small museum provides an excellent background on the mission builders and native Pima Indians. Weekend craft demonstrations, including tortilla making, basketry, and Mexican pottery, are held September through June. During the first weekend in December, La Fiesta de Tumacácori (see p39), which

Astronomy in Southern Arizona
Southern Arizona's dry air and dark, clear nights have made it an international center for astronomy. Within a 75-mile (120-km) radius of Tucson, there is a cluster of prestigious observatories located in the mountains, including the Kitt Peak National Observatory, with its large telescopes, and the Fred Lawrence Whipple Observatory, both of which can be toured. Mount Graham International Observatory features some of the world's most advanced telescope technology. Opportunities for star-gazing are exceptional, but even without high-powered equipment, anyone can enjoy the countless constellations in the night skies.

Observatories in the mountains of southern Arizona

⑩ Bisbee

Road map C5. ⛰ 6,500. 🚌 *i*
Visitor Center, 478 Dart Rd. (520) 432-3554. **W** discoverbisbee.com

This is one of the most atmospheric mining towns in the Southwest. The discovery of copper here in the 1880s sparked a mining rush, and by the turn of the century Bisbee was the largest city between St. Louis and San Francisco. Victorian buildings such as the landmark Copper Queen Hotel still dominate the historic town center, while attractive clusters of houses cling to the sides of the surrounding mountains.

Visitors can tour the mines that once flourished here, such as the deep underground Queen Mine or, a short drive south of town, the Lavender Open Pit Mine. Exhibits at the Bisbee Mining and Historical Museum illustrate the realities of mining and frontier life here.

Re-enactment of the gunfight at the OK Corral, Tombstone

The Victorian mining town of Bisbee clings to the slopes of the surrounding mountains

⑪ Tombstone

Road map C5. ⛰ 1,400. *i* Visitor Center, 395 E. Allen St. (520) 457-3929. **W** tombstonechamber.com

Tombstone is a living legend, forever known as the site of the 1881 gunfight at the OK Corral between the Earp brothers and the Clanton gang (*see p59*). The town's historic streets and buildings form one of the most popular attractions in the Southwest.

Tombstone was founded by Ed Schieffelin, who went prospecting on Apache land in 1877 despite a warning that "all you'll find out there is your tombstone." He found a silver mountain instead, and his sardonically named shanty town boomed with the ensuing silver rush. One of the wildest towns in the West, Tombstone was soon full of prospectors, gamblers, cowboys, and law-men. In its heyday, it was larger than San Francisco. More than $37 million worth of silver was extracted from the mines between 1880 and 1887, when miners struck an aquifer and flooded the mine shafts.

In 1962 "the town too tough to die" became a National Historic Landmark, and, with much of its historic downtown immaculately preserved, it attracts many visitors, all eager to sample the unique atmosphere. Allen Street, with its wooden boardwalks, shops, and restaurants, is the town's main thoroughfare. The OK Corral is preserved as a museum, and re-enactments of the infamous gunfight between the Earp brothers, Doc Holliday, and the Clanton gang are staged daily at 2pm.

Tombstone Courthouse on Toughnut Street was the seat of justice for the county from 1882 to 1929 and is now a state historic site. It contains a museum featuring the restored courtroom and many historical exhibits and artifacts, including photographs of some of the town's famous characters. Toughnut Street used to be known as "Rotten Row" as it was once lined with miners' tents, bordellos, and more than one hundred bars.

Among other buildings worth looking for in the downtown area is the Rose Tree Inn Museum, home of what is reputedly the world's largest rosebush. There is also the Bird Cage Theater, once a bawdy dance hall and bordello, and so-named for the covered "crib" compartments, or cages, hanging from the ceiling, in which ladies of the night plied their trade. Nearby is the once rowdy Crystal Palace Saloon, which is still a bar.

Just north of town, the famous Boothill Cemetery is full of the graves of those who perished in Tombstone, peacefully or otherwise. This evocative place is not without the occasional spot of humor. Look for the marker lamenting the death of George Johnson, hanged by mistake in 1882, which reads: "He was right, we was wrong, but we strung him up, and now he's gone."

🏛 **OK Corral**
Allen St. **Tel** (520) 457-3456.
Open 9am–5pm daily. 🎫 ♿
W ok-corral.com

🏛 **Tombstone Courthouse**
219 Toughnut St. **Tel** (520) 457-3311.
Open 9am–5pm daily. **Closed** Dec 25.
🎫 ♿ **W** azstateparks.com

Tombstone Courthouse in the town center is now a museum

⓬ Kartchner Caverns State Park

Road map C5. **Tel** (520) 586-2283.
Open 7am–6pm daily (summer: 8am–5pm); cave tours 8:30am–4:30pm by reservation). **Closed** Dec 25. 🅿 ♿ 🎥 obligatory. 🏛 🌐 **azstateparks. com/parks/kaca**

The Kartchner Caverns are one of Arizona's great natural wonders. Located in the Whetstone Mountains, the caves were discovered in 1974 when two cavers crawled through a sinkhole in a hillside into 7 acres (3 ha) of caverns filled with colorful formations. Out of concern to protect the caves, they kept their discovery a secret for 14 years as they explored this wonderland of speleotherms, or cave formations, made of layers of calcite deposited by dripping or flowing water over millions of years. In 1988 the land was purchased by the state, but it took 11 years to complete the development that would allow public access while conserving the special conditions that enable these "wet" caves to continue growing.

Before entering, visitors are introduced to the geology of the formations at the Discovery Center. Visitors must not touch the features, as skin oils stop their growth. Along with huge stalactites and stalagmites, there is an abundance of other types of formation such as the aptly named 21-ft (132-m) soda straw, the turnip shields, and popcorn.

Orange and white column formations at Kartchner Caverns

⓭ Amerind Foundation

Road map C5. **Tel** (520) 586-3666.
Open 10am–4pm Tue–Sun. **Closed** Mon, public hols. 🅿 🌐 **amerind.org**

The Amerind Foundation is one of the most important private archaeological and ethnological museums in the country. The name Amerind is a contraction of "American Indian," and this collection contains tens of thousands of artifacts from different Native American cultures. All aspects of Native American life are shown here, with displays covering Inuit masks, Cree tools, and sculpted effigy figures from Mexico's Casas Grandes.

The adjacent Amerind Art Gallery has a fine collection of western art by prominent artists like William Leigh (1866–1955) and Frederic Remington (1861–1909). The delightful pink buildings, designed in the Spanish Colonial Revival style (*see p26*), are also of interest.

⓮ Chiricahua National Monument

Road map D5. **Tel** (520) 824-3560.
Open 8am–4:30pm daily. **Closed** Thanksgiving, 25 Dec. 🅿 ♿ 🎥 🏛 🌐 **nps.gov/chir**

The Chiricahua Mountains were once the homeland of a band of Apache people and an impenetrable base from which they launched attacks on settlers in the late 1800s. This 19-sq-mile (49-sq-km) area now preserves stunning rock formations, which were created by a series of volcanic eruptions around 27 million years ago. Massive rocks balanced on small pedestals, soaring rock spires, and enormous stone columns make up the bizarre landscape, visible from the monument's scenic drive and hiking trails.

The nearby town of Willcox houses the **Rex Allen Arizona Cowboy Museum**, devoted to a native son who became a famous movie cowboy, starring in 19 films in the 1950s.

🏛 **Rex Allen Arizona Cowboy Museum**
150 N. Railroad Ave. **Tel** (520) 384-4583. **Open** 10am–4pm Mon–Sat. **Closed** public holidays. 🅿 ♿

Massive rock spires formed by million-year-old volcanic eruptions at Chiricahua National Monument

The iconic Welcome to Las Vegas sign ▶

LAS VEGAS

The Changing Face of Las Vegas

No other city in the US has reinvented itself so often and with such profitable results as Las Vegas. Set in an unpromising landscape, bordering three deserts, artesian waters beneath the land first supported life here. Successive groups, from Native Americans to Mexican traders, Mormons, and railroad workers, all survived the environment. They added to a unique set of factors that gave birth to a Las Vegas they would barely recognize today.

No longer unique in offering casinos, the city still draws the crowds. Associated with some of the biggest names in show business, such as Frank Sinatra and Elvis Presley, with eccentric millionaires like Howard Hughes, with mobsters such as Bugsy Siegel, and above all with glamour, Vegas continues to fire the imagination as the fun city of stretch limos, showgirls, and an "anything goes" ethos for those who can pay for it.

Helen Stewart was a local ranch owner who sold her land to the railroad, which led to the founding of the city of Las Vegas in 1905.

Downtown Las Vegas

The city grew up around Fremont Street in Downtown Las Vegas in the early 1900s. By the 1960s (see right), the area had began to suffer from competition from the Strip. Today, the area has been revived as the Fremont Street Experience (see below right and p122).

Roulette was one of the games offered in Las Vegas once gambling was legalized in Nevada in 1931. The city was a hedonistic escape from the 1930s' Depression.

Construction of the Hoover Dam, 34 miles (55 km) from Las Vegas on the Colorado River, brought a rise in the city's fortunes (see p125). By the early 1920s Las Vegas had declined, and its population had fallen to 2,300. When construction began in 1931, money and people flowed into town, and by the early 1930s the population had swelled to around 7,500. Tens of thousands of visitors arrived to see the building of the dam and to enjoy the new gambling clubs springing up.

Benjamin Siegel, *(left)* called "Bugsy" behind his back, was a New York City gangster. He moved to Los Angeles in the 1930s and created the luxurious Flamingo hotel and casino in Vegas *(see p115)*. He was killed by fellow investors only a year after the casino had opened in 1946, probably because other mobsters disliked his high profile. Although nothing remains of the original Flamingo building, there is still a tropical-themed luxury hotel on this spot.

Howard Hughes

Billionaire Howard Hughes arrived in Las Vegas in November 1966, moving into a luxurious suite on the ninth floor of the Desert Inn hotel. When the hotel's management tried to move him out a few months later, Hughes bought the place for $13.2 million. Although he never left his room in four years, he spent some $300 million buying Vegas properties. These included the Silver Slipper hotel and casino across the Strip, whose blinking neon slipper disturbed him. As owner he had it switched off.

Hughes is credited with bringing legitimate business and a sanitized image to Vegas, sounding the death knell of mob investment in the city. In the 1960s, family oriented resorts such as Circus Circus opened, and such entertainment corporations as MGM, Hilton, and Holiday Inn began legitimate building programs. However, as recently as the 1970s and 80s mobsters were caught skimming profits from some Vegas hotels.

Billionaire entrepreneur Howard Hughes

The Strip

From a few low-rise buildings along a desert road in the 1960s to the glittering neon canyon of today, the transformation of the Strip has been remarkable *(see pp106–109)*.

The Rat Pack, which included Peter Lawford, Sammy Davis Jr., Frank Sinatra, Joey Bishop, and Dean Martin, sealed Las Vegas' reputation as an entertainment mecca in the 1950s with shows at the now-demolished Sands hotel.

LAS VEGAS

Rising like a mirage out of Nevada's beautiful southern desert, Las Vegas is a glittering wonderland that promises fun to all its visitors. The city's unique attraction is its hotels with their fantastic architecture, re-creating such cities as New York and Venice. At the heart of these palaces lie the casinos where the lure of million-dollar jackpots draws almost 40 million visitors each year.

Occupied by the Ancestral Puebloan peoples until around 1150 AD, the Las Vegas area later became the home of several Native American tribes, including the Paiute, until Mexican traders arrived in the early 19th century. Mormon pioneers built a fort here in 1855, establishing the beginnings of a settlement in the area, which gradually developed. Officially founded in 1905, the city of Las Vegas expanded in the 1930s with the building of the Hoover Dam across the Colorado River, some 30 miles (45 km) away, and the legalization of gambling here in 1931. The influx of construction workers with money to burn, and the electricity and water provided by the dam, paved the way for the casino-based growth that took place in the 1940s and 1950s. Since

the 1990s, numbers of ever more extravagant resorts have been built in the city, including the impressive Bellagio, Venetian, and Cosmopolitan, and this expansion shows few signs of slowing.

For those who can tear themselves away from the city, the surrounding country has much to offer. Lake Mead and the stunning rock formations of the Valley of Fire State Park provide a range of outdoor pleasures from horseback riding to watersports.

In 2006, Las Vegas was the fastest growing city in the US, but the population has since stabilized at just under two million. Tourism and gaming remain the most successful industries – it has 20 of the 27 largest hotels in the world – but it is also known for its wedding chapels and entertainment.

Decorative stained-glass ceiling of Tropicana's elegant casino

◀ Replica Venice complete with canals and gondolas at The Venetian

Exploring Las Vegas

Las Vegas has two centers – the wonderland of the Strip, and the older Downtown area, where the city began in 1905 *(see pp100–101)*. The Downtown area focuses on Fremont Street *(see p122)*, while the Strip is a 4.5-mile- (7.2-km-) long section of Las Vegas Boulevard (Hwy 604) that runs southwest towards California. Strictly speaking, the part of the Strip that lies south of Sahara Avenue is in Clark County, while the city proper is centered around Downtown Vegas. Ringed by mountains, canyons, and desert, the Las Vegas area also has a wealth of natural beauty in a variety of parks, some just a short drive from the Strip *(see pp124–25)*.

The dazzling sight of the Las Vegas Strip, illuminated at night by myriad shimmering neon lights

Getting Around

The Strip is a long road, and driving is recommended as the best way to get around. Major hotels have free parking lots, as well as valet service. The Deuce bus runs along the Strip stopping at the major hotels, and continues to Downtown, while the monorail service operates between the MGM Grand and Sahara Avenue. Taxis are also an option and are best hailed at hotels.

Key

■ The Strip *see pp106–109*

0 kilometers |————————| 1

0 miles |————————| 1

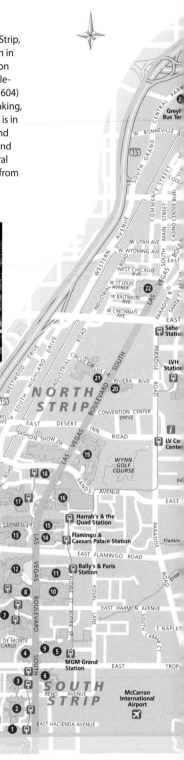

The famous Forum at Caesars Palace

Sights at a Glance

Hotels and Casinos

1 Mandalay Bay
2 Luxor
3 Excalibur
4 New York New York
5 MGM Grand
6 Tropicana
7 CityCenter
8 Cosmopolitan of Las Vegas
10 Planet Hollywood
11 Paris
12 Bellagio
13 Caesars Palace
14 Flamingo Las Vegas
16 The Venetian & Palazzo
17 Mirage
18 Treasure Island
19 Wynn Las Vegas & Encore
20 Riviera
21 Circus Circus
22 Stratosphere

Historic Towns and Cities

28 Boulder City and Hoover Dam

Streets and Malls

9 Showcase Mall
23 Fremont Street Experience

Museums and Galleries

15 Autocollections at the Quad
24 Mob Museum
25 Discovery Children's Museum
26 The Las Vegas Natural History Museum
27 Old Las Vegas Mormon State Historic Park

Areas of Natural Beauty

29 Lake Mead National Recreation Area
30 Valley of Fire State Park
31 Mount Charleston
32 Red Rock Canyon

Key

Central Las Vegas
Greater Las Vegas
Interstate
Major highway
Highway

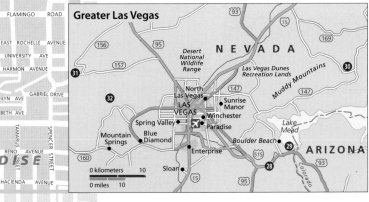

Greater Las Vegas

A View of The Strip: 1

The heart of Las Vegas lies along Las Vegas Boulevard, a sparkling vista of neon known simply as "the Strip." This southern stretch of the Strip is home to a cluster of vast, lavishly themed hotels, including Luxor, New York New York, and the Bellagio. Aiming to satisfy all a visitor's needs in one location, with restaurants, shops, and casinos, the hotels are best-appreciated at night when the lights come on and these mega-resorts become a fantasyland of such riotous design as the sphinx that fronts the Luxor hotel's striking pyramid. Change is constant along the Strip, where hotels get even larger, acclaimed chefs open new restaurants, and long-running shows close to make room for the latest stars.

The glittering Strip by night

❹ New York New York
A replica of the Statue of Liberty forms part of the façade of this hotel, which is composed of a host of Manhattan landmarks such as the Empire State Building.

❷ Luxor
The re-created Grand Staircase is one of the highlights of the Titanic Artifact Exhibition at the Luxor.

Monte Carlo's
Renaissance-style architecture comes to life at this hotel.

Mandalay Bay's interior, with its palm trees and bamboo, re-creates a 19th century tropical paradise.

Excalibur's towers are a kitsch fantasy of medieval England.

Showcase Mall is a striking building, with its giant neon Coca-Cola bottle. It contains a themed attraction run by M&M's® candy company.

❻ Tropicana
This casino has a Miami South Beach theme, with a stunning Art Nouveau-style stained-glass ceiling and glass lamps.

❺ MGM Grand
This famous statue of Leo, symbol of the Hollywood film studio, MGM, rises 45 ft (15 m) above the corner of Tropicana Avenue.

For hotels and restaurants see pp236–43 and pp248–61

⓭ Caesars Palace

reproduction Roman statuary adorns
e grounds of Caesars Palace. One of the
Strip's oldest and most glamorous hotels,
Caesars was built in 1966. Inside, the lavish
Forum Shops mall features moving statues.

⓬ Lobby of the Bellagio

Lighting the ceiling of the hotel's
elegant lobby, this colorful glass
installation was designed by
famous glass artist Dale Chihuly.

⓯ The Quad

This hotel and casino is famous for
its classic car collection that is open
to visitors.

CityCenter features
a collection of soaring
hotels and gaming resorts.

THE STRIP

FLAMINGO ROAD

| 0 meters | 300 |
| 0 yards | 300 |

Paris resort's half-scale
replica of Parisian landmark,
the Eiffel Tower, dominates
the Strip.

**Cosmopolitan
of Las Vegas**
resort's beach club lets you
escape the heat in style.

⓾ Planet Hollywood

The reputation of this hotel, which opened as the
Aladdin in 1963, as one of the glitziest on the Strip was
sealed when Elvis married Priscilla here in 1967. It retains
the old glamor under its new guise, Planet Hollywood.

⓮ Flamingo Las Vegas

The flaming pink and orange neon feathers of
the Flamingo hotel's façade is a famous Strip
icon. Redesigned in the 1970s and 1980s, the
original 1946 building was the beloved project
of gangster Bugsy Siegel (see p101).

A View of The Strip: 2

The first casino resort to open on Las Vegas' Strip in 1941 was the El Rancho Vegas Hotel-Casino, which was located on the northern section of the Strip, on the corner of Sahara Avenue. A building boom followed in the 1950s, resulting in a swathe of resorts. The Sands, Desert Inn, Sahara, and Stardust hotels began the process that has transformed the Strip into a high-rise adult theme park. The few north Strip resorts that remain are mostly unrecognizable from their earlier incarnations thanks to million-dollar rebuilding programs.

The Venetian with replica of St. Mark's Campanile

Today, resorts such as The Venetian and Mirage have established the Strip's reputation for upscale quality, and almost nothing remains of the spit-and-sawdust atmosphere the city once had.

⓮ Treasure Island
The world of Treasure Island features the spectacular Mystere™ show by Cirque du Soleil®, performed twice each evening Saturday to Wednesday.

Mirage *(see p240)* is both stylish and ornate – its beautiful, Strip-facing gardens feature an "erupting" volcano.

The Fashion Show Mall is currently the largest shopping destination in Vegas, with more than 200 stores, an entertainment complex, and a food court serving both fast and fresh food.

SPRING MOUNTAIN RD

LAS VEGAS BLVD

SANDS AVE

0 meters 300
0 yards 300

Wynn Las Vegas & Encore
This resort has it all: casinos, an exclusive golf course, oversized luxurious rooms, restaurants with award-winning chefs, nightclubs, and dozens of designer shops *(see p240)*.

Guardian Angel Cathedral
Located on Cathedral Way, this chapel has elegant marble floors and imposing buttress support columns.

⓰ The Venetian
One of the world's most luxurious hotels, this has mock canals flowing through its shopping area.

㉒ Stratosphere Tower
An observation deck at the top of this 1,149-ft (350-m) tower offers fine views of the city and the ring of mountains that rise from the desert.

㉑ Circus Circus
Lucky the clown beckons visitors to this resort, which offers circus acts and traditional carnival games on the mezzanine floor above the casino.

W. SAHARA AVE

S. MAIN STREET

THE STRIP

㉒ Riviera
The colorful, neon-lit, and seemingly jewel-encrusted façade of Riviera highlights the hotel's hit shows, and is one of the most dazzling landmarks along North Strip.

0 meters 300
0 yards 300

Neon lights at the Riviera Hotel

Las Vegas Neon

The twinkling, flashing neon sign remains the dominant icon of Las Vegas, even though several of the new themed mega-resorts here have opted for a more understated look. Neon is a gas discovered by British chemist Sir William Ramsey in 1898. But it was a French inventor, Georges Claude, who, in 1910, discovered that an electric current passed through a glass tube of neon emitted a powerful, shimmering light. In the 1940s and 1950s the craft of neon sign-making was elevated to the status of an art form in Las Vegas.

Busy traffic on the Strip at dusk

The neon-lit façade of the Mandalay Bay hotel on the Las Vegas Strip

❶ Mandalay Bay

3950 Las Vegas Blvd S. **Tel** (702) 632-7777; (877) 632-7800. 🚻 ✂
Open 24 hours *(see p239)*.
🅦 **mandalaybay.com**

The Mandalay Bay resort aims to re-create the tropics of the late 19th century. Located at the south end of the Strip, it has 3,300 rooms. Tropical plants and white stucco architectural features such as arches and decorative cornices evoke a colonial atmosphere. Even the vast 135,000-sq-ft (12,550-sq-m) casino manages to suggest elegant 1890s Singapore. One highlight is the 11-acre (4.5-ha) lagoon-style swimming pool with its sandy beach and wave machine, plus a water ride around the pool. More restrained than other Strip resorts, the Mandalay Bay includes over 20 restaurants, nightclubs, and a theater that often hosts Broadway musicals. It was also the first resort on the Strip to feature a non-gaming hotel, the Four Seasons, located on the Mandalay's top four floors.

❷ Luxor

3900 Las Vegas Blvd S. **Tel** (702) 262-4000; (877) 386-4658. **Open** 24 hours *(see p239)*. 🚻 ✂ 🅦 **luxor.com**

The Luxor's famous 30-story bronze pyramid opened in 1993 and quickly became a Las Vegas icon. Despite the fact that the resort is named after the Eygptian city of Luxor, which has no pyramid, there is impressive attention to detail in the range of Ancient Egyptian architectural features. Painted temple pillars adorn the casino, and a reproduction Cleopatra's Needle graces the entrance.

Visitors enter the pyramid through the legs of a giant sphinx to find themselves inside the casino, where the ranks of ringing slot machines are surrounded by walls decorated with copies of paintings and hieroglyphs from the original Karnak temple in Luxor.

As a tribute to Egypt's ancient religions, a beam of light is projected from the pyramid's apex nightly – so powerful that it can be seen from planes cruising above Los Angeles 250 miles (400 km) away.

Among the hotel's many attractions, a free ride in the guest elevators (named "inclinators") ranks high – they travel along the inclines of the 350-ft (110-m) pyramid at an angle of 39 degrees.

Bodies, The Exhibition showcases whole bodies and hundreds of organs that have been preserved through an innovative process. The specimens provide a unique, three-dimensional view of the human form, with all its skeletal, muscular, and circulatory systems. Also on show are organs that have been damaged by over-eating and lack of exercise.

Titanic: The Artifact Exhibition tells the story of the Titanic, a floating palace that sank on a calm night in 1912 when it struck an iceberg in the North Atlantic. Actual artifacts recovered from the ship are on display, including luggage, the

Impressive Egyptian-style entrance of the Luxor hotel

For hotels and restaurants see pp236–43 and pp248–61

ship's whistles, and an unopened bottle of champagne vintage 1900. Visitors can walk through re-created first- and third-class rooms.

🏛 Bodies, The Exhibition
Luxor. **Open** 10am–10pm daily. 🅿 ♿

🏛 Titanic: The Artifact Exhibition
Luxor. **Open** 10am–10pm daily. 🅿 ♿

Excalibur's towers are designed to create a medieval fantasy castle

❸ Excalibur

3850 Las Vegas Blvd S. **Tel** (702) 597-7777. **Open** 24 hours (see p239). ♿
🌐 **excalibur.com**

The Excalibur is a family-friendly theme park resort with a casino attached. The inspiration of the medieval world of King Arthur and his knights is obvious at first sight of the castle-like exterior, with its white towers, turrets, moat, and drawbridge. Suits of armor line the entrance, which leads into the heavily themed casino where even the one-armed bandits have signposts such as "Medieval Slot Fantasy."

The second floor houses the Medieval Village, where quaint alleyways are lined with shops and restaurants, such as Dick's Last Resort, the Roundtable Buffet, and The Steakhouse at Camelot. The shops and kiosks on Castle Walk offer merchandise and souvenirs based on the hotel's medieval theme.

The Fantasy Faire Midway features Magic Motion Machine Rides, which are thrilling three-minute sight-and-sound simulation adventures, such as a bobsled run and a runaway train. On the floor below are a variety of carnival-themed video games, including a SpongeBob Squarepants simulator ride.

❹ New York New York

3790 Las Vegas Blvd S. **Tel** (702) 740-6969; (800) 689-1797. **Open** 24 hours (see p239). ♿
🌐 **nynyhotelcasino.com**

This hotel's re-creation of the Manhattan skyline dominates the Tropicana Avenue corner of the Strip – no mean feat in a street of impressive façades. Considered one of Las Vegas' most appealing sights, New York New York is fronted by a 150-ft (46-m) replica of the Statue of Liberty, behind which are 12 of Manhattan's most famous landmark buildings, including the Empire State, the Chrysler, and Seagram's.

Every interior detail of the hotel is designed to reflect a part of New York City, including the areas around the casino floor, which feature many of the city's most famous landmarks including Times Square. This fabulous casino is entered from the Strip via a replica of Brooklyn Bridge, which is one-fifth the size of the original.

Roaring around the complex is the thrilling, Coney Island style roller coaster that twists at 180 degrees and dives at speeds of 67 mph (105 kph), passing around the building's exterior and through the casino itself.

Adding to the Manhattan flavor are versions of many popular New York eateries. Set among Greenwich Village brownstones is a wide selection of cafés, restaurants, and bars offering a choice of live music from swing and jazz to Motown and rock.

Weddings in Las Vegas

A Las Vegas wedding comes second only to the lure of the gaming tables. The kitsch style of a range of ceremonies, from a drive-in chapel to themed medieval receptions or an Elvis Presley special, persuades more than 100,000 couples to tie the knot here each year. One brave couple said their vows on a high platform in front of Circus Circus before performing a spectacular bungee jump. A host of celebrities have married here, including Elvis and Priscilla Presley, and pop star Britney Spears to Jason Alexander.

Packages start at around $100. Both parties must also first appear in person to obtain a $60 marriage license at the Clark County Courthouse (201 E. Clark Ave, 702-671-0600; open 8am to midnight daily; www.clarkcountynv.gov).

Elvis impersonator with a new bride

The roller coaster at New York New York speeding through the air

❺ MGM Grand

3799 Las Vegas Blvd S. **Tel** (702) 891-7777; (877) 880-0880. **Open** 24 hours *(see p239).* ♿ 📷
w mgmgrand.com

The emerald-green MGM Grand building is fronted by the famous Leo, a 45-ft- (15-m-) tall bronze lion that serves as the symbol of the MGM Hollywood film studio. The original MGM hotel was built in the 1970s, farther down the strip where Bally's now stands, and was named for the 1930s film, *Grand Hotel*, starring Greta Garbo. In 1980 the worst hotel fire in Las Vegas history destroyed the building and killed 84 people. After first reopening on the same site, the MGM Grand subsequently opened at its current location in 1993 at the corner of the Strip and Tropicana Avenue. It covered a mammoth 114 acres (46 ha) and was themed on the movie *The Wizard of Oz*. Subsequent refurbishments have progressively removed most of its associations with MGM movies.

The 5,000 rooms that originally made the MGM Grand the world's largest hotel have been supplemented by another 1,728 suites in its three Signature towers, not to mention 51 ultra-luxurious Sky Lofts. It also boasts a 171,500-sq-ft (16,000-sq-m) casino, and an array of big-name restaurants that include the Hakkasan with indoor and outdoor seating and the Joël Robuchon Restaurant; however, the MGM Grand is known above all for its entertainment.

The Grand Garden Arena is a 17,000-seat venue famous for hosting big-name acts, including Barbra Streisand, the Rolling Stones, and Kanye West. It also hosts major sports events and world championship boxing, most memorably the legendary 1997 fight in which Mike Tyson bit off Evander Holyfield's ear. The more intimate 750-seat Hollywood Theater attracts many top entertainers, such as David Copperfield and comedians Drew Carey and Lewis Black. It has also hosted Jay Leno's "The Tonight Show."

MGM is also home to several nightclubs, including Wet Republic, which takes over part of the hotel's huge pool complex.

During daylight hours, the major attraction for visitors is **CSI: The Experience**, in which participants make their own self-paced interactive investigation of a fictional, mocked-up murder scene.

MGM Grand figurine

🎟 **CSI: The Experience**
MGM Grand. **Tel** (702) 891-5738. **Open** 9am–9pm daily.
📷 **w** csiexhibit.com

❻ Tropicana

3801 Las Vegas Blvd S. **Tel** (702) 739-2222; (800) 462-8767. **Open** 24 hours *(see p239).* ♿ **w** tropicanalv.com

One of the few 1950s boom hotels still on the Strip, the Tropicana was built in 1957. Las Vegas' famous illusionist act, Siegfried & Roy, first appeared here at the Folies Bergères in 1973. In 2009 the resort was restyled, and it now boasts lush tropical gardens and a fine South Beach façade. A 5-acre (2-ha) water park is one of the hotel's most delightful attractions with waterfalls and exotic flowers and foliage. The huge main pool has a bar alongside and also offers somewhat unusual casino action with swim-up blackjack tables which have a waterproof surface and money dryers.

The resort also has several outdoor spas for the ultimate in relaxation. Visitors come here to escape from the bright lights and full-on action of the city and enjoy luxurious spa treatments amongst the tropical greenery.

❼ CityCenter

3740 Las Vegas Blvd S. **Tel** (702) 590-9230. **Open** varies for each attraction. ♿ **w** citycenter.com

Designed as a city within a city to exploit the vast acreage of unused land west of the Strip, CityCenter took three and a half years to complete, at a cost of $8.6 billion. It opened in 2010 as the most expensive privately funded project ever built in the US.

Consisting of five different properties, CityCenter stretches between the Monte Carlo to the south and the Bellagio to the north – a free, futuristic tram runs from one end to the other in just three minutes. Its most conspicuous component is the quartz-shaped Crystals mall, a high-end retail and dining district characterized by dazzling architecture, indoor gardens, sculptures, and water features, as well as upmarket stores including Tom Ford,

Classic Floridian 1950s style at the Tropicana

Tiffany & Co., and North America's largest branch of Louis Vuitton.

Perched away from the Strip, the Aria Hotel & Casino is a sleek monolith far removed from Las Vegas' usual ostentatious style. It boasts a collection of contemporary sculpture ranging from Maya Lin and Henry Moore to Jenny Holzer, and holds restaurants run by some of the country's top chefs, such as Julian Serrano and Michael Mina and the ultra-hip Haze nightclub. The 4,004 high-tech guest rooms with floor-to-ceiling windows provide panoramic views of the city.

The entire complex was built with green technologies in mind, using natural lighting and reclaimed water. Even Aria's slot machines promote conservation, as the bases serve as air-conditioning units, effectively cooling guests from the ground up.

❽ Cosmopolitan of Las Vegas

3708 Las Vegas Blvd S. **Tel** (702) 698-7000; (877) 551-7778. **Open** 24 hours (see p239). ♿

Ⓦ **cosmopolitanlasvegas.com**

Situated within two high-rise towers on the Strip between the Bellagio and CityCenter, The Cosmopolitan offers a 100,000-sq-ft (9,300-sq-m) casino, an oasis-inspired spa, and three pools. There are 2,995 hotel rooms, most with marble bathrooms and sliding glass doors that open onto a large terrace. Some suites even have their own kitchenettes.

Among the 13 restaurants on site, guests will find most kinds of cusine, including Chinese-Mexican fusion food from chef José Andrés at China Poblana, and authentic Italian cuisine at Scarpetta. The Chandelier, one of several bars, spans three levels, each with a different theme, while the Marquee Nightclub & Dayclub combines clubbing with poolside entertainment, complete with infinity pools and a cabana.

The giant Coca-Cola bottle at Showcase Mall

❾ Showcase Mall

3785 Las Vegas Blvd. **Tel** (702) 597-3122. **Open** varies for each attraction. ♿

Dominated by a 100-ft- (33-m-) high neon Coca-Cola bottle, the Showcase Mall entertainment and retail complex is best known as the home of M&M's® World. This promotional exhibit, spread over four stories, offers some fun chocolate-themed displays for kids and abundant opportunities to buy chocolate in a rainbow of colors.

❿ Planet Hollywood

3667 Las Vegas Blvd. S. **Tel** (702) 785-5555; (866) 919-7472. **Open** 24 hours (see p239). ♿

Ⓦ **planethollywoodresort.com**

On the site formerly occupied by the Aladdin, scene of the 1967 wedding of Elvis and Priscilla Presley, Planet Hollywood (then known as Planet Hollywood Resort & Casino) opened in 2007. The glamorous, 1930s-style lobby features eight sparkling crystal chandelier columns and the hotel's two pools offer alfresco poolside cocktails.

The focus at Planet Hollywood is firmly on adult entertainment. Major headliners – including Britney Spears, who has signed for a long-term, multi-million-dollar residency, performing around fifty times per year – regularly appear at the property's main theater, while a separate showroom hosts the Abba musical *Dancing Queen*.

The Miracle Mile shopping mall, which does indeed snake for a full mile around the casino, still features Arabian-Nights touches dating back to the Aladdin era, and offers 170 shops and 17 restaurants, as well as its own theater, which runs a continuously changing rota of shows.

⑪ Paris

3655 Las Vegas Blvd. S. **Tel** (877) 603-4386. **Open** 24 hours *(see p239)*. ♿ 💳 Ⓦ **parislv.com**

Located next to Bally's Hotel *(see p239)* on the Strip, Paris is a $760 million resort that looks like a Hollywood film set of the real French capital. The façade is composed of replicas of such Paris landmark buildings as the Louvre, the Hôtel de Ville, and the Arc de Triomphe. A 50-story, half-scale Eiffel Tower dominates the complex, and visitors can ride an elevator to the observation deck at the top or dine in its gourmet restaurant 100 ft (33 m) above the Strip. The casino contains architectural details that meticulously re-create Parisian streetlife, including cast-iron street lamps, and everything is set beneath a fabulous painted sky.

Half-size model of the Eiffel Tower in the Paris hotel complex

Cocktail waitress Cobblestone streets wind along the edge of the casino and are filled with shops selling an array of expensive French goods including clothes, wine, cheese, and chocolate. The resort also boasts five lounges, a spa, and two wedding chapels. There are nine restaurants, including the brasserie-style Mon Ami Gabi *(see p254)*. This restaurant has tables situated outside overlooking the Strip, where diners can enjoy fine French cuisine in true Paris style.

⑫ Bellagio

3600 Las Vegas Blvd. S. **Tel** (702) 693-7111; (888) 987-6667. **Open** 24 hours *(see p239)*. ♿ 💳 Ⓦ **bellagio.com**

This $1.6 billion luxury resort opened in 1998 on the site of a previous hotel called the Dunes. Its design is based on the northern Italian town of Bellagio, with ocher- and terracotta-colored Mediterranean buildings set back from the Strip behind an 8-acre (3-ha) lake modeled on Italy's Lake Como. One of the hotel's many attractions is the sublime fountain display on the lake that springs into action at regular intervals through the day and evening. Crowds gather to watch the free show – a choreographed water dance set to music, accompanied by visual effects including a rolling mist and, at night, stunning light effects.

No expense has been spared on the Bellagio's interior either; delicate Carrara marble mosaics adorn all the entrance hall floors, and the main lobby ceiling is hung with Dale Chihuly's sculpted glass flowers of every color. Even the casino manages to be light and airy; powerful air-conditioning helps banish the smoky atmosphere. The parade of upscale shops includes some of the most stylish names in Italian design, including exclusive Bottega Veneta, discerning Armani, and trend-setting Prada.

Perhaps the most popular aspect of the Bellagio for visitors is its Conservatory, adjoining the lobby, which is planted with colorful, ever-changing displays of seasonal flowers. Set farther back from the Strip, the hotel's **Gallery of Fine Art** features temporary exhibitions by big-name artists.

🏛 **Gallery of Fine Art**
Bellagio. **Tel** (702) 693-7871. **Open** 10am–8pm daily.

The Bellagio's famous dancing fountains shooting high into the air

Caesars Palace, seen from the Strip at night

⓭ Caesars Palace

3570 Las Vegas Blvd S. **Tel** (702) 731-7110; (866) 227-5938. **Open** 24 hours (see p239). 🚻 ⓦ **caesarspalace.com**

Roman statues, Greek columns, and cocktail waitresses in togas could all be found at Caesars Palace when it opened in 1966. The decor and waitresses remain part of the ambience here, but in a less kitsch, more upscale way since more than $600 million was spent refurbishing the resort during the 1990s.

This classic Vegas casino was the first themed hotel on the Strip and quickly established a reputation for attracting top artists, from Andy Williams in the 1960s to the singer Celine Dion and the magician David Copperfield in the 1990s. Since the 1980s Caesars has also hosted international sports events, including championship tennis, featuring stars such as John McEnroe and Andre Agassi, and boxing, with such names as world champions Muhammad Ali and Mike Tyson.

Today the hotel houses three casinos, four lounges, a health spa, and the 4.5-acre (1.8-ha) Garden of the Gods – a pleasant landscaped area with four swimming pools. Caesars' elegant façade is fronted by fountains and cypress trees. The casinos have all been refurbished and, with their high ceilings and light

decor, create an elegant and upbeat atmosphere.

The entrance to the chic and highly exclusive Forum Shops (see p128) continues the ancient Greek and Roman theme and is as impressive as the hotel and casinos. The grand portico features a *trompe l'oeil* sky ceiling and is adorned with statues and relief sculpture.

Replicas of the Trevi and Triton Fountains in Rome adorn a sweeping plaza that is topped by a glass dome ceiling and has a large reflective pool at its center. There is also a majestic spiral escalator leading to the shopping mall itself, which offers more than 150 upscale clothes stores, specialty stores, and 13 different restaurants including Italian, Chinese, and seafood.

⓮ Flamingo Las Vegas

3555 Las Vegas Blvd S. **Tel** (702) 733-3111; (888) 902-9929. **Open** 24 hours (see p239). 🚻 ⓦ **flamingolv.com**

The brilliant pink and orange neon plume of the Flamingo hotel's façade is, to many, the archetypal Las Vegas icon. However, nothing remains of the original 1946 casino: the last vestiges of this building, including mobster Bugsy Siegel's private suite, were bulldozed in 1976 (see p101). One of the few remaining signs of this notorious gangster's involvement in the hotel is a display of 1940s and 1950s black-and-white photos, situated at the east entrance. In the 1990s a $130-million renovation created one of the most elegant pool areas in Vegas. Set among 15 acres (6 ha) of landscaped gardens, two Olympic-sized pools are veiled by tropical plants and palm trees, with islands providing a home to pink flamingoes, swans, turtles, and huge Japanese Koi fish. There is a kids' pool, two Jacuzzis, and a water slide leading to three additional pools. The hotel's pretty wedding chapel is also set in the pool area. Both guests and visitors may use the renown-ed tennis club, which has four floodlit night courts, a practice court, and a tennis shop.

Lush palms surround the pool at the Flamingo Las Vegas

Glittering Parisian landmarks at the Paris hotel complex on the Strip ▶

⓰ Autocollections at the Quad

3535 Las Vegas Blvd. S. **Tel** (702) 794-3174. **Open** 10am–6pm daily. 🐾 ♿
W autocollections.com

Located on the fifth floor of the Quad's parking lot, this multi-million-dollar collection of classic cars from around the world will impress even

An example of the celebrity-owned cars on show at the Quad

the most auto-phobic of visitors. Ralph Engelstad, the former owner of the Imperial Palace (as the Quad used to be known), began his collection with a 1929 Ford Model A Roadster in 1979. Two years later, the museum was opened with enough space for 200 cars.

As well as vintage Fords, the exhibition includes such classics as Mercedes, Chevys, Cadillacs, and a range of military vehicles. Today, many of the cars are for sale, some with price tags of more than one million dollars.

The collection is constantly changing as cars are sold and new ones replace them. At various times the exhibits have

included a Duesenberg Murphy Roadster owned by Howard Hughes. More recent, but no less stylish, are the Cadillacs, Lincolns, and Chevrolets of the 1950s and 1960s with their elongated tail fins, leather seats, and chrome accessories, such as the 1961 Lincoln Continental used by Jacqueline Kennedy. A 1976 Cadillac that once belonged to Elvis Presley is another former exhibit.

⓱ The Venetian & Palazzo

3355 Las Vegas Blvd. S. **Tel** (702) 414-1000; (877) 883-6423. **Open** 24 hours (see p239). ♿ 🅿 **W** venetian.com

An astounding piece of architecture that re-creates the city of Venice, the Venetian hotel currently holds, along with its sister resort the Palazzo, more than 7,000 suites. Together they typify the new breed of luxury Vegas mega-resorts. The Venetian opened in 1999 on the site of the legendary Sands Hotel, formerly the home of the

"Rat Pack" (see p101) and a famous swim-up craps table, and was demolished in 1996.

The Venetian's Strip façade consists of facsimiles of the Doge's Palace, the Campanile, and the Ca d'Oro, which overlook the blue waters of the Grand Canal – complete with a gondola park beneath a Rialto Bridge. Craftsmen have made sure that every detail is authentic – even the concrete has been aged to look like 400-year-old stone.

The colonnade of the Doge's Palace offers visitors one of the best views of the Strip. Inside the building, and up the stairs, another separate section of canal, also plied by gondolas, winds through the Grand Canal Shoppes. The Venetian fantasy continues here with high-quality stores and restaurants set among cobblestone walkways and bridges beneath a blue, painted sky that resembles a Renaissance painting. Acres of lavish marble flooring, statues, and replicas of

Entertainer at the Venetian

famous Venetian paintings are found throughout this elegant complex. The stunning front lobby has a dome decorated with scenes from Venetian master paintings, while the entrance to the Grand Canal Shoppes boasts a copy of Veronese's 1538 painting, *The Apotheosis of Venice*.

At the far end of the Shoppes, walkways lead into the similar Palazzo, completed in 2008, which holds more upscale stores, restaurants, and nightclubs.

⓲ Mirage

3400 Las Vegas Blvd. S. **Tel** (702) 791-7111; (800) 374- 9000. **Open** 24 hours (see p240). ♿ 🅿 **W** themirage.com

Mirage hotel-casino opened in the fall of 1989 at the staggering cost of $620 million. At the time it was the largest hotel in the

The stylish Venetian Hotel, complete with reproduction Campanile

alm trees and gentle rapids at the lagoon fronting Treasure Island resort and casino

S, with 3,044 rooms. This new negaresort aimed to cater not nly to gamblers but also to acationers and conventioneers. erhaps more than any other otel, the Mirage revolutionized he Strip, setting out to draw isitors with attractions other han just the casino – a kind of antasyland for adults.

The Mirage occupies an ntire block along Las Vegas oulevard, between Caesars alace and Treasure Island, nd offers a range of attractions o its own guests and Vegas isitors alike. Its traffic-stopping açade introduces the omplex's South Sea island heme, with tropical gardens,

waterfalls, and a lagoon. But the star of the show is undoubtedly a volcano that erupts, spewing fire and smoke, every hour from dusk to midnight. Inside the complex, an atrium filled with exotic plants (some real, some fake) is kept suitably steamy by computerized misters. Behind the main desk a 20,000-gallon (90,000-liter) aquarium is filled with brightly colored fish and small sharks.

As well as gaming, visitors can shop in designer stores, eat in one of 15 restaurants and bars, or see rare animal breeds, such as the Royal White tiger and white lions, in Siegfried

and Roy's Secret Garden. This delightful zoo and research center is set amongst the hotel's lush, landscaped gardens. Adjacent to the zoo is the Dolphin Habitat, home to Common Bottlenose dolphins.

⑱ Treasure Island

3300 Las Vegas Blvd. S. **Tel** (702) 894-7111; (800) 228-7206. **Open** 24 hours (see p239). 🚻 Ⓦ **treasureisland.com**

This hotel resort and casino offers luxurious accommodation and award-winning service. Originally pirate-themed, the hotel is now a more generic young-adult resort, and often abbreviates its name to the less piratical TI. Guests can relax in the hotel spa or sip cocktails by the heated outdoor pool. There are eight restaurants to choose from, including a branch of Señor Frog's, the Mexican-themed chain of restaurants, as well as several bars and lounges; nightclubs include the Kahunaville Party Bar.

The hotel is host to the exhilarating contemporary circus *Mystère*™ by Cirque du Soleil®, performed in a specially customized showroom (see p131).

he exotic rainforest atrium in the Mirage

The towers of Wynn Las Vegas & Encore

⑲ Wynn Las Vegas & Encore

3131 Las Vegas Blvd. S. **Tel** (702) 770-7000; (877) 321-WYNN. **Open** 24 hours *(see p240)*. 🚻
W wynnlasvegas.com

While the exteriors are not as flamboyant as other hotels on the Strip, the bronze-glass façades of the Wynn Las Vegas and its sister resort, Encore, are nevertheless stunning. Set against the desert and a forest-clad mountain range, the hotel offers wonderful views.

Within the two gigantic 60-story towers, opulence and exclusivity reign. The resort carries a reputation for being the most expensive and fashionable place in town.

Upon arriving at the main entrance of the Wynn, visitors are guided to the Atrium, with its tree-lined walkways. At the center of the hotel is the Lake of Dreams and the man-made mountain, which soars over the lake while curtains of water cascade in a dramatic waterfall. The Wynn also boasts a magnificent 18-hole golf course, which has hosted PGA and LGPA tour events.

Encore ranks among the city's most prominent nightlife destinations. The indoor-outdoor Encore Beach Club achieved worldwide notoriety thanks to Prince Harry in 2012, while the acclaimed XS has a 10-ft (3-m) rotating chandelier and a patio with poolside bars. The resorts' casinos are known for high gambling stakes: Encore's Sky Casino only takes bets over $300,000. However, for the less serious gamer, there are slot machines, table games, and poker tournaments.

⑳ Riviera

2901 Las Vegas Blvd S.
Tel (702) 734-5110; (800) 634-3420.
Open 24 hours *(see p239)*. 🚻
W rivierahotel. com

Bronze sculpture of showgirls at the Riviera

One of the group of Las Vegas hotels that were built on the Strip during the post-World War II building boom, the Riviera opened in 1955. Its nine-story tower made the hotel the city's first high-rise. Some of the key characters of Las Vegas' past have featured in the hotel's history. The famous entertainer Liberace was the first headliner here, appearing with legendary Hollywood actress Joan Crawford, who was the official hostess on opening night. Liberace was paid a record-breaking $50,000 a week. Over the next ten years the Riviera consolidated its reputation for offering glamorous entertainment, attracting such Hollywood stars as Orson Welles, Ginger Rogers, and Marlene Dietrich.

Today the Riviera occupies 1,000 ft (300 m) of the north Strip, and boasts 2,075 rooms. While its glamor is somewhat faded, the Riviera nevertheless retains an "old Vegas" atmosphere, symbolized by its large, brash casino. The hotel's neutral theme also makes it a good shooting location for scenes in feature films, such as *Ocean's Eleven* (1960), *Casino* (1995), and *The Hangover* (2009). This is one of the less expensive big Strip hotels, but it still offers an impressive range of facilities, including an

Sparkling neon stars light up the Riviera façade at night

Seen from the Strip, the brightly lit Circus Circus façade features Lucky the clown

Olympic-sized swimming pool, tennis courts, and a health spa. There are several restaurants, cafés, bars, and stores, and six live shows including a comedy showcase and a legendary topless show, *Crazy Girls*.

㉑ Circus Circus

2880 Las Vegas Blvd S. **Tel** (702) 734-0410; (800) 634-3450. **Open** 24 hours.
♿ Ⓦ circuscircus.com

Located at the north end of the Strip, Circus Circus opened in 1968 and is a themed resort offering family entertainment. The hotel has a choice of reasonably priced restaurants and buffets, including a delicious steak house.

This vast property covers over 68 acres (27.5 ha) and has the largest indoor theme park in the country. The huge **Adventuredome** is housed inside a pink dome, with a re-created Southwest landscape of sandstone cliffs, caves, and a waterfall, and is maintained at a temperature of 72°F (21°C) year round. The range of rides here includes the terrifying double loop, double corkscrew roller coaster, a water flume ride that races down a mountain, and the Fun House Express – an IMAX™ simulator ride. The three casinos here cover an incredible 100,000 sq ft (9,500 sq m). Above the main casino is the Big Top with its circular walkway of

traditional games where the children are the winners – they can often be seen here carrying lots of stuffed toys. This is also the place to find the seating for the live circus acts that perform half-hourly from 11am to midnight. World-class acrobats can be seen flying high above the heads of the gamblers filling the slot machines below.

Neon sign rising above the Stratosphere

🎡 The Adventuredome
Circus Circus. **Tel** (702) 794-3939. **Open** daily (times vary). 📷 ♿

㉒ Stratosphere

2000 Las Vegas Blvd S. **Tel** (702) 380-7777. **Open** 24 hours (*see p239*). ♿
Ⓦ stratospherehotel.com

Somewhat isolated at the north end of the Strip, away from the main attractions, this resort hotel boasts the 1,149-ft-(350-m-) high Stratosphere Tower – a Vegas landmark and the tallest building west of the Mississippi River. The summit has indoor and outdoor observation decks, which offer unparalleled views of the city and the surrounding desert and mountains, and a popular revolving restaurant (*see p254*).

The tower elevators take just 30 seconds to whisk visitors to the top, where several thrilling

rides are located, including **X-Scream**, a giant teeter-totter that propels riders 27 ft (8 m) over the tower edge; **Big Shot**, which shoots visitors 160 ft (49 m) up in the air; and **SkyJump**, a terrifying 855-ft (260-m) free-fall (the highest controlled free-fall in the world).

The Stratosphere hotel itself also offers two shows, and several restaurants and stores.

🎢 X-Scream, Big Shot, and SkyJump
Stratosphere. **Open** 11am–1am Sun–Thu, 11am–2am Fri, Sat & hols. 📷 ♿ for observation deck only.

The Stratosphere Tower, landmark of Las Vegas' north Strip

Evening light show at the Fremont Street Experience

㉓ Fremont Street Experience

Light shows: hourly 6pm–midnight daily. ♿ 🖥 vegasexperience.com

Long known as "Glitter Gulch," Fremont Street has been at the heart of Downtown Las Vegas since the city was founded in 1905. This is where the first casinos were located, complete with stylish neon signs, and famous illuminated icons such as Vegas Vic and Vickie lit up the night sky. However, as the Strip boomed during the 1980s and early 1990s, Fremont Street became ever more run-down in comparison.

The spectacular Fremont Street Experience, an ambitious $70-million project to revitalize the area, was unveiled in 1994. A vast steel canopy was erected over the central stretch of downtown, rising 90 ft (27 m) above a 1,500-ft- (457-m-) long five-block section of Fremont Street. After sunset every night, on the hour, sound and light shows are projected onto the canopy, using over 12 million synchronized LED modules, and backed by a sound system comprised of 208 speakers.

Fremont Street is pedestrianized, so visitors can easily stroll from casino to casino, stopping to snack and shop at stalls along the way. Some of the famous 1950s and 1960s neon signs have gone, but

many of the dazzling old façades remain. One way to see them, if you have the nerve, is from the Slotzilla zipline, a thrill ride that allows visitors to fly the full length of the street.

For many years the landmark casino in Vegas was Binion's Horseshoe, established by the legendary Benny Binion, who is said to have arrived in town in 1946 wearing a ten-gallon hat and carrying a suitcase filled with $2 million in cash. **Binion's**, as the casino is now known, is famous for its poker heritage – the World Series of Poker started here in 1970, and the Binion's Hall of Fame Poker Room is lined with photos of historic poker games and respected players. Visitors can pose for photos alongside a stack of $1 million in banknotes.

The dazzling **Golden Nugget**, opposite, was where entrepreneur Steve Wynn made his reputation in the 1970s. Its eponymous golden nugget is

Binion's, one of Fremont Street's most traditional casinos

the world's largest, weighing an incredible 61 lbs 11 oz (27 kg). There are other historic casinos nearby. **The Plaza** was built in 1971 on the site of the original Union Pacific Railroad depot, while the friendly **El Cortez**, with its Mexican styling, is one of the few casinos to retain features from its original 1950s building. The **Four Queens** was built in 1966 and named for the owner's four daughters; the casino's gilt mirrors and chandeliers evoke 19th-century New Orleans.

Binion's
128 E. Fremont St. **Tel** (702) 382-1600.
Open 24 hours. ♿ 🖥 binions.com

Golden Nugget
129 E. Fremont St. *(see p238)*.
Tel (702) 385-7111. **Open** 24 hours.
♿ 🖥 goldennugget.com

The Plaza
1 Main St. **Tel** (702) 386-2110. **Open** 24 hours. ♿ 🖥 plazahotelcasino.com

El Cortez
600 E. Fremont St. *(p238)*. **Tel** (702) 385-5200. **Open** 24 hours. ♿
🖥 elcortezhotelcasino.com

Four Queens
202 E. Fremont St. **Tel** (702) 385-4011.
Open 24 hours. ♿
🖥 fourqueens.com

㉔ Mob Museum

300 Stewart Ave. **Tel** (702) 229-2734. **Open** 10am–7pm Sun–Thu, 10am–8pm Fri–Sat. **Closed** Jan 1, Thanksgiving, Dec 25. 📷 ♿
🖥 themobmuseum.org

Las Vegas these days is a far cry from the city of the 1950s and 1960s, when many casino owners had close links with organized crime, and profits were regularly "skimmed" to line the pockets of shady mobsters. That era is recalled at the Mob Museum, opened in 2012 as the pet project of former mayor Oscar Goodman, who as a lawyer himself defended many Mob-associated figures. Three floors of displays tell the story of the gory deeds and flamboyant lifestyles of the city's gangsters and of the dedicated lawmen and politicians who eventually brought them to justice.

Discovery Children's Museum located in Symphony Park

㉕ Discovery Children's Museum

360 Promenade Place. **Tel** (702) 382-5437. **Open** 9am–4pm Tue–Fri (Jun–Labor Day: 10am–5pm), 10am–5pm Sat, noon–5pm Sun. **Closed** Mon (except school holidays), Jan 1, Thanksgiving, Dec 25. 🅿 ♿
W discoverykidslv.org

Relocated in 2013 to Symphony Park, on the western edge of Downtown, this excellent museum remains devoted to interactive exhibits that are fun for both adults and children. It centers on a 12-level tower known as the Summit, where visitors can experiment with exhibits that show the connections between scientific concepts and real-life applications. Other displays include a laboratory for young inventors; a water tank designed to replicate and explain the Hoover Dam and Lake Mead; the Eco City, a child-sized town laid out along a boulevard complete with banks, groceries, and a wind turbine; and Toddler Town, a glorified desert sandpit aimed at younger kids. Changing exhibitions cover a range of subjects from world cultures to art and wildlife.

㉖ The Las Vegas Natural History Museum

900 Las Vegas Blvd. N. **Tel** (702) 384-3466. **Open** 9am–4pm daily. **Closed** Jan 1, Thanksgiving, Dec 25. 🅿 ♿
W lvnhm.org

A popular choice with the families who need a break from the Strip resorts, this museum has an appealing range of exhibits. Dioramas re-create the African savannah and display a variety of wildlife from leopards and cheetahs to several African antelope species such as nyalas, bush boks, and duikers.

The Wild Nevada Room features the flora and fauna of the Mojave desert. Animatronic dinosaurs include a 35-ft- (10.5-m-) long *Tyrannosaurus rex*, while the marine exhibit has live sharks and eels. In the hands-on discovery room visitors can dig for fossils and explore the five senses.

㉗ Old Las Vegas Mormon State Historic Park

500 East Washington Blvd. **Tel** (702) 486-3511. **Open** 8am–4:30pm Mon–Sat. **Closed** Nov–May: Mon.
W parks.nv.gov/olvmf.htm

This diminutive soft-pink adobe building is the oldest in Las Vegas and all that remains of a fort built by Mormon settlers – the first non-Natives who arrived in the area – in1855. The fort, built on the banks of Las Vegas Creek, was arranged around a 150-ft- (45-m-) long *placita* (small rectangular plaza) with 14-ft- (4-m-) high walls, but the settlers abandoned it three years later. It became part of a ranch in the 1880s and was run by Las Vegas pioneer Helen Stewart (*see p100*). The City of Las Vegas bought the site in 1971.

Today, the Visitor Center is a reconstruction of the original adobe house with its simply furnished interior much as it would have been when the Mormon settlers lived here. The building also contains an exhibition that describes the Mormon missions and their impact on Las Vegas.

An animatronic *Tyrannosaurus rex* in roaring form at the Las Vegas Natural History Museum

Neat lawns and houses in the Boulder City suburbs

㉘ Boulder City and Hoover Dam

Road map A3. 🏔 12,500. 🚏 🚌 ℹ️ Hoover Dam Visitor Center: summer: 9am–5pm daily; winter: 9am–4pm daily. **Tel** (702) 494-2517. 🚿 ♿

Just eight miles (13 km) west of the colossal Hoover Dam, Boulder City was built as a model community to house dam construction workers. With its neat yards and suburban streets, it is one of Nevada's most attractive and well-ordered towns. Its Christian founders banned casinos, and there are none here today. Several of its original 1930s buildings remain, including the restored 1933 Boulder Dam Hotel, which houses the quaint yet engaging **Hoover Dam Museum**.

The Hoover Dam was built between 1931 and 1935 across the Colorado River's Black Canyon, 30 miles (48 km) east of Las Vegas. Hailed as an engineering victory, the dam gave this desert region a reliable water supply and provided inexpensive electricity. Today, the dam supplies water and electricity to the three states of Nevada, Arizona, and California, and has created Lake Mead – a popular tourist center. Visitors to the dam can take the Hoover Dam Powerplant Tour, which includes a trip to the observation deck where there are panoramic views of eight of the dam's 17 huge generators. The guided tour leads through old construction tunnels and explains how the dam was built.

🏛 **Hoover Dam Museum**
1305 Arizona St., Boulder City.
Tel (702) 294-1988. **Open** 10am–5pm Mon–Sat, noon–5pm Sun. **Closed** public hols. 🚿 ♿ 🆆 **bcmha.org**

㉙ Lake Mead National Recreation Area

Road map A3. **Tel** (702) 293-8906; Alan Bible Visitor Center (702) 293-8990. 🚌 Las Vegas. **Open** 8:30am–4:30pm daily. **Closed** Jan 1, Thanksgiving, Dec 25. 🚿 ♿ limited. 🏕 🆆 **www.nps.gov/lake**

After the completion of the Hoover Dam, the waters of the Colorado River filled the deep canyons that once towered above the river to create a huge reservoir. This lake, with its 700 miles (1,130 km) of shoreline, is the centerpiece of Lake Mead National Recreation Area, a 2,344-sq-mile (6070-sq-km) tract of land. The focus is on water sports, especially sailing, waterskiing, and fishing. Striped bass and rainbow trout are popular catches. There are also several campgrounds and marinas.

Power boating on Lake Mead

㉚ Valley of Fire State Park

Road map A3. **Tel** (702) 397-2088. 🚌 Las Vegas. **Open** 8:30am–4:30pm daily. 🚿 ♿ partial. 🏕 🆆 **parks.nv.gov/vf.htm**

This spectacularly scenic state park has a remote, desert location some 60 miles (97 km) north-east of Las Vegas. Its name derives from the red sandstone formations that began as huge, shifting sand dunes

Extraordinary rock formations in the Valley of Fire State Park

For hotels and restaurants see pp236–43 and pp248–61

about 150 million years ago. There are four well-maintained trails across this wilderness, including the Petroglyph Canyon Trail, an easy half-mile (0.8-km) loop, which takes in several fine prehistoric Ancestral Puebloan rock carvings. Here, summer temperatures often reach 112°F (30°C). The best time to visit is in spring or fall.

The nearby town of Overton lies along the Muddy River. Ancestral Puebloan people *(see pp30–31)* settled here in around 300 BC but left some 1,500 years later, perhaps because of a long drought. Archaeologists have unearthed hundreds of prehistoric artifacts in the area since the first digs began in the 1920s. Overton's **Lost City Museum of Archaeology**, just outside the town, has a large collection of pottery, beads, woven baskets, and delicate turquoise jewelry.

Ⅲ Lost City Museum of Archaeology
721 S. Moapa Valley Blvd., Overton.
Tel (702) 397-2193. **Open** 8:30am–4:30pm Thu–Sun. **Closed** Jan 1, Thanksgiving, Dec 25. 🚫 ♿

❸ Mount Charleston

Road map A3. **Tel** (702) 872-5486; (702) 515-5400 (Forest Service).
🚌 Las Vegas. ⛰ 🌐 **fs.fed.us/htnf**

About 45 miles (72 km) northwest of Las Vegas, Mount Charleston rises to 11,918 ft (35,754 m) out of Toiyabe National Forest, clad with pine, mountain mahogany, fir, and aspen. Also known as the Spring Mountain Recreation Area, it offers refuge from the Las Vegas summer heat, with a variety of hiking trails and picnic areas. In the wintertime, skiing and snowboarding are popular *(see p271)*.

A range of hikes is available, including two demanding trails that snake up to the summit: the 11-mile (18-km) North Loop Trail and the 9-mile (14-km) South Loop Trail. Easier walks on the forested slopes are also marked, including a one-hour hike up Cathedral Rock. This walk starts from a picnic area at

Rainbow Mountain in Red Rock Canyon National Conservation Area

the end of Nevada State Hwy 157. This is the more southerly of the two by-roads leading to Mount Charleston off Hwy 95; the other is Hwy 156, which runs to the Lee Canyon Ski Area, catering to both skiers and snowboarders.

❸ Red Rock Canyon

Road map A3. **Tel** (702) 515-5350. 🚌 Las Vegas. **Open** 8am–4:30pm daily. **Closed** public hols. 🅿 ♿ limited.
⛰ 🌐 **nv.blm.gov/redrockcanyon**

From downtown Las Vegas, it is a short, 10-mile (16-km) drive west to the low hills and steep gullies of the Red Rock Canyon

National Conservation Area. A gnarled escarpment rises out of the desert, its gray limestone and red sandstone the geological residue of an ancient ocean and the huge sand dunes that succeeded it. Red Rock Canyon is easily explored on an enjoyable 13-mile (21-km) scenic road that loops off Hwy 159. Beside the road are picnic spots and trailheads for a series of short hikes that cover the area's steep winding canyons. The visitor center at the start of the road has useful displays on the Canyon's flora and fauna. There are more some 80 to 100 bighorn sheep in the conservation area.

The Construction of the Hoover Dam

Hoover Dam sign

More than 1,400 miles (2,250 km) in length, the Colorado River flows through seven states on its journey from the Rocky Mountains to the Gulf of California. A treacherous, unpredictable river, it used to be a raging torrent in spring and a trickle in the heat of summer. As a source of water it was therefore unreliable and, in 1928, the seven states it served signed the Boulder Canyon Project Act to define how much water each state could siphon off. The agreement paved the way for the Hoover Dam, and its construction began in 1931. It was a mammoth task, and more than 5,000 men toiled day and night to build what was, at 726 ft (218 m), the world's tallest dam. Named after Herbert Hoover, the 31st president of the US (1929–33) and an avid supporter of the project, it contains 17 hydroelectric generating units.

View of the Hoover Dam

PRACTICAL INFORMATION

Las Vegas has become one of the world's most popular playgrounds. The Strip at night, in all its blazing glory, is a sight that never seems to tire visitors. Vegas is a city that knows how to cater to its guests, and a wealth of information about hotels, casinos, dining, and entertainment is available.

However, with so much to choose from it is a good idea to do some advance planning. Most visitors spend most of their time around the Strip and the Downtown area, but there are many rewarding day trips to be had exploring other nearby sights including Grand Canyon *(see pp 62–67)*.

Façade of the Las Vegas Convention Center

General Information

Choosing when to go to Vegas can be tricky if you are looking for a bargain deal. These days the city is a highly popular destination year round, but unless you have prebooked, it is generally best to avoid the major conventions when the hotels can be full. New Year is also an extremely busy time.

Summers are very hot here with an average July temperature of 105°F (40°C). Spring and fall are sunny without such intense heat, and winters can also be warm but with occasional cold winds.

The **Las Vegas Convention and Visitor's Authority (LVCVA)** runs an excellent website, which offers information on every aspect of your trip, and will also mail out information packs. In the city itself, you can get many free papers such as *What's On*, as well as the combined daily editions of the *Las Vegas Review Journal* and the *Las Vegas Sun*, which contain reviews of the current shows and restaurants.

Although Las Vegas is no longer the low-cost destination it once used to be, hotel prices

do vary greatly *(see pp238–40)*. Different room rates are likely to be charged for each specific day of your stay, and are almost always lower on weekdays; avoid the weekends if you're planning a touring itinerary. All the major hotels have their own websites, each with a reservations facility holding details of all sorts of offers and discounts *(see under individual hotel pp238–40)*. Many are linked to other properties run by the same owners, making it easy to compare prices, and also offer toll-free phone numbers.

Tipping

Tipping for services rendered is part of life in Las Vegas. Bellhops expect $1 per bag (generally with a $2 minimum), bartenders $1 a drink, waiters 15 percent of the check, and cab drivers 10–15 percent of the fare. Leave a dollar a day for the chamber maids, and a tip for croupiers, if you are lucky and win.

Getting around Las Vegas

The Las Vegas transit authority, the **Regional Transportation Commission (RTC)**, runs the Deuce bus, which stops at all the major hotels along the Strip for a flat fare of $6 for a 2-hour pass, or $8 for 24 hours. Exact change is required; dollar bills are accepted. There is also the **Las Vegas Monorail**, which travels between the MGM Grand and Sahara Avenue ($5 per ride, $12 per day, or $28 for a 3-day pass), with stops at Bally's/Paris, the Flamingo/Caesars Palace, Harrah's/The Quad, the Las Vegas Convention Center, and the LV Hotel. There are three free tram services: the first runs between the Excalibur, the Luxor, and the Mandalay Bay; the second runs through CityCenter, between Monte Carlo in the south and the Bellagio in the north; and the third connects the Mirage with Treasure Island. These services can save a great deal of pounding up and down the Strip between hotels.

Regional Transportation Commission (RTC)

If used a lot, taxis here can be an expensive way of getting around. They have an initial charge of $3.30, plus $2.60 for each mile. A cab from the airport to the south end of the Strip (a 5-minute trip) costs around $20, while a trip to the north end can be as much as $30. Cabs cannot be hailed on the street so are usually picked up at one of the hotel lines. Despite the fact that the majority of your time will be spent on one street, the Strip is a very long stretch of road, and while the properties along it appear to be near, this is an optical illusion caused by

Tram linking the Excalibur, Luxor, and Mandalay Bay resorts

their vast size. Renting a car in Las Vegas allows you to see everything without getting footsore or spending a fortune on taxis. Parking is easy in Las Vegas; all the large Strip hotels have free parking lots. All the major car rental companies are represented here, and cars may be picked up and dropped off at the **McCarran Rent-A-Car Center**, three miles southwest of the airport, which is connected with the terminals by free shuttle buses. Rates can be as low as $30 a day. (For more information about arriving in Las Vegas, see *pp286–7*).

Perhaps the ultimate Las Vegas travel experience is the limousine, particularly the stretch limo. It is possible to rent a wide range of these vehicles, including stretch and super-stretch versions that come fitted out with TV, cocktail bar, and even Jacuzzi, typically costing between $75 and $100 per hour. Several companies in the city, such as **AWG Ambassador** and **Las Vegas Limousines**, rent their vehicles by the hour as

well as for picking up and dropping off visitors at the airport. **On Demand Sedan & Limousine Service** provides chauffeur-driven vehicles.

Sightseeing Trips

For a break from the Strip's attractions, there is a variety of day trips on offer to Las Vegas' surrounding sights. These include the gigantic Hoover Dam, a major tourist attraction, and nearby Lake Mead, with its extensive opportunities for every kind of water sport *(see p124)*. Organized trips by **Pink Jeep Tours** include drives through the scenic Red Rock Canyon National Conservation Area *(see p125)*, and **Lake Mead Cruises** offers several cruises aboard the Desert Princess on Lake Mead.

Many Las Vegas visitors take a day trip to Grand Canyon by air *(see pp62–7)*. Grand Canyon West, home to the Skywalk, can be quickly reached by airplane or helicopter, while the more spectacular South

Rim, within the National Park, lies 270 miles (435 km) away by road, and can only be seen on a day trip by airplane; **Scenic Airlines** and **Papillon Helicopter Tours** fly to both. Papillon also offers exciting night flights over Las Vegas itself, soaring 500 ft (150 m) above the Strip, and taking in all the major resorts in their amazing neon-lit settings.

Most hotels have plenty of information on the trips available and also usually provide a booking service.

DIRECTORY

Useful Numbers

AWG Ambassador
Tel (702) 740-3461.
[w] awgambassador.com

Lake Mead Cruises
Tel (702) 293-6180.
[w] lakemeadcruises.com

Las Vegas Convention and Visitors Authority
3150 Paradise Rd.
Tel (877) 847-4858.
[w] visitlasvegas.com

Las Vegas Limousines
Tel (888) 696-4400.
[w] lasvegaslimo.com

Las Vegas Monorail
Tel (702) 699-8200.
[w] lvmonorail.com

McCarran Rent-A-Car Center
[w] mccarran.com

On Demand Sedan & Limousine Service
Tel (800) 990-0417.
[w] odslimo.com

Papillon Helicopter Tours
Tel (888) 635-7272.
[w] papillon.com

Pink Jeep Tours
Tel (888) 900-4480.
[w] pinkjeep.com

Regional Transportation Commission
Tel (702) CAT RIDE (228-7433).
[w] rtcsnv.com

Scenic Airlines
Tel (702) 638-3300.
[w] scenic.com

A helicopter from Papillon Helicopter Tours

SHOPPING IN LAS VEGAS

Las Vegas continues to consolidate its reputation as a shopper's paradise. Fun and tacky souvenirs are available in small stores along the Strip, whereas jewelry and designer clothes can be found everywhere, from hotel shops to malls. Given the city's hot climate, indoor shopping malls are the norm. All the major resorts have their own covered parades of shops, and some, such as the Forum Shops in Caesars Palace, are as flamboyant as the hotels themselves. Several malls in Las Vegas, such as the Strip's Fashion Show Mall, house upscale department stores such as Saks Fifth Avenue and Neiman Marcus. For bargains on clothes and shoes as well as a variety of household items, head to a discount mall such as Las Vegas Premium Outlets, which has a South branch three miles south of Mandalay Bay, and a North branch a mile west of Downtown. Everyday items like shampoo and toothbrushes can be expensive in hotel shops, but 24-hour stores are scattered along the Strip.

Marble floors and a glass ceiling house elegant stores at Via Bellagio

Hotel Shopping

The indoor malls in many of the mega-resorts take shopping to a new dimension. Themed styling for the large hotels means that their resort streets are designed to look like Venice, Paris, or ancient Rome.

The **Forum Shops** at Caesars Palace are decorated with columns, arches, statuary, and a *trompe l'oeil* sky, which simulates the changes from dawn to dusk through the day. The statues adorning one ornate fountain spring to life every 90 minutes and move with light and sound depicting the Atlantis myth. Among the 160 stores found here are designer clothes and shoes at Louis Vuitton, DKNY, and Emporio Armani. There are specialty candy and chocolate shops, as well as a choice of restaurants including a franchise for renowned Los Angeles chef Wolfgang Puck's Spago.

The beautiful **Grand Canal Shoppes** extends from the upper floor of the Venetian into the Palazzo, along a canal full of gondolas, and runs through an amazing replica of St. Mark's Square. Stores flanking the canal to either side sell the usual designer apparel, such as Kenneth Cole's shoes and clothes by Caché, as well as expensive jewelry and antiques, imported Italian goods, and Venetian-themed souvenirs. The mall also holds Italian ice cream stands, bakeries, and restaurants.

Novelty magnets on display in a hotel store

Miracle Mile Shops at Planet Hollywood has 170 stores and 15 restaurants encircling a huge theater. Streaming images displayed on an outdoor LED sign welcome shoppers as they arrive. Hip store H&M stocks European-influenced fashions, while trendy Urban Outfitters has urban-inspired furniture, and retro and modern clothing. Restaurants range from casual eateries to upscale fine dining establishments.

Le Boulevard at the Paris hotel is a Francophile's joy, with authentically styled Parisian stores selling French goods including children's clothes, cheese, wine, and chocolate. The elegant **Via Bellagio** at the Bellagio hotel offers several upscale boutiques such as Chanel, Prada, and Gucci arranged around a marble-floored walkway with natural sunlight streaming in through an ornate glass ceiling *(see p107)*.

Roman statues and a painted sky at Caesars Palace's Forum Shops

Visitors entering the Fashion Show Mall on the Strip

The Malls

Immediately north of Treasure Island, the **Fashion Show Mall** is Nevada's largest mall, housing seven department stores, including Neiman Marcus, Dillard's, Macy's, and Saks Fifth Avenue, as well as the ubiquitous Gap and Abercrombie & Fitch. For everyday items and lower prices, head off the Strip to the 1.2-million square-ft (111,500 sq-m) **Boulevard Mall**. The vast range of shops here includes such all-American favorites as Sears and JC Penney, as well as toy, gift, and jewelry stores. There is also a food court. **Town Square Las Vegas** is designed to resemble a local village center and has a range of eclectic shops, including H&M and Sephora.

If you're searching for real bargains, outlet malls lie within easy reach of both the Strip and Downtown. These sell branded goods with minor faults or excess stock, at discounts that can reach up to 70 percent. The enormous **Las Vegas Premium Outlets (North)**, a mile west of downtown and served by SDX buses, tends to offer the best deals, in outlets ranging from Disney to Tommy Hilfiger and Nike, while stores at the less bargain-oriented **Las Vegas Premium Outlets (South)**, 3 miles (5 km) south along Las Vegas Boulevard from Mandalay Bay, include Gap, Nike, and Banana Republic.

Souvenirs and Specialty Stores

The Las Vegas of old is often associated with the tacky and kitsch, and souvenirs here can be all those things. All along the Strip stores sell memorabilia; always popular are the Elvis sunglasses, some even have sideburns attached. The largest emporium, the **Bonanza Gift Shop** offers a wide range of gifts, from the cheapest pair of slot machine earrings to luxury sets of poker chips. The gambling store, **JP Slot Emporium**, offers a wide range of gaming merchandise from the serious to the frivolous. It also stocks an impressive collection of bargain-price one-armed bandits. **Serge's Wigs** is one of the largest wig showrooms in the country and is a great place to experiment with different looks.

1970s retro Elvis sunglasses

Sign for Bonanza Gift Shop, a landmark on the Strip

DIRECTORY

Hotel Shopping

Forum Shops at Caesars
Open 10am–11pm Sun–Thu, 10am–midnight Fri & Sat.
Tel (702) 893-4800.

Grand Canal Shoppes
Open 10am–11pm Sun–Thu, 10am–midnight Fri & Sat.
Tel (702) 414-4500.

Le Boulevard
Open 10am–11pm Sun–Thu, 10am–midnight Fri & Sat.
Tel (702) 946-7000.

Miracle Mile Shops
Open 10am–11pm Sun–Thu, 10am–midnight Fri & Sat.
Tel (702) 866-0703.

Via Bellagio
Open 10am–midnight daily.
Tel (702) 693-7111.

The Malls

Boulevard Mall
3528 S. Maryland Pkwy.
Open 10am–9pm Mon–Sat, 11am–6pm Sun.
Tel (702) 735-7430.

Fashion Show Mall
3200 Las Vegas Blvd. S. **Open** 10am–9pm Mon–Sat, 11am–7pm Sun. **Tel** (702) 369-8382.

Las Vegas Premium Outlets (North)
875 S. Grand Central Parkway.
Open 10am–9pm Mon–Sat, 10am–8pm Sun.
Tel (702) 474-7500.

Las Vegas Premium Outlets (South)
7400 Las Vegas Blvd S. **Open** 10am–9pm Mon–Sat, 10am–8pm Sun. **Tel** (702) 896-5599.

Town Square Las Vegas
6605 Las Vegas Blvd. S. **Open** 10am–9:30pm Mon–Thu, 10am–10pm Fri & Sat, 11am–8pm Sun. **Tel** (702) 269-5000.

Specialty Stores

Bonanza Gift Shop
2400 Las Vegas Blvd. S.
Tel (702) 385-7359.

JP Slot Emporium
5280 S. Valley View Blvd. Suite C.
Tel (888) 988-SLOT (7568).

Serge's Wigs
4515 W. Sahara Ave.
Tel (702) 207-7494.

ENTERTAINMENT IN LAS VEGAS

Las Vegas makes a good claim to be the world's entertainment capital. From free acts performing on Strip-front stages or in casino lounges, to lavishly produced shows in purpose-built theaters, a full range of nightlife is available. Sinatra and Elvis may be gone but headliners still appear regularly in the city's showrooms, offering a rare chance to see a favorite star in a surprisingly intimate setting. Most of the major venues are concentrated in the hotels along the Strip and Downtown, and range from small lounges to 1,000-seater showrooms. While visitors can still enjoy the kitsch appeal of a Vegas burlesque show such as *Jubilee!*, high-quality productions featuring the latest in lighting and special effects are a big draw. Comedy, magic, and music from jazz to salsa are also widely available and often for free or the price of a cocktail.

Information

There is no shortage of information on the lively entertainment scene in Las Vegas. A variety of free publications lists all the major productions as well as the latest big acts in town. Magazines and free newspapers such as *Las Vegas*, *What's On*, and *Las Vegas Weekly* can usually be picked up in all the major hotels. Even Las Vegas taxis carry free guides to the city, with information on shows and attractions. The **Las Vegas Convention and Visitors Authority** provides up-to-date showguides, and their website has current listings and reviews (see p127).

Buying Tickets

The easiest way to book tickets to the major shows or visiting headliners is via the venue or hotel, using either their website or toll-free number. Prices can vary, ranging from around $45 to $175 per ticket. The ticket may also include drinks, a free program, tips, and even dinner. All the big shows have pre-assigned seating; for smaller shows, where seating is not reserved, you can tip the maitre d' to get a better seat.

If you know you want to see a particular show, it is always best to reserve in advance. The eight different Cirque du Soleil® extravaganzas, for example, which include the Beatles' musical *Love* at the Mirage, *Michael Jackson One* at Mandalay Bay (see p110), and the stunning *Mystère*™ at Treasure Island, are liable to be booked months ahead.

If you are happy simply to catch whatever is available, your chances are better on weekdays than on weekends, although most shows have one or two days off during the week. Call or visit the relevant box office, or, for bargain deals, try **Tix4tonight**, which has multiple outlets along the Strip, and sells same-day tickets at discounts of up to fifty percent.

For sports events, such as world championship boxing, or the big rock and pop concerts, frequently held at the impressive 17,000-seater MGM Grand Garden Arena (see p112), tickets can also be purchased through **Ticketmaster** and other agency outlets. Discounts for children and senior citizens may be available, and free tickets may be offered to the hotel casino's big winners.

Showgirls in full regalia for the production of *Jubilee!* at Bally's Las Vegas

Headliners

Ever since the Strip's early days in the 1940s, Las Vegas resorts have lured some of the world's most famous performers to entertain their gambling guests. Stars such as Frank Sinatra, Dean Martin, Liza Minnelli, and Elvis Presley played regularly here, often in relatively small "headliner" showrooms. The

Lavish production number at Kà (Cirque du Soleil®)

Relaxing with a round of golf just minutes from the Strip

construction of the 4,000-seat **The Colosseum** at Caesars Palace in 2003, however, brought things to a new level, and enticed a new generation of headliners to the city. Built to showcase Celine Dion, who still appears frequently, it also hosts regular residencies by the likes of Shania Twain, Elton John, and Rod Stewart. Several other casinos have since followed suit, including Planet Hollywood, which has a long-term deal with Britney Spears *(see p113)*.

Lounge Acts

The time-honored tradition of the Las Vegas lounge – a bar open to the casino floor, and providing free entertainment – is still going strong. All the mega-resorts hold one or two indoor lounges, and several also have outdoor stages, with bars, facing the Strip. Lively lounges include dueling-piano bars like New York New York's Bar at Times Square *(see p111)*, and Napoleon's in Paris *(see p114)*, where there is much boisterous audience participation.

These performances are free except for the price of buying a drink. However, each venue has a minimum drink purchase charge or cover. The wonderful views from the Stratosphere Top of the World Lounge *(see p254)* will cost you the additional price of an elevator ticket.

Outdoor Activities

One of the most popular outdoor activities in Las Vegas is golf. There are dozens of superbly designed golf courses, some positioned in the midst of spectacular scenery. As well as private courses there are many public ones, some just a short distance from the Strip itself. The concierge desk in your hotel will advise and book time at one of the many nearby courses. There are also excellent tennis facilities at some hotels, including Caesars Palace *(see p115)*, the Monte Carlo *(see p239)* , and the Riviera *(see p239)*.

Luxurious health spas are a standard element in the big hotels providing services such as weight rooms, personal trainers, and massages.

Hiking is available at Red Rock Canyon National Conservation Area, a short way west of downtown *(see p125)*.

Production Shows

The first production show to be staged at a Strip resort was the musical revue *Lido de Paris*, at the Stardust, which began in 1958 and ran for 33 years. This prompted other hotels to stage their own productions. Traditionally these shows have long runs – the Tropicana staged the French *Folies Bergère* in 1959, and it ran for almost 50 years. Often performed in built-to-order showrooms, Vegas shows usually have two performances each evening. Among today's long-running, popular shows are *Mystère™* at Treasure Island, *Kà* at MGM Grand *(see p112)*, *Jubilee!* at Bally's Las Vegas, and *Love* at the Mirage.

DIRECTORY

Venues and Tickets

The Colosseum
Caesars Palace **Tel** (866) 227-5938. Showtimes and prices vary.
W thecolosseum.com

Ticketmaster
Tel (800) 745-3000.
W ticketmaster.com

Tix4tonight
Tel (877) 849-4868.
W tix4tonight.com

Shows

Listed below is a choice of recommended Las Vegas shows.

Blue Man Group
A multimedia experience of art, percussion, and clowning. **Monte Carlo**: **Tel** (800) 258-3626. 7pm Sun–Thu, 7pm & 9.30pm Fri & Sat. Price: $83.50 to $158.90.
W blueman.com

Jubilee!
Long-running showgirl revue. **Bally's Las Vegas**: **Tel** (702) 777-2782; (855) 234-7469. Two shows nightly at 7:30pm and 10:30pm, Sat–Thu. Price: $57.50 to $117.50.

Love
Cirque du Soleil®'s dramatic re-imagining of the Beatles, performed to a remixed soundtrack. **Mirage**: **Tel** (702) 792-7777; (800) 963-9634. Two shows at 7pm and 9:30pm Thu–Mon. Price: $79 to $180.
W cirquedusoleil.com

Mystère™
Cirque du Soleil®'s impressive contemporary circus performed in its own built-to-order theater. **Treasure Island**: **Tel** (702) 894-7722; (800) 392-1999. Two shows at 7pm and 9:30pm Sat–Wed. Price: $60 to $119

"O"
Enchanting Cirque du Soleil® show involving water acrobatics. **Bellagio**: **Tel** (702) 796-9999; (888) 488-7111. Two shows nightly at 7:30pm and 10pm Wed–Sun. Price: $109 to $180.

Terry Fator
Singing ventriloquist with an amazing array of impressions. **Mirage**: **Tel** (702) 792-7777; (800) 963-9634. One show nightly at 7:30pm Mon–Thu. Price: $60 to $150.

GAMBLING IN LAS VEGAS

Despite its fame as an all-round adult amusement park, Las Vegas remains famous for its casinos. Almost 40 million visitors come to the city every year and, on average, each visitor spends around $150 gambling every day. Do not come expecting to make your fortune; with a combined annual income from gambling of almost $7 billion, the casinos appear to have the advantage.

The secret pleasure of gambling is the lure of the unknown – you never know what the next card will be. Casinos know this and aim to keep you playing for as long as possible. Free drinks are usually brought around to gamblers, but it is not a good idea to gamble without a clear head. Before you start, decide on an amount that you can afford to lose and be sure to stick to it.

For a first timer, a casino can seem daunting, but, with a basic understanding of the rules, most of the games are relatively simple to play *(see p134–35)*. Some hotels have gaming guides on their in-house TV channels and Las Vegas' visitor center supplies printed guides. Several large casinos give free lessons at the tables.

Row upon row of "slots" on the gaming floor of New York New York Casino *(see p111)*

General Information

Always carry ID if you are young-looking and tend to be carded in bars, because it is illegal to gamble under the age of 21. Children are not welcome on the casino floor, which can make it difficult for families with children in some hotels *(see pp238–40)*.

Be aware that if you are winning it is casino etiquette to tip the dealers. It can also be to your advantage to tip when you first sit down at a table, as it is always a good idea to get the dealer on your side. Dealers can prevent inexperienced gamblers from making silly mistakes and will usually explain the finer points of the games, if asked. Head for the tables where players are talking and laughing. The chances are that a row of glum faces means that you may be in for an equally dull gambling experience.

Slot Machines

Slots of every kind dominate Las Vegas casinos. The simple one-armed bandit, where pulling a handle spun the reels and a win resulted from a row of cherries or some other icon, has been largely superceded by computerized push-button machines offering a bewildering variety of plays. There are basically two kinds of slots: flat-top machines and progressive machines. A flat-top machine has a range of fixed payouts depending on different arrangements of winning symbols. There will usually be a choice of stakes, from one to three coins, and if you hit a winning display, you will win less for a one-coin stake than if you play the limit. On progressive slots, you give up smaller jackpots in exchange for winning a progressive jackpot. The payout on these machines increases as you play, and the rising jackpot figure is displayed above each machine. The biggest payout is currently from the Megabucks slots, which operate all across Nevada. A software engineer won $39 million on a machine at the Excalibur Hotel in 2003, the highest payout ever. The majority of machines are now coinless and use prepaid electronic cards, but there are a few coin machines left in the down-town casinos. There are also high-roller slots, which take anything from $10 to $500 for a single play.

Casino loyalty card

Tips

• Usually located together, progressive machines pay out at a certain limit. It is a good idea to ask an attendant what this limit usually is, and when it was last hit. If the jackpot hits at around $10,000 and the machines are displaying $9,000, this could be a good time to start playing.
• Always play the machine limit because if you win, you will be sure to receive the maximum amount.
• Wins on both types of machine allow you to cash out your win or else rack up credits, which you can use for subsequent bets. Monitoring your display of credits will help keep track of how much you are spending. If your original stake was 10 quarters and you win 30, using credits allows you to decide to walk away when the credit display is down to 20, leaving you 10 quarters up on the game.
• Choose to play at the busier banks of machines, as rows of unoccupied machines could mean that they are not paying out well.
• Join a slot club. All the casinos have clubs that offer a range of incentives to get you to play with them; which range from cash back to discounts on hotel

rooms. Members are issued with an electronic-strip plastic loyalty card that inserts into the machine; the more money a gambler spends, the greater the rewards.

Blackjack

This card game is one of the most popular games on the floor; casino blackjack tables offer minimum bet games from $2 to $500. The aim is to get as close to 21 without going over, and to beat the dealer. Cards are worth their numerical value, with all the face cards worth 10 and an ace worth 1 or 11. Generally the dealer will deal from a "shoe" (a box containing up to six decks of cards). Each player receives two cards face up, while the dealer's second card is face down. Players must not touch the cards and should use hand signals to indicate if they wish to take another card, or "hit" (scratch the table with their forefinger to receive another card) or not take a card, "stand" (wave a flat hand over their cards.) Once each player has decided to stand or hit the 21

Traditional slot machine

limit, the dealer turns over his second card and plays his hand, hitting 16 or less and standing with 17 or more. This is important because it is an

essential part of "basic strategy" blackjack. The assumption behind basic strategy is that the dealer's second card will be a ten and that the next card in the shoe will also be a ten. This is because there are more tens in the deck than any other card (there are 96 tens in six decks).

Tips

• In basic strategy if the dealer's top card is a "bad" card (from 2 to 6), then the player should stand from 12 up and not risk taking another card. This is because the dealer has to get to 17, so it is most likely that he will go over 21 when he hits his hand.
• If the player has between 12 and 16 and the dealer's first card is seven or higher, the player should gamble on drawing an extra card, as the probability is that the dealer's other card is a ten, which beats a hand of under 17.
• If your first two cards add up to 10 or 11, then you can "double down," or bet the same amount again. If you have a $5 chip on the table then you add another, hoping to get a ten card thereby reaching a winning total of 20 or 21 and doubling your winnings. Be aware that you are only allowed one extra card if you double down.
• Another betting option is to split your hand. If you are dealt two cards of the same value, you can choose to separate them into two hands, placing a second bet by the first on the table. Do this when you have aces and eights.

A winning hand on a blackjack table at Circus Circus *(see p121)*

Craps

Often the most fun game on the floor, a sense of camaraderie develops in craps because players are betting either with or against the "shooter" (whoever has the dice) on what the next number rolled will be. The aim of the shooter's first roll, or "coming out," is to make 7 or 11 in any combination (say 3/4, 5/6) to win. A roll of 2, 3, or 12 is craps; everyone loses and the shooter rolls the dice again. If a total of 4, 5, 6, 8, 9, or 10 is rolled, this becomes the "point" number, and the shooter must roll this number again before rolling a 7 to win. Craps etiquette says that you put your money on the table rather than handing it to the dealer; wooden holders around the table will keep your chips. Always roll with one hand; the dice must hit the end of the table. All betting and laying down of chips must be completed before the next roll.

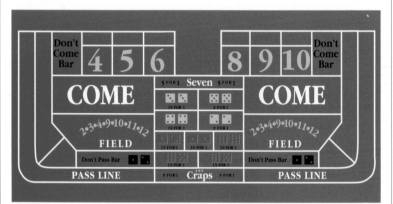

Craps table seen from above, showing the various boxes and areas for the many bets

Bets

Craps can seem confusing as there appears to be a lot going on at any one time; this is largely due to the wide variety of bets it is possible to lay. If you are a beginner the following bets are

Laying bets during a craps game at Caesars Palace

The Pass Line Bet

With this one you are basically betting that the shooter will roll a 7/11 on the first roll in order for you to win. The odds at this point are even, so if you do win you get the same amount you laid down. If a

point number is rolled, the shooter has to throw the same number before he rolls another 7. Since there are more ways to roll a 7 than any point number, it pays to take the odds once the shooter has a point, which means placing an additional bet behind your pass line bet. This will pay you the true house odds if the shooter rolls his point. The odds change according to the number, so check with the dealer first.

The Don't Pass Bet

This is the opposite of a pass line bet. The aim here is for the shooter to lose by throwing a 2 or 3 on the first roll, or by rolling a losing 7, which happens before he makes his point number.

The Come Bet

This is an optional bet you can make during the game, when your money comes to the next number that rolls. For example; if the point is 6 you make a come bet, and the shooter rolls an 8. Your come bet "comes" to the 8, and now you have two numbers in play. You can also take odds on a come bet.

The Place Bet

Another way of getting additional numbers is by making a place bet. In this case, you simply pick the number you want and make a place bet on that number. The advantage of place bets is that you pick the number yourself and you can remove your bet at any time. The disadvantage is that the casino charges you from 50 cents to $1 for each $5 bet you place.

Poker

There are several different versions of poker, including video poker, played in Las Vegas casinos. It is important to know the hierarchy of poker hands to play any of these: starting with a pair as the lowest hand, and a royal flush as the highest.

Caribbean Stud Poker

A type of five-card stud poker played on a table with a layout like a blackjack table, where the aim is to beat the dealer. There is a progressive jackpot where winnings increase according to a player's hand. Players win all or part of a progressive jackpot with a Royal Flush, Straight Flush, Four of a Kind, Full House, or Flush.

Pai Gow Poker

Combining the ancient Chinese game of Pai Gow with American poker, this game includes a joker in the standard 52-card pack. The joker is used as an ace or to complete a straight or flush. Each player has to make the best two-card and five-card hand possible to beat the banker's two hands.

Casino poker chips

Texas Hold 'Em

This is the most popular form of poker played in the poker rooms of Las Vegas casinos. It is also the game of the famous World Series of Poker that is held each year at the Rio. Players are dealt two cards and they must make their best hand from five communal cards dealt face up on the table.

Roulette

Roulette is quite a simple game but with a great variety of bets. A ball is spun on a wheel containing numbers 1 to 36 divided equally between red and black, plus a single and a double zero, colored green. Each player's chips are a different color so they can be easily identified on the table. The aim is to guess the number

A croupier setting up roulette in a private gaming room

that will come up on the spin of the wheel. Bets are placed on the table, which has a grid marked out with the numbers and a choice of betting options. The highest payout odds are 35 to 1 for a straight bet on one number such as 10 black. You can also make a "split bet" on two numbers, which pays 17 to 1 if either number comes up. The most popular bets are the outside bets, which are those placed in the boxes outside the numbered grid. These only pay even money, but allow you to cover more numbers such as Odd or Even, Red or Black, First 18 Numbers or Second 18 Numbers. You can also make a Column Bet covering 12 numbers, which pays 2 to 1.

Baccarat

A variation of *chemin de fer*, baccarat is played at a leisurely pace with eight decks of cards, the deal rotating from player to player. The object of the game is to guess

Two cards in each hand of baccarat

which hand will be closest to 9: the player's or the banker's. You can bet on either hand.

Keno

One of the easiest games to play, keno is a close relative of bingo. Out of the 80 numbers on a keno ticket, players may choose up to 20. A range of bets is possible and winning depends on your chosen numbers coming up. The prize depends on the amount of numbers matched.

A screen showing a keno game in progress at Circus Circus

Race and Sports Book

Giant video screens adorn these areas of the casino, where you can bet on almost any sport. The race book is for betting on thoroughbred horse racing and features live coverage from racetracks across the US. The sports book covers the main sporting events taking place around the country, as well as the major tournaments staged in Las Vegas itself. Watch the progress of your team on the nearby TVs.

The flame-colored hoodoos of Bryce Canyon ▶

SOUTHERN UTAH

Southern Utah

Southern Utah contains an abundance of stunning natural landscapes, and boasts the highest concentration of national parks in the US. The region, which lies to the north of Grand Canyon and centers on the blue waters of Lake Powell, owes much of its dramatic beauty to the geological wonder of the Grand Staircase, a series of steep terraces of colored rock. Weather and river erosion have sculpted this feature into the fine scenery found at Bryce, Arches, Capitol Reef, Zion, and Canyonlands National Parks. Hiking, boating, and mountain-biking are popular here, with equipment rentals available in such towns as Moab and St. George.

View of the peaks of Zion National Park in spring

Visitors on horseback following the winding trails of the high country at Bryce Canyon National Park

For **additional map symbols** *see back flap*

Getting Around

The best way to explore Southern Utah is by car: every road is a scenic route, and public transportation is limited. One train passes through the region, an Amtrak Superliner, which stops at Green River, 50 miles (80 km) northwest of Moab. Greyhound buses travel to some of the region's larger towns. Two Interstate Highways, I-15 and I-70, pass close to Zion and Arches National Parks, respectively. Smaller paved highways include Highway 191 via Moab, and the scenic Highway 12, which skirts Grand Staircase-Escalante National Monument. A high-clearance 4WD vehicle is advisable for many of the unpaved roads.

SOUTHERN UTAH

Key

━━ Highway
━━ Major road
┅┅ Minor road
─── Main railroad
━━ State border
△ Summit

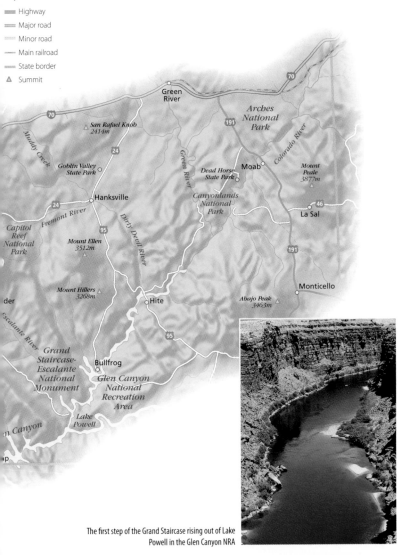

The first step of the Grand Staircase rising out of Lake Powell in the Glen Canyon NRA

The Mormons

The Church of Jesus Christ of Latter Day Saints was founded by Joseph Smith (1805–44), a farm worker from New York State. In 1820 Smith claimed to have had visions of the Angel Moroni. The angel led him to a set of golden tablets, which he translated and later published as the *Book of Mormon*, leading to the founding of the Mormon church. This new faith grew rapidly but attracted hostility because of its political and economic beliefs, and because it practised polygamy. Seeking refuge, the Mormons moved to Illinois in 1839, where Smith was killed by an angry mob. Leadership passed to Brigham Young (1801–77), who led church members westward. Salt Lake City was founded and Young led his followers to establish farms across Utah's wilderness. Today, over 60 percent of Utah's citizens are Mormons.

19th-century depiction of Joseph Smith's vision. The Angel Moroni is seen delivering the tablets which became the Mormon scriptures.

On the great trek westward, pilgrims rode or walked for a year, leaving Illinois in 1846 and arriving in Utah in July, 1847.

Mormon pioneers were intrepid and successful; after they had established themselves in the Salt Lake valley, church members fanned out across the west, establishing agricultural colonies in their wake. One of these colonies was in Las Vegas *(see p123)*, where 30 Mormons, sent here by Brigham Young, built a mission and a small fort.

The Great Mormon Trek West

In 1846, Brigham Young led a band of Mormons west in the hope of escaping persecution and founding a safe haven in the Salt Lake valley. Young wished to find "a place on Earth that nobody wants." It was an extraordinary enterprise in which the pioneers traveled across bleak prairies and over mountains in primitive wagons, braving the fierce winter and summer weather. Those who could not afford oxen hauled all their possessions in hand carts.

Brigham Young and his wives, nine of whom are seen here, illustrated Mormonism's most controversial practice, polygamy. It was outlawed in 1890 to appease the US Government and pave the way for Statehood in 1896.

INTRODUCING SOUTHERN UTAH | 141

Salt Lake City was painstakingly laid out in a grid system over the unpromising, and previously unsettled, landscape of Utah's Salt Lake Basin. The grid ensured wide streets, decent-sized houses, and enough land so that each family could be self-sufficient. By 1900, many farms and more than 300 towns had been founded across the West and Southwest.

Brigham Young

Born in Vermont in 1801 of a Protestant family, Brigham Young, carpenter, painter, and glazier, joined the Mormons in Ohio in 1832. He took charge of the great migration west from Illinois in 1846, arriving in Salt Lake City in 1847. In 1849 he established the territory of Deseret, which encompassed present-

Brigham Young in middle-age

day Utah. "Deseret" means "Honeybee" in the *Book of Mormon* and symbolizes industry. Young's vision and organizational skills helped the settlers turn the desert into fruitful farmland. During his long life, he had several disputes with the federal government, whose authority he both resisted and recognized. Despite being removed from political office in 1857, Young was head of the Mormon church until his death in 1877.

Mormon missionaries preach their faith through-out the world, placing great emphasis on their social and philosophical concerns. The church enjoys a high rate of conversion, and church membership continues to grow rapidly.

The St. George Mormon Temple was constructed under the aegis of Brigham Young. For the fifteen million Mormons worldwide, it is a potent symbol of a faith based on work, sobriety, and cooperation, with the emphasis on humanitarian service.

SOUTHERN UTAH

Wherever you go in southern Utah, it is hard to find a road that does not dazzle the visitor with unforgettable scenery. Winding highways lead through stunning red rock canyons, stark deserts of wind-polished rock, and cool, mountain realms of tall pines and sparkling streams. The five national parks in this region are favorite destinations, such that each is inundated with up to three million visitors a year. Despite this, even in summer there are quiet, undiscovered corners to be found across the region. The Grand Staircase–Escalante National Monument offers visitors a chance to experience this living wilderness by driving such unpaved scenic routes as the Hole-in-the-Rock Road *(see p151)*.

The first people to live here were Paleo-Indians 12,000 years ago. Later, the Ancestral Puebloan people thrived in southeastern Utah, building cliff dwellings along the San Juan River. The Mormons arrived here in 1847, successfully establishing settlements in this harsh land.

Today, most people come to the area to enjoy the outdoors. Hiking, mountain biking, and 4-wheel driving are all popular activities, as well as riverfloat trips and whitewater adventures. St. George and Cedar City are the biggest towns in southern Utah. A number of smaller communities, however, such as Springdale, Torrey, and Bluff, have good motels and restaurants. Moab meanwhile offers outdoor activities by day, and entertainment by night.

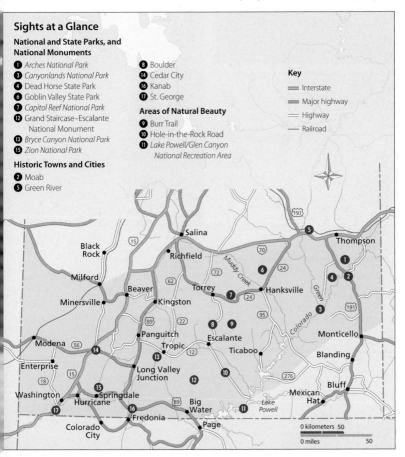

Sights at a Glance

National and State Parks, and National Monuments
- ① Arches National Park
- ③ Canyonlands National Park
- ④ Dead Horse State Park
- ⑥ Goblin Valley State Park
- ⑦ Capitol Reef National Park
- ⑫ Grand Staircase–Escalante National Monument
- ⑬ Bryce Canyon National Park
- ⑮ Zion National Park

- ⑧ Boulder
- ⑭ Cedar City
- ⑯ Kanab
- ⑰ St. George

Areas of Natural Beauty
- ⑨ Burr Trail
- ⑩ Hole-in-the-Rock Road
- ⑪ Lake Powell/Glen Canyon National Recreation Area

Historic Towns and Cities
- ② Moab
- ⑤ Green River

Key
- ▬▬ Interstate
- ▬▬ Major highway
- ▭▭ Highway
- ── Railroad

Map labels: Salina, Thompson, Black Rock, Richfield, Milford, Muddy Creek, Torrey, Hanksville, Beaver, Minersville, Kingston, Panguitch, Escalante, Monticello, Modena, Tropic, Ticaboo, Blanding, Enterprise, Long Valley Junction, Bluff, Washington, Springdale, Mexican Hat, Hurricane, Big Water, Fredonia, Lake Powell, Colorado City, Page, Green, Colorado

0 kilometers 50
0 miles 50

◀ One of the numerous graceful stone arches in Arches National Park

For additional map symbols *see back flap*

❶ Arches National Park

Arches National Park contains the highest number of natural stone arches found anywhere in the world. More than 80 of these natural wonders have formed over millions of years. The park "floats" on a salt bed, which once liquefied under the pressure exerted by the rock above it. About 300 million years ago, this salt layer bulged upward, cracking the sandstone above. Over time the cracks eroded, leaving long "fins" of rock. As these fins eroded, the hard overhead rock formed arches, which range today from the solid looking Turret Arch to the graceful Delicate and Landscape arches.

Devil's Garden
This area contains several of the park's finest arches, including Landscape Arch, a slender curve of sandstone more than 300 ft (91 m) long, thought to be the longest natural arch in the world.

Sunset watch at Delicate Arch
A natural amphitheater surrounds the arch, creating seating from which vistas of the La Sal Mountains are framed.

The Windows Section
In the park's Windows Section, a one-mile loop trail leads to Turret Arch, then the North and South Windows arches, situated side by side. With excellent viewing spots available, many visitors photograph North and South arches framed by the sandstone Turner Arch, as seen here.

Exploring the Park

The park's highlights can be seen from the many viewpoints dotted along the scenic drive. The drive starts at the visitor center at the park's south end, just off Hwy 191. Several easy trails start from parking lots at the road's viewpoints. The loop at Balanced Rock is a short and easy trail suitable for children, while Delicate Arch Viewpoint Trail has disabled access. The Windows loop is suitable for families.

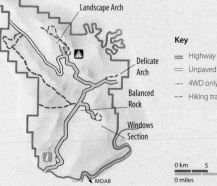

Landscape Arch

Delicate Arch

Balanced Rock

Windows Section

MOAB

Key

═══ Highway
═══ Unpaved road
--- 4WD only
-- Hiking trail

0 km   5
0 miles   5

For additional map symbols *see back flap*

Delicate Arch
The most celebrated of all the arches here, and a state symbol, Delicate Arch appears on many Utah license plates. It is reached via a moderate 45- minute walk over sandstone.

Arches are formed through a process that takes millions of years; today's arches continue to erode and will eventually collapse.

Western-style, timber-clad gift store on Main Street, Moab

❷ Moab

Road map 2C. 6500. *i* Main and Center Sts. (435) 259-8825. **Open** mid-Mar–Oct: 8am–7pm Mon–Sat, 9am–6pm Sun; Nov–mid-Mar: 9am–5pm Thu–Mon, 1–5pm Tue, 9am–2pm Wed. *w* discovermoab.com

A town of dramatic ups and downs, Moab is once again booming. It is lively and has good facilities. In 1952 a local prospector discovered the first of several major uranium deposits outside town. Overnight, Moab became one of the wealthiest communities in America. When the uranium market declined in the 1970s, the town was saved by tourism and its proximity to Arches and Canyonlands national parks.

Today, Moab is one of the top destinations for lovers of the outdoors. Mountain bikers come here to experience the famous Slick Rock Trail. They also come for the challenging ride to Moab Rim, a strenuous journey that entails a trek of about 10 miles (17 km). There is also a vast choice of hiking and 4WD routes taking in some of this region's fabulous landscapes.

Matheson Wetlands Preserve off Kane Creek Blvd has 2 miles (3 km) of hiking trails along a riverside wetland that is home to birds and wildlife. Moab is also a center for whitewater rafting on the Colorado River.

Matheson Wetlands Preserve Off Kane Creek Blvd. **Tel** (435) 259-4629. **Open** dawn–dusk daily.

Balanced Rock
This precariously balanced boulder atop a sandstone spire is one of the park's landmarks. Good views are available from the trail as well as the scenic road route.

Park Avenue and the Courthouse Towers
The large, rock monoliths known as Courthouse Towers bear an uncanny resemblance to city skyscrapers. They can be seen from Park Avenue, an easy, short trail.

❸ Canyonlands National Park

Millions of years ago, the Colorado and Green Rivers cut winding paths deep into rock, creating a labyrinth of rocky canyons that form the heart of this stunning wilderness. At its center, the rivers' confluence divides the park's 527 sq miles (1,365 sq km) into three districts: the Needles, the Maze, and the grassy plateau of the Island in the Sky. Established as a national park in 1964, Canyonlands is growing in popularity. Most wilderness travel, whether on foot or by vehicle, requires a permit.

VISITORS' CHECKLIST

Practical Information
Road map C2. 🛈 Horseshoe (435) 259-2652; Island In The Sky (435) 259-4712; The Maze (435) 259-2652; Needles District (435) 259-4711. 🆆 **nps.gov/cany**
Visitor center: **Open** 8am–4:30pm daily (longer in spring, summer & fall). **Closed** Jan 1, Thanksgiving, Dec 25. 🅿️ ♿ 🚻 📷 ⛺

Mesa Arch
An easy and rewarding 500-yard (0.5-km) trail leads to Mesa Arch, a long, low curve of stone that perfectly frames the snow capped La Sal Mountains in the distance.

Key

═══ Highway

▬▬▬ 4WD only

▪ ▪ ▪ Hiking route

───── National Park boundary

Horseshoe Canyon contains 6000-year-old petroglyphs, said to be the oldest in existence.

Upheaval Dome Overlook

White Rim Road is a 100-mile (160-km) trail accessed via the exhilarating Shafer Road, a 4WD drive track down a steep cliff

Grand View Point Overlook

Maze Overlook

The Maze canyons, where outlaw Butch Cassidy hid out in the late 1800s, offer a challenge to skilled hikers.

Needles District
The most interesting features in this remote district are the hundreds of red rock spires, or needles, for which it was named

Island in the Sky
Easy access by car makes this the most visited district of the park. A popular stop here is the Grandview Overlook, which offers panoramic views of the rocky canyons of the Green and Colorado rivers.

| 0 km | 5 |
| 0 miles | 5 |

The stunning desert-scape visible from the Green River Overlook in Canyonlands National Park

Dead Horse Point State Park

Road map C1. [i] State Route 313 (435) 259-2614. **Open** 6am–10pm daily. Visitor center **Open** Apr–Oct: 8am–6pm daily; Nov–Mar: 8am–5pm daily. [icons] **stateparks.utah.gov**

The high mesa of Dead Horse Point lies just outside the entry to the Island in the Sky of Canyonlands National Park. Unforgettable views of the Colorado River and the maze of deep canyons are a highpoint here. Legend has it that this park owes its name to the fact that it was once used as a natural corral for wild mustangs. A group of horses not chosen for taming were once left in this dry site, eventually dying of thirst within

View of dramatic cliffs from Dead Horse Point State Park

sight of the Colorado River far below. The Park also features several short hiking trails that follow the cliff edge, offering variations on the truly amazing view. The drama of this place has not been lost on Hollywood *(see pp34–5)*. Famous as the spot where Thelma and Louise drove off the edge in the 1991 film of the same name, in 2000 these cliffs were scaled by Tom Cruise in *Mission Impossible: 2*.

❺ Green River

Road map C1. [icon] 1,000. [i] 1765 E. Main St (435) 564-3427. **Open** Apr–Oct: 8am–7pm; Nov–Mar: 9am–5pm daily.

Located in a broad, bowl-shaped valley, the town grew around a ford of the wild Green River in the 19th and early 20th centuries. Primarily a service town, it is also a launching spot for those braving the whitewater of the Green and Colorado Rivers.

John Wesley Powell *(see p29)* began his intrepid exploration of the Colorado River and Grand Canyon from here in 1871. The **John Wesley Powell River History Museum** has 20,000 sq ft (1,860 sq m) of displays tracing the history of the area's exploration.

[icon] John Wesley Powell River History Museum
1765 E. Main St. **Tel** (435) 564-3427. **Open** Apr–Oct: 8am–7pm daily; Nov–Mar: 9am–5pm daily. **Closed** public hols. [icons]

Eroded rock formations of Goblin Valley State Park

❻ Goblin Valley State Park

Road map C1. **Tel** (435) 275-4584. **Open** 6am–10pm daily. [icons] **stateparks.utah.gov**

The "Goblins" of Goblin Valley State Park are a group of mushroom-shaped rocks or hoodoos, intricately carved by erosion. Visitors are free to wander among these rocks, which are up to 10 ft (3 m) in height. Two paved and several unpaved trails lead down to the valley floor.

The great red dome of the Golden Cathedral, Grand Staircase–Escalante National Monument ▶

❼ Capitol Reef National Park

Around the turn of the 20th century, prospectors coming across the desert were forced to stop at the Waterpocket Fold, a vast 100-mile- (160-km-) long wall of rock that runs north–south through the desert. They likened it to an ocean reef and thought its round white domes looked like the nation's Capitol Building, hence the park's name. Covering 378 square miles (980 sq km), many people pass through the park via Fremont Canyon on Hwy 24. The park is famous for its long record of human habitation; Ancestral Puebloan petroglyphs and a preserved Mormon homestead can still be seen here.

VISITORS' CHECKLIST

Practical Information
Road map 2C. 10 miles E. of Torrey, Hwy 24. **ℹ** Capitol Reef Visitor Center (435) 425-3791.
W nps.gov/care
Open Jun–Sep: 8am–6pm daily (Oct–May: to 4:30pm). **Closed** Dec 25.

Cathedral Valley
The vast rock monoliths that tower over the desert here give the valley its name. An unpaved road crosses this stunning area.

The Fremont Petroglyphs were created by the Ancestral Puebloans between 700 and 1250, and can be seen on a rock wall in the Fremont Canyon.

Bicknell

Hanksville

The Gifford Farmhouse
Visitors can tour the 1908 Gifford home, which is now a cultural center dedicated to the 1880s Mormon settlement that once flourished here.

Capitol Gorge
Capitol Gorge can be reached from the scenic route that extends about 10 miles (16 km) into the heart of the park. Guided walking tours are available during summer, but only experienced hikers should explore the back country here.

Notom-Bullfrog Road is an adventurous drive along a partly unpaved road for 70 miles (112 km) south to Lake Powell. Cars can negotiate the road in dry weather but extra gas and water are essential.

Waterpocket Fold was formed 65 million years ago as the Earth's crust buckled upward. The multicolored ripples of rock that run the length of the park continue to be shaped by erosion.

Key

= Highway
= Unmade road
= 4WD only

0 kilometers   10
0 miles   1

Boulder

Road map C2. **i** Anasazi State Park
Museum (435) 335-7308. **Open** Mar–
Oct: 8am–6pm daily; Nov–Feb:
9am–5pm daily.

The tiny town of Boulder nestles
picturesquely among the
surrounding peaks. The town is
home to the Anasazi State Park,
which offers restored ruins and
a museum detailing the history
of the Ancestral Puebloans that
lived here between AD 1050
and 1200. Before Hwy 12 was
built, Boulder was virtually
isolated as the last town in
America to receive its mail by
pack mule. Today, Boulder
makes a welcome rest stop
along Hwy 12, which connects
Hwy 89 and Capitol Reef
National Park. This road boasts
what may be the most
spectacular and diverse array of
landscapes found along any
road in the country.

Between Escalante and
Boulder, Hwy 12 winds through
an unforgettable landscape of
vividly colored, towering rock
formations and twisting
canyons. Visitors can stop at
Calf Creek Campground to hike
the 6-mile (10-km) round-trip
trail to Lower Calf Creek Falls.
The falls are one of the hidden
treasures of the Southwest, a
126-ft (38-m) plume that drops
past lush hanging gardens
into an emerald-green pool.
Continuing along Hwy 12, just
before Boulder, the road offers
white-knuckle excitement as it
traverses the Hogsback, a knife-
edge ridge of rock with
guardrails and steep drops on
either side. Beyond Boulder,
Hwy 12 climbs to the 9,400-ft
(2,820-m) summit of
Boulder Mountain.

❾ Burr Trail

Road map C2. **i** 755 W. Main St,
Escalante (435) 826-5499.

The Burr Trail is another partly
paved scenic road, winding
through the Grand Staircase–
Escalante National Monument.
The first 40 miles (64 km) are
paved and follow Deer Creek,
rising through the winding red-
rock maze of Long Canyon. At
the canyon end, the view
opens out to reveal the pristine
valleys of the Circle Cliffs and
Capitol Reef. The trail crosses
Capitol Reef as an unpaved
road before reaching Bullfrog
Marina at Lake Powell (see
pp154–5) and is passable only
by four-wheel drive, high-
clearance vehicles.

❿ Hole-in-the-Rock Road

Road map C2. **i** 755 W. Main St,
Escalante (435) 826-5499.

In 1879 a determined group of
230 Mormon settlers headed
out from Panguitch, hoping to
create a new settlement in
southeastern Utah. Instead they
were brought to a halt by the
yawning 2,000-ft- (600-m-)
deep abyss of Glen Canyon.
Undeterred, they dynamited a

View of Lake Powell from the end of
Hole-in-the-Rock Road

narrow hole through a wall of
rock and constructed a primitive
road down the sheer sides of
the canyon. Lowering their
wagons and cattle down the
path by ropes they finally
reached the bottom, only to
repeat the whole process in
reverse to ascend the far side.
They finally founded the town
of Bluff in 1880 (see p176).

Today, their original route,
Hole-in-the-Rock Road, offers an
impressive trip through the wild
interior of the Grand Staircase–
Escalante National Monument.
About 18 miles (29 km) along
the road, intrepid hikers can
explore Peekaboo and Spooky
canyons, two slot canyons
barely one foot (30 cm) wide in
places. 4WD is necessary to
traverse the last 6 miles (10 km)
to the pioneers'"Hole in the
Rock," a 50-ft (15-m) slit in the
rock which offers a fine view of
Lake Powell.

Hell's Backbone Bridge, with steep mountain drops on either side, west of the town of Boulder

⓫ Lake Powell

See pp154–5.

⓬ Grand Staircase–Escalante National Monument

Road map C2. ℹ️ 755 W. Main St., Escalante (435) 826-5499. **Open** mid-Mar–mid-Nov: 7:30am–5:30pm daily; mid-Nov–mid-Mar: 8am–4:30pm Mon–Fri. 🖥️ ut.blm.gov/monument

Established by President Clinton in 1996, this national monument encompasses 2,970 sq miles (7,690 sq km) of pristine rock canyons, mountains, and high desert plateaus. One of the last areas in the US to be explored, the Grand Staircase–Escalante National Monument abuts Capitol Reef National Park, Glen Canyon National Recreation Area, and Bryce Canyon National Park. It was named for the four cliff faces, called Vermilion, Grey, White, and Pink, that rise in tiered steps across the Colorado Plateau (see pp22–3). Geologically speaking, they are a recent phenomenon, having been raised just 12 million years ago.

This vast area has a special importance, as the Bureau of Land Management intends to preserve its wild and largely pristine state. No new roads, facilities, or campgrounds will be built in the monument, while those roads that already exist will not be improved.

The spectacular beauty of the monument is best explored on scenic drives combined with day-long hikes. Several paved and dirt roads offer access to various parts of the park. Highway 89 follows the southern boundary, in places hugging the base of the towering Vermilion cliffs. Just 10 miles (16 km) east of the town, a road leads north into Johnson Canyon, where there is a mock Western town that has been used for many movies and TV shows (see p34).

Information on guided and independent tours in this vast region can be found at the Escalante visitor center.

A few miles east of Bryce Canyon and 9 miles (14 km) south of Hwy 12 stands **Kodachrome Basin State Park**, a distinctive landscape noted for 67 free-standing sand pipes, or rock chimneys, formed millions of years ago as geyser vents.

🏕️ **Kodachrome Basin State Park**
Tel (435) 679-8562; (800) 322-3770.
Open 6am–10pm daily. 🅿️ 🚻 ⛺

⓭ Bryce Canyon National Park

See pp156–7.

Stage of the Globe Theatre in Cedar City

⓮ Cedar City

Road map B2. 🚇 29,000. ✈️ 🚌
ℹ️ 581 N. Main St. (435) 586-5124.
🖥️ scenicsouthernutah.com

Founded in 1851 by Mormons, this town developed as a center for mining and smelting iron in the latter part of the 19th century. Today, it offers hotels and restaurants within an hour's drive of the lovely Zion National Park (see pp158–9). In town, the **Frontier Homestead State Park Museum** pays tribute to the early Mormons indomitable pioneering spirit and features an extensive collection of more than 300 wagons and early vehicles, including an original Wells Fargo overland stagecoach. Cedar City's Shakespeare Festival, which runs annually from June to October, is staged in a replica of London's neo-Elizabethan Globe Theatre and attracts large audiences from the area.

Vintage wagon, Frontier Homestead Museum

Petrified ancient sand pipes rising out of the desert in the Kodachrome Basin State Park

For hotels and restaurants see pp236–43 and pp248–61

An ATV (all-terrain vehicle) rider at the Coral Pink Sand Dunes State Park

Around 20 miles (32 km) east of the town, along Hwy 14, **Cedar Breaks National Monument** features a small but spectacular array of vibrant pink and orange limestone cliffs, topped by deep green forest. Carved by erosion, sculpted columns rise in ranks of color, and resemble a smaller, less-visited version of Bryce Canyon (see pp156–7). The area remains open to cross-country skiers in winter.

Frontier Homestead State Park Museum
635 N. Main St. **Tel** (435) 586-9290. **Open** 9am–5pm Mon–Sat.

Cedar Breaks National Monument
Tel (435) 586-9451. **Open** daily. Visitor center **Open** late May–mid-Oct: 9am–6pm daily. **W** nps.gov/cebr

⓯ Zion National Park

See pp158–9.

⓰ Kanab

Road map B2. 3,900. **i** 78 South 100 E. (435) 644-5033. **Open** Mar–Oct: 9am–7pm Mon–Fri, 10am–6pm Sat, 9am–4pm Sun; Nov–Feb: 9am–5pm Mon–Fri. **W** kaneutah.com

This small town was named originally for Fort Kanab, built in 1864 but abandoned two years later because of frequent Indian attacks. Founded in 1874 by Mormon settlers, the main occupation of today's town is offering reasonably priced food and accommodations to vacationers traveling between Grand Canyon, Zion, and Bryce Canyon National Parks. Often referred to as the "gateway to Lake Powell," Kanab is also known as Utah's "Little Hollywood," a reference to the 200 or so movies and TV shows that have been filmed in and around the town since 1963 (see pp34–5). Details of film sets open to the public may be obtained from the Visitor Center.

Environs
About 10 miles (16 km) west of Kanab and a few miles south of the small town of Mount Carmel Junction, the **Coral Pink Sand Dunes State Park** is a sea of ever-shifting pink dunes that cover more than 4.7 sq miles (12 sq km). This distinctive, harsh desert landscape was created when wind eroded the rich red sandstone cliffs surrounding the site, slowly depositing sand in the valley below. Interpretive signs relate the story of the dunes' geological formation. A path leads out into the dunes where you can enjoy the thrill of sliding down their faces. The park is a popular destination for riders of ATVs (all-terrain vehicles) and dune buggies.

Coral Pink Sand Dunes State Park
Tel (435) 648-2800. **Open** dawn–dusk daily. **W** stateparks.utah.gov

⓱ St. George

Road map B2. 75,000. **i** 1835 Convention Center Blvd (435) 634-5747. **Open** 10am–6pm Mon–Sat. **W** utahstgeorge.com

Established in 1861 by Mormons (see pp140–2), the town of St. George has since experienced a population boom as retirees from all over the US discover its mild climate and tranquil atmosphere. The towering gold spire that can be seen over the town belongs to Utah's first Mormon Temple, finished in 1877. A beloved project of Mormon leader and visionary Brigham Young (1801–77), it remains a key site. Only Mormons are allowed inside the temple, but the Visitor Center, which relates its history, is open to all. St. George's association with Brigham Young began when he decided to build a winter home here in 1871. The elegant and spacious **Brigham Young Winter Home Historic Site** is now a museum and has preserved much of its first owner's original furnishings.

Five miles (8 km) northwest of town on Hwy 18 lies Snow Canyon State Park. The park features hiking trails that lead to volcanic caves and million-year-old-lava flows. A paved bike path leads through the park and back to St. George.

Brigham Young Winter Home Historic Site
67 West St. N. **Tel** (435) 673-2517. **Open** Jun–Sep: 10am–7pm daily; Sep–May: 9am–5pm daily.

Façade of Brigham Young's winter home in St. George

⓫ Lake Powell and Glen Canyon National Recreation Area

The Glen Canyon National Recreation Area (NRA) was established in 1972 and covers more than one million acres of dramatic desert and canyon country around the 185-mile- (298-km-) long Lake Powell. The lake was created by damming the Colorado River. The recreation area is "Y"-shaped, following the San Juan River east almost to the town of Mexican Hat and heading northeast toward Canyonlands National Park *(see pp146–7)*. Today, the lake hosts watersports enthusiasts, though droughts since the early 2000s have repeatedly lowered the water level and restricted or closed many boating channels – call ahead for boat launch information. Glen Canyon is also one of the most popular hiking, biking, and 4WD destinations in the US.

Rainbow Bridge National Monument
Rising 309 ft (94 m) above Lake Powell, Rainbow Bridge is the largest natural bridge in North America, only accessible by boat from Wahweap or Bullfrog marinas.

General View of Lake Powell
The blue waters of the man-made Lake Powell are encircled by colorful sandstone coves – once Glen Canyon's side canyons – and dramatic buttes and mesas.

Glen Canyon Dam was completed in 1963 and rises 710 ft (213 m) above the bedrock of the Colorado River.

Antelope Canyon
Bands of sandstone curve sinuously together, sometimes just a few feet apart, in this famously deep "slot" canyon.

Escalante River

Fiftymile Mountains

Dangling Rope Marina

Lake Powell

West Canyon

Wahweap

Navajo Canyon

•**Page**

98

To Grand Canyon

Lees Ferry was a Mormon settlement in the 19th century. Today, this outpost offers tourist facilities, including a ranger station and campground.

Wahweap Marina
One of the best ways of touring the area is by boat; Wahweap Marina offers tours and boat hire.

Henry Mountains

 Hite

Lake Powell

Red Rock Plateau

 Bullfrog

San Juan River

Boating on Lake Powell
On summer weekends, the lake is a busy place as powerboats, waterskiers, houseboat parties, jetskis, and catamarans explore its myriad sandstone side canyons. The Colorado river float trips, available below Glen Canyon dam, are a special attraction.

Halls Crossing has a marina and is the starting point for the regular ferry service to Bullfrog Bay.

Canyon Controversy

The completion of Glen Canyon dam in 1963 flooded the area described by explorer John Wesley Powell *(see p29)* as "a curious ensemble of wonderful features." The project was controversial right from the start; environmentalists deplored the drowning of the pristine canyon, and many continue to campaign for the restoration of Glen Canyon, believing that ancient ecosystems are being ruined. Pro-dam advocates point out the value of the dam's ability to store water, generate power, and provide recreation.

Lake Powell behind vast Glen Canyon Dam

0 km   20
0 miles   20

Key
Highway
Unpaved road

For additional map symbols *see back flap*

⑬ Bryce Canyon National Park

A series of deep amphitheaters filled with flame- colored rock formations called hoodoos are the hallmark of Bryce Canyon National Park. Bryce is high in altitude, reaching elevations of 8,000–9,000 ft (2,400–2,700 m), with a scenic road traveling for 18 miles (30 km) along the rim of Paunsaugunt Plateau. The highlights here are the views of vast fields of pink, orange, and red spires; the Paiute Indians, once hunters here, described them as "red rocks standing like men in a bowl-shaped recess." The canyon's maze of pillars and channels is best appreciated on foot.

• Shakespear Point

• Mos Cav

Pink Cliffs

Fairyland Point

Queen's Garden Trail

Navajo Loop Trail

Sunrise Point
From this lookout it is easy to see why early settler and Mormon farmer Ebenezer Bryce, after whom the park is named, called it "a helluva place to lose a cow."

Thor's Hammer
Carved into the pink cliffs of the highest "step" of the Grand Staircase *(see p152)*, this unusual landscape consists of eroded sandstone. Hoodoos such as Thor's Hammer are formed as rain and wind erode "fins" of harder rock that become columns, then further erode into strangely shaped hoodoos. The high altitude, ice, and wind continue the "carving" process today.

Sunset Point is one of the major lookouts in Bryce Canyon. In spite of its name, it faces east, so while sunrises can be spectacular here, sunsets can be a little anticlimactic.

Navajo Loop
This 1.4-mile (2-km) round-trip trail zig-zags sharply down the cliff face for 500 ft (150 m) to finish in a slow meander among slot canyons and rock stands. The climb back up the trail is particularly strenuous.

Key

= Highway

■ ■ Hiking route

Bryce Amphitheater
This panoramic vista of snow-covered rock spires, is among the most popular views of the park. In both winter and summer the amphitheater is best seen from Inspiration Point.

Natural Bridge
This graceful natural bridge is located a few yards from the park's scenic highway. It frames a picturesque view of the distant valley far below. Officially, it is a natural arch and not a bridge, as it was formed not by a river, but by the same natural forces (of wind, rain, and ice) that created the park's hoodoos.

Agua Canyon
This overlook features some of the most delicate and beautiful of the park's formations, as well as a good view of the layered pink sandstone cliffs typical of the Paunsaugunt Plateau.

Rainbow Point

Ponderosa Canyon

Yovimba Point

Noon Canyon Butte

Pink Cliffs

0 km 2
0 miles 2

Utah Prairie Dog
Now threatened, the Utah prairie dog lives only in southern Utah: those living in the park today constitute the largest remaining group.

For hotels and restaurants see pp236–43 and pp248–61

⑮ Zion National Park

Zion Canyon lies at the heart of this beautiful national park and is arguably the most popular of all of Utah's natural wonders. The canyon was carved by the powerful waters of the Virgin River and then widened, sculpted, and reshaped by wind, rain, and ice. The canyon walls rise up to 2,000 ft (600 m) on both sides, and are shaped into jagged peaks and formations in shades of red and white.

Although you can drive through the park year-round, between April and October the only way to explore the inner core of Zion Canyon is via the park's frequent shuttle buses. Numerous stops along the way offer access to hiking trails; some lead to nearby waterfalls and alcoves, while others, like the demanding East and West Rim trails, climb right out of the canyon.

Horseback and Mule Tours
Half- and full-day mule- and horseback tours follow trails in the park. The Sand Bench Trail leads to a high plateau that offers fine vista

River Walk
At the end of Zion Canyon Scenic Drive lies the park's most popular trail. Involving no climbing, the 1.3-mile (2-km) paved River Walk follows the Virgin River to where the canyon walls rise to over 2,000 ft (600 m). The trail offers beautiful views of the river as it winds between red sandstone walls.

Exploring Zion Canyon

Once inside the park, the 6-mile (10-km) Scenic Drive follows the Virgin River into the ever-narrowing canyon. In summer shuttle buses operate both along the drive and between the visitor center and the nearby town of Springdale.

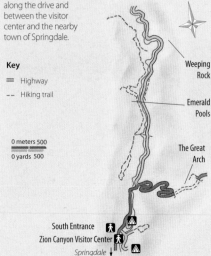

Key

≡ Highway

‑‑ Hiking trail

0 meters 500
0 yards 500

Weeping Rock

Emerald Pools

The Great Arch

South Entrance
Zion Canyon Visitor Center
Springdale ↓

Zion Canyon

The lower reaches of the Virgin River meander quietly through the banks of cottonwood, oak, and willow trees that grow beneath the gradually sloping walls at the start of the canyon. The river bank is bordered with wild meadows that, in spring, sport a profusion of wild flowers. However, sudden summer rainstorms may cause floods and areas of the park near the river to be closed. Visitors are advised to check conditions first.

For additional map symbols *see back flap*

Hiking

Numerous guided walking and hiking tours of Zion's geology and history leave daily from the visitor center. Popular trails are Emerald Pools Trail, and Canyon Overlook Trail, which leads to a superb west-facing viewpoint over the canyon.

Sculpted monoliths of rock rise above the Virgin River as it flows along the canyon.

VISITORS' CHECKLIST

Practical Information
Road map 2B. Hwy 9, near Springdale. *i* Zion Canyon Visitor Center (435) 772-3256. **w** nps.gov/zion
Open 8am–5pm daily (to 7:30pm Jun–Aug). partial.

Weeping Rock

An easy, self-guided trail leads to the rock and its hanging gardens, which are full of wildflowers in spring. This spot owes its fertility to the spring- and seep-water that flows from the rock.

Luxuriant foliage along the banks of the Virgin River provides shade for the area's abundant wildlife, including birds, mule deer, and bobcats.

The Virgin River seems gentle, but the force of its current is responsible for forming the canyon.

Zion–Mt. Carmel Highway

The only driving route through the park, the dramatic Zion–Mt. Carmel highway climbs out of the canyon via a set of hairpin switchbacks with splendid views, then burrows through a mile-long tunnel to reach the pastel-colored sandstone of the surrounding peaks.

THE FOUR CORNERS

Exploring The Four Corners

The Four Corners region is the only place in the United States where four states meet at a single point. Here, parts of Utah, Colorado, Arizona, and New Mexico make up an area of national monuments and parks, ancient ruins, and dramatic canyonlands, many set on Native American reservations. World-famous vistas include the buttes of Monument Valley, and Colorado's San Juan Skyway, where both the highway and the Durango-Silverton Narrow Gauge Railroad travel through picturesque old alpine towns.

The Keet Seel ruins at the Navajo National Monument in Arizona

"The Mittens", one of the distinctive buttes in Monument Valley

The spectacular desert landscape of Canyon de Chelly National Monument, at the heart of the Navajo Nation

Getting Around

A car is essential for getting around the Four Corners; a high-clearance 4WD vehicle is recommended for traveling many interesting, unpaved regional roads. Secondary (paved) highways are generally good, while unpaved roads are categorized as follows: Good roads are suitable for all passenger cars; high clearance roads are suitable for 2 or 4WD; 4WD roads should be tackled by only experienced drivers in high-clearance vehicles. Always check on road and weather conditions.

THE FOUR CORNERS

Key

— Major road

═══ Minor road

━━ State border

△ Summit

0 kilometers 50

0 miles 50

Mountain view on the San Juan Skyway
between Durango and Silverton

For additional map symbols see back flap

The Ancestral Puebloans

The hauntingly beautiful and elaborate ruins left behind by the Ancestral Puebloan people are a key factor in the hold that this ancient culture has over the public imagination. Also known as "Anasazi," a name coined by the Navajo meaning "Ancient Enemy Ancestor," today they are more accurately known as the Ancestral Puebloan people, and are seen as the ancestors of today's Pueblo peoples.

The first Ancestral Puebloans *(see p42)* are thought to have settled at Mesa Verde in around AD 550, where they lived in pithouses. By around AD 800 they had developed masonry skills and began building housing complexes using sandstone. From AD 1100 to 1300, impressive levels of craftsmanship were reached in weaving, pottery, jewelry, and tool-making.

Ceramics, such as this bowl, show the artistry of the Ancestral Puebloans. Pottery is just one of many ancient artifacts on display in Southwestern museums.

Kivas are round pit-like rooms dug into the ground and roofed with beams and earth.

Jackson Stairway in Chaco Canyon is evidence of the engineering skills of the Ancestral Puebloans. They also built networks of roads between their communities and extensive irrigation systems.

Bone awl

Tools of various types were skillfully shaped from stone, wood, and bone. The Ancestral Puebloans did not work metal, yet they managed to produce such beautiful artifacts as baskets, pottery, and jewelry.

Needle

Drills

The blue corn growing on the Hopi reservation in Arizona today is a similar plant to that grown by Ancestral Puebloans. They were also skilled at utilizing the medicinal properties of plants, including cottonwood bark, which contains a painkiller.

The kiva was the religious and ceremonial center of Ancestral Puebloan life. Still used by modern Pueblo Indians today, a *kiva* usually had no windows and the only access was through a hole in the roof. Small kivas were used by a single family unit, while large *kivas* were designed to accommodate the whole community.

Where to Find Ancestral Puebloan Ruins

Canyon de Chelly National Monument *(p172)*; Chaco Culture National Historical Park *(p178)*; Mesa Verde National Park *(p184)*; Navajo National Monument *(p170)*; Hovenweep National Monument *(p176)*; Aztec Ruins National Monument *(p177)*.

Petroglyphs were often used by Ancestral Puebloans as astronomical markers for the different seasons. This one was found at the Petrified Forest National Park in Arizona *(see p77)*.

Pueblo Bonito features many examples of the masonry skills used by the Puebloan peoples.

The Pueblo People

By AD 1300 the Ancestral Puebloans had abandoned many of their long-established settlement sites and migrated to areas where new centers emerged. Theories on why this occurred include a 50-year drought; the strain that a larger population placed on the desert's limited resources; and a lengthy period of social upheaval, perhaps stimulated by increasing trade with tribes as far away as central Mexico. Archaeologists agree that the Ancestral Puebloans did not disappear but live on today in Puebloan descendants who trace their origins to Mesa Verde, Chaco, and other sacred ancestral sites.

Chaco Canyon's Pueblo Bonito

At Chaco Canyon (see pp178–9) the largest "great house" ever built was Pueblo Bonito with more than 600 rooms and 40 kivas. One current theory is that these structures did not house populations but were, in fact, public buildings for commerce and ceremonial gatherings. The lives of the Ancestral Puebloans were short, barely 35 years, and as harsh as the environment in which they lived. Their diet was poor, and arthritis and dental problems were common. Women often showed signs of osteoporosis or brittle bones as early as their first childbirth.

Painstaking excavation at an Ancestral Puebloan *kiva* in Chaco Canyon

THE FOUR CORNERS

Dominated by the Navajo reservation, which is the size of Connecticut, and presenting sweeping panoramas of mesas, canyons, and vast expanses of high desert, the Four Corners is the perfect destination for those wanting to experience native culture and the real west.

Although it receives less than 10 in (25 cm) of rainfall per year, this arid land has supported life since the first Paleo-Indians arrived perhaps 12,000 years ago. The people now known as the Ancestral Puebloans lived here from about AD 500 until the 13th century. They were responsible for the many evocative ruins found here, including those at Mesa Verde, Chaco Canyon, and Hovenweep National Monument. Their descendants include the Hopi, whose pueblos are said to be the oldest continually occupied towns in North America. The Navajo arrived here in the 15th century and their spiritual center is Canyon de Chelly with its 1,000-ft (330-m) red rock walls. Monument Valley's impressive landscape has been used as a backdrop for countless movies and TV shows. The region is also popular for hiking, fishing, and whitewater rafting.

Sights at a Glance

Historic Towns and Cities
- ❸ Tuba City
- ❻ Window Rock
- ❽ Bluff
- ❾ Blanding
- ⓮ Farmington
- ⓯ Aztec
- ⓱ Telluride
- ⓲ Ouray
- ⓳ Silverton
- ⓴ Durango

Areas of Natural Beauty
- ❶ *Monument Valley*
- ⓰ San Juan Skyway Tour

Indian Reservations
- ❹ Hopi Indian Reservation
- ⓫ Ute Mountain Indian Reservation

National Parks and Monuments
- ❷ Navajo National Monument
- ❼ *Canyon de Chelly National Monument*
- ❿ Hovenweep National Monument
- ⓬ Four Corners Monument
- ⓭ Chaco Culture National Historic Park
- ㉑ *Mesa Verde National Park*

Historic Sites
- ❺ Hubbell Trading Post National Historic Site

Key
- ▭▭▭ Interstate
- ▬▬▬ Major highway
- ═══ Highway
- ——— Railroad

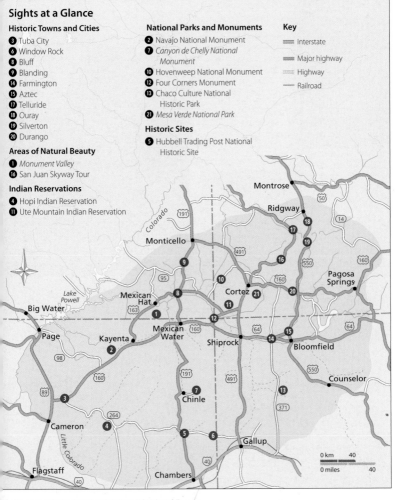

◄ The slopes of the San Juan mountain range, Colorado, in fall

❶ Monument Valley

From scenic Highway 163, which crosses the border of Utah and Arizona, it is possible to see the famous towering sandstone buttes and mesas of Monument Valley. These ancient rocks, soaring upward from a seemingly boundless desert, have come to symbolize the American West, largely because Hollywood has used these breathtaking vistas as a backdrop for hundreds of movies, TV shows, and commercials since the 1930s *(see p34)*.

The area's visitor center sits within the boundary of Monument Valley Tribal Park, but many of the valley's spectacular rock formations and other sites are found just outside the park boundary.

Guided Tours
A row of kiosks at the visitor center offer Navajo-guided 4WD tours of the valley. The marketing tactics can be aggressive but the tours offer an excellent way to see places in the park that are otherwise inaccessible.

Three Sisters
The Three Sisters are one of several distinctive pinnacle rock formations at Monument Valley. Others include the Totem Pole and the "fingers" of the Mittens. The closest view of the sisters can be seen from John Ford's Point, and is one of the most photographed sights here.

Left Mitten

Art and Ruins
Petroglyphs such as this bighorn sheep can be seen on Navajo-guided tours of rock art sites, which are dotted around the valley's ancient ruins.

Exploring the Valley

The awe-inspiring beauty of Monument Valley's buttes and mesas can be viewed by travelers from Hwy 163. Visitors can also pay a fee to travel on a 17-mile (27-km) self-guided drive along a well-marked dirt road. (Fees are collected at the visitor center.) Alternatively, Navajo guides may be hired for hiking, horseback, or 4WD tours to fascinating and less-visited parts of the valley.

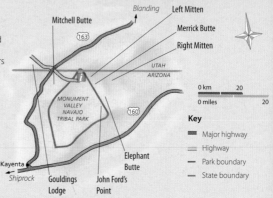

Blanding
Mitchell Butte
Left Mitten
Merrick Butte
Right Mitten
163
UTAH
ARIZONA
MONUMENT VALLEY NAVAJO TRIBAL PARK
160
Kayenta
Shiprock
Gouldings Lodge
John Ford's Point
Elephant Butte

0 km   20
0 miles   20

Key
▬ Major highway
▭ Highway
▬ Park boundary
▬ State boundary

John Ford's Point
The most popular stop along the valley drive is John Ford's Point, which is said to be the film director's favorite view of the valley. Various stands offer a range of Navajo handicrafts. A nearby native *hogan* (Navajo dwelling) serves as a gift shop where Navajo weavers demonstrate their craft.

VISITORS' CHECKLIST

Practical Information
Road map C2. 🛈 PO Box 360289, Monument Valley, UT 84536. (435) 727-5870.
Open sunrise–sunset daily.
Closed Dec 25. 🚫 🚻 visitor center only. 🅿 🍴 🚻 🏔
🖢 navajonationparks.org

Right Mitten

Merrick Butte

Navajo Weaver
Navajo women are usually considered to be the finest weavers in the Southwest. One rug can take months to complete and sell for thousands of dollars. Using the natural colors of the land, the weavers often add a "spirit line" to their work to prevent their spirit being "trapped" within the rug.

Monument Valley
Monument Valley is not really a valley. The tops of the mesas mark what was once a flat plain. Millions of years ago, this plain was cracked by upheavals within the earth. The cracks widened and eroded, until all that is left today are the formations rising from the desert floor.

Gouldings Lodge
The lodge offers accommodations, a restaurant, and guided bus tours of the valley. The original trading post is now a museum of the valley's cinematic history.

Ancestral Puebloan ruins of Keet Seel at Navajo National Monument

❷ Navajo National Monument

Road map C3. **Tel** (928) 672-2700.
Open 8am–5:30pm daily (8am–5pm
end May–mid-Sep). **Closed** Jan 1,
Thanksgiving, Dec 25. 🚗 🅿
w nps.gov/nava

While named because of its
location on the Navajo
Reservation, this monument is
actually known for its Ancestral
Puebloan ruins. The most accessible ruin here is the beautifully
preserved, 135-room pueblo of
Betatakin, which fills a vast,
curved niche in the cliffs of Tsegi
Canyon. An easy one-mile
(1.6-km) trail from the visitor
center leads to an overlook
where Betatakin is clearly visible
on the far side, near the canyon
floor. This is a lovely hike through
piñon pines and juniper trees.
From late May to early
September there are daily five-
hour hiking tours to Betatakin,
which allow a close look at the
ruins of these ancient houses.

A much more demanding
17-mile (27-km) round-trip hike
leads to Keet Seel, a more
impressive ruin. Only a limited
number of permits to visit the

ruin are issued each day. This
hike requires overnight
camping at a camp site with
only the most basic facilities.
Keet Seel was a larger and more
successful community than
Betatakin. Construction began
on Keet Seel in about 1250, but
the site is thought to have been
abandoned by 1300.

These two sites are
considered to mark the pinnacle
of development of the area's
Ancestral Puebloan people.

❸ Tuba City

Road map C3. 🔼 8,900. 🛈 Tuba City
Trading Post, 10 N. Main St (928) 283-
5441.

Named for Tuuvi, a Hopi Indian
who converted to the Mormon
faith, Tuba City is best known for
the 65-million-year-old dinosaur
tracks found just off the main
highway, 5 miles (8 km)
southwest of the town. This is
the largest community in the
western section of the Navajo
Reservation and a good spot
from which to explore the
Navajo National Monument and
the Hopi Reservation.

❹ Hopi Indian Reservation

Road map C3. 🔼 10,000. 🛈
Highway 264, Second Mesa (928) 734-
2401. **Open** May–Sep: 6am–9pm
daily; Oct–Apr: 7am–8pm daily.
Closed Jan 1, Thanksgiving, Dec 25.

Arizona's only Pueblo Indians
(see p31), the Hopi, are the
direct descendants of the
Ancestral Puebloan people,
whom they call the Hisatsinom.
The Hopi Reservation is
surrounded by the lands of the
Navajo. The landscape is harsh
and barren, yet the Hopi have
cultivated the land here for a
thousand years. They worship,
through the *kachina*, the living
spirits of plants and
animals, believed to
arrive each year to
stay with the tribe
during the
growing season
(see p31). Most of the
Hopi villages are on
or near one of three
mesas (flat-topped
elevations), named
First, Second, and
Third Mesa. The
artisans on each of
the mesas specialize
in particular crafts: on
First Mesa these are
carved figures
(representing the *kachina*
spirits) and painted pottery; on
Second Mesa, silver jewelry and
coiled baskets are made; and on
Third Mesa, craftspeople fashion
wicker baskets and woven rugs.

Walpi, the ancient pueblo on
First Mesa, was first inhabited
in the 12th century. To reach
Walpi, visitors drive up to the
Mesa from the Pollaca
settlement to the village of
Sichomovi. Nearby, the Ponsi
Visitor Center is the departure

*Kachina
figure*

Historic pueblo town of Walpi on First Mesa on the Hopi Indian Reservation

For hotels and restaurants see pp236–43 and pp248–61

A range of merchandise in the general store at Hubbell Trading Post

point for the one-hour Walpi tours. Walpi was built to be easily defended, and straddles a dramatic knife edge of rock, extending from the tip of First Mesa. In places Walpi is less than 100 ft (33 m) wide with a drop of several hundred feet on both sides. The Walpi tour includes several stops where visitors can purchase *kachina* figurines and distinctive hand-crafted pottery, or sample the Hopi *piki* bread.

Those wishing to shop further can continue on to Second Mesa, where several galleries and stores offer an array of Hopi arts and crafts. The Hopi Cultural Center is home to a restaurant *(see p256)*, the only hotel *(see p241)* for miles around, and a museum that has a collection of photographs depicting scenes of Hopi life.

On Third Mesa, Old Oraibi pueblo, thought to have been founded in the 12th century, is of note because of claims that it is the oldest continually occupied human settlement in North America.

🏛 Walpi
i (928) 737-2670. Walking tours available 9am–3pm daily. 🖼

❺ Hubbell Trading Post National Historic Site

Road map D3. A2264, near Ganado. Tel (928) 755-3475. Open late May–early Sep: 8am–6pm; early Sep–late May: 8am–5pm. W nps.gov/hutr

Located at the heart of the Navajo reservation in the small, bustling town of Ganado, the

Hubbell Trading Post was established in the 1870s by John Lorenzo Hubbell and is the oldest continually operating trading post in the Navajo Nation. Trading posts like this one were once the economic and social centers of the reservations. The Navajo traded sheep, wool, blankets, turquoise, and other items in exchange for tools, household goods, and food. The trading posts were also a resource during times of need. When a smallpox epidemic struck in 1886, John Lorenzo helped care for the sick, using his house as a hospital.

Today, the trading post still hums with traditional trading activities. One room is a working general store, the rafters hung with frying pans and hardware, and shelves stacked with cloth, medicines, and food. Another room is filled with Navajo baskets, Hopi *kachina* dolls, and beautiful hand-woven rugs – the Ganado

Navajo bracelet at Hubbell Trading Post

Red style of rug arose in the late 1800s from local weavers' creative response to J. L. Hubbell's suggestion of what might sell to customers of the trading post. In another department a long row of glass cases displays an impressive array of silver and turquoise jewelry.

Visitors can tour Hubbell's restored home and view the significant collection of South-western art. At the visitor center Navajo women demonstrate rug weaving.

❻ Window Rock

Road map D3. 🏔 4,500. 🚌
i Highway 264 (928) 871-6436.

Window Rock is the capital of the Navajo Nation. The town is named for the natural arch found in the sandstone cliffs located about a mile north of the main strip on Hwy 12.

The **Navajo Nation Museum** located here is one of the largest Native American museums in the US. The huge hogan-shaped building houses displays that cover the history of the Ancestral Puebloans and the Navajo.

🏛 Navajo Nation Museum
Hwy 264 & Post Office Loop Rd. (928) 871-7941. Open 8am–5pm Mon, 8am–6pm Tue–Fri, 9am–6pm Sat. W navajonationmuseum.org

Eroded sandstone opening of Window Rock, near Highway 12

❼ Canyon de Chelly National Monument

Few places in North America can boast a longer or more eventful history of human habitation than Canyon de Chelly. Archaeologists have found evidence of four periods of Native culture, starting with the Basketmaker people around AD 300, followed by the Great Pueblo Builders, who created the cliff dwellings in the 12th century. They were succeeded by the Hopi, who lived here seasonally for around 300 years, taking advantage of the canyon's fertile soil. In the 1700s, the Hopi left the area and moved to the mesas, returning to the canyon to farm during the summer months. Today, the canyon is the cultural and geographic heart of the Navajo Nation. Pronounced "d'Shay," de Chelly is a Spanish corruption of the Navajo word *Tsegi*, meaning Rock Canyon.

Yucca House Ruin
Perched just below the mesa top, this ruin of an Ancestral Puebloan house sits in a rock hollow, precariously overhanging a sheer drop to the valley floor.

Mummy Cave Ruin
The two pueblos in Mummy Cave, separated by a central tower, were built in the 1280s by Ancestral Puebloans who had inhabited the area for more than 1,000 years. An impressive overlook provides a good view of the ruin.

Stone and adobe cliff dwellings were home to the Ancestral Puebloans from the 12th to the 14th century and were built to face south toward the sun, with cooler areas within.

Navajo Fortress
This imposing rock tower was the site of a three-month siege in 1864, after a group of Navajos reached the summit via pole ladders to escape Kit Carson and the Army. The persistence of Carson (*see p175*) and starvation led them to surrender and they were marched to a camp in New Mexico.

Canyon Landscape
The sandstone cliffs of Canyon de Chelly reach as high as 1,000 ft (300 m), towering above the neighboring meadows and desert landscape in the distance. The canyon floor around the cliffs is fringed with cotton wood bushes, watered by the Chinle Wash.

The pale walls of the White House cliff drop 550 ft (160 m) to the canyon floor.

Hogan Interior
The *hogan* is the center of Navajo family life. Made of horizontal logs, a smoke hole in the center provides contact with the sky, while the dirt floor gives contact with the earth. A door faces east to greet the rising sun.

White House Ruins

This group of rooms, tucked into a tiny hollow in the cliff, seems barely touched by time. The dwellings were originally situated above a larger pueblo, much of which has now disappeared. It is the only site within the canyon that can be visited without a Navajo guide, and is reached via a steep 2.5-mile (5-km) round-trip trail that winds to the canyon floor and offers magnificent views.

Massacre Cave

The canyon's darkest hour was in 1805, when a Spanish force under Lieutenant Antonio Narbona entered the area. The Spanish wanted to subdue the Navajo, claiming they were raiding their settlements. While some Navajo fled by climbing to the canyon rim, others took refuge in a cave high in the cliffs. The Spanish fired into the cave, and Narbona boasted that he had killed 115 Navajo including 90 warriors. Navajo accounts are different, claiming that most of the warriors were absent (probably hunting) and those killed were mostly women, children, and the elderly. The only Spanish fatality came when a Spaniard attempting to climb into the cave was attacked by a Navajo woman and both plunged over the cliff, gaining the Navajo name "Two Fell Over." The Anglo name is "Massacre Cave."

Pictograph on a canyon wall showing invading Spanish soldiers

Exploring Canyon de Chelly

Canyon de Chelly ("de shay") is very different from the sparse desert landscape that spreads from its rim. Weathered red rock walls, just 30-ft- (9-m-) high at the canyon mouth, rise to more than 1,000-ft- (300-m-) high within the canyon, creating a sheltered world. Navajo *hogans (see p173)* dot the canyon floor; Navajo women tend herds of sheep and weave rugs at outdoor looms, and everywhere Ancestral Puebloan ruins add to the canyon's appeal. Navajo-led 4WD tours along the scenic North and South rims are a popular way to view the site.

Antelope House Ruin
Named for a pictograph of an antelope painted by Navajo artists in the 1830s, the oldest ruins at Antelope House date from AD 700. They can be seen from the Antelope House Overlook.

Canyon Vegetation
Within the canyon, cottonwood and oak trees line the river washes; the land itself is a fertile oasis of meadows, alfalfa and corn fields, and fruit orchards.

0 km   3
0 miles   3

Chinle

Chinle Wash

Ledge Ruin Overlook

Sta Cov

Antelope House Overloo

White House Overlook

Canyon de Chelly

South Rim Drive

Canyon Tour
Half- and full-day tours from Sacred Canyon Lodge carry passengers in open flatbed or large 6WD army trucks. Of varying length and difficulty, the tours are the best way to see ruins up close.

Tsegi Overlook
This high curve along the South Rim offers good general views of the farm-studded canyon floor and surrounding landscape.

For additional map symbols *see back flap*

Hiking in the Canyon

Canyon de Chelly is a popular destination for hikers, but only the White House Ruins Trail may be walked without a guide. The visitor center *(see p173)* offers Navajo-guided hikes on trails of varying lengths.

Key

⎓ Highway

▪▪ Hiking route

To Tsaile Window Rock

North Rim Drive

Canyon del Muerto

☀ **Massacre Cave Overlook**

☀ **Mummy Cave Overlook**

Black Rock Canyon

Spider Rock

Rising more than 800 ft (245 m), Navajo legends say it was here that Spider Woman lived and gave them the skill of weaving.

Spider Rock Overlook

7

Kit Carson and the "Long Walk"

In 1863, the US government sent Kit Carson under the command of General James A. Carlton to settle the problem of Navajo raids. To avoid outright slaughter Carson led his soldiers through the region, destroying villages and livestock as the Navajo fled ahead of them. In January 1864 Carson entered Canyon de Chelly, capturing the Navajo hiding there. In 1864, they were among 9,000 Navajo who were driven on the "Long Walk," a forced march of 370 miles (595 km) from Fort Defiance to Bosque Redondo in New Mexico. There, in a pitiful reservation, more than 3,000 Navajo died before the US government accepted the resettlement as a failure and allowed them to return to the Four Corners.

Fur trapper and soldier Kit Carson (1809–68)

Dramatic mesas and buttes in the Valley of the Gods near Bluff

❽ Bluff

Road map D2. 🏞 300. 🏕
🌐 bluffutah.org

The charming town of Bluff was settled in 1880 by the Mormons of "Hole-in-the-Rock-Road" fame *(see p151)*. It is a good base for exploring Utah's southeast corner. Float trips along the gentle San Juan River include stops at Ancestral Pueblo ruins that can be reached only by boat.

Environs
About 12 miles (20 km) south of town, a marked turn leads onto the 17-mile (27-km) dirt road through the Valley of the Gods. Like a smaller version of Monument Valley *(see pp168–9)*, this place features high rock spires, buttes, and mesas, but none of the crowds. On a quiet day visitors may have the place to themselves and be able to imagine what it looked like to the first settlers.

❾ Blanding

Road map D2. 🏞 3,800. ℹ️ 12 N. Grayson Parkway. (435) 678-3662. 🏕
Open 8am–7pm Mon–Sat.
🌐 blandingutah.org

A tidy Mormon town at the base of the Abajo Mountains, Blanding is home to the **Edge of the Cedars State Park**. The park contains modest Ancestral Puebloan ruins, including a small *kiva*, or religious chamber. The museum has well-thought-out displays on the history of these ancient people and other cultures that have inhabited the region.

🏛 Edge of the Cedars Museum
660 W. 400 N. **Tel** (435) 678-2238.
Open 9am–5pm Mon–Sat. **Closed** Jan 1, Thanksgiving, Dec 25. 🏕

❿ Hovenweep National Monument

Road map D2. East of Hwy 191. **Tel** (970) 562-4282. **Open** 8am–5pm daily (6pm Apr–Sep). **Closed** Jan 1, Thanksgiving, Dec 25. 🏕 📷 🏕
🌐 nps.gov/hove

One of the most mysterious Ancestral Puebloan sites in the Southwest, the ruins at Hovenweep lie along the rims of shallow canyons on a remote high plateau in the southwest corner of Colorado. These well-preserved ruins, which include unique round, square, and D-shaped towers, have neither been restored nor rebuilt. Indeed, they look much as they did when W.D. Huntington, leader of a Mormon expedition, first came upon the site in 1854. The site was named later in 1874, after an

Ute word meaning "Deserted Valley." The culture here reached its peak between 1200 and 1275. Little is known of these people beyond the clues found in the pottery and tools that they left behind. Researchers have speculated that the towers at Hovenweep might have been defensive fortifications, astronomical observatories, storage silos, or religious structures.

Self-guided hiking trails explore each of the six separate sets of ruins at Hovenweep, which lie a few miles apart.

⓫ Ute Mountain Tribal Park

Road map D2. ℹ️ Junction of Highway 160 and Highway 491. (970) 565-9653. 📷 9am daily (obligatory; reserve ahead). 🏕

The Ute Mountain Tribal Park ruins are one of the South-west's better kept secrets. The Ancestral Puebloan people first arrived in this region in about AD 400. They closely followed

Ancient brick tower at Hovenweep National Monument

the Mesa Verde (see pp184–5) development pattern, eventually creating numerous fine cliff dwellings, including the 80-room Lion House. These ruins have few visitors because of their inaccessibility. Visitors can use their own vehicles and join the dusty tours led by local Ute guides, or pay an extra charge to be driven.

⓬ Four Corners Monument Navajo Tribal Park

Road map D2. Junction of Hwys 160 and 41. **Tel** (928) 871-6647. **Open** May–Sep: 8am–7pm; Oct–Apr: 8am–5pm. **Closed** Jan 1, Thanksgiving, Dec 25. 🅿️ ♿
W navajonation parks.org

There is something oddly compelling about being able to put one foot and hand in each of four states. The Four Corners Monument is the only place in the US where four states meet at one point.

⓭ Chaco Culture National Historical Park

See pp178–9.

⓮ Farmington

Road map D2. 🅰️ 46,000. ✈️ 🚌
ⓘ 3041 E. Main St. (505) 326-7602.
W farmingtonnm.org

A dusty, hard-working ranch town, Farmington is a good base for exploring the surrounding monuments. It is also home to one of the most unusual museums in the Southwest. Just south of town, on the family-run B-Square Ranch, the vast **Bolack Museum of Fish and Wildlife** houses the largest accumulation of mounted game animals in the world – over 2,500 specimens collected over 70 years by oilman and rancher Tom Bolack. It is divided into nine themed game rooms, including African, Asian, European, and Russian. The **Farmington Museum** focuses on the local history and geology

of this area and features a popular children's gallery with several interactive exhibits.

Environs

About 25 miles (40 km) west of Farmington is Shiprock, named for the spectacular 1,500-ft (457-m) rock peak that thrusts up from the valley floor about 5 miles (8 km) west of town. To the Navajo, this rock is sacred; to early Anglo-American settlers it was a landmark visible for many miles that reminded them of a ship's prow, hence the name. Now it is only possible for visitors to observe the peak from the roadsides of Hwys 64 or 33.

Eight miles (12 km) south are the **Salmon Ruins**, which were once an outlying Chaco settlement. These ruins were protected from grave diggers by the Salmon family, who homesteaded here in the 1870s. As a result, a century later archaeologists recovered more than a million artifacts, many of which are on display in the excellent on-site museum. Outside, trails lead to the Salmon homestead and the ruins, which show the exceptional level of skill of these ancient stonemasons.

🏛️ Bolack Museum of Fish and Wildlife
3901 Bloomfield Hwy. **Tel** (505) 325-4275. **Open** 9am–3pm Mon–Sat, appointment only. 🅿️ ♿ 🎥 obligatory.

🏛️ Farmington Museum
3041 E. Main St. **Tel** (505) 599-1174. **Open** 8am–5pm Mon–Sat. 🅿️ ♿ 🎥
W farmingtonmuseum.org

🏠 Salmon Ruins
6131 Hwy 64. **Tel** (505) 632-2013. **Open** May–Oct: 8am–5pm Mon–Fri, 9am–5pm Sat & Sun; Nov–Apr: 8am–5pm Mon–Sat, noon–5pm Sun. 🅿️ ♿ 🎥

Interior of the Great Kiva at Ancestral Puebloan Salmon Ruins

⓯ Aztec

Road map D2. 🅰️ 6,000. ⓘ 110 North Ash St. (505) 334-9551.

The small town of Aztec was named for its ruins, which are Ancestral Puebloan – and not Aztec as early settlers believed. Preserved as a national monument, the site's 500-room pueblo flourished in the late 1200s. Visitors can look inside a rebuilt kiva.

🏠 Aztec Ruins National Monument
North of Hwy 516 on Ruins Rd. **Tel** (505) 334-6174. **Open** 8am–5pm daily (6pm in summer). **Closed** Jan 1, Thanksgiving, Dec 25. 🅿️ ♿ 🎥
W nps.gov/azru

The spectacular red peak of Shiprock near Farmington

⑬ Chaco Culture National Historical Park

Chaco Canyon is one of the most impressive cultural sites in the Southwest, reflecting the sophistication of the Ancestral Puebloan civilization that existed here. With its six "great houses" (pueblos containing hundreds of rooms) and many lesser sites, the canyon was once the political, religious, and cultural center for settlements that covered much of the Four Corners. At its peak during the 11th century, Chaco was one of the most impressive pre-Columbian cities in North America. Despite its size, it is thought that Chaco's population was small because the land could not have supported a larger community. Archaeologists believe that the city was mainly used as a ceremonial gathering place, with a year-round population of less than 3,000. Probably the social elite, the inhabitants supported themselves largely by trading.

Architectural Detail
Chaco's skilled builders had only stone tools to work with to create this finely wrought stonework.

Pueblo Bonito
Pueblo Bonito is an example of a "great house." Begun around AD 850, it was built in stages over the course of 300 years. This reconstruction shows how it might have looked, with its D-shaped four-story structure that contained more than 650 rooms.

Chetro Ketl
A short trail from Pueblo Bonito leads to another great house, Chetro Ketl. Almost as large as Pueblo Bonito, at 3 acres (2 ha), Chetro Ketl has more than 500 rooms. The masonry used to build the later portions of this structure is among the most sophisticated found in any Ancestral Puebloan site.

Casa Rinconada
Also known as a great *kiva*, Casa Rinconada is the largest religious chamber at Chaco, measuring 62 ft (19 m) in diameter. It was used for spiritual gatherings.

Pueblo Alto

Pueblo Alto was built atop the mesa at the junction of several ancient Chacoan roads. Reaching the site requires a two-hour hike, but the views over the canyon are well worth it.

Early Astronomers at Fajada Butte

Measurement of time was vital to the Chacoans for crop planting and the timing of ceremonies. A spiral petroglyph, carved on Fajada Butte, is designed to indicate the changing seasons through the shadows it casts on the rock.

Exploring Chaco

The site is accessed via a 13-mile (21-km) dirt road that is affected by flash floods in wet weather. Drivers can follow the paved loop road that passes several of Chaco's highlights. There is parking at all major sites. From the visitor center, a trail leads to Una Vida and the petroglyphs.

Key

= Highway

= Unpaved road

-- Hiking route

— Park boundary

KEY

① **The many kivas** here were probably used by visitors arriving for religious ceremonies.

② **This great house** was four stories high.

③ **Hundreds of rooms** within Pueblo Bonito show little sign of use and are thought to have been kept for storage or for guests arriving to take part in ceremonial events.

Kin Kletso

Pueblo del Arroyo

Pueblo Bonito

Casa Rinconada

Pueblo Alto

Chetro Ketl

Una Vida

7950

Wijiji

57

Chaco Canyon

0 km 2

0 miles 2

For additional map symbols *see back flap*

The mesas of Monument Valley, with the Left Mitten in the foreground ▶

⓰ San Juan Skyway Tour

The San Juan Skyway is a 236-mile (380-km) loop through some of America's finest scenery. The route travels three highways (550, 145, and 160) over the San Juan Mountains, past 19th- century mining towns and through forests and canyons. There are 14 peaks above 14,000 ft (4,200 m). Between Silverton and Ouray the road is also known as the Million Dollar Highway, having been named for the gold-rich gravel used in the road's construction or, according to another theory, because the road was expensive to build.

Tips for Drivers

Tour Route: Highway 550 from Durango, then 145 and 160.
Length: 236 miles (380 km).
Stopping-off points: Ridgeway State Park on Hwy 550 offers great views of the San Juan Mountains.

④ Telluride
Smaller than the ski resorts of Aspen and Vail, Telluride's gentrified Western persona attracts both wealthy jet setters and serious skiers.

③ Ouray
Another very Western mining town with a history similar to Silverton's, Ouray has the added attraction of the Ouray Hot Springs.

⑤ Atlas Lake
One of many lovely alpine lakes to be found along the San Juan Skyway, Atlas Lake lies south of Telluride and just north of the high-mountain Lizard Head Pass.

⑥ Dolores
Two 12th-century Ancestral Pueblos have been preserved here as part of the Anasazi Heritage Center, together with a museum on pueblo life.

↑ *Montrose*

● **Ridgway**

62

③

● **Placerville**

④

⑤

● **Ophir**

Animas River

②

145

● **Rico**

550

Dolores River

● **Stoner**

San Juan National Forest

⑥

184

Mancos River

La Plata River

160

①

Farmington ↓

0 km ——— 10
0 miles ——— 10

Key

▬ Tour route
═ Other roads

THE FRENCH QUARTER CAFE

① Durango
The start of the Durango and Silverton steam train trip, the town of Durango has a charming Victorian district and hot springs.

② Silverton
Silver was discovered here in 1874. Today, this classic frontier town is the scene of daily mock gunfights along Blair Street.

Spectacular views of the Rockies from Telluride's main street

🄗 Telluride

Road map D2. ⛰ 2,400. ✈ 🚌
ℹ 700 W. Colorado Ave. (888) 605-2578. **Open** 9am–5pm daily.
🆆 visittelluride.com

Once a mining town like Silverton, today Telluride is a noted ski resort, as popular with Hollywood celebrities as the equally famous Aspen in northern Colorado. Its late Victorian center boasts upscale ski shops, boutiques, and restaurants. Yet Telluride retains its authentic charm; it is still possible to imagine the days when the notorious outlaw Butch Cassidy lived here.

The ski resort's exclusive Mountain Village lies across a mountain ridge easily reached by a free 12-minute gondola ride. In winter there is a variety of sports available. In summer there are walks and riding trails, and fishing in the lakes and rivers. The town also hosts an annual international film festival.

🄘 Ouray

Road map D2. ⛰ 1,000. ℹ 1230 North Main St. (970) 325-4746; (800) 228-1876. **Open** daily.
🆆 ouraycolorado.com

The wonderfully preserved old mining town of Ouray lies 23 miles (37 km) north of Silverton on Hwy 550. Its stunning setting, amid mountain peaks,

has made it a popular base for hikers and 4WD enthusiasts. To the north of town are the Ouray Hot Springs. To the south, a loop road leads to Box Canyon Falls Park. A short trail leads across a swinging bridge to the falls' dramatic cascade.

🄙 Silverton

Road map D2. ⛰ 600. ℹ 414 Greene St. (970) 387-5654; (800) 752-4494. ⛰ 🆆 silvertoncolorado.com

Silverton is set among snow-covered peaks, and is one of the best preserved 19th-century mining towns in the Southwest. The entire town is registered as a National Historic Landmark, and the façades along Blair Street have altered little since the days of the 1880s silver-mining boom that gave the town its

Plaque from Silverton County Jail

name. On Greene Street, most of the buildings date from the late 19th and early 20th centuries, including the 1902 County Jail, which houses the **San Juan County Historical Museum**. Greene Street East leads 13 miles (21 km) north to the ghost town, Animas Forks, abandoned after the mines ran out of silver.

🏛 San Juan County Historical Museum
1512 Greene St. **Tel** (970) 387-5838. **Open** late May–mid-Oct: 9am–5pm daily. **Closed** late Oct–mid-May. ♿

🄚 Durango

Road map D2. ⛰ 14,700. ✈ 🚌
ℹ 111 S. Camino del Rio (970) 247-3500; (800) 463-8726. **Open** Jun–Sep: 8am–6pm Mon–Fri, 9am–5pm Sat, 11am–4pm Sun; Oct–May: 8am–5pm Mon–Fri. 🆆 durango.org

Durango is a lovely town with shady tree-lined streets and splendid Victorian architecture. Its attractive setting, on the banks of the Animas River, draws increasing numbers of residents, making the town the largest community in this part of Colorado. It is famous as the starting point of the **Durango and Silverton Narrow Gauge Railroad**, perhaps the most scenic train ride in the US. A 1920s coal-fired steam train ferries more than 200,000 visitors each year along the Animas River valley, up steep gradients through canyons and mountain scenery, to Silverton. Passengers may choose to ride in either Victorian or open-sided "gondola" cars that offer great views. Several stops along the way allow hikers and anglers access to the pristine back-country of the San Juan National Forest. A good time to make the trip is September when fall colors cover the mountainsides. This is a popular attraction, and booking ahead is recommended.

🚂 Durango and Silverton Narrow Gauge Railroad
479 Main Ave. **Tel** (970) 247-2733; reservations (888) 872-4607. **Open** most days year round.
🆆 durangotrain.com

Steam train on Durango and Silverton Narrow Gauge Railroad

For hotels and restaurants see pp236–43 and pp248–61

㉑ Mesa Verde National Park

This high, forested mesa overlooking the Montezuma Valley was home to the Ancestral Puebloan people *(see p42)* for more than 700 years. Within canyons that cut through the mesa are some of the best preserved and most elaborate cliff dwellings built by these people. Mesa Verde, meaning "Green Table," was a name given to the area by the Spanish in the 1700s, but the ruins were not widely known outside the area until the late 19th century. This site provides a fascinating record of these people from the Basketmaker period, beginning around AD 550, to the complex society that built the many-roomed cliff dwellings between 1000 and 1250. Displays at the Visitor and Research Center and the Chapin Mesa Museum provide a good introduction.

Spruce Tree House
Tucked into an alcove in a cliff, these three-story structures probably housed as many as 100 people.

Guided Tours
Ranger-led tours give visitors a chance to actually enter the ruins and get a feel for the daily lives of these ancient people.

Cliff Palace
With 150 rooms, this is the largest Ancestral Puebloan cliff dwelling found anywhere, and is the site that most visitors focus on. The location and symmetry suggest that architecture was important to the builders. Begun around 1200, it was vacated around 1275.

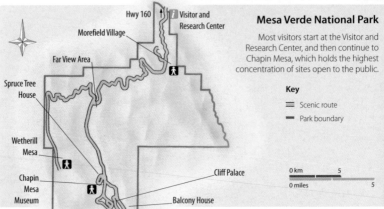

Hwy 160 — Visitor and Research Center
Morefield Village
Far View Area
Spruce Tree House
Wetherill Mesa
Chapin Mesa Museum
Cliff Palace
Balcony House

Mesa Verde National Park

Most visitors start at the Visitor and Research Center, and then continue to Chapin Mesa, which holds the highest concentration of sites open to the public.

Key

═══ Scenic route

▬▬ Park boundary

0 km — 5
0 miles — 5

Balcony House

Possibly built or adapted for defense, Balcony House could not be seen from above. Access was (and still is) difficult. Visitors must climb three ladders high above the canyon floor, then crawl through a tunnel to exit the site.

Towers were probably used for signalling or as lookouts for defense.

VISITORS' CHECKLIST

Practical Information
Road map D2. ℹ PO Box 8, Mesa Verde, CO 81330 (970) 529-4465. Visitor and Research Center: **Open** daily. Chapin Mesa Archaeological Museum: **Open** daily.
🏛 ♿ 📷 🛍 📷 🚫
Ⓦ nps.gov/meve

Transport
🚗 Cortez and Durango. No public transport to the park.

Square Tower House

Early cowboys named this site for the prominent, tower-like central structure, which was actually a vertical stack of rooms that was once surrounded by other rooms. It may have been used as a dwelling or for ceremonial purposes.

The 23 *kivas* at this site may have served a variety of ceremonial, social, and utilitarian purposes, and may indicate that many different clans lived here at various times.

Wetherill Mesa Long House

A scenic 12-mile (17-km) drive on a winding mountain road leads to Wetherill Mesa, named for the local rancher, Richard Wetherill, who found Cliff Palace in the 1880s. Two cliff dwellings here, Step and Long houses, are open to visitors.

The Rio Chama near Abiquiu in O'Keeffe Country, New Mexico ▶

NEW MEXICO

Introducing New Mexico

New Mexico's scenic beauty, rich cultural heritage, and unique mix of Native American, Hispanic, and Anglo-American people make it a fascinating place to visit. The forested peaks of the Rocky Mountains in the north offer ski resorts in winter and cool retreats in the hot summers. Northern New Mexico is also noted for its quality of light, with stark shadows and soft colors that have attracted generations of artists to the region, especially to the creative centers of Santa Fe and Taos. Albuquerque is the state's centrally located largest city, and, to the south, visitors can explore ancient Native ruins at Gila Cliff Dwellings National Monument, as well as such natural wonders as the gleaming dunes of White Sands National Monument and the cave systems of Carlsbad Caverns.

Adobe in Albuquerque's Old Town
(see pp214–15)

0 kilometers 50

0 miles 50

Key

▬▬ Highway

▬ Major road

▭▭ Minor road

▬ State border

△ Summit

Getting Around

New Mexico has two major Interstate Highways, I-25 and I-40, which cross each other in Albuquerque. Interstate 25 cuts north into Colorado and south into Mexico. Interstate 40 cuts east to west, into Texas and Arizona respectively. To the south, Interstate 10 connects the city of Las Cruces with Arizona. Albuquerque airport is New Mexico's main hub for both international and domestic flights. Greyhound buses run between Albuquerque and several major US cities.

SANTA FE AND NORTHERN NEW MEXICO

ALBUQUERQUE AND SOUTHERN NEW MEXICO

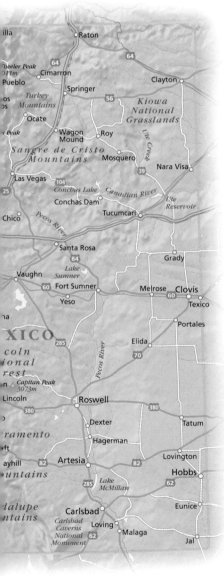

Ancestral Puebloan cliff dwellings at Bandelier National Monument (see p204)

Soaptree yucca plant growing among the dunes at White Sands National Monument (see p227)

The Atomic Age

During World War II, fears that the Germans were developing an atomic bomb led the US to begin its own nuclear weapons program. In 1942 Britain and the US combined their research efforts; Los Alamos was chosen as the location for the Manhattan Project, which resulted in the world's first nuclear explosion in July 1945. The clear skies, level ground, and sparse population made it an ideal top-secret testing ground. Today, Los Alamos National Laboratory and Sandia National Laboratory in Albuquerque are the largest nuclear research facilities in the US, and remain important centers for military research and development. Visitors can find out more at museums in Los Alamos (see p204) and White Sands (see p227).

Fat Man and Little Boy were atomic bombs dropped on the Japanese cities of Hiroshima and Nagasaki in August 1945. Reproductions can be seen at the Bradbury Science Museum in Los Alamos (see p204).

The Nike Ajax missile at the International New Mexico Museum of Space History in Alamogordo (see p228) was one of the first guided missiles. It was tested at the White Sands Missile Range in 1951. Other rockets from the period are on display in the museum grounds.

Robert Goddard did not live to see the age of spaceflight. At the time of his death in 1945, he held 214 patents in rocketry.

The Manhattan Project

In 1943 an innocuous former boys' school, the Los Alamos Ranch School set high in New Mexico's remote Pajarito Plateau, was chosen as the research site for the top secret Manhattan Project. Work began immediately under the direction of physicist J. Robert Oppenheimer and General Leslie R. Groves. In just over two years they had developed the first atomic bomb, detonated at the secluded Trinity Test Site, now the White Sands Missile Range, 230 miles (370 km) south of Los Alamos on July 16 1945. The decision to explode the bomb in warfare was highly controversial, and some of the scientists who developed the bomb signed a petition against its use. Displays on the project can be seen at the Bradbury Science Museum and the Los Alamos Historical Museum.

Oppenheimer and Groves at Los Alamos, 1944

Dr. John P. Stapp testing acceleration in his Sonic Wind I rocket sled in 1954 at Holloman Air Force Base near White Sands Missile Range. His research improved aircraft seatbelt technology.

oddard's assistants (left o right) in his workshop ere N.T. Ljungquist, A.W. sk, and C.W. Mansur.

Ham the space chimp is helped out of his capsule after becoming the first living creature to be sent into space in 1961.

Rocket Science

Robert Goddard (1882–1945) is often referred to as "the father of modern rocketry," developing rocket science in his workshop in Roswell, New Mexico (see p231). He launched his first liquid-fueled rocket in Massachusetts in 1926 and performed 56 flight tests in Roswell in the 1930s. By 1935 he had developed rockets that could carry cameras and record instrument readings. An altitude record was set in 1937 when a Goddard rocket reached 2 miles (3 km) above the earth.

A Goddard rocket without its casing, being studied on an "assembly frame."

The space shuttle touching down on the Northrup strip at the White Sands Missile Range on March 30, 1982. This was the first time in its three-flight history that the shuttle landed in New Mexico. The shuttle program ended in 2011, but White Sands remains a designated missile testing ground.

New Mexico is a major center for astronaut training and selection. Here astronaut Steven Robinson is training in a buoyancy tank to simulate life in space in preparation for his 1998 mission on the *Discovery* shuttle.

Hispanic Culture in New Mexico

The heart of Hispanic culture in the Southwest is found in New Mexico. Here, the Hispanic population, descendants of the original Spanish colonizers from the 17th century onwards, outnumbers that of the Anglo-Americans. The Spanish introduced sheep and horses to the region, and Catholicism with its saints'festivals and colorful church decorations.

Centuries of mixing with the Southwest's native and Anglo cultures have also influenced all aspects of modern Hispanic society, from language and cooking to festivals and the arts. Many contemporary New Mexican residents bear the Hispanic surnames of their ancestors, and speak English with a Spanish accent. Even English speakers use Spanish terms.

Pueblo pottery traditions go back centuries. Today Hispanic potters use New Mexico's micaceous clay to produce items such as this 1997 jar by Jacobo de la Serna.

Navajo rugs are considered a native handicraft, but their designs also show signs of Moorish patterns brought from Spain by the colonizers who first introduced sheep into the New World.

A Bulto (carved wooden figure) of St. Joseph sits on the altar of the Morada at El Rancho de las Golondrinas *(see pp202– 203)*. It is an example of a form of Hispanic folk art, which combined religious beliefs and artistic expression.

The well was always located in the middle of the main courtyard to be easily accessible.

Hacienda Martínez was built south of Taos in 1804 by Don Antonio Martínez, an early mayor of the town. It is one of the few Spanish haciendas to be preserved in more or less its original form. Today it is open to visitors who can watch local artisans demonstrating a variety of folk arts.

Decorations made from tin originated in Mexico where this metal was a cheap substitute for silver. Shapes were cut out and painted with translucent colors.

Cockerel

Mexican bird

Bull

Fiestas are an important element of Hispanic culture, and there are many throughout the year, particularly on saints' days *(see pp36–9)*. Fiestas often combine both indigenous and Spanish influences. Elements of Hispanic celebrations have also been incorporated into events in other cultures; here, young girls perform traditional dances at celebrations for the Fourth of July.

Adobe beehive ovens *(hornos)* were introduced by the Spanish for baking bread. They were originally of Moorish design.

Spanish Influence

The restored El Rancho de las Golondrinas (see pp202–203) is a living museum showing the way of life – centered on the hacienda – pioneered in the Southwest by the Spanish colonists. In a hacienda, a large number of rooms (approximately 20) would be set around one or two courtyards, reflecting the extended family style of living favored by the Spanish settlers. The Spanish Colonial style is also seen in the layout of many towns, including central Santa Fe (see pp196–7).

Chili ristras are garlands of dried red chilies sold as souvenirs in New Mexico. Chilis were a Native American food, unknown in Europe before Columbus landed in the Americas in 1492. However, they were adopted wholeheartedly by the Spanish.

Luminarias fill the square outside San Felipe de Neri church in Albuquerque's Old Town. These Mexican lanterns (also called *farolitos*) consist of a candle set in sand in a paper bag, and are displayed during religious festivals.

SANTA FE AND NORTHERN NEW MEXICO

The beauty of the landscape and the wealth of cultural attractions make northern New Mexico one of the most popular destinations in the Southwest. Visitors drive through the forests of the San Juan Mountains and the peaks of the Sangre de Cristo Range, part of the southern Rocky Mountains, then through picturesque villages to meet the Rio Grande valley. It was this fertile landscape that probably attracted Ancestral Puebloan people in the 1100s. Their descendents still live today in pueblo villages, and are famous for producing distinctive crafts and pottery. Taos Pueblo is the largest of the pueblos, its fame due both to its adobe architecture and its ceremonial dances performed on feast days.

Southward lies the beautiful city of Santa Fe. Founded by Spanish colonists in 1610, Santa Fe is now one of the most visited cities in the United States, renowned for its art galleries and adobe buildings. Today, tourism dominates this historic trading center, with its appealing mix of Hispanic, Native, and Anglo-American cultures. Many specialty vacations and outdoor activities are available in the area, including archaeological tours, skiing, and white-water rafting.

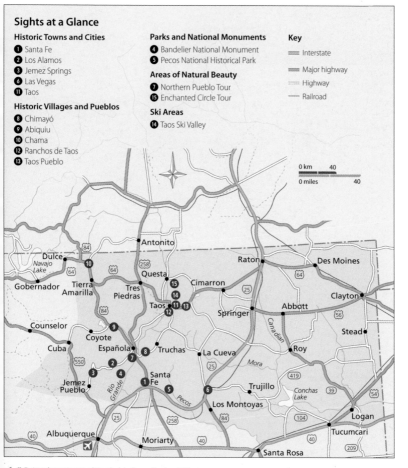

Sights at a Glance

Historic Towns and Cities
1 Santa Fe
2 Los Alamos
3 Jemez Springs
6 Las Vegas
11 Taos

Historic Villages and Pueblos
8 Chimayó
9 Abiquiu
10 Chama
12 Ranchos de Taos
13 Taos Pueblo

Parks and National Monuments
4 Bandelier National Monument
5 Pecos National Historical Park

Areas of Natural Beauty
7 Northern Pueblo Tour
15 Enchanted Circle Tour

Ski Areas
14 Taos Ski Valley

Key
═══ Interstate
═══ Major highway
═══ Highway
─── Railroad

◄ Chili *ristra* decorating a traditional adobe home, Ranchos de Taos

● Street-by-Street: Santa Fe Plaza

The oldest state capital in North America, Santa Fe was founded by the Spanish conquistador Don Pedro de Peralta, who created a colony here in 1610 *(see p43)*. This colony was abandoned in 1680 following the Pueblo Revolt, but settlers recaptured it in 1692 *(see p44)*. When Mexico gained independence in 1821, Santa Fe was opened up to the wider world and traders and settlers from the US arrived via the Santa Fe Trail *(see p29)*.

The central plaza has been the heart of Santa Fe since its founding, and there is no better place to begin exploring the city. Today, it houses a Native American market under the portal of the Palace of the Governors, and the square is lined with shops, cafés, and galleries.

★ New Mexico Museum of A
This museum focuses on the paintings and sculpture of Southwestern artists.

The Plaza
The obelisk at the center of this main square commemorates the Anglo defeat of New Mexico's Native peoples. The Plaza is dominated by the Palace of the Governors and lined with old colonial buildings.

0 meters 100
0 yards 100

Original Trading Post
This historic trading post sells Hispanic art, antiques, and Native American crafts.

Key

— Suggested route

★ Palace of the Governors
This single-story adobe building dates back to the early 17th century. Now part of the New Mexico History Museum, the palace houses displays on the city's history.

VISITORS' CHECKLIST

Practical Information
Road map E3. 🅜 69,000. ℹ️ 491 Old Santa Fe Trail. (505) 827-7336. 🎭 Spanish Market (Jul); Indian Market (Aug); Fiestas de Santa Fe (Sep). 🆆 **santafe.org**

Transport
✈️ Santa Fe Municipal Airport, 10 miles (16 km) SW. of Santa Fe. 🚉 Lamy, 18 miles S. of city. Rail Runner: Santa Fe Railyard. (866) 795-7245. 🆆 **nmrailrunner.com**

Museum of Contemporary Native Arts

CATHEDRAL PLACE

E. SAN FRANCISCO STREET

PLAZA

OLD SANTA FE TRAIL

E. WATER STREET

La Fonda Hotel

Loretto Chapel
Built in Gothic style by French architects in the 1870s, the Loretto Chapel was modeled on Ste. Chappelle in Paris. The building and elegant spiral staircase inside were commissioned for the Sisters of Loretto.

Saint Francis Cathedral
This colorful, carved wooden statue of the Virgin stands in a chapel belonging to the original 17th-century church on which the cathedral was built in 1869.

Exploring Central Santa Fe

Santa Fe's rich history and beautiful architecture have made it one of the most popular destinations in the US. Sitting 7,000 ft (2,100 m) up on a high plateau, surrounded by the splendor of the Sangre de Cristo mountains, it basks in clear light and sunshine. The blending of three distinct cultures – Hispanic, Native American, and Anglo – contribute to the city's vibrancy. Santa Fe is an artists' town. About one in six residents work in the arts, and their legacy is everywhere, from the dozens of private galleries along Canyon Road to the fine collections at the New Mexico Museum of Art. Still, Santa Fe has a relaxed atmosphere, and a setting that offers plenty of opportunities for such outdoor activities as hiking or skiing.

Exploring Santa Fe

Many of the main attractions in Santa Fe are within easy walking distance of the Plaza *(see p196)*. This is also the city's main shopping district for arts, crafts, and souvenirs, and many cafés and restaurants line the nearby streets. Santa Fe is home to several superb museums, including four run by the state of New Mexico. Good-value four-day passes can save on admission fees.

🏠 Santuario de Guadalupe

417 Agua Fria St. **Tel** (505) 983-8868. **Open** 9am–noon & 1–4pm Mon–Sat.

This 1795 adobe church is dedicated to the Virgin of Guadalupe, patron saint of both the Mexican and Pueblo peoples. Santuario de Guadalupe marked the end of the old Camino Real (Royal Road), the main trade route from Mexico. A painted altarpiece of the Virgin, dating from 1783, graces the interior, also used for classical concerts.

🏛 Georgia O'Keeffe Museum

217 Johnson St. **Tel** (505) 946-1000. **Open** 10am–5pm daily (to 7pm Fri). **Closed** Easter, Thanksgiving, Dec 25. Other closures may occur – check before visiting. 🅿 ♿ 🇼 okeeffemuseum.org

This museum is dedicated to New Mexico's most famous resident artist, Georgia O'Keeffe (1887–1986; *see p207*). Some of her best-loved paintings are on display here, including *Jimson Weed* (1932), *Purple Hills II*, and *Ghost Ranch, New Mexico* (1934),

Jimson Weed (1932), painting at the Georgia O'Keeffe Museum

as well as her sculpture and less well-known works, such as paintings of New York.

🏛 New Mexico Museum of Art

107 W. Palace Ave. **Tel** (505) 476- 5072. **Open** 10am–5pm Tue–Sun (also Mon in summer), 10am–8pm Fri. **Closed** Jan 1, Easter, Thanksgiving, Dec 25. 🅿 ♿ 🇼 nmartmuseum.org

Built to showcase New Mexico's growing art scene and completed in 1917, this building is one of the earliest examples of modern Pueblo Revival-style architecture *(see p27)*. The design owes much to the nearby Pueblo mission churches. Exhibition spaces have square beams, hand-carved decoration, and other traditional features. The collection comprises over 20,000 pieces of Southwestern art from the 19th century onward.

🏛 Palace of the Governors and New Mexico History Museum

105 W. Palace Ave. **Tel** (505) 476- 5100. **Open** 10am–5pm Tue–Sun (to 8pm Fri; also Mon in summer). **Closed** public hols. 🅿 ♿

The Palace of the Governors dominates the north side of the Plaza and is the oldest public building in continuous use in America. Built in 1610, it was the seat of regional government for 300 years. Exhibits here trace the history and culture of New Mexico from 1540 to 1912.

The adjacent New Mexico History Museum presents the stories of the American West through historic artifacts, documents, and interactive exhibits.

🏛 Museum of Contemporary Native Arts

108 Cathedral Pl. **Tel** (505) 983-1777. **Open** 10am–5pm Mon–Sat, noon–5pm Sun. **Closed** Nov–May: Tue; public hols. 🅿 ♿

Housed in a striking Pueblo Revival-style building, this museum contains the National Collection of Contemporary Indian Art. Traditional pottery, textiles, and beadwork are displayed alongside modern

Sculpture in the courtyard of the New Mexico Museum of Art

The decorative façade of St. Francis Cathedral

paintings and mixed-media works by leading Native American artists.

🏠 St. Francis Cathedral

131 Cathedral Pl. **Tel** (505) 982- 5619. **Open** daily. ♿

The Cathedral's French Romanesque-style façade is an anomaly in the heart of this adobe city, yet its honey-colored stone, glowing in the afternoon light, makes it one of its loveliest landmarks. It was built in 1869 under Santa Fe's first Archbishop,

Jean Baptiste Lamy. The building replaced most of an earlier adobe church called *La Parroquia*, except for the side chapel of Our Lady of the Rosary. This houses the oldest statue of the Virgin Mary in North America, known as *La Conquistadora*. Carved in Mexico in 1625, the figure was brought to Santa Fe where it gained mythical status as settlers fleeing the Pueblo Revolt in 1680 *(see p44)* claimed to have been saved by the Virgin's protection.

🏠 Loretto Chapel

207 Old Santa Fe Trail. **Tel** (505) 982-0092. **Open** 9am–5pm Mon–Sat, 10:30am–5pm Sun. 📷 ♿

w lorettochapel.com

This Neo-Gothic chapel was fashioned after Ste. Chapelle in Paris by the architect of Santa Fe's St. Francis Cathedral. It is most famous though for its staircase, a dramatically curved spiral that winds upward for

21 ft (6 m) with 33 steps that make two complete 360 degree turns. The spiral has no nails or center support – only its perfect craftsmanship keeps it aloft. When the chapel was built it lacked access to the choirloft. A mysterious carpenter appeared, built the spiral, and vanished without payment.

The elegant curves of the spiral staircase at the Loretto Chapel

Santa Fe Plaza

① Santuario de Guadalupe
② Georgia O'Keeffe Museum
③ New Mexico Museum of Art
④ Palace of the Governors and New Mexico History Museum
⑤ Museum of Contemporary Native Arts
⑥ St. Francis Cathedral
⑦ Loretto Chapel
⑧ Canyon Road
⑨ San Miguel Mission
⑩ New Mexico State Capitol
⑪ Santa Fe Southern Railway Depot

Key

▇ Santa Fe Street-by-Street map *see pp 196–7*

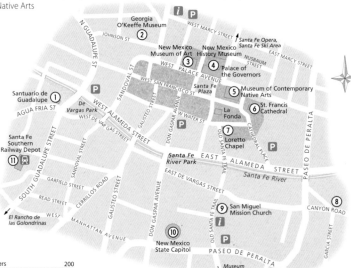

Museum of International Folk Art

This charming museum houses a stunning collection of folk art from all over the world, including toys, miniature theaters, dolls, and paintings, as well as religious and traditional art. The eastern gallery holds the fine Girard Wing, the largest collection of cross-cultural works in existence. Thousands of objects from more than 100 countries are displayed, including icons and paintings. The highlights are ceramic figures arranged in attractive scenes, ranging from a Polish Christmas to a Mexican baptism. The Hispanic Heritage Wing contains Spanish colonial decorative art, such as rare hide paintings, while the Neutrogena Wing offers textiles from Africa, Asia, and South America.

★ Girard Collection Figures
Created in 1960 in Oaxaca, Mexico, this baptism scene is made up of over 50 painted earthenware villagers.

Neutrogena Wing
Specializing in rugs, textiles, blankets, and costumes, this gallery spans world culture to reveal a depth of craft and detail in each piece, as shown in this former exhibit – a 19th-century dyed Japanese bridal sleeping cover.

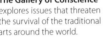

The Gallery of Conscience
explores issues that threaten the survival of the traditional arts around the world.

Hispanic Heritage Wing
This hand-carved New-Mexican icon, from 1830–50, represents Mary, Our Lady of Sorrows. It is typical of the Spanish colonial and Hispanic folk art found in this wing.

Temporary exhibitions

Library

Entra

VISITORS' CHECKLIST

706 Camino Lejo. **Tel** (505) 476-1200. **Open** 10am–5pm Tue–Sun (also Mon in summer). **Closed** public hols.

★ **Girard Collection Toy**
This Bangladeshi toy is a 1960s addition to the more than 100,000 artifacts collected by US designer Alexander Girard from 1930 to 1978.

Canyon Road

Originally an Indian track between the Rio Grande and Pecos pueblos, Canyon Road was later used by burros (donkeys) hauling firewood down from the mountains. This upscale road is today lined with more than 100 private art galleries, restaurants, and shops, with their premises in historic adobe houses. Canyon Road runs parallel to the river and the former Acequia Madre, or "mother ditch," the city's first irrigation channel, which today is lined with adobe buildings.

Ancient male figurine

San Miguel Mission

401 Old Santa Fe Trail. **Tel** (505) 983-3974. **Open** daily.
The chapel of San Miguel is thought to have been built around 1610, making it one of the oldest churches in the US. The original dirt floor and adobe steps are still visible at the front of the altar. It was built by Tlaxcala Indians, who traveled from Mexico with the early Spanish settlers.

This simple church has great roof beams that were restored in 1692, having been burned 12 years earlier in the Pueblo Revolt. A carved wooden *reredos* (altarpiece) frames the centrally placed statue of the patron saint, San Miguel, while the side walls boast paintings of religious scenes on deerskin and buffalo hide.

Museum Hill

Alongside the Museum of International Folk Art, three other important museums are found on Museum Hill. **The Museum of Indian Arts and Culture** is dedicated to traditional Native American arts and culture. Its main exhibit, *Here, Now & Always*, tells the story of the Southwest's oldest communities in the words of native Pueblo, Navajo, and Apache people.

The Wheelwright Museum of the American Indian, established in 1937 by wealthy philanthropist Mary Cabot Wheelwright of Boston, was built to resemble a Navajo *hogan (see p173)*. The museum's focus is on its changing exhibitions of contemporary work by Native American artists. In the basement, the excellent Case Trading Post re-creates the first trading posts established on the Navajo reservation.

The Museum of Spanish Colonial Art holds one of the world's most extensive collections of Spanish Colonial art, with over 3,000 objects including textiles, furniture, religious santos, and ceramics.

The Museum of Indian Arts and Culture

710 Camino Lejo. **Tel** (505) 827-6344. **Open** 10am–5pm Tue–Sun (also Mon in summer).

The Wheelwright Museum of the American Indian

704 Camino Lejo. **Tel** (505) 982-4636. **Open** daily. **Closed** public hols.
wheelwright.org

The Museum of Spanish Colonial Art

750 Camino Lejo. **Tel** (505) 982-2226. **Open** 10am–5pm Tue–Sun (also Mon in summer).

Key

- Girard Wing
- Neutrogena Wing
- Hispanic Heritage Wing
- Bartlett Wing
- Non-exhibition space

Detail of the carved wooden *reredos* at San Miguel Mission

El Rancho de las Golondrinas

Established in the early 1700s, El Rancho de las Golondrinas (Ranch of the Swallows), is a historic stopping place on the Camino Real, the old royal road trading route that ran from Mexico City to Santa Fe. Home to successive occupants for three centuries, including the Baca family for 200 years, the 200-acre (89-ha) ranch was used by settlers and explorers to rest up and water their animals before heading on to the city. Located in a fertile valley just south of Santa Fe, this living history museum, with its restored buildings and historic features, re-creates life on a typical 18th-century Spanish ranch. Authentic historic crops such as squash and corn are grown here, and burros and horses are used to work the fertile land.

Villager Weaving
On weekends, costumed workers demonstrate assorted traditional skills, including weaving.

*Sapel
and S
Village*

★ La Placita
This small central courtyard contains the *hornos*, or beehive-shaped ovens that were used to bake bread and cookies.

★ Baca House Kitchen
The kitchen, like the rest of the Baca house, dates from the early 1800s. It features a bell-shaped oven and a built-in wall cabinet *(alacena)* to keep food cool.

★ Chapel
This pretty painted wooden *retablo* (screen) graces the chapel. Having such a chapel was essential for devout Catholic settlers.

Sapello Mill
This 1870s water mill was moved here from a New Mexican village in 1972. Its millstones still grind wheat into flour on festival days.

🎭 Santa Fe Opera
5 miles N. of Santa Fe on Hwy 84/285. **Tel** (505) 986-5900; (800) 280-4654. **Open** Jun–Aug. 🕙
w santafeopera.org

Located just north of Santa Fe near the pueblo of Tesuque, the outdoor auditorium is the setting for one of the finest summer opera companies in the world. It is renowned for innovative productions, which attract international stars. A state-of-the-art electronic system allows the audience to read translations of the libretti on the seats in front of them. Backstage tours are available in July and August.
Visitors are advised to come prepared for Santa Fe's changeable weather with warm clothing, umbrellas, rugs, and waterproof gear.

🎿 Santa Fe Ski Area
Hwy 475. **Tel** (505) 982-4429. **Open** Nov–early Apr: 9am–4pm daily, weather permitting. 🖼
w skisantafe.com

Just a 30-minute drive from central Santa Fe, the ski area sits in a 12,000-ft- (4,000-m-) high basin of the Sangre de Cristo mountains. The resort has 77 trails to suit skiers of every ability, from beginners to experts, and snowboarding runs are also open. Check the website for the latest snow report. A lodge, equipment rentals, ski school, and child care are available, as are a variety of ski packages. From late September to early October, chairlift rides offer splendid views of the fall colors.

The façade of the New Mexico State Capitol with Puebloan sun motif

🏛 New Mexico State Capitol
Old Santa Fe Trail & Paseo de Peralta. **Tel** (505) 986-4589. **Open** Sep–May: 7am–6pm Mon–Fri; Jun–Aug: 7am–6pm Mon–Fri, 9am–5pm Sat & public hols. 📷 🕙 **w** nmlegis.gov

Built to resemble the sun symbol of the Zia Pueblo people, the circular State Capitol houses works by New Mexican artists from the Capitol Art Collection. Paintings, photographs, sculptures, furniture, and weavings are displayed on four

Buffalo sculpture at State Capitol

levels. A highlight is the sculpture *The Buffalo* (1992), by Holly Hughes, which uses paintbrushes and film for hair.

🏛 Santa Fe Railyard
Guadalupe St. 🛈 (505) 982-3373.
w railyardsantafe.com

As well as serving as the terminus for the exemplary Rail Runner light rail system that connects Santa Fe with Albuquerque, 60 miles (97 km) southwest, this lively urban park holds shops, galleries, and cafés, and hosts Saturday's open-air Farmers' Market. There is also a performance space for special events and festivals.

The Santa Fe Railyard district, a successful redevelopment of disused rail lands

❷ Los Alamos

Road map E3. 🗺 12,000. 🛈 109 Central Park Square (505) 662-8105.
🌐 visit.losalamos.com

The town of Los Alamos is famous as the location of the Manhattan Project *(see p190)*, the US Government's top-secret research program for the development of the atomic bomb during World War II. Government scientists took over this remote site in 1943. In 1945 the first atomic bomb was detonated at the Trinity test site in the southern New Mexico desert near Alamogordo *(see p228)*.

Today, the town is home to scientists from the Los Alamos National Laboratory, a leading defense facility. The **Bradbury Science Museum** showcases its work, with security and technology exhibits, and replicas of Little Boy and Fat Man, the atomic bombs dropped on Hiroshima and Nagasaki in 1945. The **Los Alamos Historical Museum** covers local geology and history.

🏛 **Bradbury Science Museum**
15th & Central Ave. **Tel** (505) 667-4444. **Open** 10am–5pm Tue–Sat, 1–5pm Sun & Mon. **Closed** public hols. ♿

Façade of Bradbury Science Museum in Los Alamos

🏛 **Los Alamos Historical Museum**
1050 Bathtub Row. **Tel** (505) 662-6272. **Open** 10am–4pm Mon–Fri (9:30am–4:30pm in summer), 11am–4pm Sat, 1–4pm Sun. **Closed** public hols. ♿

❸ Jemez Springs

Road map E3. 🗺 450. 🛈 Highway 4.
🌐 jemezsprings.org

The small town of Jemez Springs lies in San Diego Canyon, by the Jemez River, on land once occupied by the Giusewa Pueblo. Its ruins and those of a 17th-century mission church are now part of the **Jemez State Monument**. Remnants of the mission walls and a reconstruction of its huge main gates are here. A few miles south on Hwy 4, Jemez Pueblo is open only on feast days and festivals; call Jemez Springs visitor center for dates.

The region is famous for its hot springs. Spence Hot Springs, 7 miles (11 km) north of town, has several outdoor hot pools linked by waterfalls.

🏛 **Jemez State Monument**
Off Hwy 4. **Tel** (575) 829-3530. **Open** 8:30am–5pm Wed–Sun. **Closed** Mon, Tue, public hols. 📷 ♿ partial.

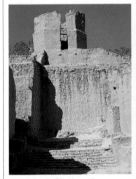
Mission church of San Jose at Jemez State Monument

❹ Bandelier National Monument

Road map E3. Off Hwy 4. **Tel** (505) 672-3861. **Open** sunrise–sunset daily; visitor center: 9am–4:30pm daily (8am–6pm Memorial Day to Labor Day). **Closed** Jan 1, Dec 25. 📷 ♿ partial. No pets. 🏔 🌐 nps.gov/band

Set in the rugged cliffs and canyons of the Pajarito Plateau, Bandelier National Monument has over 3,000 archaeological sites that are the remains of an Ancestral Pueblo culture. The site is thought to have been occupied by ancestors of the

The Rio Grande

One of America's great rivers, the Rio Grande evokes romantic images of frontier legends, from Billy the Kid to John Wayne. Its mythic status grew up from movies and TV westerns, but its historical and geographical importance is no less fascinating. From its source in Colorado, the fifth-longest river in the United States flows southeast for 1,885 miles (3,000 km) to the Gulf of Mexico. It crosses New Mexico, then forms the entire boundary between Texas and Mexico. Used for irrigation since ancient times by the pueblos, in the 16th century, Spanish settlers established towns and villages along the length of the river. Today, crops including cotton, citrus fruits, and vegetables are grown along its fertile banks.

The dramatic Rio Grande Gorge carved by the river, south of Taos

Puebloan peoples for around 500 years from the 12th to the 16th centuries when successive communities grew corn and squash, as well as hunting. The earliest occupants are thought to have carved the soft volcanic rock of the towering cliffs to make cave dwellings; later people built houses and pueblos from rock debris.

One of the most fascinating sights here is the ruin of the 400-room Tyuonyi village. The settlement is laid out with semicircular lines of houses on the floor of Frijoles Canyon.

From the visitor center, also in the canyon, the Main Loop Trail leads past Tyuonyi to some of the cave dwellings and the Long House, multistoried dwellings built into an 800-ft (240-m) stretch of the cliff. Petroglyphs can be spotted above the holes which once held the roof beams. Another short trail leads to the Alcove House, perched 150 ft (45 m) up in the rocks and reached by ladders.

❺ Pecos National Historical Park

Road map E3. Hwy 63. **Tel** (505) 757-7241. **Open** Jun–Aug: 8am–6pm daily; Sep–May: 8am–4:30pm daily. **Closed** Dec 25. 🏞 ♿ 🌐 nps.gov/peco

Located across Hwy 63, about 25 miles (40 km) southeast of Santa Fe, Pecos National Historical Park includes the ruins of the once-influential Pecos Pueblo. Situated in a pass through the Sangre de Cristo Mountains, the pueblo dominated trade routes between the Plains Indians and the Pueblo peoples between 1450 and 1550.

The façade of the Plaza Hotel in the main square of Las Vegas

Pecos Puebloans acted as a conduit for goods like buffalo skins and meat, and Puebloan products including pottery, textiles, and turquoise. The village is thought to have been among the largest in the Southwest. It stood up to 5 stories high, with nearly 700 rooms housing over 2,000 people, a quarter of them warriors. When the Spanish arrived in the early 1540s, it was a strong regional power. But by 1821 Comanche raids, disease, and migration had taken their toll; the pueblo was almost deserted, and the inhabitants moved to Jemez Pueblo.

The pueblo site can be seen on a 1.25-mile (2-km) trail that winds past them and the ruined remains of two Spanish mission churches. There are also two reconstructed *kivas* (sacred ceremonial sites). The visitor center has exhibits of historic artifacts and crafts, and a video covering 1,000 years of Puebloan history in the area.

❻ Las Vegas

Road map E3. 🚹 13,500. 🚌 🚃
🛈 1224 Railroad Ave. (505) 425-8631.
🌐 lasvegasnewmexico.com

Not to be confused with its Nevada cousin *(see pp98–135)*, Las Vegas, New Mexico has its own high-rolling past. Vegas means "meadows" in Spanish, and the town's old Plaza was established along the lush riverfront by Spanish settlers in 1835. A lucrative trade stop on the Santa Fe Trail, Las Vegas soon became a wild frontier town. Doc Holliday, who briefly owned a saloon here, was among its legendary characters *(see p59)*. The coming of the railroad in 1879 brought even greater prosperity, and new building took place around the station.

Grand Victorian architecture still prevails and self-guided tours are available from the visitor center.

Outdoor activities are popular in the area, with golf resorts and the water sports of Storrie Lake just a few miles out of town.

One of the ruined Spanish mission churches in Pecos National Historical Park

❼ Northern Pueblos Tour

The fertile valley of the Rio Grande between Santa Fe and Taos is home to eight pueblos of the 19 Native American pueblos in New Mexico. Although geographically close, each pueblo has its own government and traditions, and many offer attractions to visitors. Nambe gives stunning views of the surrounding mountains, mesas, and high desert. San Idelfonso is famous for its fine pottery, while other villages produce handcrafted jewelry or rugs.

Tips for Drivers

Starting point: Tesuque Pueblo, north of Santa Fe on Hwy 84. **Length:** 45 miles (70 km). Local roads leading to pueblos are often dirt tracks, so allow extra time. **Note:** Visitors are welcome, but must respect their laws and etiquette *(see p278–9)*. ℹ️ Indian Pueblo Cultural Center (866) 855-7902. **indianpueblo.org**

⑤ Santa Clara Pueblo

This small pueblo is known for its artisans and their work. As in many pueblos, it contains a number of craft shops and small studios, often run by the Native artisans themselves.

⑥ Puyé Cliff Dwellings

Now deserted, this site contains over 700 rooms, complete with stone carvings, that were home to Native peoples until 1500.

⑦ Ohkay Owingeh

Declared the first capital of New Mexico in 1598, and known until 2005 as San Juan Pueblo, this village is a center for the visual arts and has an arts cooperative.

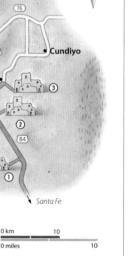

④ San Ildefonso Pueblo

Occupied since 1300, this pueblo is best known for its etched black pottery, the proceeds of which saved its people from the Depression of the 1930s.

Taos

285 · 68
Alcalde
⑦
74 · 76
Española ·
⑥
565 · ⑤ · 84 · **Cundiyo**
30 · **Nambe** · ③
Los Alamos · 502 · ④
Pojoaque · ②
White Rock · 84
Rio Grande
①
Santa Fe

③ Nambe Pueblo

Set in a beautiful fertile valley, this village is bordered by a lakeside hiking trail with waterfall views and a buffalo ranch.

② Pojoaque Pueblo

The Peoh Museum here is an excellent introduction to the pueblo way of life in these small communities.

① Tesuque Pueblo

The Tewa people here have concentrated on farming and pottery-making for centuries.

0 km		10
0 miles		10

Key

▬ Tour route
═ Other road

The adobe-and-timber façade of the Santuario de Chimayó

Georgia O'Keeffe

One of the 20th century's foremost artists, Georgia O'Keeffe (1887–1986) managed to achieve both critical and popular acclaim for her paintings, which, either as studies of single blooms or sun-washed landscapes of the Southwest, are universally loved. Wisconsin-born and raised, she studied art in Chicago and New York but fell in love with the light of New Mexico when her friend and patron, Mabel Dodge Luhan, invited her to her home in the area. O'Keeffe bought an old adobe in Abiquiu and there created the abstract paintings that brought the beauty of New Mexico to national attention.

Artist Georgia O'Keeffe

❽ Chimayó

Road map E3. 2,800. (505) 351-4889. Church open: 9am–5pm daily.

This village lies 25 miles (40 km) north of Santa Fe on the eastern flanks of the Rio Grande valley. Chimayó was settled by Spanish colonists in the 1700s on the site of an Indian pueblo famous for having a healing natural spring. The site of the spring is now occupied by the Santuario de Chimayó, built by a local landowner in 1813–16 after he experienced a vision telling him to dig the foundations in earth blessed with healing powers. While digging here he found a cross that once belonged to two martyred priests, and the church became a place of healing pilgrimage. The chapel contains a beautiful *reredos* surrounding the crucifix and a tiny side-room with a pit of "the holy dirt," which visitors are allowed to take away.

Chimayó is also known for its woven blankets and rugs, which have been produced by the Ortega family for generations. Their workshop is just off the junction with Hwy 76, while farther along, Cordova and Truchas villages are also known for their fine craftwork.

❾ Abiquiu

Road map E3. 500.

This small adobe village with its sunlit dusty streets was the home of the Southwest's most famous artist, Georgia O'Keeffe, from 1946 until her death in 1986. Her village home and studio can be toured only by reservation and bookings need to be made in advance on (505) 685-4539. The country around Abiquiu, with its red rocks, mesas, and corrugated slopes, is now known as O'Keeffe Country because it inspired so many of her abstract landscape paintings.

A few miles north of town, the fascinating **Ghost Ranch**, a retreat established and now run by Presbyterians, features two small but fascinating museums, which highlight local archaeology and palaeontology. Several hiking trails also start from the ranch.

Ghost Ranch
HC77, Box 11, Abiquiu. **Tel** (575) 685-4333. **Open** Museums: 9am–5pm Tue–Sat, 1–5pm Sun. donation.
ghostranch.org

❿ Chama

Road map E2. 1,000. 2372 Hwy 17, (505) 756-2306; (800) 477-0149. chamavalley.com

Founded during the 1880s silver-mining boom, the main attraction in today's Chama is the **Cumbres and Toltec Scenic Railroad**. This narrow-gauge steam train makes a spectacular 64-mile (102-km) daily trip over the Cumbres Pass and through the Toltec Gorge into Colorado, with views of the San Juan and Sangre de Cristo mountains.

Cumbres and Toltec Scenic Railroad
Hwy 17. **Tel** (575) 756-2151; 1 (888) 286-2737. **Open** late May–mid-Oct: 10am daily.

Dramatic red rock landscape near Abiquiu

⓫ Taos

The small community of Taos is set between the dramatic peaks of the Sangre de Cristo Mountains and the Rio Grande River. Like Santa Fe, it is an important center for the arts but is more bohemian and relaxed in style. Its plaza and the surrounding streets are lined with craft shops, cafés, and galleries, many housed in original adobe buildings.

Taos Indians have lived in the area for around 1,000 years. With the arrival of the Spanish missionaries in 1598, a few settlers followed, but it was not until Don Diego de Vargas resettled the area, after the Pueblo Revolt in 1680, that the town's present foundations were laid *(see p44)*. In 1898, artists Ernest Blumenschein and Bert Phillips stopped in Taos to repair a broken wagon wheel, and never left. In 1915 they established the Taos Society of Artists, which still supports local artists today.

Exploring Taos

There are three parts to Taos: the central historic district, Taos Pueblo to the north, and Rancho de Taos to the south *(see p210)*. Paseo del Pueblo Norte, the main street, leads north then curves west, becoming Hwy 64. It leads to Taos Ski Valley, the Millicent Rogers Museum, and Rio Grande Gorge Bridge.

Furniture displayed in the Blumenschein Museum

Ernest Blumenschein (1874–1960), along with Bert Phillips and Joseph Henry Sharp, was instrumental in founding the Taos Society of Artists in 1915. The Society promoted their own work and that of other Taos artists. The Museum is located in Blumenschein's former home, sections of which date from the 1790s. Paintings by Blumenschein and his family, as well as representative works produced by the Taos Society of Artists, hang in rooms decorated with Spanish Colonial furniture and European antiques.

🏛 Harwood Museum of Art

238 Ledoux St. **Tel** (575) 758-9826. **Open** 10am–5pm Mon–Sat, noon–5pm Sun. **Closed** Mon Nov–Mar. 🅿 ♿ 🅦 harwoodmuseum.org

This museum occupies a 19th-century adobe compound run by the University of New Mexico. It provides a tranquil setting for paintings, sculpture, prints, drawings, and photography. Work by members of the original Taos Society of Artists is displayed alongside that of contemporary local artists. A collection of Hispanic works is also featured.

🏛 Blumenschein Home and Museum

222 Ledoux St. **Tel** (575) 758-0505. **Open** Apr–Oct:10am–5pm Mon–Sat, noon–5pm Sun; Nov–Mar: 10am–4pm Mon, Tue, Thu–Sat. 🅿 ♿ partial. 🅦 taoshistoricmuseums.com

Shops and cafés line the narrow streets around Taos Plaza

🏙 Taos Plaza

Taos Plaza, built by the Spanish and fortified after the Pueblo Revolt of 1680, has been remodeled several times but remains the centerpoint of the town. Its shady trees and benches make it a relaxing spot to sit and people-watch. The copper-topped bandstand was a gift from Mabel Dodge Luhan, New Mexico's leading arts patron in the 1920s. A flag has flown continuously from the flagpole since the Civil War, when Kit Carson and a band of citizens raised the Union Flag to protect Taos from Confederate supporters.

🏛 Kit Carson Home and Museum

113 Kit Carson Rd. **Tel** (575) 758-4945. **Open** 10am–5:30pm daily. 🅿 ♿ partial. 🅦 kitcarsonhomeand museum.com

At the age of 17, Christopher "Kit" Carson (1809–68) ran away to join a wagon train and became one of the most famous names in the West. He led a remarkable life, working as a cook and interpreter, a fur-trapping mountain man, a scout for mapping expeditions, an Indian agent, and a military officer *(see p175)*. He purchased this house in Taos in 1843 for his 14-year-old bride, Josefa Jaramillo, and lived here for the rest of his life. Carson's remarkable story, and the unpredictable nature of frontier life, are the focus of the museum exhibits, which feature antique firearms, trapping equipment, photographs, and furniture.

Cover of a Kit Carson book

🏛 Taos Art Museum at Fechin House

227 Paseo del Pueblo Norte. **Tel** (575) 758-2690. **Open** 10am–5pm Tue–Sun (call for winter hours). 🅿 ♿ 🅦 taosartmuseum.org

Born in Russia in 1881, Nicolai Fechin learned woodcarving from his father. He became a talented artist, producing paintings, drawings, and

Handcrafted, wooden swing doors in the Fechin House

sculpture. Fechin moved to Taos with his family in 1927 and set about restoring his adobe home with Russian-influenced wood-work including handcrafted doors, windows, and furniture. Today his house is the Taos Art Museum, containing examples of his work as well as that of numerous early Taos artists.

Millicent Rogers Museum

1504 Millicent Rogers Rd. **Tel** (575) 758-2462. **Open** Apr–Oct: 10am–5pm daily; Nov–Mar: 10am–5pm Tue–Sun. **Closed** public hols.

Beautiful heiress and arts patron Millicent Rogers (1902–53) moved to Taos in 1947.

Fascinated by the area, she created one of the country's best museums of Southwestern arts and design. Native silver and turquoise jewelry and Navajo weavings form the core of the exhibits, which are housed in a historic hacienda. Also featured is the pottery of the famous Puebloan artist Maria Martinez (1887–1980), with its distinctive black-on-black style.

Governor Bent House and Museum

117a Bent St. **Tel** (575) 758-2376. **Open** Apr–Oct: 9:30am–5pm daily; Nov–Mar: 10am–4pm daily.

Charles Bent became the first Anglo-American governor of New Mexico in 1846. In 1847 he was killed by Hispanic and Indian residents who resented American rule. The hole hacked in the adobe by his family as they attempted to flee can still be seen. Today, exhibits include guns, native artifacts, and animal skins.

Rio Grande Gorge Bridge

The dramatic Rio Grande Gorge Bridge, which was built in 1965, is the second-highest suspension bridge in the country. At 650 ft (195 m) above the Rio Grande, its dizzying heights offer awesome views of the gorge and the surrounding stark, sweeping plateau.

Central Taos

1. Harwood Museum of Art
2. Blumenschein Home and Museum
3. Taos Plaza
4. Kit Carson Home and Museum
5. Governor Bent House and Museum
6. Taos Art Museum at Fechin House

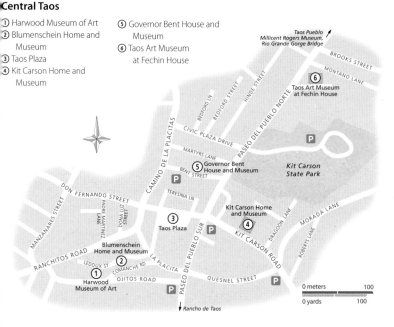

For keys to symbols *see back flap*

Restored early 19th-century kitchen at the Hacienda Martínez

⓬ Ranchos de Taos

Road map E3. **ℹ** Taos Visitor Center, 1139 Paseo de Pueblo Sur, Taos (575) 758-3873. **W** taosvacation guide.com

Three miles (5 km) southwest of central Taos, this separate community is centered on a peaceful plaza. Ranchos de Taos is also home to the striking adobe church of **San Francisco de Asis**, built during 1710–55. It is one of the best examples of mission architecture in the Southwest and provided inspiration for many artists. It was often painted by Georgia O'Keeffe (*see p207*).

The **Hacienda Martínez** is a Spanish Colonial house built in 1804 and one of few still in existence (*see p192*). Its adobe walls are 2 ft (60 cm) thick and have heavy *zaguan* (entry) gates. Inside, 21 rooms surround two courtyards. The first owner, Antonio Severino Martínez, prospered through trade with Mexico and later became mayor of Taos. The merchandise he sold is displayed here.

🏠 San Francisco de Asis
60 St Francis Plaza. **Tel** (575) 758-2754. **Open** 9am–4pm Mon–Sat. **Closed** 1st two weeks Jun. **♿**

🏛 Hacienda Martínez
708 Hacienda Rd. **Tel** (505) 758-1000. **Open** Apr–Oct:10am–5pm Mon–Sat, noon–5pm Sun; Nov–Mar: 10am–4pm Mon, Tue, Thu–Sat. **📷**

⓭ Taos Pueblo

Road map E3. Hwy 150. **ℹ** Taos Pueblo Tourism Office, P.O. Box 1846, Taos (575) 758-1028. **📷 🎫**
W taospueblo.com

This is one of the oldest communities in the US, having been occupied continuously for around 1,000 years. Two multistory adobe communal houses sit on opposite sides of the open central "square." Known as North House and South House, they are the largest pueblo buildings in the country and are thought to date from the early 1700s. More than 100 people live year-round at the pueblo, as their ancestors did, with no electricity, and

water supplied only from a stream. Sights include the 1850 St. Jerome Chapel, the ruins of the earlier 1619 San Geronimo Church, and the central plaza, with its corn and chili drying-racks and adobe ovens, or *hornos*. Several ground-floor dwellings are now craft shops. Guided tours are available but there is a fee of $6 for each camera; permission must be granted prior to photographing a resident. No cameras are permitted during ceremonial dances, but several festivals are open to visitors throughout the year.

Downhill view of one of the celebrated ski slopes at Taos

⓮ Taos Ski Valley

Road map E2. **Tel** (575) 776-2291. **♿** village only. **W** skitaos.org

A century ago Taos Ski Valley was a bustling mining camp. In 1955, Swiss-born skier Ernie Blake began developing a world-class ski resort on the northern slopes and snow bowls of Wheeler Peak, the 13,161-ft (3,950-m) summit that is the highest in New Mexico. Located 15 miles (24 km) north of Taos, it has 14 lifts and 113 runs for all abilities, but it is particularly known for its challenging expert terrain. The ski season itself generally runs from Thanksgiving to early April depending on the weather. The valley also makes a spectacular summer retreat, popular with those seeking relief from the summer heat. Some 100 residents live in the village year-round.

Adobe buildings at the Taos pueblo, inhabited to this day by villagers

⓯ Enchanted Circle Tour

The scenery around Taos rises from high desert plateau with its sagebrush and yucca plants to the forested Sangre de Cristo Mountains. The Enchanted Circle tour follows a National Forest Scenic Byway through some of the area's most breathtaking landscapes. Circumnavigating the highest point in New Mexico, Wheeler Peak (13,161 ft/ 3,950 m), it continues through the ruggedly beautiful Carson National Forest. Lakes and hiking trails lie off the tour, which passes through a number of small towns.

Tips for Drivers

Length: 111 miles (178 km).
Starting point: North of Taos on Hwy 522, continuing east and south on Hwys 38 & 64.
Getting around: While the main roads offer smooth and rapid driving, bear in mind that many sights are located on dirt tracks and minor roads.

① Río Grande del Norte National Monument
Established in 2013 by President Obama, this area stretches up the Rio Grande Gorge to Colorado. The visitor center has information on hiking and is a launch point for rafting trips.

② Questa
This hamlet is the gateway to Carson National Forest, with rivers, mountains, and lakes set against a rocky backdrop.

③ Red River
Once a gold-mining town, this hill village retains its Old West-style architecture, and offers a base for hiking and skiing in this scenic area.

Cerro ②

① 522

150

San Cristobal

Rio Grande

③

38

④ Eagle Nest Lake

Idlewild •

Cimarron

64

⑥

Taos Pueblo

Taos

64

68

0 km 7
0 miles 7

⑥ DAV Vietnam Veterans Memorial State Park
Located northeast of Angel Fire, this modern chapel honors all the US troops who lost their lives in Vietnam.

⑤ Angel Fire
Winter sports are foremost here, with sleigh rides, snowmobiling, and horseback trips through the snowy landscape available at this growing resort.

④ Eagle Nest
Growing in popularity as a base for sports trips, this small town is conveniently located and offers ski and boat rental for the nearby mountains and lakes.

Key
▨ Tour route
═ Other road

For additional map symbols *see back flap*

ALBUQUERQUE AND SOUTHERN NEW MEXICO

Southern New Mexico is home to natural wonders such as the Carlsbad Caverns, as well as modern cities thriving on hi-tech research industries. Albuquerque is the state's largest city, with an Old Town plaza and fine museums. West of here is Acoma Pueblo, the oldest continually inhabited settlement in the country. The southern third of the state is dominated by the Chihuahua Desert, which is one of the driest in the region. Despite this, the area was cultivated by Hohokam farmers for centuries. The Gila Cliff Dwellings preserve a remarkable settlement built by the Mogollon people. By the 17th century Apaches occupied much of the region, whose reputation as a "Wild West" outpost stems from the 19th-century exploits of characters such as Billy the Kid.

Sights at a Glance

Historic Towns and Cities

1. Albuquerque
3. Bernalillo
6. Grants
8. Socorro
9. Truth or Consequences
11. Silver City
12. Deming
14. Las Cruces
15. Mesilla
16. El Paso
18. Alamogordo
19. Cloudcroft
20. Ruidoso
21. Lincoln
23. Carlsbad
24. Roswell

Areas of Natural Beauty

2. Sandia Peak Tramway
4. The Turquoise Trail
5. Acoma Pueblo

National Parks and Monuments

7. El Morro National Monument
10. Gila Cliff Dwellings National Monument
13. Fort Selden State Monument
17. White Sands National Monument
22. *Carlsbad Caverns National Park*

Key

— Interstate
— Major highway
— Highway
— Railroad

0 km 75
0 miles 75

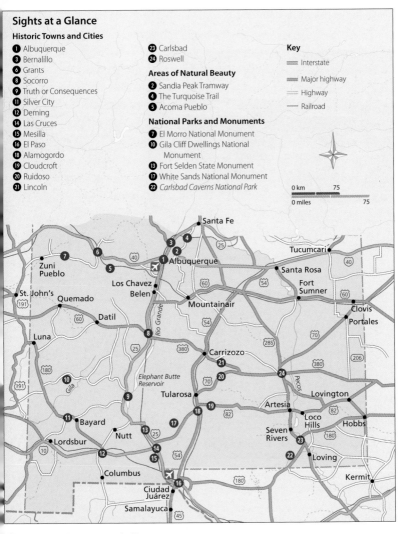

◄ Adobe San Miguel Mission, just outside of Socorro

❶ Street-by-Street: Albuquerque Old Town

Occupied by Native peoples from 1100 to 1300 AD, Albuquerque grew up from a small colonial group of pioneers who first settled by the Rio Grande in the wake of late 16th-century Spanish explorers of the region. In 1706, a band of 18 families won formal approval for their town from the Spanish crown by naming the city after the Spanish Duke of Alburquerque (the first "r" in the name was later dropped).

Today's Old Town still boasts many original adobe buildings dating from the 1790s. The city's first civic structure, the imposing San Felipe de Neri church was completed in 1793. Despite many renovations, the church retains its original adobe walls. The adjacent plaza forms the heart of the Old Town and is a pleasant open space where both locals and visitors relax on benches, surrounded by the lovely adobe buildings that house craft shops, restaurants, and museums.

Agape Pueblo Pottery
This store features a selection of pueblo pottery such as this handcrafted pc from Santa Clara Pueblo.

Church Street Café
Said to occupy the oldest house in the city, this café serves excellent New Mexican cuisine and is famous for its spicy chili.

Christmas shop

San Felipe de Neri church

CHURCH ST NW

ROMERO NW

NORTH P

RIO GRANDE BOULEVARD NW

SOUTH

★ Old Town Plaza
The plaza was the center of Albuquerque for over 200 years. Today, this charming square makes a pleasant rest stop for visitors strolling around the nearby streets lined with museums and colorful stores.

For hotels and restaurants see pp236–43 and pp248–61

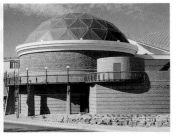

Museum of Natural History
The space-age dome of the LodeStar Astronomy Center houses a planetarium and an observatory *(see p216)*.

MOUNTAIN ROAD NW

19TH STREET

0 meters   50

0 yards   50

Key

— Suggested route

★ Albuquerque Museum of Art and History
This full-scale model of a conquistador on horseback illustrates the kind of Spanish Colonial art and artifacts that dominate this museum's excellent displays. There is also a delightful outdoor sculpture gallery.

FELIPE NW

American International Rattlesnake Museum
This Eastern diamond-back rattlesnake (right) is one of many species of rattler here. There are displays on the snake's role in medicine, history, and Native American culture.

Exploring Albuquerque

Albuquerque is New Mexico's largest city, filling the valley that stretches westward from the foothills of the Manzano and Sandia Mountains and across the banks of the Rio Grande. The coming of the railroad during the 1880s brought large numbers of settlers and great prosperity. The city center shifted 2 miles (3 km) east from the Old Town Plaza to what is now the Downtown area. Today, the city has a contemporary buzz with many shops, museums, and high-tech industries concentrated in and around Downtown. At the eastern end of this area lies the University of New Mexico, with its collection of museums and galleries.

San Felipe de Neri Church lies at the north end of Old Town Plaza

Exploring Albuquerque

The best way to see the city is by car. The major sights here are all located near highway exits, which are surprisingly close to areas of historic and architectural interest such as the Old Town. Two Interstate highways cross the center of Albuquerque. Highway 25 travels north to south just east of Downtown, while Highway 40 cuts west to east running just north of Downtown and close by the university campus.

🦋 ABQ BioPark

2601 Central Ave. NW. **Tel** (505) 768-6200. **Open** 9am–5pm daily, until 6pm Sat & Sun in summer. **Closed** Jan 1, Thanksgiving, Dec 25. 🅿 &
W cabq.gov

The Albuquerque Aquarium, in the ABQ BioPark, focuses on the marine life of the Rio Grande *(see p204)*, and features a fascinating walk-through eel cave and an impressive 285,000-gallon (627,000-liter), floor-to-ceiling shark tank. The park also encompasses Rio Grande Botanic Garden, the Rio Grande Zoological Park *(see p217)*, and Tingley Beach, where boats can be rented.

🏛 Turquoise Museum

2107 Central Ave. NW.
Tel (505) 247-8650.
🕐 11am & 1pm Mon–Sat (reserve ahead). 🅿 &
W turquoisemuseum.com

The entrance to this museum is a replica mine tunnel that leads to the "vault," which contains an unsurpassed collection of rare and varied turquoise specimens from more than fifty mines around the world.

🏛 New Mexico Museum of Natural History and Science

1801 Mountain Rd. NW.
Tel (505) 841-2800. **Open** 9am–5pm daily. **Closed** Jan 1, Thanksgiving, Dec 25. 🅿 &
W nmnaturalhistory.org

This museum has a series of interactive exhibits. Visitors can stand inside a simulated volcano or explore an ice cave. The "Evolator" is a six-minute ride through 38 million years of the region's evolution using the latest video technology. Replica

Glasshouse at Rio Grande Botanic Garden, ABQ BioPark

For hotels and restaurants see pp236–43 and pp248–61

Sculpture outside the Albuquerque Museum of Art and History

dinosaurs, a state-of-the-art planetarium, and a large-screen film theater are all highly popular with children.

Albuquerque Museum of Art and History

2000 Mountain Rd. NW. **Tel** (505) 242-4600. **Open** 9am–5pm Tue–Sun. **Closed** public hols. 🅿 ♿
W cabq.gov/museum

This excellent museum depicts four centuries of history in the middle of Rio Grande Valley. The well-chosen Spanish Colonial artifacts *(see p41)* are expertly arranged and include a reconstructed 18th-century house and chapel. From March to December, walking tours of the Old Town leave from the museum.

American International Rattlesnake Museum

202 San Felipe Ave. N. **Tel** (505) 242-6569. **Open** 10am–6pm Mon–Sat (Sep–May: 11:30am–5:30pm), 1–5pm Sun. **Closed** public hols. 🅿 ♿
W rattlesnakes.com

This animal conservation museum explains the life-cycles and ecological importance of some of Earth's most misunderstood creatures. It contains the world's largest collection of different species of live rattlesnakes, including natives of North, Central, and South America.

The snakes are displayed in glass tanks that simulate their natural habitat, and have explanatory notices suitable for both adults and children. The museum also features other much-maligned venomous animals, including a Gila monster lizard, tarantulas, and scorpions.

KiMo Theatre

423 Central Ave. NW. **Tel** (505) 768-3522. **Open** 11am–8pm Wed–Sat, 11am–3pm Sun. 🅿 ♿
W kimotickets.com

Built in 1927, the KiMo Theatre was one of many entertainment venues constructed in the city during the 1920s and 1930s. The theater's design was inspired by that of the nearby Native American pueblos, and created a fusion of Pueblo Revival and Art Deco styles. Today, the KiMo Theatre presents an eclectic range of musical and theatrical performances.

Rio Grande Zoological Park

903 10th St. SW. **Tel** (505) 768-6200. **Open** 9am–5pm daily (to 6pm Sat & Sun in summer). **Closed** Jan 1, Thanksgiving, Dec 25. 🅿 ♿

The Rio Grande Zoo forms part of the Albuquerque BioPark. The zoo is noted for its imaginative layout with enclosures designed to simulate the animals' natural habitats, including the African savanna. Among the most popular species here are lowland gorillas and white Bengal tigers.

Explora! Science Center and Children's Museum

1701 Mountain Rd. NW. **Tel** (505) 224-8300. **Open** 10am–6pm Mon–Sat, noon–6pm Sun. **Closed** public hols. 🅿 ♿ **W** explora.us

Explora's kids-oriented science center is enjoyable for adults and children alike with its many interactive exhibits, such as stepping inside a soap bubble. In the Children's Museum, youngsters can look through kaleidoscopes, build wind cars, or practice weaving.

MARQUETTE AVE NW
KENT AVE NW
TEJERAS AVE NW
MARBLE AVE NW
8TH ST NW
7TH ST NW
COPPER AVE SW
KiMo Theatre ⑦
CENTRAL AVE SW
5TH STREET SW
6TH AVE SW
5TH AVE SW
GOLD AVE SW
4TH AVE SW
DOWNTOWN
LEAD AVE SW
3RD AVE SW
2ND AVE SW
COAL AVE SW
1ST STREET SW
8TH AVE SW
HAZELDINE AVE SW
5TH STREET SW
4TH STREET SW

Anderson-Abruzzo
Albuquerque
International
Balloon Museum

National Museum
of Nuclear Science
and History

University
of New Mexico

Amtrak
Station

Greyhound
Station

Albuquerque
International Airport
6 km (4 miles)

Grande
ogical Park

Key

▪ Albuquerque Old Town Street-by-Street map *see pp214–15*

meters   500
yards   500

Sights at a Glance

For additional map symbols *see back flap*

Indian Pueblo Cultural Center

This impressive cultural center is run by New Mexico's 19 Indian Pueblos, which are largely concentrated along the Rio Grande north of Albuquerque, but also occupy lands as far west as the border with Arizona. The complex history and varied culture of the Puebloan peoples is traced through their oral history and is presented from their viewpoint.

The building is designed to resemble Pueblo Bonito, located at Chaco Canyon and one of the largest pueblo dwellings from the pre-Columbian era. The center also includes a restaurant serving Native-fusion cuisine and an excellent gift shop offering authentic Native arts and craft.

Two Puebloan dancers in front of a mural in the central courtyard

Puebloan Central Courtyard
Red adobe walls decorated with murals and hung with chilis emulate the layout of a Pueblo dwelling. Each weekend exuberant dance performances are held here.

Key

- Museum (featuring Puebloan history)
- Arts and Crafts Exhibition
- Theater
- Pueblo Kitchen Restaurant
- Gift shops
- Non-exhibition space

Main entrance

Arts and Crafts Exhibition
A flower and leaf motif, colored with bold strokes of black and orange on yellow, are typical of the kind of pottery found in some villages today.

VISITORS' CHECKLIST

Practical Information
2401 12th St. NW. **Tel** (866) 855-7902. **Open** 9am–5pm daily.
Closed major holidays.
🎨 ♿ 📷 🚫 📷
W indianpueblo.org

Transport
🚌

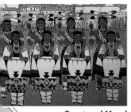

Courtyard Mural
Painted by Jemez Pueblo artist Jose Rey Toledo in 1979, this mural shows the turtle rain dance.

Museum
entrance

★ **Museum**
This wooden baby carrier from Taos Pueblo is one of many artifacts, from ancient to modern, that highlight Puebloan cultural life.

🏛 University of New Mexico
ℹ Welcome Center, Central and Cornell. **Tel** (505) 277-1989. **Open** 8am–5pm Mon–Fri. **W** unm.edu

The campus of New Mexico's largest university is known for its Pueblo Revival-style architecture (see p27) and its museums. The **University Art Museum** contains one of the largest fine art collections in the state, including Old Master paintings, sculpture, and other works from the 17th to the 20th centuries.

The **Maxwell Museum of Anthropology** emphasizes the culture of the Southwest, with an important collection of art and artifacts. There are also traveling exhibits on regional and international themes, as well as a permanent exhibition, "Ancestors," which traces human development.

🏛 University Art Museum
Tel (505) 277-4001. **Open** 10am–4pm Tue–Fri, 1–4pm Sat & Sun. **Closed** university holidays. ♿

🏛 Maxwell Museum of Anthropology
Tel (505) 277-4405. **Open** 10am–4pm Tue–Sat. ♿

🏛 Anderson-Abruzzo International Balloon Museum
9201 Balloon Museum Dr. NE. **Tel** (505) 880-0500. **Open** 9am–5pm Tue–Sun. 📷 **W** balloonmuseum.com

This museum features soaring gallery spaces that contain the world's most extensive collection of modern and historic balloons, and ballooning memorabilia. Named after two of the city's legendary balloonists, the exhibits tell how balloons have been used in adventurous exploits, warfare, and space

Petroglyphs in Petroglyph National Monument

exploration, and include artifacts that date from the earliest days of ballooning.

🏛 National Museum of Nuclear Science & History
601 Eubank at Southern Blvd. SE. **Tel** (505) 245-2137. **Open** 9am–5pm daily. **Closed** Jan 1, Easter, Thanksgiving, Dec 25. 📷 **W** nuclearmuseum.org

This museum presents the stories of nuclear pioneers and the history of nuclear development (see pp190–91). The exhibits explore the many applications of nuclear energy in the past, present, and into the future. Energy Encounter illustrates the amount of wind, solar, or hydro power required to match the output from one nuclear reactor, while Little Albert's Lab introduces children to the concepts of physics. Outdoors, the Heritage Park displays unique military missile systems, rockets, and historic planes including a B-52 bomber.

🏛 Petroglyph National Monument
ℹ 6001 Unser Blvd. NW. **Tel** (505) 899-0205. **Open** 8am–5pm daily. **Closed** Jan 1, Thanksgiving, Dec 25. 📷 ♿ limited. **W** nps.gov/petr

This site lies on the western outskirts of Albuquerque. The area was established in 1990 to preserve nearly 20,000 images carved into rock along the 17-mile (27-km) West Mesa escarpment. The earliest petroglyphs date back to 1,000 BC, but the most prolific period is thought to be between 1300 and 1680. The pictures from this time range from human figures such as musicians and dancers to animals, including snakes, birds, and insects. Spirals and other geometric symbols are common, as are hands, feet, and animal tracks. Though the meaning of many petroglyphs has been lost over time, others have great cultural significance to today's Puebloan population. Hundreds of petroglyphs are accessible along Boca Negra Canyon, 2 miles (3 km) north of the park visitor center, where three self-guided trails wind past them. Do not touch the petroglyphs.

Sandia Peak Tramway rising over pine forest and mountains near Albuquerque

❷ Sandia Peak Tramway

10 Tramway Loop NE. **Tel** (505) 856-7325. **Open** 9am–9pm daily. **Closed** 2 weeks spring & fall for maintenance.
sandiapeak.com

The Sandia Peak Tramway is a breathtaking ride from the foothills at the northeastern edge of Albuquerque to Sandia Peak at 10,378 ft (3,113 m). The tram was constructed in the mid-1960s, and carries tourists from the outskirts to the summit's viewing platform. The 15-minute ride passes through low desert to ponderosa pine forests and rugged mountains. The summit offers outstanding panoramic views of Albuquerque and of the surrounding landscape.

❸ Bernalillo

8,400. (505) 867-8687.
sandovalcounty.org

The farming community of Bernalillo was settled by Spanish colonists in 1698. Here, against a striking backdrop on the banks of the Rio Grande, is the **Coronado State Monument**, which encompasses the partially restored ruins of the Kuaua pueblo. Spanish explorer Francisco Vasquez de Coronado is believed to have been here in 1540 on a quest to find Cibola, the fabled seven cities of gold *(see p43)*.

Nearby Sandia Pueblo is home to around 300 people. Their festival on San Antonio's Day in June features tribal dancing *(see p37)*.

Environs

Around 16 miles (26 km) northwest of Bernalillo, Zia Pueblo is famous for its redware pottery. Visitors are welcome to buy the pottery and watercolors made in this small community.

Coronado State Monument
485 Kuaua Rd. **Tel** (505) 867-5351. **Open** 8:30am–5pm Wed–Mon. **Closed** Jan 1, Easter, Thanksgiving, Dec 25.

❹ The Turquoise Trail

P.O. Box 303, Sandia Park 87047 (505) 281-5233. **turquoisetrail.org**

Known as the Turquoise Trail, Hwy 14 offers a scenic, alternative 52-mile (84-km) route between Albuquerque and Santa Fe. Passing through the spectacular scenery of the Sandia Mountains and Cibola National Forest, it takes in the old mining towns of Golden, Madrid, and Cerillos.

Golden is the first stop in a northward direction. It is a small ghost town with ruined buildings, and an atmospheric adobe mission church, which dates back to 1830. Madrid was a busy coal-mining town in the early 20th century. Its ramshackle houses are now full of artists and New

The interior of the Trading Post store at Cerillos

Age entrepreneurs, and there are over 20 galleries, craft, and antique shops. **The Old Coal Mine Museum** in town displays a variety of old locomotives, vintage vehicles, buildings, and mining gear, and stages Victorian melodramas in the nearby Engine House Theater.

Tiny Cerillos has a 2,000-year history of mining turquoise, gold, copper, and coal. Today, its sleepy streets attract browsing tourists who enjoy the fine **Casa Grande Trading Post** with its turquoise mining museum, rock and gift shop, and petting zoo.

Old Coal Mine Museum
2846 Hwy 14, Madrid. **Tel** (505) 474-0344. **Open** 10:30am–4:30pm daily (Fri–Sun in winter).

Casa Grande Trading Post
17 Waldo St., Cerillos. **Tel** (505) 438-3008.

An old mining cottage in Madrid, midway on the Turquoise Trail

➎ Acoma Pueblo

Rte 23, off I-40. **Open** year round. **Closed** some pueblo festivals. partial. obligatory. Sky City Cultural Center (505) 470-0181; (800) 747-0181. **Open** mid-Feb–mid-Nov: 8am–7pm daily; mid-Nov–mid-Feb: 9:30am–4pm Sat & Sun.
w sccc.acomaskycity.org

The incredible beauty of Acoma Pueblo's setting on the top of a 357-ft- (107-m-) high mesa, has earned it the sobriquet "Sky City." Looking out over a stunning panorama of distant mountains, mesas, and plains, its high position afforded the Puebloan people natural defense against enemies and helped delay submission to Spanish rule. Acoma is one of the oldest

Centuries-old houses at Acoma Pueblo on a high plateau

continuously inhabited towns in the US, occupied since before the 12th century *(see p43)*. Today, fewer than 30 people live on the 70-acre (40-ha) mesa top year round; 6,000 others from local towns return to their ancestral home for festivals and celebrations.

As well as original pueblo buildings, the village features the 1629 mission church, San Esteben del Rey. There are also seven ceremonial *kivas (see p165)*. Acoma can be visited only on a guided tour, where expert guides explain its rich history.

➏ Grants

9,200. 100 N. Iron Street. (800) 748-2142. grants.org

Between the 1950s and the 1980s, Grants was famous as a center for uranium mining. Yellow rocks of the mineral were found by Navajo farmer Paddy Martinez on top of Haystack Mountain, 10 miles (16 km) from town in 1951. The industry has now declined but visitors can relive its heyday at the **New Mexico Mining Museum** – tours go underground to see a re-created mine.

Grants is well-placed along Hwy 40/Route 66 for exploring the sights in the area, such as the badlands of El Malpais National Monument.

New Mexico Mining Museum
100 N. Iron Street. **Tel** (505) 287-4802. **Open** 9am–4pm Mon–Sat. **Closed** public hols.

➐ El Morro National Monument

Tel (505) 783-4226. **Open** visitor center: Oct–late May: 9am–5pm, Jun–Sep: 9am–7pm; Hiking Trail: Oct–late May: 9am–4pm; May–Sep: 9am–6pm. **Closed** Jan 1, Dec 25.
w nps.gov/elmo

Rising dramatically from the surrounding plain, El Morro is a long sandstone cliff that slopes gently upward to a high bluff, where it suddenly drops off. Its centerpiece is the 200-ft- (60-m-) tall Inscription Rock, which is covered with more than 300 petro-glyphs and pictographs from early pueblo people, as well as some 2,000 inscriptions left by Spanish and Anglo travelers. For centuries, people were drawn to this remote spot by a pool of fresh water, formed by runoff and snowmelt, beneath the bluff. Here they carved their initials into the rock.

Among the signatures is that of the Spanish colonizer Don Juan de Oñate *(see p43)*, who, in 1605, wrote "pasó por aquí," meaning "passed by here." An easy half-mile (1-km) trail leads past the pool and the inscriptions on the rock.

Handcrafted pot from Zuni

Environs

The people of the Zuni Pueblo, 32 miles (50 km) west of El Morro, are descendants of the early mesa dwellers of the region. Today, Zuni artists are known for their fine pottery and shell mosaic jewelry. Murals depicting Zuni history can be seen in the pueblo's 17th-century mission church.

Façade of San Miguel Mission in Socorro

❽ Socorro

Road map E4. 🏔 9,000. ℹ️ 217
Fisher Ave. (575) 835-8927.
Ⓦ socorronm.gov

Socorro, meaning "aid" in
Spanish, was named by explorer
Juan de Oñate in 1598 when his
party received help from the
people of the Pilabo Pueblo,
which once stood here. The
area was resettled in the early
1800s, and it was during the
silver boom of the 1880s that
many of the town's delightful
Victorian buildings were
constructed, including those
surrounding the plaza. Just
north of here is the 1821 San
Miguel Mission, featuring
massive adobe walls,
supported by curved arches.

Environs
The **Bosque del Apache
National Wildlife Refuge**, a
renowned bird-watching area,
lies 18 miles (32 km) south of
Socorro. It attracts thousands of
migrating snow geese and
sandhill cranes in winter.

🦅 **Bosque del Apache National
Wildlife Refuge**
Hwy 1. **Tel** (575) 835-1828. **Open** daily.
Closed Jan 1, Thanksgiving, Dec 25. ♿

❾ Truth or Consequences

Road map E4. 🏔 6,500. ℹ️ 529 N.
Broadway. (575) 894-1968. ⚠️

Known by locals as "T-or-C,"
this town changed its name
from Hot Springs to Truth or
Consequences for the

10th anniversary of the game
show of the same name, held
here in 1950. The original hot
springs still exist in the form of
bath houses dotted around the
town. For centuries the thermal
springs had drawn Native
Americans to the area, notably
the famous Geronimo (see p46).
The **Geronimo Springs
Museum** has displays on local
history, including a life-sized
statue of the Apache warrior.
Hot mineral water from an
underground spring flows
down the ceramic mountains of
an elaborate fountain in the
plaza next to the museum. The
town is now a mecca for artists
and other free spirits.

Truth or Consequences is a
popular summer resort, close to
both the **Elephant Butte Lake**
and the Caballo Lake State

Parks. These are famous for
a wide range of outdoor
activities, including such water
sports as fishing, boating,
jetskiing, and windsurfing.

🏛 **Geronimo Springs Museum**
211 Main St. **Tel** (575) 894-6600.
Open 9am–5pm Mon–Sat, noon–
4pm Sun. **Closed** public hols. ♿ ♿

🦅 **Elephant Butte Lake State Park**
Off I-25. **Tel** (575) 744-5923.
Open 24 hours. Visitor center:
Open 7:30am–4pm daily. ♿ ♿ ⚠️

❿ Gila Cliff Dwellings National Monument

Road map D4.**Tel** (575) 536-9461.
Open late May–early Sep: 8am–5pm
daily; early Sep–late May: 8am–
4:30pm daily. **Closed** Jan 1, Dec 25.
🅿️ Ⓦ nps.gov/gicl

The Gila (pronounced hee-la)
Cliff Dwellings are one of the
most remote archaeological
sites in the Southwest, situated
among the piñon, juniper, and
ponderosa evergreens of the
Gila National Forest. The
dwellings occupy five natural
caves in the side of a sandstone
bluff high above the Gila River.

Hunter-gatherers and farmers
called the Tularosa Mogollon
established their 40-room
village here in the late 13th
century. The Mimbres Mogollon

Chili Peppers
The chili pepper is a potent symbol of New
Mexico. Chilies were first brought to the region
by Spanish colonists in 1598, and flourished in
the hot, dry climate. Today, some 47 sq miles
(120 sq km) are devoted to growing many
varieties of the crop, including the
chipotle, poblano, New Mexico (or
NuMex), and jalapeño peppers. New
Mexican cooking is dominated by the
chili, either fresh (green) or dried (red). The
center of the chili-growing industry is the
town of Hatch, which holds a chili festival

Wreath of red dried chilies

every September on Labor Day Weekend
(see p38). The chili has a reputation as a cure
for a range of health problems. In the 18th century, it was used to
relieve toothache. Today, capsaicin, the chemical that gives chili its
heat, is added to ointments for muscle and joint pain. The chili's high
vitamin C content (a large green chili contains as much as an orange),
is believed to help prevent colds and flu.

One of the entrances to the Gila Cliff Dwellings, situated high above the Gila River

people, famous for their abstract black-and-white pottery designs, also lived in this area *(see p42)*. The ruins are accessed by a one-mile (1.6-km) round-trip hike from the footbridge crossing the Gila River's West Fork. Allow two hours to drive to the site from Silver City as the road winds and climbs through mountains and canyons.

⓫ Silver City

Road map D5. 🏔 10,000. 🚌
ℹ️ 201 N. Hudson St. (800) 548-9378.
🏔 🌐 silvercity.org

As its name suggests, Silver City was a mining town. Located in the foothills of the Pinos Altos Mountains, the town's ornate Victorian architecture dates from its boom period between 1870 and the 1890s. In 1895, a flood washed away the city's main street, and in its place today is Big Ditch Park, an *arroyo* (or waterway) running 50-ft-(15-m-) deep through the town. This area was the site of the cabin where Billy the Kid *(see p229)* spent much of his youth.

Silver City has three defined historic districts – Chihuahua Hill, Gospel Hill, and the old business district – all containing buildings that evoke the town's Wild West boom-town past. The **Silver City Museum** is located in the beautiful 1881

H.B. Ailman House, and contains frontier-era memorabilia, while the **Western New Mexico University Museum** holds the Southwest's largest collection of Mimbres pottery.

Silver City is a good base for exploring the surrounding region. The nearby forest is home to elk, deer, and bear, and there are several hiking trails and picnic areas.

🏛 Silver City Museum
312 W. Broadway. **Tel** (575) 538-5921.
Open 9am–4:30pm Tue–Fri,
10am–4pm Sat & Sun. **Closed** public hols. ♿ 🌐 silvercitymuseum.org

🏛 Western New Mexico University Museum
1000 W. College Ave. **Tel** (575) 538-6386. **Open** 9am–4:30pm Mon–Fri,
10am–4pm Sat & Sun. **Closed** public hols. ♿ 🌐 wnmumuseum.org

⓬ Deming

Road map D5. 🏔 14,500. 🚆 🚌
ℹ️ 800 E. Pine St. (575) 546-2674. 🏔
🌐 demingchamber.com

The town of Deming lies 60 miles (96 km) west of Las Cruces. The Deming Luna Mimbres Museum contains excellent pieces of Mimbres pottery, frontier artifacts, and a fine gem and mineral display. Rockhounding (amateur rock and mineral collecting) takes place in **Rockhound State Park** where jasper, agate, and other minerals can be found. The town is also known for its Great American Duck Race, run every August *(see p37)*.

🏕 Rockhound State Park
Highway 141. **Tel** (575) 546 6182.
Open 7am–sunset daily. 🅿️ ♿

The H.B. Ailman House, home to the Silver City Museum

Ruins tucked inside a sandstone cave, Gila Cliffs Dwellings National Monument ▶

Remains of the 1865 Fort Selden in Mesilla Valley

⑬ Fort Selden State Monument

Road map E5. **Tel** (575) 526-8911. **Open** 8:30am–5pm Wed–Mon. 🅿 ♿

This adobe fort was built in 1865 to protect settlers and railroad construction crews in the Mesilla Valley from attacks by Apaches and outlaws. Its buildings, now in ruins, once housed four companies of the 125th Infantry, a black infantry unit known as the Buffalo Soldiers. Douglas MacArthur, who was to command Allied troops in the Pacific in World War II, lived here for two years as a boy in the 1880s when his father was post commander. The fort was abandoned in 1891. Living history demonstrations are sometimes offered on weekends, where rangers in period uniforms portray 19th-century army life. There are also exhibits on frontier life in the visitor center.

Sentinel statue at Fort Selden

⑭ Las Cruces

Road map E5. 🅰 100,000. ℹ 211 N. Water St. (575) 541-2444. 🅦 lascrucescvb.org

Spreading out at the foot of the Organ Mountains, *Las Cruces*, or The Crosses, was named for the graves of early settlers ambushed here by the Apache in 1787 and again in 1830. It has always been a crossroads – of frontier trails, of the railroads, and now two Interstate Highways (10 and 25). Today, it is New Mexico's second-largest city and a busy manufacturing and farming center, as well as the home of New Mexico State University.

While the town is best used as a base for exploring the region, there are a number of interesting museums to be found here. They include the **Branigan Cultural Complex**, which houses a Cultural Center with a historical museum and fine arts museum. Tours can also be arranged here of the nearby Bicentennial Log Cabin, a late 19th-century pioneer house of hand-hewn timber furnished with period antiques and artifacts.

🏛 Branigan Cultural Complex

Downtown Mall, 501 N. Main St. **Tel** (575) 541-2155. **Open** Cultural Center and Fine Arts Museum: 9am–4:30pm Tue–Sat. **Closed** public hols. ♿

⑮ Mesilla

Road map E5. 🅰 2,250. ℹ 2231 Avenida de Mesilla (575) 524-3262. 🅦 oldmesilla.org

This town was established in 1850 by a group of residents who preferred to remain in Mexican territory, when most of New Mexico came under American rule. However, with the Gadsden Purchase of 1854

(*see p45*), Mesilla became part of the United States.

Today, Mesilla exudes the atmosphere of a late 19th-century frontier town, especially around the historic plaza. It was here, in Mesilla's former courthouse, that Billy the Kid (*see p229*) was sentenced to hang in 1881. **The Gadsden Museum** contains exhibits on local history and cultures.

🏛 Gadsden Museum

Hwy 28 & Boutz Rd. **Tel** (575) 526-6293. **Open** by appointment only. **Closed** public hols. 🅿 ♿

Billy the Kid gift shop in the 19th-century town of Mesilla

⑯ El Paso

Road map E5. 🅰 675,000. ✈ 🚃 🚌 ℹ 1 Civic Center Plaza (915) 534-0600; (800) 351-6024. 🅦 visitelpaso.com

Large and sprawling, El Paso, Texas, is a key entry point to New Mexico and the Southwest. Facing El Paso on the other side of the Rio Grande is its Mexican sister town of Ciudad Juárez. They share the border, which was established in 1963 after disputes concerning the Rio Grande had been resolved. From the city, Interstate I-10 travels north to Las Cruces and west across southern Arizona. The Amtrak train *Sunset Limited* (*see p288*) stops at El Paso three times a week.

The Spanish named their early settlement here *El Paso del Norte* (Northern Pass) in the late

The 1692 Socorro Mission on El Paso's Mission Trail

16th century. It was a stopping place on the famous King's Highway *(Camino Real, see p29)*, which linked Mexico to Spain's northern territories. The city's history as a major hub is reflected today in its typically Southwestern mix of Native American, Hispanic, and European cultures.

El Paso has a series of outstanding mission churches, including the Ysleta and the Socorro, which both date from 1692, while the lovely Chapel San Elizario was built in 1789. **Mission Socorro** combines Native and Spanish styles, with *vigas* (wooden ceiling beams).

El Paso's western heritage is further reflected in its links with the famous outlaw Billy the Kid *(see p229)*, who visited the town in 1876 to get his partner out of jail. Today, El Paso is a center for Western wear, with many stores selling cowboy boots and hats.

Mission Socorro
328 S. Nevarez Rd. **Tel** (915) 859-7718. **Open** 10:30am–3pm Mon–Sat. 🅿️ ♿ 📷 obligatory.

❶ White Sands National Monument

Road map E4. **Tel** (575) 479-6124. Visitor Center: **Open** 8am–7pm daily (to 5pm winter); Dunes Drive: 7am–sunset daily. **Closed** Dec 25. 🅿️ ♿ 📷 🅆 nps.gov/whsa

The glistening dunes of the White Sands National Monument rise up from the Tularosa Basin at the northern end of the Chihuahuan Desert. It is the world's largest gypsum dune field, covering around 300 sq miles (800 sq km). Gypsum is a water-soluble mineral, rarely found as sand. But here, with no drainage outlet to the sea, the sediment washed by the rain into the basin becomes trapped. As the rain evaporates, dry lakes form, and strong winds blow the gypsum up into the vast fields of rippling dunes.

Visitors can explore White Sands by car on the Dunes Drive, a 16-mile (26-km) loop. Four signposted trails lead from points along the way, including the wheelchair-accessible Interdune Boardwalk. Year-round ranger-led walks introduce visitors to the dunes' flora and fauna. Only plants that grow quickly enough not to be buried survive, such as the soaptree yucca. Most of the animals are nocturnal, and include coyotes and porcupines.

The park is surrounded by the White Sands Missile Range. For safety, the park and road leading to it (Hwy 70) may shut for up to 2 hours during testing. **White Sands Missile Range Museum** displays many of the missiles tested here.

🏛 White Sands Missile Range Museum
US 70, 25 m (40 km) E. of Las Cruces. **Tel** (575) 647-1116. **Open** 8am–4pm Mon–Fri, 10am–3pm Sat. **Closed** Sun, pub. hols. ♿ 🅆 wsmr-history.org

Soaptree yucca plants growing at White Sands National Monument

Colorful shops along Ruidoso's attractive main street

⓲ Alamogordo

Road map E4. 🏔 31,300. ✈ 🛈 1301 N. White Sands Blvd. (575) 437-6120; (800) 826-0294. 🅦 **alamogordo.com**

Alamogordo was established as a railroad town in 1898 by two New York entrepreneurs, Charles and John Eddy. Its wide streets are lined with cottonwood trees, which reflect its origins and are at the root of its name – Alamogordo means "fat cottonwood" in Spanish. Located at the foot of the Sacramento Mountains, the town was a sleepy backwater until World War II, when construction of the nearby Holloman Air Force Base sparked its development as a major defense research center.

The town is only 13 miles (21 km) from White Sands National Monument (*see p227*) and offers many opportunities for such outdoor activities as hiking, biking, and golf, especially in the Lincoln National Forest on Alamogordo's eastern border. In town the **New Mexico Museum of Space History** is a fascinating museum housed in a golden-glass, cube-shaped building. The museum focuses on the history of the space race, with exhibits detailing living conditions inside a space station, a full-size replica of Sputnik, the first space satellite, and a simulated walk in space to repair the Hubble Space Telescope. Another simulator offers the

Launch vehicle, Museum of Space History

chance to land the space shuttle. The Space Hall also includes the IMAX™ Dome, a large-screen theater.

🏛 New Mexico Museum of Space History
Scenic Drive. **Tel** (575) 437-2840; (877) 333-6589. **Open** 9am–5pm daily. **Closed** Thanksgiving, Dec 25. 🅿 ♿ 🅦 **nmspacemuseum.org**

⓳ Cloudcroft

Road map E4. 🏔 700. 🛈 Cloudcroft Chamber of Commerce, Hwy 82 (575) 682-2733. 🅰 🅦 **cloudcroft.net**

The picturesque mountain town of Cloudcroft was established in 1898 as a center for the lumber trade. Perched at 8,650 ft (2,600 m) in the Sacramento Mountains, the village soon became a favorite vacation spot for those escaping the summer heat of the valley below. Cloudcroft remains a popular resort, with its summer population more than doubling the number of year-round residents. Burro Avenue, running parallel to the main highway, looks much as it did at the turn of the 20th century with its rustic timber buildings (many are quaint gift shops). Surrounded by Lincoln National Forest, the town offers many outdoor sports – mountain biking, hunting, fishing, skiing, and golf.

⓴ Ruidoso

Road map E4. 🏔 8,000. 🛈 720 Sudderth Drive (575) 257-7395. 🅰 🅦 **ruidoso.net**

Nestled high in the Sacramento Mountains, surrounded by cool pine forest, Ruidoso is one of New Mexico's fastest growing resorts. Sudderth Drive is the long main street lined with shops, art galleries, cafés, and restaurants. Here, specialty shops sell everything from candles to cowboy boots.

Outdoor activities are the area's major attraction, with hiking, horseback riding, and fishing. There are several golf courses including the **Links at Sierra Blanca**, a top-rated 18-hole course. Northwest of the town is **Ski Apache**. Owned and operated by the Mescalero Apache Tribe, it is famous for its warm-weather powder snow. The town is best known for horse racing. Quarter horse (fast over a quarter of a mile) and thoroughbred racing at **Ruidoso Downs Racetrack**. The track hosts the All American Futurity, held each Labor Day (the first Monday in September). The world's richest quarter horse race, it has prize money in excess of $2 million. The Ruidoso Downs Racehorse Hall of Fame exhibits racing memorabilia. The **Hubbard Museum of the American West** contains Western memorabilia, the heart of which is a collection of more than 10,000 pieces assembled by a wealthy New Jersey horsewoman, Anne Stradling

Billy the Kid

When he died, Billy the Kid was one of the Old West's most notorious outlaws. Born Henry McCarty in 1859, it is believed he changed his name to William Bonney in 1877, when he killed his first victim in Arizona.

Billy fled to Lincoln, where he was hired by John Tunstall and Alexander McSween, who had set up a store competing with one run by Lawrence Murphy and James Dolan. In February 1878, when Dolan's men murdered Tunstall, Billy helped to form the Regulators, who set out to get justice. The Lincoln County War followed, culminating with a violent battle in July. Billy escaped, but was captured by Sheriff Pat Garrett two years later and returned to Lincoln to be hung. Once again, however, he escaped.

Billy was eventually shot, by Garrett, at Fort Sumner on July 14, 1881. In spite of his violent life, Billy was a local hero. His story and deeds are memorialized in the little town of Lincoln.

Wild West outlaw, Billy the Kid

One of the historic buildings along Lincoln's main street

㉑ Lincoln

Road map E4. 100. Hwy 380E Lincoln (575) 653-4372. **Open** 8:30am–4:30pm daily. **Closed** public hols. **nmmonuments.org**

The peacefulness of this small town, surrounded by the beautiful countryside of the Capitan Mountains, belies its violent past. It was the center of the 1878 Lincoln County War, a battle between rival ranchers and merchants involving the legendary Billy the Kid. In those days, Lincoln County covered one-quarter of the state, and Lincoln itself was the county seat.

Lincoln is now a state monument, with 11 buildings kept as they were in the late 1800s. At the Lincoln County Courthouse you can see where Billy the Kid was held, and the bullet hole in the wall from his escape. Tunstall Store has its shelves stocked with original 19th-century merchandise. The Historic Lincoln Visitor Center & Museum has displays on the Apache people, the early Hispanic settlers, and the Buffalo Soldiers all-black regiment from Fort Stanton, as well as the Lincoln County War.

(1913–92). Formerly known as the Museum of the Horse, its artifacts range from fine art to horse-drawn carriages. Outside is the fabulous *Free Spirits at Noisy Water* (1995), a monument of seven larger-than-life-sized horses by local artist Dave McGary (b.1958). Every October, the town celebrates life in the Old West with the Lincoln County Cowboy Symposium, which features country music and dancing, celebrity roping, and a chuck wagon cook-off.

Set on a high mesa a few miles north at Alto is the **Spencer Theater for the Performing Arts**, a state-of-the-art venue for theater, music, and dance. Built by Albuquerque architect Antoine

Predock in 1997, this sandstone building has a spectacular mountain backdrop.

Links at Sierra Blanca
105 Sierra Blanca Dr. **Tel** (575) 258-5330.

Ski Apache
skiapache.com

Ruidoso Downs Racetrack
Hwy 70. **Tel** (575) 378-4431.
Open May–early Sep.

Hubbard Museum of the American West
26301 Hwy 70 West. **Tel** (575) 378-4142. **Open** 10am–4:30pm daily.
Closed Thanksgiving, Dec 25.
hubbardmuseum.org

Spencer Theater for the Performing Arts
108 Spencer Rd. **Tel** (575) 336-4800; (888) 818-7872.

The bronze monument, *Free Spirits at Noisy Water* (1995), at the Hubbard Museum of the American West

㉒ Carlsbad Caverns National Park

Located in the remote southeastern corner of New Mexico, Carlsbad Caverns National Park protects one of the world's largest cave systems. Geological forces carved out this complex of chambers, and their decorations began to be formed around 500,000 years ago when dripping water deposited drops of the crystalized mineral calcite. Native pictographs near the Natural Entrance indicate that they had been visited by Native peoples, but it was cowboy Jim White who brought them to national attention, after exploring them in 1901. The caverns were made a national park in 1930, and a United Nations World Heritage Site in 1995, one of 21 in the US.

Underground Lunchroom
A paved section of the cavern is home to a popular underground diner, a kitsch souvenir store, and restrooms.

Natural Entrance

Visitor Information Center

King's Palace Tour
This tour takes in the deepest cave open to the public, 830 ft (250 m) below ground.

The Boneyard is a complex maze of dissolved limestone rock.

Queens Chamber and Papoose Room

Doll's Theater
This small cave is named for its size. The Doll's Theater resembles a fairy grotto, filled with fine, luminous soda-straw formations.

The Big Room
A self-guided tour takes in the 14-acre (5.6-ha) Big Room and passes features such as the Bottomless Pit.

Rock of Ages

Bottomless Pit

VISITORS' CHECKLIST

Practical Information
Road map F5. 3225 National Parks Hwy, Carlsbad. **Tel** (575) 785-2232; (877) 444-6777 (tour reservations). **Open** late May–early Sep: 8am–4pm daily; early Sep–late May: 8am–3:30pm (Natural Entrance) call for last entry times. **Closed** Dec 25. ⚡ partial. 📷 W nps.gov/cave

Transport
✈ to Carlsbad. 🚌 to White's City.

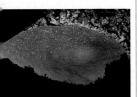

Bat Cave
Most summer evenings at dusk, clouds of free-tailed bats emerge from the bat cave to cross the desert in search of food.

Doll's Theater

Painted Grotto

```
0 meters        100
0 yards         100
```

Tours
— Big Room route
— Natural Entrance route
— King's Palace tour (Ranger guided only)

Butterfly and lobelia flowers, Living Desert State Park

㉓ Carlsbad

Road map: F5. ⛰ 26,000. 🛈 302 S. Canal St. (575) 887- 6516. 🏔 W carlsbadchamber.com

The town of Carlsbad is located just 20 miles (32 km) northeast of Carlsbad Caverns National Park. There are plenty of hotels as well as opportunities for outdoor activities. (Whites City also has accommodations; *see p243*.) The Pecos River winds through town, there are three lakes, and fishing, boating, and water-skiing are popular pastimes. At the northern edge of town, the Living Desert State Park has exhibits focusing on the ecology of the Chihuahuan Desert (*see p24*).

Roswell's Alien Zone symbol

㉔ Roswell

Road map F4. ⛰ 48,300. 🛈 912 N. Main St. (575) 624-6860. **Open** 8am–5pm Mon–Fri.
W roswellnm.com

Once a small ranching town, Roswell is now a byword for aliens and UFOs, due to the Roswell Incident. The **International UFO Museum and Research Center** is devoted to the investigation of visitors from outer space and features an extensive collection of newspaper clippings, photographs, and maps of the crash site. A 70-minute film contains over 400 interviews with people connected to the crash.

Roswell's highly respected **Museum and Art Center** houses a collection of 2,000 artifacts on the history of the American West. The fascinating Robert H. Goddard Collection details 11 years of his experiments (*see p191*).

🏛 **International UFO Museum and Research Center**
114 N. Main St. **Tel** (575) 625-9495. **Open** 9am–5pm daily. ⚡ W roswellufomuseum.com

🏛 **Roswell Museum and Art Center**
100 W. 11th St. **Tel** (575) 624-6744. **Open** 9am–5pm daily (from 1pm Sun). **Closed** Jan 1, Thanksgiving, Dec 25. ⚡ W roswellmuseum.org

The Roswell Incident

Near midnight on July 4, 1947 an unidentified airborne object crash-landed during a storm in the Capitan Mountains, 75 miles (120 km) northwest of town. Jim Ragsdale was camping nearby and claims to have seen a flash and a craft, 20 ft (6 m) in diameter, hurtling through the trees and the bodies of four "little people," with skin like snakeskin. However, Ragsdale did not tell his story until 1995.

The US Air Force issued a statement that a flying saucer had been recovered, and the story spread around the world. By July 9, however, they said it was just a weather balloon. Witnesses were allegedly sworn to secrecy, fueling rumors of a cover-up and alien conspiracy theories to this day.

Officers examine "alien" material

TRAVELERS' NEEDS

WHERE TO STAY

The Southwest has a long history of hospitality that is reflected in the wide variety of accommodations on offer. There is a wealth of options – from luxurious five-star resorts to simple rustic lodges. Guests have a choice of modern hotels, historic or cozy bed and breakfasts (B&Bs) or inns, convenient motels, or fully equipped apartments. For those seeking Western-style adventure, there are dude ranches, many of which provide luxurious lodgings and horseback riding. Across the range, all establishments are likely to offer private bathrooms and clean, comfortable rooms. Las Vegas hotels are noted for their themes and size, and have widely varying prices, which fluctuate depending on the number of rooms vacant and whether it is mid-week or a weekend. Across the rest of the region, prices also tend to vary according to the season.

Traditional adobe architecture of the Hotel Santa Fe façade (see p242)

Hotel Classifications

The tourist industry throughout the Southwest is recognized for its quality lodgings. A guideline for travelers is the diamond rating system of the **American and Canadian Automobile Associations** (AAA and CAA). Every accommodation, from the one-diamond motel to the five-diamond resort hotel, is rated for service, cleanliness, and the facilities offered. AAA members also benefit from discounts when they book in advance.

Taxes

Accommodation tax varies across the region as it is charged by both state and city or county governments. Expect to pay between 10 and 14 percent. Prices provided in the hotel listings on pages 236–243 include taxes.

Luxury Hotels

In the Southwest, hotels come in every shape and size. There are historic showplaces, such as Grand Canyon's El Tovar (see p236), originally built in the early 1900s to impress East Coast investors and prove that the Southwest was an exciting tourist destination. Today, some of the most lavish hotels in the US are located in the region, from the extravagant, themed mega-resorts of Las Vegas (see pp238–40) to the Wigwam Resort in Phoenix (see p237), with its three championship 18-hole golf courses, tennis courts, and gourmet dining. The area around Phoenix and Southern Arizona is famous for both its luxury and golf resorts.

Chain Hotels and Motels

For the most part, travelers can count on efficient service, moderate prices, and comfortable (if bland) surroundings at a chain hotel. The two most popular chains are **Best Western** and **Comfort Inn**. Motels provide rooms that are usually accessible from the parking area. They are often the only option in remote areas, and can vary from nostalgic Route 66 places (see pp54–55) to such bargain lodgings as **Motel 6**.

Historic Inns and Bed and Breakfasts

There are many excellent inns and B&Bs across the Southwest. Inns tend to be larger, with more spacious public areas and a dining room. B&Bs are usually noted for their more homey atmosphere. Both inns and B&Bs may be found in restored or reconstructed historic buildings, and many are located in charming Victorian houses in historic towns. These lodgings pride themselves on providing a warm welcome and friendly service. Many are furnished with antiques or decorated with the works of local artisans. Some have gardens where guests are welcome to relax or even dine. There are **Bed and Breakfast and Inn Associations** in each state that can help guests select and make bookings.

Western Hotels and Dude Ranches

If you want to indulge your "Old West" fantasies, there are plenty of historic hotels in which to do so. Between 1880 and 1920, Western towns gained prestige through the quality and grandeur of their hotels, and many built during this time boast ornate decor. Many of these establishments have been restored and offer great settings for a vacation. Durango's Strater Hotel (see p241), for example, is a historic hotel and a museum. Dude ranches, such as White

Imposing exterior of The Phoenician resort in Scottsdale (*see p238*)

Stallion Ranch located between Phoenix and Tuscon (*see p238*), offer visitors the chance to experience Western life. They first appeared in the 1920s – the name "dude" is a colloquialism for a city-dweller unfamiliar with life on the range. Some offer relaxing vacations that include leisurely horseback rides while others are working ranches where guests participate in such activities as cattle roundups. Meals, accommodations, and horses are usually included in the price. Arizona and Colorado have **Dude Ranch Associations** to help you find the perfect Western vacation.

National Park Fees

An entrance fee is charged at many – but not all – state and national parks. The national park fee is usually charged per vehicle and must be paid separately to access hotels and restaurants within national park areas. If you plan to visit several national parks during your trip, consider buying an $80 annual pass. See the **National Park Service** website for more details. Fees for entry to state parks are not included in national park passes.

Campgrounds and RV Parks

Campgrounds for both tents and RVs (recreational vehicles) are found all over the Southwest – those located in national parks are especially popular. The **National Forest Service** provides information on forest campgrounds, which range from extremely basic to those that have running water and limited RV hookups.

Recommended Hotels

The lodging options listed on pages 236–43 have been selected across a wide price range for their excellent facilities, good location, and value. From rustic, family-owned inns and opulent resorts to historic hotels soaked in atmosphere, these venues run the gamut across all price levels and environments.

Luxury options offer the region's very best in service and amenities. The Southwest is awash in noteworthy historic hotels, many of which date back to the 19th century. For a more intimate experience, consider a cozy, atmospheric Inn or B&B. Budget lodgings, ranging from casual hostels to clean yet non-descript motels and motor lodges, help to keep vacation costs down. If traveling with family, consider the region's world-class resorts, several of which include activity packages.

For the best of the best, look out for venues labeled as DK Choice. These have been highlighted in recognition of an exceptional feature – a stunning location, breathtaking views, notable history, inviting atmosphere and service, excellent amenities, or a combination of these.

DIRECTORY

Hotel Classifications

American Automobile Assocation (AAA)
W aaa.com

Canadian Automobile Association (CAA)
W caa.ca

Chain Hotels and Motels

Best Western
Tel (800) 528-1234.
W bestwestern.com

Comfort Inn
Tel (800) 221-2222.
W comfortinn.com

Motel 6
Tel (800) 466-8356.
W motel6.com

Historic Inns and Bed and Breakfasts

Arizona Association of B&B Inns
Tel (800) 752-1912.
W arizona-bed-breakfast.com

B&B Innkeepers of Colorado
Tel (800) 265-7696.
W innsofcolorado.org

B&B Inns of Utah
W bbiu.org

New Mexico B&B Association
Tel (800) 661-6649.
W nmbba.org

Western Hotels and Dude Ranches

Arizona Dude Ranch Association
Tel (520) 823-4277.
W azdra.com

Colorado Dude and Guest Ranch Association
Tel (866) 942-3472.
W coloradoranch.com

Campgrounds and RV Parks

National Forest Service
Tel (877) 444-6777.
W recreation.gov

National Park Service
W nps.gov

Where to Stay

Grand Canyon and Northern Arizona

CAMP VERDE: Camp Verde Comfort Inn $
Budget   Map B4
340 N. Goswick Way, AZ 86322
Tel *(928) 567-9000*
W choicehotels.com
Near Montezuma Castle, this is a good alternative to pricier hotels in Sedona or Jerome.

COTTONWOOD: Best Western Cottonwood Inn $
Budget   Map B3
993 S. Main St, AZ 86326
Tel *(928) 634-5575*
W bestwesterncottonwoodinn.com
A comfortable motel, Cottonwood Inn has a friendly atmosphere and serves great breakfasts.

FLAGSTAFF: Hotel Monte Vista $
Historic   Map C3
100 N. San Francisco St, AZ 86001
Tel *(928) 779-6971*
W hotelmontevista.com
This 1926 hotel has an illustrious past and rooms named for Hollywood stars who stayed here.

FLAGSTAFF: Weatherford Hotel $
Historic   Map C3
23 North Leroux St, AZ 86001
Tel *(928) 779-1919*
W weatherfordhotel.com
In an 1897 sandstone building with a veranda, this elegant hotel is decorated in period style.

FLAGSTAFF: DoubleTree by Hilton Flagstaff $$
Luxury   Map C3
1175 W. Route 66, AZ 86001
Tel *(928) 773-8888*
W flagstaff.doubletree.com
A modern, smart hotel situated near downtown.

FLAGSTAFF: Little America Hotel $$
Resort   Map C3
2515 E. Butler Ave, AZ 86004
Tel *(928) 779-7900*
W flagstaff.littleamerica.com
Set in pine forest, this hotel has luxurious rooms and suites, a hot tub and outdoor pool.

GRAND CANYON: Bright Angel Lodge $
Historic   Map B3
Grand Canyon Village,
South Rim, AZ 86023
Tel *(928) 297-2757*
W grandcanyonlodges.com
These log-and-stone cabins were designed by famed architect Mary Elizabeth Colter in 1935.

GRAND CANYON: Grand Canyon Lodge $
Historic   Map B3
North Rim, AZ 86052
Tel *(877) 386-4383*
W grandcanyonlodgenorth.com
This rustic lodge has motel-style rooms in the woods, and timber cabins on the Canyon rim's edge.

GRAND CANYON: Maswik Lodge $
Historic   Map B3
Grand Canyon Village,
South Rim, AZ 86023
Tel *(928) 297-2757*
W grandcanyonlodges.com
A family-friendly, modern lodge set amid pine forest.

GRAND CANYON: Phantom Ranch $
Historic   Map B3
North Kaibab Trail, AZ 86023
Tel *(303) 297-2757*
W grandcanyonlodges.com
The only lodge below the Canyon rim, Phantom Ranch has wood-and-stone cabins and

> **Price Guide**
> Prices are for a standard double room per night, inclusive of service charges and any additional taxes.
>
> | $ | up to $150 |
> | $$ | $150–$250 |
> | $$$ | over $250 |

dormitories. It is accessible only by mule or foot, or by rafting the Colorado River.

GRAND CANYON: El Tovar Hotel $$
Historic   Map B3
Grand Canyon Village,
South Rim, AZ 86023
Tel *(928) 638-2631*
W grandcanyonlodges.com
The design of this luxurious landmark lodge incorporates natural stone and Douglas fir.

JEROME: Ghost City Inn Bed & Breakfast $
Inn/B&B   Map B4
541 N. Main St, AZ, 86331
Tel *(928) 634-4678*
W ghostcityinn.com
This elegant 1890s inn is in a former miners' boarding house.

LAKE HAVASU CITY: Hampton Inn $
Inn/B&B   Map A4
245 London Bridge Rd, AZ 86403
Tel *(928) 855-4071*
W hamptoninn.com
The modern Hampton Inn boasts well-equipped rooms. Some balconies offer lake views.

LAKE HAVASU CITY: Heat $$
Luxury   Map A4
1420 McCulloch Blvd, AZ 86403
Tel *(888) 898-4328*
W heathotel.com
The rooms at this stylish, modern hotel offer views of London Bridge and Bridgewater Channel.

PAGE: Best Western Plus at Lake Powell $
Budget   Map C2
208 N. Lake Powell Blvd, AZ 86040
Tel *(928) 645-5988*
W bestwesternarizona.com
This hotel with views of Glen Canyon Dam and Vermillion Cliffs has a large outdoor pool.

PAGE: Courtyard by Marriott $$
Resort   Map C2
600 Clubhouse Dr, AZ 86040
Tel *(928) 645-5000*
W courtyard.com
Surrounded by Lake Powell National Championship Golf Course, this modern hotel has comfortable rooms.

Stone cabin at the Phantom Ranch, nestled at the bottom of the Grand Canyon

Enchantment Resort in Sedona, against a backdrop of the the Boynton Canyon

SEDONA: Amara Resort $$
Resort   Map C3
100 Amara Lane, AZ 86336
Tel *(928) 282-4828*
W amararesort.com
A chic boutique resort and spa with a warm ambience and excellent service. Swim in the saltwater pool or star-gaze by the fire pit, sipping a glass of wine.

SEDONA: Cozy Cactus $$
Inn/B&B   Map C3
80 Canyon Circle Dr, AZ 86351
Tel *(928) 284-0082*
W cozycactus.com
Family-friendly and close to hiking trails, Cozy Cactus offers stunning views of the red rock landscape.

SEDONA: Enchantment Resort $$$
Resort   Map C3
525 Boynton Canyon Rd, AZ 86336
Tel *(928) 282-2900*
W enchantmentresort.com
The *casitas* here have luxurious rooms and suites with Native American-inspired decor.

WAHWEAP: Lake Powell Resort $
Resort   Map C2
100 Lakeshore Dr, AZ 86040
Tel *(928) 645-2433*
W lakepowell.com
Overlooking Wahweap Marina, this lodging has upscale rooms with balconies and patios.

WILLIAMS: Grand Canyon Railway Hotel $$
Historic   Map B3
235 N. Grand Canyon Blvd, AZ 86046
Tel *(928) 635-4010*
W thetrain.com
This elegant hotel adjoins the century-old railroad terminus.

DK Choice
WINSLOW: La Posada $
Historic   Map C3
303 E. Route 66, AZ 86047
Tel *(928) 289-4366*
W laposada.org
This magnificent former railroad hotel, designed in 1929 by Southwestern architect Mary Elizabeth Colter to resemble a Spanish hacienda, was a famous retreat for Hollywood stars, including John Wayne and Bob Hope. Rooms have traditional Native American and Hispanic decor. Not as luxurious as its modern counterparts, but a unique experience.

Phoenix and Southern Arizona

APACHE JUNCTION: Best Western Apache Junction Express Inn $
B&B   Map C4
1101 W. Apache Trail, AZ 85120
Tel *(480) 982-9200*
W bestwestern.com
Comfortable rooms, an outdoor pool, and mountain views feature at this inn near the Apache Trail.

BISBEE: Copper Queen Hotel $
Historic   Map C5
11 Howell Ave, AZ 85603
Tel *(520) 432-2216*
W copperqueen.com
This early-1900s hotel has antique-filled rooms decorated with period wallpaper.

BISBEE: Shady Dell $
Historic   Map C5
1 Douglas Rd, AZ 85603
Tel *(520) 432-3567*
W theshadydell.com
Nine 1950s travel trailers with period furnishings offer a vintage experience in the Mule Mountains.

DOUGLAS: The Gadsden Hotel $
Historic   Map D5
1046 G Ave, AZ 85607
Tel *(520) 364-4481*
W hotelgadsden.com
An opulent lobby with a Tiffany stained-glass mural features at this 1920s-style hotel.

DRAGOON: Triangle T Guest Ranch $$
Historic   Map C5
I-10 exit 318, 4190 Dragoon Rd, AZ 85609
Tel *(520) 586-7533*
W triangletguestranch.com
These rustic cabins are set amid stunning rock formations.

PHOENIX: Clarendon Hotel & Suites $
Budget   Map B4
401 W. Clarendon Ave, AZ 85013
Tel *(602) 252-7363*
W theclarendon.net
This trendy hotel in the business district offers a stylish pool and rooftop deck.

PHOENIX: Quality Inn & Suites $
Budget   Map B4
202 E. McDowell Rd, AZ 85004
Tel *(602) 528-9100*
W qualityinn.com
A comfortable downtown base with an outdoor pool.

PHOENIX: Arizona Biltmore Resort & Spa $$
Resort   Map B4
2400 E. Missouri Ave, AZ 85016
Tel *(602) 955-6600*
W arizonabiltmore.com
Enjoy lawn chess or golf at this 1930s resort, known for its Frank Lloyd Wright-inspired architecture.

PHOENIX: Arizona Grand Resort $$
Resort   Map B4
7777 S. Pointe Pkwy, AZ 85044
Tel *(602) 438-9000*
W arizonagrandresort.com
This family-friendly resort offers golf, tennis, horseback riding, and a waterpark with a wave pool.

PHOENIX: Hotel Palomar Phoenix $$
Luxury   Map B4
2 E. Jefferson St, 85004
Tel *(602) 253-6633*
W hotelpalomar-phoenix.com
A contemporary hotel located at the CityScape entertainment hub.

PHOENIX: The Wigwam Resort $$
Resort   Map B4
300 E. Wigwam Blvd, Litchfield Pkwy, AZ 85340
Tel *(623) 935-3811*
W wigwamresort.com
A sprawling complex of elegant *casitas*, a spa, and four pools.

DK Choice
SCOTTSDALE: Hotel Valley Ho $$
Luxury   Map B4
6850 E. Main St, AZ 85251
Tel *(480) 248-2000*
W hotelvalleyho.com
Built in 1956 and once frequented by Humphrey Bogart and Marilyn Monroe, Hotel Valley Ho has retro-chic rooms, a yoga-Pilates studio, and a pool. Close to downtown, it is a short walk from shops, restaurants, and art galleries.

**SCOTTSDALE: Fairmont
Scottsdale Princess** $$$
Resort Map B4
7575 E. Princess Dr, AZ 85255
Tel *(480) 585-4848*
W fairmont.com
A retreat with Spanish-style
architecture and luxurious rooms.

**SCOTTSDALE: Hyatt Regency
Scottsdale Resort & Spa at
Gainey Ranch** $$$
Resort Map B4
*7500 E. Doubletree Ranch Rd,
AZ 85258*
Tel *(480) 444-1234*
W scottsdale.hyatt.com
Exquisite rooms, ten pools, luxury
spa, and golf course feature here.

**SCOTTSDALE: The
Phoenician** $$$
Resort Map B4
6000 E. Camelback Rd, AZ 85251
Tel *(480) 941-8200*
W thephoenician.com
Superb amenities and numerous
dining options are to be enjoyed
at this world-famous resort.

**TOMBSTONE: Landmark
Lookout Lodge** $
Inn/B&B Map C5
781 N. Hwy 80, AZ 85638
Tel *(520) 457-2223*
W lookoutlodgeaz.com
A convenient place to stay for
exploring the town's key sights.

**TOMBSTONE: Silver Nugget
Bed & Breakfast** $
Inn/B&B Map C5
520 E. Allen St, AZ 85638
Tel *(520) 457-9223*
W tombstone1880.com
This historic B&B overlooks dusty
Allen Street, the site of the
famous gunfight at the OK Corral.

TUCSON: Hotel Congress $
Budget Map C5
311 E. Congress St, AZ 85701
Tel *(520) 622-8848*
W hotelcongress.com
Hotel Congress has retro rooms,
plus multiple bars and restaurants.

TUCSON: Lodge on the Desert $
Historic Map C5
306 N. Alvernon Way, AZ 85711
Tel *(520) 325-2000*
W lodgeonthedesert.com
This urban oasis dates back to 1936
and has hacienda-style rooms.

**TUCSON: Windmill Suites at
St. Philip's Plaza** $
Inn/B&B Map C5
4250 N. Campbell Ave, AZ 85718
Tel *(520) 577-0007*
W windmillinns.com
Two-room suites are offered at
this comfortable B&B.

**TUCSON: Hacienda del Sol
Ranch Resort** $$
Resort Map C5
5601 N. Hacienda del Sol Rd, AZ 85718
Tel *(520) 299-1501*
W haciendadelsol.com
The rooms at this luxurious resort
have warm Southwestern tones
and Spanish Colonial design.

**TUCSON: Royal Elizabeth
Bed & Breakfast Inn** $$
Inn/B&B Map C5
204 S. Scott Ave, AZ 85701
Tel *(520) 670-9022*
W royalelizabeth.com
This meticulously restored 1878
adobe mansion boasts original
antiques and beautiful woodwork.

**TUCSON: Tanque Verde
Guest Ranch** $$
Resort Map C5
14301 E. Speedway Blvd, AZ 85748
Tel *(520) 296-6275*
W tvgr.com
Enjoy cowboy-style breakfasts
and horseback riding at this
1868 ranch at the base of the
Rincon Mountains.

**TUCSON: White
Stallion Ranch** $$
Historic Map C5
9251 W. Twin Peaks Rd, AZ 85743
Tel *(520) 297-0252*
W wsranch.com
See longhorn cattle and weekly
rodeos at this working ranch.

Las Vegas

**BOULDER CITY: El Rancho
Boulder Motel** $
Budget Map A3
725 Nevada Hwy, NV 89005
Tel *(702) 293-1085*
W elranchoboulder.com
This family-run motel has rooms
with kitchens and is a 30-minute
drive to the Vegas Strip.

Elegant room with wood-beamed ceiling at
Tanque Verde Guest Ranch, Tucson

**DOWNTOWN: The D Hotel &
Casino Las Vegas** $
Budget Map A3
301 E. Fremont St, NV 89101
Tel *(702) 388-2400*
W thed.com
Towering over downtown, this
34-story hotel with a pool offers
far-reaching views.

DOWNTOWN: El Cortez $
Budget Map A3
600 E. Fremont St, NV 89101
Tel *(702) 385-5200*
W elcortezhotelcasino.com
Open since 1941, this hotel and
casino preserves a vintage feel. It
has a range of comfortable,
modern suites and rooms .

**DOWNTOWN: Golden Nugget
Hotel & Casino** $
Historic Map A3
129 E. Fremont St, NV 89101
Tel *(702) 385-7111*
W goldennugget.com
This family-friendly hotel features
deluxe rooms and suites, a huge
shark aquarium, and the world's
largest gold nugget on display.

**DOWNTOWN: Main Street Station
Casino Brewery & Hotel** $
Budget Map A3
200 N. Main St, NV 89101
Tel *(702) 387-1896*
W mainstreetcasino.com
With an old-West theme, this
hotel has gas lamps, stained-
glass windows, and tin ceilings,
plus an excellent buffet.

**HENDERSON: Green Valley
Ranch Resort, Spa & Casino** $
Resort Map A3
2300 Paseo Verde Pkwy, NV 89052
Tel *(702) 617-7777*
W greenvalleyranchresort.com
This luxurious resort has spacious
rooms with large bathrooms and
a spa. It offers a free shuttle
service to the Strip.

**OFF STRIP: Hard Rock
Hotel & Casino** $$
Resort Map A3
4455 Paradise Rd, NV 89109
Tel *(702) 693-5000*
W hardrockhotel.com
Famous musicians perform live at
this hotel that has musical
memorabilia in every corner.

**OFF STRIP: Palms
Casino Resort** $$
Resort Map A3
4321 W. Flamingo Rd, NV 89103
Tel *(702) 942-7777*
W palms.com
Guests can enjoy a 14-screen
movie complex, a nightclub, and
a tattoo studio at this trendy
resort with deluxe amenities.

THE STRIP: Excalibur $
Budget **Map** A3
3850 Las Vegas Blvd S., NV 89109
Tel *(702) 597-7777*
W excalibur.com
Complete with court jesters and
a dinner show, this medieval-
themed resort is family friendly.

THE STRIP: Flamingo $
Historic **Map** A3
3555 Las Vegas Blvd S., NV 89109
Tel *(702) 733-3111*
W flamingolv.com
This hotel with stylish, modern
rooms, has a pool set in a large
garden with cascading waterfalls.

**THE STRIP: New York New York
Hotel & Casino** $
Resort **Map** A3
3790 Las Vegas Blvd S., NV 89109
Tel *(702) 740-6969*
W nynyhotelcasino.com
The NYC replicas here range from
the Statue of Liberty to a Coney
Island arcade.

THE STRIP: Riviera $
Historic **Map** A3
2901 Las Vegas Blvd S., NV 89109
Tel *(702) 734-5110*
W rivierahotel.com
One of the Strip's oldest hotels,
the Riviera opened in 1955 and
features a huge, busy casino.

THE STRIP: Stratosphere $
Budget **Map** A3
2000 Las Vegas Blvd S., NV 89104
Tel *(702) 380-7777*
W stratospherehotel.com
The 113-floor tower provides
classic views, comfortable rooms,
and the world's highest thrill rides.

**THE STRIP: Aria Resort
& Casino** $$
Luxury **Map** A3
3730 Las Vegas Blvd S., NV 89109
Tel *(702) 590-7757*
W arialasvegas.com
The ultra high-tech rooms and
suites here have floor-to-ceiling
windows with panoramic views.

THE STRIP: Bally's Las Vegas $$
Luxury **Map** A3
3645 Las Vegas Blvd S., NV 89109
Tel *(702) 967-4111*
W ballyslv.com
Bally's has sizable rooms, a great
buffet, tennis courts, an Olympic-
sized pool, and a show-girl revue.

**THE STRIP: Cosmopolitan of
Las Vegas** $$
Luxury **Map** A3
3708 Las Vegas Blvd S, NV 89109
Tel *(702) 698-7000*
W cosmopolitanlasvegas.com
Sleek hotel with a casino, bars,
restaurants, pool areas, and a spa.

Reconstruction of the canals of Venice inside The Venetian, Las Vegas

THE STRIP: Luxor $$
Luxury **Map** A3
3900 Las Vegas Blvd S., NV 89119
Tel *(702) 262-4000*
W luxor.com
Housed in a glass pyramid with
replicas of the Sphinx and
Cleopatra's needle, the rooms at
Luxor have Art Deco accents.

THE STRIP: MGM Grand $$
Luxury **Map** A3
3799 Las Vegas Blvd S., NV 89109
Tel *(702) 891-7777*
W mgmgrand.com
This complex has modern rooms,
a vast casino, and an events arena.

**THE STRIP: Monte Carlo
Resort & Casino** $$
Resort **Map** A3
3770 Las Vegas Blvd S., NV 89109
Tel *(702) 730-7777*
W montecarlo.com
Comfortable rooms with subtle
Mediterranean touches are
housed in tall towers.

THE STRIP: Paris $$
Luxury **Map** A3
3655 Las Vegas Blvd S., NV 89109
Tel *(702) 946-7000*
W parislv.com
This hotel has replicas of the Eiffel
Tower and Arc de Triomphe. It is
great for people-watching.

THE STRIP: Planet Hollywood $$
Resort **Map** A3
3667 Las Vegas Blvd S., NV 89109
Tel *(702) 785-5555*
W planethollywoodresort.com
Planet Hollywood has several
restaurants, a spa, a huge
shopping complex, and a casino.

THE STRIP: Treasure Island $$
Resort **Map** A3
3300 Las Vegas Blvd S., NV 89109
Tel *(702) 894-7111*
W treasureisland.com
A popular hotel, this is aimed at
the young adult party crowd.

THE STRIP: Tropicana $$
Historic **Map** A3
3801 Las Vegas Blvd S., NV 89109
Tel *(702) 739-2222*
W tropicanalv.com
This 1957 hotel has gardens with
waterfalls spilling into lagoons.

**THE STRIP: The Venetian
Las Vegas** $$
Luxury **Map** A3
3355 Las Vegas Blvd S., NV 89109
Tel *(702) 414-1000*
W venetian.com
Guests here ride gondolas along
canals, while marveling at replicas
of Venice's main landmarks.

DK Choice

THE STRIP: Bellagio $$$
Luxury **Map** A3
3600 Las Vegas Blvd S., NV 89109
Tel *(702) 693-7111*
W bellagio.com
An Italian-themed hotel, the
Bellagio is opulently decorated
with marble and silk. Best known
for its fountains that dance to
music, this full-service resort has
plenty of shopping and dining
options. Its Gallery of Fine Art
has outstanding exhibitions.

THE STRIP: Caesars Palace $$$
Luxury **Map** A3
3570 Las Vegas Blvd S., NV 89109
Tel *(702) 731-7110*
W caesarspalace.com
A Vegas institution with its
Classical sculptures and façades,
Caesars Palace boasts big-name
entertainers and plush rooms.

THE STRIP: Mandalay Bay $$$
Luxury **Map** A3
3950 Las Vegas Blvd S., NV 89119
Tel *702) 632-7777*
W mandalaybay.com
Top amenities and luxurious
rooms with spectacular views of
the South Strip feature here.

For more information on types of hotels *see page 234–5*

THE STRIP: Mirage $$$
Luxury   Map A3
3400 Las Vegas Blvd S., NV 89109
Tel *(702) 791-7111*
W mirage.com
Fronted by a volcano, the Mirage houses the famous Secret Garden full of exotic animals.

THE STRIP: Wynn Las Vegas $$$
Luxury   Map A3
3131 Las Vegas Blvd S., NV 89109
Tel *(702) 730-7777*
W wynnlasvegas.com
This opulent casino resort has a championship golf course and a Maserati car dealership.

SUMMERLIN: Red Rock Casino, Resort & Spa $$
Resort   Map A3
11011 W. Charleston Blvd, NV 89135
Tel *(702) 797-7777*
W redrocklasvegas.com
The sleek rooms here have great views of Red Rock Canyon. There are on-site cinemas and bowling.

Southern Utah

BOULDER: Boulder Mountain Lodge $$
Resort   Map C2
20 N. Hwy 12, UT 84716
Tel *(435) 335-7460*
W boulder-utah.com
Hike through sandstone canyons and spot nature in the bird sanctuary at this eco-lodge.

BRYCE CANYON: Best Western Ruby's Inn $
Inn/B&B   Map B2
1000 S. Hwy 63, Bryce, UT 84764
Tel *(435) 834-5341*
W rubysinn.com
An all-purpose complex, this has restaurants, an art gallery, general store, post office, and gas station.

BRYCE CANYON: The Lodge at Bryce Canyon $$
Historic   Map B2
Bryce Canyon National Park, UT 84717
Tel *(435) 834-8700*
W brycecanyonforever.com
Built from sandstone and pine in the 1920s, this hotel has rooms and cabins with gas-log fireplaces.

CEDAR BREAKS NATIONAL MONUMENT: Cedar Breaks Lodge & Spa $$
Resort   Map B2
223 Hunter Ridge Rd, Brian Head, UT 84719
Tel *(435) 677-3000*
W cedarbreakslodge.com
This modern complex, popular with skiers, has an inviting spa, fireside Jacuzzi, and spacious rooms.

CEDAR CITY: Crystal Inn Cedar City $
Budget   Map B2
1575 W. 200 North St, UT 84720
Tel *(435) 586-8888*
W crystalinncedar.com
Located at the gateway of several parks, this inn has a pool, an indoor hot tub, and a sauna.

ESCALANTE: Prospector Inn $
Budget   Map C2
380 W. Main St, UT 84726
Tel *(435) 826-4653*
W prospectorinn.com
In the beautiful Grand Staircase Escalante National Monument, this family-run inn has spacious rooms and a restaurant.

KANAB: Parry Lodge $
Historic   Map B2
89 E. Center St, UT 84741
Tel *(435) 644-2601*
W parrylodge.com
Steeped in movie history, this 1931 hotel has rooms named after Hollywood stars.

MOAB: Kokopelli Lodge $
B&B   Map D2
72 S. 100 East St, UT 84532
Tel *(435) 259-7615*
W kokopellilodge.com
Built in the 1950s, this eco-friendly hotel offers good-value rooms. Pets are welcome.

MOAB: The Gonzo Inn $$
B&B   Map D2
100 W. 200 South St, UT 84532
Tel *(435) 259-2515*
W gonzoinn.com
Southwestern and '70s retro decor are combined at this trendy inn with an outdoor pool and hot tub.

MOAB: Sunflower Hill $$
Inn/B&B   Map D2
185 N. 300 East St, UT 84532
Tel *(435) 259-2974*
W sunflowerhill.com
This historic ranch house has individually decorated rooms.

DK Choice
MOAB: Sorrel River Ranch Resort & Spa $$$
Luxury   Map D2
Hwy 128, Mile 17, UT 84532
Tel *(435) 259-4642*
W sorrelriver.com
Set in the gorgeous Castle Valley, the rooms at this upscale resort have log furniture, a kitchenette, sitting area, and a porch swing. The full-service spa and activities, such as horseback riding, make this an excellent one-stop destination for relaxation.

The Mirage mega-resort, fronted by a lagoon at the heart of the Las Vegas Strip

PANGUITCH: New Western Motel $
Budget   Map B2
180 E. Center St, UT 84759
Tel *(435) 676-8876*
W newbrycewesterninn.com
A seasonal heated pool features at this motel close to many national parks.

ST. GEORGE: Seven Wives Inn $$
Inn/B&B   Map B2
217 N. 100 West St, UT 84770
Tel *(435) 628-3737*
W sevenwivesinn.com
Charming, individually styled rooms can be found at these neighboring Victorian houses.

SPRINGDALE: Best Western Zion Park Inn $$
Inn/B&B   Map B2
1215 Zion Park Blvd, UT 84767
Tel *(435) 772-3200*
W zionparkinn.com
This motel-lodge, with a winter fire and relaxing pool in summer, sits amid towering red-rock mountains near Zion's entrance.

SPRINGDALE: Majestic View Lodge $$
Inn/B&B   Map B2
2400 Zion Park Blvd, UT 84767
Tel *(435) 772-0665*
W majesticviewlodge.com
The large rooms at this beautiful lodge have handmade furniture and views of Zion's peaks.

TORREY: Broken Spur Inn $
Budget   Map C2
955 E. Hwy 24, UT 84775
Tel *(435) 425-3775*
W brokenspurinn.com
This comfortable motel, close to Capitol Reef National Park, boasts a glass-enclosed pool.

ZION NATIONAL PARK: Zion Lodge $$
B&B   Map B2
Springdale, UT 84767
Tel *(888) 297-2757*
🅦 zionlodge.com
The cabins and rooms here are in a wood surrounded by the sandstone walls of Zion Canyon.

The Four Corners

BLUFF: Recapture Lodge $
Inn/B&B   Map D2
Hwy 191, UT 84512
Tel *(435) 672-2281*
🅦 recapturelodge.com
These simple accommodations are perfectly located for kayaking and rafting on the San Juan River.

CAMERON: Cameron Trading Post $
Inn/B&B   Map C3
Route 89, AZ 86020
Tel *(928) 679-2231*
🅦 camerontradingpost.com
This Native American trading post and motel has historic Southwestern decor.

CHINLE: Sacred Canyon Lodge $
Inn/B&B   Map D3
Canyon de Chelly Navajo Route 7, AZ 86503
Tel *(928) 674-5841*
🅦 sacredcanyonlodge.com
The only hotel in Canyon de Chelly is this adobe, Navajo-owned lodge.

CORTEZ: Kelly Place B&B $
Inn/B&B   Map D2
14537 Rd G, CO 81321
Tel *(970) 565-3125*
🅦 kellyplace.com
A family-friendly retreat nestled in the orchards of McElmo Canyon.

DURANGO: General Palmer Hotel $$
Historic   Map D2
567 Main Ave, CO 81301
Tel *(970) 247-4747*
🅦 generalpalmer.com
Expect Victorian elegance and great hospitality at this 1898 hotel.

DURANGO: Strater Hotel $$
Historic   Map D2
699 Main Ave, CO 81301
Tel *(970) 247-4431*
🅦 strater.com
This red-and-white gingerbread Victorian building has individually decorated rooms with antiques.

HOPI RESERVATION: Hopi Cultural Center Inn $
Inn/B&B   Map C3
Second Mesa, Route 264, AZ 86043
Tel *(928) 734-2401*
🅦 hopiculturalcenter.com
This pueblo-style inn makes a great base for touring the mesas.

MESA VERDE NATIONAL PARK: Far View Motor Lodge $
Budget   Map D2
Mile Marker 15, Mancos, CO 81328
Tel *(602) 331-5210*
🅦 visitmesaverde.com
This quiet, modern retreat near the park's visitor center overlooks the Montezuma Valley.

MONUMENT VALLEY: Goulding's Lodge $$
Inn/B&B   Map C2
1000 Main St, off Hwy 163, UT 84536
Tel *(435) 727-3231*
🅦 gouldings.com
Goulding's Lodge is tucked beneath a mesa opposite the entrance to Monument Valley. The balconies have spectacular views.

DK Choice

MONUMENT VALLEY: The View Hotel $$
Inn/B&B   Map C2
Hwy 163 Monument Valley Tribal Park, UT 84536
Tel *(435) 727-5555*
🅦 monumentvalleyview.com
Enjoy stunning views from the only hotel perched right on the edge of Monument Valley. The well-appointed rooms at this Navajo-owned establishment have balconies – perfect vantage points for watching the sunrise. The top floors are great for star-gazing. Guided tours and day trips are available.

TELLURIDE: The Victorian Inn $
Inn/B&B   Map D2
401 W. Pacific Ave, CO 81435
Tel *(970) 728-6601*
🅦 thevictorianinn.org
This good-value option is near the historic downtown district.

TELLURIDE: New Sheridan Hotel $$
Historic   Map D2
231 W. Colorado Ave, CO 81435
Tel *(970) 728-4351*
🅦 newsheridan.com
Built in 1891, this small hotel has antique-filled rooms, some with mountain views.

TELLURIDE: The Peaks Resort & Golden Door Spa $$$
Resort   Map D2
136 Country Club Dr, CO 81435
Tel *(970) 728-6800*
🅦 thepeaksresort.com
The luxurious Peaks Resort has splendid mountain views. It provides access to skiing in winter and golf in summer.

WINDOW ROCK: Quality Inn Navajo Nation Capital $
Budget   Map D3
48 W. Hwy 264, AZ 86515
Tel *(928) 871-4108*
🅦 qualityinnwindowrock.com
Rooms at this good-value hotel with friendly staff have refrigerators and microwaves.

Santa Fe and Northern New Mexico

CHAMA: Branding Iron Motel $
Budget   Map E2
1511 W. Main St, NM 87520
Tel *(575) 756-2162*
🅦 brandingironmotel.com
Walk to America's highest and longest narrow-gauge railroad from this pleasant motel.

CHIMAYÓ: Casa Escondida Bed & Breakfast $$
Inn/B&B   Map E3
64 County Rd 100, NM 87522
Tel *(505) 351-4805*
🅦 casaescondida.com
A great base for exploring the area, the rooms here are decorated with antiques.

CIMARRON: St. James Hotel $
Historic   Map E2
17th & Collinson sts, NM 87714
Tel *(575) 376-2664*
🅦 exstjames.com
This 1880s hotel has 12 antique-filled rooms (10 more rooms are in the modern annex), a restaurant, café, and saloon.

The grand Strater Hotel in Durango, built in 1887

For more information on types of hotels *see page 234–5*

LAS VEGAS: Historic Plaza Hotel $
Historic   Map E3
230 Plaza, NM 87701
Tel *(505) 425-3591*
W plazahotel-nm.com
Built in 1882, this beautifully
restored Victorian property has
period decor. Breakfast is included.

SANTA FE: El Rey Inn $
Inn/B&B   Map E3
1862 Cerrillos Rd, NM 87505
Tel *(505) 982-1931*
W elreyinnsantafe.com
El Rey Inn is a white adobe-style
complex set among gardens
with fountains and chile *ristras*.

SANTA FE: Don Gaspar Inn $$
Inn/B&B   Map E3
623 Don Gaspar, NM 87505
Tel *(505) 986-8664*
W dongaspar.com
In three historic buildings with
lovely gardens, Don Gaspar Inn is
a short walk to major attractions.

SANTA FE: Hotel St. Francis $$
Historic   Map E3
210 Don Gaspar Ave, NM 87501
Tel *(505) 983-5700*
W hotelstfrancis.com
This elegant 1923 landmark has
spacious rooms and antiques.

SANTA FE: Hotel Santa Fe $$
Historic   Map E3
1501 Paseo de Peralta, NM 87501
Tel *(505) 982-1200*
W hotelsantafe.com
Owned by Native Americans, this
hotel has Indian artifacts, native
storytelling sessions, and tribal
dance performances.

**SANTA FE: The
Bishop's Lodge $$$**
Luxury   Map E3
1297 Bishop's Lodge Rd, NM 87501
Tel *(505) 983-6377*
W bishopslodge.com
An upscale adobe-style lodge, this
was once an archbishop's retreat.

Cozy room with a fireplace and balcony at
the Rosewood Inn of the Anasazi, Santa Fe

For key to prices *see page 236*

**SANTA FE: Inn on
the Alameda $$$**
Luxury   Map E3
303 East Alameda, NM 87501
Tel *(505) 984-2121*
W innonthealameda.com
This pueblo-style boutique hotel
serves complimentary wine and
cheese late every afternoon.

**SANTA FE: The Inn of the
Five Graces $$$**
Luxury   Map E3
150 E. DeVargas, NM 87501
Tel *(505) 992-0957*
W fivegraces.com
With Asian and Latin American
decor, this all-suite hotel offers an
exotic, romantic ambience.

**SANTA FE: Inn of the
Turquoise Bear $$$**
Inn/B&B   Map E3
342 E. Buena Vista St, NM 87505
Tel *(505) 983-0798*
W turquoisebear.com
Sumptuous rooms with *kiva*
fireplaces grace this adobe villa .

DK Choice

**SANTA FE: La Fonda on the
Plaza $$$**
Luxury   Map E3
100 E. San Francisco St, NM 87501
Tel *(505) 982-5511*
W lafondasantafe.com
On the site of a 1610 adobe
inn, this grande dame is full
of original artworks by local
artists, including handpainted
headboards, blanket boxes,
and even light switches.
Amenities include a pool,
fitness center, and spa.

**SANTA FE: La Posada de
Santa Fe $$$**
Luxury   Map E3
330 E. Palace Ave, NM 87501
Tel *(505) 986-0000*
W laposadadesantafe.com
This romantic retreat has adobe
casitas, a spa, and gardens.

**SANTA FE: Rosewood Inn of
the Anasazi $$$**
Luxury   Map E3
113 Washington Ave, NM 87501
Tel *(505) 988-3030*
W innoftheanasazi.com
Native tapestries and wooden
furniture exude elegance here.

**TAOS: American Artists Gallery
House Bed & Breakfast $**
Inn/B&B   Map E3
132 Frontier Lane, NM 87571
Tel *(575) 758-4446*
W taosbedandbreakfast.com
Rooms here have fireplaces and
works by Southwestern artists.

TAOS: Palacio de Marquesa $$
Luxury   Map E3
405 Cordoba Rd, NM 87571
Tel *(575) 758-4777*
W marquesataos.com
Wood-beamed ceilings, native
artworks, and *kiva* fireplaces
feature here.

TAOS: Taos Inn $$
Historic   Map E3
125 Paseo del Pueblo Norte, NM 87571
Tel *(575) 758-2233*
W taosinn.com
The brightly colored rooms at
Taos Inn have antiques and
fireplaces. There is a popular bar.

ZUNI: The Inn at Halona $
Inn/B&B   Map D3
23B Pia Mesa Rd, NM 87327
Tel *(505) 782-4547*
W halona.com
Enjoy the unique experience of
staying in the heart of Zuni
Pueblo. Rooms here are
decorated with Zuni artworks.

Albuquerque and
Southern New
Mexico

**ALAMOGORDO: Quality
Inn & Suites $**
Budget   Map E4
1020 S. White Sands Blvd, NM 88310
Tel *(575) 434-4200*
W choicehotels.com
This motorlodge near White Sands
National Monument has a pool,
fitness center, and sizable rooms.

DK Choice

**ALBUQUERQUE: Casas de
Sueños $**
Inn/B&B   Map E3
*310 Rio Grande Blvd SW.,
NM 87104*
Tel *(505) 247-4560*
W casasdesuenos.com
An artists' colony during the
1930s, the "House of Dreams"
today features adobe-style
casitas hidden in the gardens.
Each room is uniquely
decorated and some feature
either a patio or a Jaccuzi.
Guests can enjoy breakfast in
the sunny garden studio.

**ALBUQUERQUE: MCM
Eleganté Hotel $**
Budget   Map E3
2020 Menaul Blvd NE., NM 87107
Tel *(505) 884-2511*
W mcmelegantealbuquerque.com
Some of the rooms at this modern
hotel have balconies and views of
the Sandia Peak Mountains.

Patio with pool and palms at the Hotel Encanto, Las Cruces

ALBUQUERQUE: Bottger Mansion of Old Town $$
Inn/B&B   **Map** E3
110 San Felipe NW., NM 87104
Tel (505) 243-3639
w bottger.com
The only B&B in the historic district, the cosy patio here faces the San Felipe de Neri church.

ALBUQUERQUE: Crowne Plaza Albuquerque $$
Luxury   **Map** E3
1901 University Blvd NE., NM 87102
Tel (505) 884-2500
w ihg.com
This sprawling resort-like property has a pool and fitness center.

ALBUQUERQUE: DoubleTree by Hilton Hotel Albuquerque $$
Luxury   **Map** E3
201 Marquette Ave NW., NM 87102
Tel (505) 247-3344
w doubletreealbuquerque.com
An underground concourse links this modern hotel with spacious rooms to the Convention Center.

ALBUQUERQUE: Mauger Estate Bed & Breakfast Inn $$
Inn/B&B   **Map** E3
701 Roma Ave NW., NM 87102
Tel (505) 242-8755
w maugerbb.com
A lovely Queen Anne-style house, offering an old-world atmosphere.

ALBUQUERQUE: Sheraton Albuquerque Uptown $$
Luxury   **Map** E3
2600 Louisiana Blvd NE., NM 87110
Tel (505) 881-0000
w starwoodhotels.com
The spacious, tastefully designed rooms here have mountain views.

CARLSBAD: Hampton Inn & Suites $$
Luxury   **Map** F5
120 Esperanza Circle, NM 88220
Tel (575) 725-5700
w hamptoninn.hilton.com
A comfortable hotel in a scenic location on the Pecos River.

CEDAR CREST: Elaine's Bed & Breakfast $
Inn/B&B   **Map** E3
72 Snowline Rd, NM 87008
Tel (505) 281-2467
w elainesbnb.com
This log home with delightful rooms is adjacent to Cibola Forest.

CLOUDCROFT: The Lodge $$
Historic   **Map** E4
601 Corona Place, NM 88317
Tel (575) 682-2566
w thelodgeresort.com
Antique-filled rooms dating back to 1911 exude casual elegance. There is an attractive golf course.

GILA: Casitas de Gila Guesthouses $$
Inn/B&B   **Map** D4
50 Casita Flats Rd, NM 88038
Tel (575) 535-4455
w casitasdegila.com
In remote Apache country, this complex has five adobe houses.

GRANTS: Days Inn Grants $
Budget   **Map** D3
1504 E. Santa Fe Ave., NM 87020
Tel (505) 287-8883
w daysinn.com
A 45-minute drive from El Morro National Monument, Days Inn Grants has large rooms.

JEMEZ SPRINGS: Cañon del Rio Bed & Breakfast $$
Inn/B&B   **Map** E3
16445 Hwy 4, Jemez Springs, NM 87025
Tel (575) 829-4377
w canondelrio.com
Pleasant rooms here, named after local tribes, feature Native art.

LAGUNA: Apache Canyon Ranch Bed & Breakfast $$
Inn/B&B   **Map** D3
4 Canyon Dr, NM 87026
Tel (505) 908-2220
w apachecanyon.net
Luxurious suites and a lovely cottage make up this adobe home in a peaceful setting.

LAS CRUCES: Hotel Encanto $
Luxury   **Map** E5
705 S. Telshor Blvd, NM 88011
Tel (575) 522-4300
w hotelencanto.com
This hotel, with Spanish Colonial architecture, overlooks the striking Mesilla Valley. It caters to both business and leisure travelers.

LINCOLN: Ellis Store Country Inn $
Historic   **Map** E4
Hwy 380, NM 88338
Tel (575) 653-4609
w ellisstore.com
A relic of the Lincoln County War, this charming inn is where Billy the Kid stayed during his house arrest.

ROSWELL: Best Western Sally Port Inn & Suites $
Budget   **Map** F4
2000 N. Main St, NM 88201
Tel (575) 622-6430
w bestwestern.com
Located close to the New Mexico Military Institute, rooms here are spacious. There is a large indoor pool and a nearby golf course.

RUIDOSO: Dan Dee Cabins $
Inn/B&B   **Map** E4
310 Main Rd, NM 88345
Tel (575) 257-2165
w dandeecabins.com
The comfortable family lodgings in Upper Canyon are surrounded by snow-capped peaks. Cabins have wood-burning fireplaces.

RUIDOSO: The Lodge at Sierra Blanca $$
Resort   **Map** E4
107 Sierra Blanco Dr, NM 88345
Tel (575) 258-5500
w thelodgeatsierrablanca.com
An upscale property in the heart of Lincoln National Forest, the Lodge offers modern rooms, and a pool. Breakfast is included.

SILVER CITY: Bear Mountain Lodge $
Inn/B&B   **Map** D5
2251 Cottage San Rd, NM 88061
Tel (575) 538-2538
w bearmountainlodge.com
Rooms have handcrafted furnishings in this beautifully restored 1920s hacienda.

WHITES CITY: Rodeway Inn $
Budget   **Map** F5
12 Carlsbad Caverns Hwy, NM 88268
Tel (575) 785-2291
w rodewayinn.com
Locted near the Carlsbad Caverns, this hotel has spacious rooms with Southwestern decor. Continental breakfast is included.

For more information on types of hotels see pages 234–5

WHERE TO EAT AND DRINK

In addition to offering travelers a top-class, regional cuisine, which is rapidly gaining international recognition, the Southwest also offers a diverse range of eating experiences, especially in its larger cities. Las Vegas rivals any city in the country for the quality of ingredients and variety of cuisine available, and Santa Fe, Phoenix, Albuquerque, and Tucson all offer endless culinary options with ambiences ranging from rustic to romantic. Southwestern cuisine is widely served in casual cafés, as well as more stylish restaurants. Mexican food is best eaten in New Mexico, Arizona, and Colorado, while Utah favors American fare. Restaurants with a cowboy or Mexican theme are usually inexpensive and can be entertaining. Hotel restaurants often serve the best food in small towns.

Informal dining area of Shevek & Co. Restaurant, Silver City *(see p261)*

Eating Hours

As found elsewhere in the US, breakfast is often a banquet: restaurants have extensive breakfast menus to choose from while hotels often have large buffets. Bacon, eggs, hash brown potatoes, pancakes, waffles, cereals, toast, and muffins appear on most menus. Sunday brunch is a feast to be lingered over, with seafood, meat, and poultry dishes served as well. Breakfast times range from 6 or 6:30am to 10:30 or 11am, though "all-day breakfasts" are popular at many cafés. Brunch is frequently served until 2pm.

Lunch is generally served from around 11:30am until 2:30 or 3pm. Many of the pricier restaurants offer scaled-down versions of their evening menu, which can be good value. Evening meals are served from 5:30 or 6pm, and the last seating is seldom later than 9pm. In small towns, many restaurants are closed in the evening. At the other extreme, Las Vegas' 24-hour culture offers a variety of meals and endless buffets at any time of the day or night.

Prices and Tipping

Eating out is very reasonable, and even the most expensive eateries offer good value. Light meals in cafés and diners usually cost between $10 and $15, while many chain restaurants serve complete dinners such as chicken or steak with potatoes and vegetables or salad for under $15. Mexican restaurants generally offer huge combination plates for $8 to $12. At finer restaurants and upscale cafés, dinner entrées range from $15 to over $30, and a three-course meal, excluding wine, can still be found for under $50. In Las Vegas, the casino buffets serve myriad dishes, such as roasts, salads, pasta, and fish, to a high standard at reasonable prices (usually all-you-can-eat for $15 to $30).

The standard tip is 15 to 20 percent of the cost of the meal, after tax. Tipping should be based on service, and if it is outstanding, leave up to 20 percent. Bartenders expect to be tipped for each round of drinks.

Sales taxes will not be shown on menu prices, but apply to each item of food and drink.

Although they vary from state to state and from city to city, sales taxes usually add between 5 and 10 percent to the cost of a meal.

Types of Restaurants

Dining establishments in the Southwest come in a wide variety of shapes and sizes, from small and friendly diners offering hearty burgers and snacks to gourmet restaurants serving the latest Southwestern and fusion cuisine, to the lavish dining rooms in some of the area's top resorts, particularly in Phoenix and Las Vegas.

Fast food is a way of life throughout the country, and a string of outlets such as McDonald's, Burger King, Wendy's, and Taco Bell are found along the main strips of most towns in the region. They serve the usual inexpensive variations on burgers, fries, and soft drinks. Chains such as Applebee's and Denny's offer more variety, with soups, salads, sandwiches, meals, and desserts. These are generally good value, but the quality can vary from one establishment to the next. Pizza chains are also ubiquitous in the region.

Mid-range restaurants can include a variety of ethnic cuisine, such as Italian, Greek, Chinese, Japanese, and Indian food. Many good restaurants within this range can be found at shopping malls.

Many of the region's finest restaurants serve Southwestern cuisine, a fusion of Hispanic, Native American and international flavors. Renowned chefs are often in residence – Eric Di Stefano, for example, is executive chef at two of Santa Fe's most lauded restaurants, Geronimo and Coyote Café *(see p259)*. Las Vegas is also home to some of the most elegant restaurants in the country. In the 1990s, several of the city's best hotels recruited celebrity chefs. Now, every hotel has at least one upscale restaurant with a world-class menu and the involvement of influential names such as Hollywood's Wolfgang Puck, who is the owner of several restaurants on The Strip.

Coffee Houses and Cafés

Coffee houses are popular throughout Southwest resorts and major cities. Along with specialty coffees, they generally serve pastries, bagels, desserts, and delicatessen fare. Cafés range from simple places serving sandwiches to trendy eateries offering local cuisine.

Mexican Food

Mexican restaurants proliferate in the region, especially in New Mexico and southern Arizona, and vary from roadside stands and snack bars to upscale restaurants where the food is complemented by traditional adobe architecture; such places often have a romantic courtyard as well.

Southwestern Cuisine

Among North American regions, the Southwest has one of the most clearly defined and beloved set of native culinary traditions. Alongside the ubiquitous Mexican restaurants and steakhouses (many of which feature a ranch theme), many of the region's top-rated restaurants focus on native Southwestern recipes, most of which feature fresh, local ingredients such as smoky green chiles or earthy homemade tortillas. Attentive diners will note a heavy emphasis on fiery Mexican spices and intricate sauces, many of which garner national acclaim. Those adverse to spice can usually find something on the menu to suit their tastes; it is wise to speak with the server if you have any concerns over a particular dish's heat quotient.

Vegetarian

Southwestern and American cuisine is largely meat based. Vegetarians may not find much variety outside the larger cities and resorts. Salads can be a meal in themselves; they usually come with meat and seafood, but vegetarian orders are often accommodated. Many fast food chains now serve salads, soups, or baked potatoes to cater to the more health-conscious customer.

Alcohol

Beer, particularly the *cervezas* imported from Mexico, is the most popular drink in the region, although most cities now foster a growing cocktail scene fueled by the nationwide mixology craze. Visitors need to be 21 to buy alcohol. Be sure to carry your I. D. as it is often requested before you are served. Utah's licensing laws, influenced by the Mormon community, are stricter, with liquor stores open for shorter hours and never on a Sunday. Alcohol is forbidden on all Native reservations.

Disabled Facilities

Establishments are required to provide wheelchair access and a ground-level rest room by law, but check with older venues in advance.

Dress Codes

Dining is casual throughout the Southwest. Even in upscale restaurants, there is seldom a need for a jacket and tie. In the land of cowboys, jeans are acceptable almost everywhere. In Las Vegas, however, dressing smartly for the classier restaurants is recommended.

Smoking

Almost all restaurants have smoking and nonsmoking areas, although many ban smoking entirely throughout the eatery, including the bar area.

Recommended Restaurants

The restaurants listed on pages 248–61 have been selected across a wide price range for their value, good food, atmosphere, and location. From authentic, no-frills snack shacks to pricey temples of gastronomy, these restaurants run the gamut across all cuisine types.

Throughout the listings, certain venues are highlighted as DK Choice. These offer an exceptional feature – a celebrity chef, historic setting, exquisite food, stunning location, or an inviting atmosphere. The majority of these venues are very popular, so be sure to inquire about a reservation or you may be facing a lengthy wait for a table.

Colorful Southwestern decor at La Cocina restaurant in Tucson *(see p251)*

The Flavors of the Southwest

Southwestern food reflects the region's strong Hispanic and Native cultures. One of the pleasures of a visit to the region is discovering the great variety of dishes available, made with the freshest ingredients, and cooked with expertise. Those with tender tastebuds need not fear the chili pepper, which is at the heart of the cuisine – chilies can pack a powerful bite, but milder varieties add flavor without heat. Most menus in restaurants frequented by tourists provide an explanation of the dishes, and staff are happy to offer advice. The region's other great staple is beef, and there is no shortage of good steaks and burgers in most areas.

Kidney beans

Prime beef steaks on the griddle at a southwestern barbecue

Southwestern Food

"Red or green?" You'll often hear this question when you order food. This refers to the chili, which is more of a staple than a specialty in much of the region. Many dishes can be served with either green or red chili on top. One is not necessarily hotter than the other. The heat depends on the variety of chili, how many seeds it contains, and on the soil conditions that year. Restaurants used by locals generally serve hotter chilies than those catering to tourists. If you're unsure, many places will serve a little dish of each on the side – this is known as "Christmas". There are more than 100 types of chili available, including jalapeño, poblano, mulato, and chipotle.

Very hot varieties include cayenne and habanero. This is ranching country, so sirloins, T-bones, and other cuts of steak are in plentiful supply, and regional cooking features some great meat dishes. *Carne asada* means roasted or sometimes grilled meat, while *carne seca* is beef that has been dried in the sun before cooking. Poultry also appears in many regional dishes. Fish

Some of the fresh and dried chilies used in regional dishes

Labels: Dried habanero, Poblano, Serrano, Dried mulato, Fresh habaneros, Classic New Mexican, Jalapeño

Regional Dishes and Specialties

Tortillas are flat pancakes made of wheat or corn. They are the basis of many local dishes, and can be stuffed or rolled, served soft or crispy (fried). Variations on the tortilla include the burrito, or larger *burro*, a soft, floury pancake, that becomes a crispy *chimichanga* when deep-fried. *Flautas*, also fried, are similar but are folded rather than rolled. Salsa is found on almost every table in the region. This cold spicy sauce of tomatoes, onions, chilies, herbs, and spices is served with many dishes. Guacamole is another topping or dip, made from avocados, lime or lemon juice, chili, cilantro (coriander), and spices. Popular desserts include *sopaipilla*, a light pastry that puffs up when fried and is served with honey to drizzle over the top, and *flan*, a firm, creamy, caramel custard.

Avocados

Enchiladas are rolled tortillas filled with cheese, chicken, or beef, topped with a red chili sauce and melted cheese.

Mural on the wall of a café in Tucson's Presidio Historic District

and seafood are popular, and the quality is high since fresh fish is flown in from California.

Mexican Flavors

The main ingredients of Southwestern cuisine are similar to those found in Mexican cooking, including corn, beans, cheese, tomatoes and, of course, chili. But there the similarity ends. New Mexican cuisine has its roots in the Pueblo culture, whose foods and cooking methods were adapted by early settlers. The distinctive taste of many local dishes comes from ingredients such as nuts from the *piñon* pine which are considered a delicacy; *nopales*, the fruit of the prickly pear cactus; the *chayote* (similar to zucchini); and tomatillos, a walnut-sized green berry fruit. Mexican sauces are often tomato-based with chili added as a spice. New Mexican sauces use puréed green or red chili diluted with water; garlic, salt, and sometimes herbs for seasoning, and flour to thicken, are added. Meat may also be added. Mexican food and its Anglo version, Tex-Mex, are found all over the Southwest.

Ice-cold Corona beer, served with a wedge of lime

Native American Specialties

There are few specifically Native American restaurants. Indian fry bread – a flat, fried dough served with honey or other toppings – is often sold at food stands outside tourist attractions or at events. Navajo tacos are made with a base of fry bread rather than tortilla. Hopi piki bread is made from ground corn and boiling water and is cooked in a thin layer over a hot surface. At festivals, special foods may be offered to visitors, such as fried rabbit meat, or Three Sisters Stew made with corn, beans, and squash.

WHAT TO DRINK

Beer is known to cool burning chili mouths, and popular brands include San Miguel, Corona, and Tecate. A margarita, a tequila cocktail served in a salt-rimmed glass, is a typical aperitif. California wines feature on most wine lists, but consider trying some of the little-known regional wines. There are small wineries in southern Arizona and New Mexico. Sonoita Vineyards, near Elgin, Arizona, has received national recognition for its Pinot Noir and Cabernet wines. New Mexico's winemaking tradition stretches back to the first Spanish missionaries. Among its forty wineries, the Gruet winery is known for its excellent sparkling wines.

Huevos rancheros, fried eggs on a soft tortilla with chili, cheese, and refried beans, are eaten at breakfast.

Tacos are crisp-fried tortillas filled with ground beef, beans, cheese, and salad, and served with guacamole.

Chili relleno is a whole green chili stuffed with cheese, meat, or rice, dipped in light batter and then deep-fried.

Where to Eat and Drink

Grand Canyon and Northern Arizona

FLAGSTAFF: Beaver Street Brewery & Whistle Stop Café $
American   Map C3
11 S. Beaver St, AZ 86001
Tel *(928) 779-0079*
Burgers and wood-fired pizzas are served from an open kitchen. The seasonal beer garden has views of the San Francisco Peaks.

FLAGSTAFF: Downtown Diner $
American   Map C3
7 E. Aspen Ave, AZ 86001
Tel *(928) 774-3492*
Photos of local landscapes line the walls at this neighborhood favorite for breakfast. The lunch menu includes giant burgers and fresh trout.

FLAGSTAFF: San Felipe's Cantina $
Mexican   Map C3
103 N. Leroux St, AZ 86001
Tel *(928) 779-6000*
Grilled *mahi-mahi* (dolphinfish) and chicken with mango salsa feature on the menu at this Baja-style cantina. The choco-taco with ice cream is popular with kids.

FLAGSTAFF: Charly's $$
American   Map C3
23 N. Leroux St, AZ 86001
Tel *(928) 779-1919*
Charly's varied menu includes soups, steaks, Navajo tacos, and vegetarian dishes. The sidewalk patio is popular. Nightly live music.

FLAGSTAFF: Pasto $$
Italian   Map C3
19 E. Aspen Ave, AZ 86001
Tel *(928) 779-1937*
This casual downtown haunt serves a range of classic dishes. Diners sit inside beneath a

Elegant table settings at the Cottage Place Restaurant, Flagstaff

painted copper ceiling or outside in the relaxing garden. There are fresh flowers and photos of Italy.

FLAGSTAFF: Black Bart's Steakhouse $$$
Steakhouse   Map C3
2760 E. Butler Ave, AZ 86004
Tel *(928) 779-3142*
A family-owned hangout named after an 1870s stagecoach robber, Black Bart's serves corn-fed steaks and fresh seafood. A musical revue is performed by the staff in the evenings.

FLAGSTAFF: Cottage Place Restaurant $$$
American/Continental   Map C3
126 W. Cottage Ave, AZ 86001
Tel *(928) 774-8431*   **Closed** *Mon & Tue*
The inspired Continental dishes at this airy restaurant include pan-seared tenderloin topped with gorgonzola with a port demi-glaze. Extensive wine list.

GRAND CANYON: Bright Angel Restaurant $
American   Map B3
Grand Canyon Village, South Rim, AZ 86023
Tel *(928) 638-2631*
This family-friendly restaurant offers classic dishes such as *quesadillas* and steaks. No reservations accepted.

GRAND CANYON: Maswik Cafeteria $
International   Map B3
Grand Canyon Village, South Rim, AZ 86023
Tel *(928) 638-2631*
Favorites at this self-service café include burgers, hot sandwiches, pasta, and Mexican fare.

GRAND CANYON: Phantom Ranch Canteen $
American   Map B3
North Kaibab Trail, AZ 86023
Tel *(928) 638-2631*
Breakfast and dinner are served at specific hours here for adventurers who have traveled to the bottom of the canyon. Reserve in advance.

GRAND CANYON: El Tovar $$
Southwestern   Map B3
Grand Canyon Village, South Rim, AZ 86023
Tel *(928) 638-2631*
Perhaps the finest dining option in the park, but few tables have canyon views at El Tovar. The menu offers a mix of classic and Southwestern flavors.

GRAND CANYON: Grand Canyon Lodge $$$
American   Map B3
North Rim, AZ 86052
Tel *(928) 638-2611*
This beautiful, remote restaurant offers astounding views of the Kaibab Plateau and sophisticated cuisine. Reserve well ahead.

JEROME: Flatiron Café $
American   Map B4
416 Main St, AZ 86331
Tel *(928) 634-2733*   **Closed** *Tue*
A tiny café with hearty breakfasts and an impressive lunch menu. Try the smoked salmon *quesadilla* with dill cream cheese and homemade cilantro pesto.

JEROME: Asylum Restaurant $$$
Contemporary American Map B4
200 Hill St, AZ 86331
Tel *(928) 639-3197*
With great views of the Verde valley, the menu highlights here are Pacific king salmon with prickly pear barbecue sauce, and grilled pork tenderloin with chipotle apricot sauce. There is an excellent wine list.

KINGMAN: Mr. D'z Route 66 $
American   Map B3
105 E. Andy Devine Ave, AZ 86401
Tel *(928) 718-0066*
Great burgers are served at this gas-station-turned-diner filled with 1950s memorabilia. Admire vintage vehicles from the hot-pink picnic tables outside.

LAKE HAVASU CITY: Mudshark Brewing Co. $
American   Map A4
210 Swanson Ave, AZ 86403
Tel *(928) 453-2981*
Popular for its handcrafted beer on tap, Mudshark offers an eclectic menu of burgers, sandwiches, and slow-cooked pork chops.

LAKE HAVASU CITY: Shugrue's $$$
American   Map A4
1425 N. McCulloch Blvd, AZ 86403
Tel *(928) 453-1400*
Enjoy open views of the Bridgewater Channel and London Bridge from this restaurant. Try the halibut baked in Dijon garlic crust with sea scallops.

Cozy dining room with picture window at Elote Café, Sedona

PAGE: Dam Bar and Grille $$
American **Map** C2
644 N. Navajo Dr, AZ 86040
Tel *(928) 645-2161*
Fine steaks, pasta, and seafood are served in this contemporary setting. An elegant, etched-glass wall celebrates the Glen Canyon Dam just west of here.

SEDONA: Black Cow Café $
American **Map** C3
229 N. Hwy 89A, AZ 86336
Tel *(928) 203-9868*
Decorated like an old-time parlor with photos from the '50s, the Black Cow serves up sundaes, filling sandwiches, pastries, gourmet coffee, and smoothies.

SEDONA: El Rincon Restaurante Mexicano $
Mexican **Map** C3
Tlaquepaque Village, 336 State Route 179, AZ 86336
Tel *(928) 282-4648*
Arched doorways and Spanish-style furnishings form a backdrop to the Arizona-style Mexican dishes, from burritos to tamales, with a touch of Navajo influence.

SEDONA: Oaxaca Restaurante & Rooftop Cantina $
Mexican **Map** C3
321 N. Hwy 89A, AZ 86336
Tel *(928) 282-4179*
A lively, long-running restaurant with a seasonal rooftop cantina offering stunning views. Sample the specialty – marinated and grilled cactus in a zesty sauce.

SEDONA: Barking Frog Grille $$
Southwestern **Map** C3
2620 W. State Route 89A, 86336
Tel *(928) 204-2000*
Creative interpretations of popular favorites are part of the varied menu here. There is a choice of three casual dining rooms, a bar, and outdoor patios. There is an impressive wine list.

SEDONA: Elote Café $$
Mexican **Map** C3
771 State Route 179, AZ 86336
Tel *(928) 203-0105*
Local wines, cheese, and other produce are complemented by smoked chilies and inventive sauces at this colorful venue.

SEDONA: Takashi $$
Japanese **Map** C3
465 Jordan Rd, AZ 86336
Tel *(928) 282-2334* **Closed** *Mon*
The vast menu here includes sushi, soft-shell crabs, *teriyaki, sukiyaki, tempura,* and *teppanyaki* dishes.

SEDONA: Dahl & Di Luca $$$
Italian **Map** C3
2321 W. State Route 89A, AZ 86336
Tel *(928) 282-5219*
The extensive menu at this romantic restaurant includes cheese-filled olives and linguine with wild mushrooms.

SEDONA: The Heartline Café $$$
International **Map** C3
1610 W. Hwy 89A, AZ 86336
Tel *(928) 282-0785*
A mix of Asian, European, and Mediterranean dishes, made with ingredients fresh from the garden, can be enjoyed in the casual atmosphere of this restaurant.

DK Choice

SEDONA: Shugrue's Hillside Grill $$$
American **Map** C3
671 Hwy 179, AZ 86326
Tel *(928) 282-5300*
The eclectic menu here features local, organic produce and offers superb steaks and seafood prepared in a number of ways – grilled, sautéed, or blackened. Floor-to-ceiling windows offer stunning views of Sedona's Thunder Mountain.

WILLIAMS: Twisters Soda Fountain & The Route 66 $
American **Map** B3
417 E. Route 66, AZ 86046
Tel *(928) 635-0266* **Closed** *Sun*
Complete with retro tunes, a black-and-white checkerboard floor, and red-vinyl soda-fountain chairs, Twisters Soda pulls off a '50s vibe. Menu highlights include burgers, chili dogs, and banana splits.

WILLIAMS: Red Raven $$
American **Map** B3
135 W. Route 66, AZ 86046
Tel *(928) 635-4980*
This unexpected gem offers a creative menu of Southwestern-inspired steaks, burgers, fish, salads, soups, and pasta dishes. A choice of quality wines and beers is available.

WILLIAMS: Rod's Steakhouse $$$
Steakhouse **Map** B3
301 E. Route 66, AZ 86046
Tel *(928) 635-2671* **Closed** *Sun*
Look for the red neon sign of this restaurant's mascot, Domino the Steer – a landmark on Route 66. Excellent steaks and slow-cooked prime ribs are the specialties.

Phoenix and Southern Arizona

APACHE JUNCTION: Mining Camp Restaurant $
American **Map** C4
6100 E. Mining Camp St, AZ 85119
Tel *(480) 982-3181* **Closed** *mid-May–mid-Oct.*
Heaped platters of delicious roast chicken, oven-baked ham, and barbecued ribs are served on tin plates at long wooden tables in this family-friendly former miners' shanty.

Bench seating at the Mining Camp Restaurant, Apache Junction

For more information on types of restaurants *see pages 244–5*

GLOBE: Chalo's Casa Reynoso $
Mexican   Map C4
902 E. Ash St, AZ 85501
Tel *(928) 425-0515*   **Closed** *Sun*
This cozy local hangout is known for its traditional home cooking. The house specialty is Mexican *sopaipillas* (fried pastry) filled with spicy pork or beef.

GLOBE: Jerry's Restaurant $
American   Map C4
699 E. Ash St, AZ 85501
Tel *(928) 425-5282*
Jerry's serves all the American classics – burgers, chicken dishes, steaks, and corn bread. The service is friendly and portions are large. Open 24 hours.

PARADISE VALLEY: El Chorro $$$
American   Map B4
5550 E. Lincoln Dr, AZ 85253
Tel *(480) 948-5170*
The menu of classic regional favorites with Southwestern influences highlights fresh, organic, and locally grown ingredients. The Sunday brunch features legendary sticky buns.

PHOENIX: Aunt Chilada's $
Mexican   Map B4
7330 N. Dreamy Draw Dr, AZ 85020
Tel *(602) 944-1286*
Authentic, south-of-the-border dishes are served in casual, rustic environs spilling over with flowers. There is pleasant patio seating for alfresco dining.

PHOENIX: Matt's Big Breakfast $
American   Map B4
825 N. 1st St, AZ 85004
Tel *(602) 254-1074*
The excellent breakfast menu here has only grain-fed meats, free-range eggs, and organic produce. The decor features 1950s dinette tables and vintage artwork.

PHOENIX: Barrio Café $$
Mexican   Map B4
2814 N. 16th St, AZ 85004
Tel *(602) 636-0240*   **Closed** *Mon*
Classic southern Mexican cuisine as well as original creative dishes are served in three dining rooms filled with vivid art. The tiny bar offers over 250 tequilas and perfect margaritas.

PHOENIX: Courtyard Café $$
Southwestern   Map B4
2301 N. Central Ave, AZ 85004
Tel *(602) 251-0204*   **Closed** *Mon*
Housed in the Heard Museum, this lunch spot offers salads and gourmet sandwiches, as well as the house specialty, *posolé* (spicy corn stew), served with roasted pork and all the trimmings.

DK Choice

PHOENIX: Pizzeria Bianco $$
Pizzeria   Map B4
623 E. Adams St, AZ 85004
Tel *(602) 258-8300*   **Closed** *Sun*
Foodies from all over the world flock to this downtown restaurant to sample the gourmet pizza pies that some claim to be the best in the country. A simple menu of salads and wood-fired pizzas incorporates a variety of local, seasonal ingredients such as fennel sausage and house-smoked mozzarella.

PHOENIX: Rustler's Rooste $$
Steakhouse   Map B4
8383 S. 48th St, AZ 85044
Tel *(602) 431-6474*
This cowboy-themed eatery is located on a butte overlooking the lights of Phoenix. At the mine-like entrance, guests can opt to ride the slide to the dining room.

PHOENIX: Avanti $$$
Italian   Map B4
2728 E. Thomas Rd, AZ 85016
Tel *(602) 956-0900*   **Closed** *Sat & Sun lunch*
This local institution with Art Deco accents and a welcoming bar area has been famous for its homemade pasta dishes since 1974. Special wine dinners are held for oenophiles.

PHOENIX: Compass Arizona Grill $$$
Contemporary American   Map B4
122 N. 2nd St, AZ 85004
Tel *(602) 252-1234*
Housed in the Hyatt Regency hotel, Phoenix's revolving restaurant offers splendid views. Seasonal menus feature selections inspired by the region.

PHOENIX: Durant's $$$
Steakhouse   Map B4
2611 N. Central Ave, AZ 85004
Tel *(602) 264-5967*
Spot local celebrities dining on large appetizers and generous portions of steaks and seafood at this bustling steakhouse, a mainstay since the 1950s.

PHOENIX: T. Cook's $$$
Mediterranean   Map B4
5200 E. Camelback Rd, AZ 85018
Tel *(602) 808-0766*
Located in a resort filled with elegant Old World touches, this restaurant has a seasonal menu of Mediterranean-inspired dishes made with organic ingredients.

PHOENIX: Vincent's on Camelback $$$
American   Map B4
3930 E. Camelback Rd, AZ 85018
Tel *(602) 224-0225*   **Closed** *Sun*
A local favorite since 1986, Vincent's offers an inventive menu blending Southwestern ingredients with a Provençal flair. The wine list is extensive.

SCOTTSDALE: Frank & Lupe's $
Mexican   Map B4
4121 N. Marshall Way, AZ 85251
Tel *(480) 990-9844*
This small eatery serves favorites such as *enchiladas*, tamales, and tacos, with red or green chili sauce, *charro* beans, fresh salsa, and crispy homemade chips.

SCOTTSDALE: FnB $$
Contemporary American   Map B4
7125 E. 5th Ave, Suite 31, AZ 85251
Tel *(480) 284-4777*   **Closed** *Sun & Mon*
The creative seasonal menu here has dishes such as crispy squash blossoms stuffed with tomato and a wide range of Arizona wines.

Patio dining with mountain views at EL Chorro, Paradise Valley

For key to prices *see page 248*

SCOTTSDALE: Zuzu $$
Contemporary American **Map** B4
6850 E. Main St, AZ 85251
Tel *(480) 421-7997*
Savor seasonal dishes made with fresh, local ingredients, along with hand-crafted cocktails, and well-chosen wines in this mid-1950s-style restaurant.

SCOTTSDALE: Cowboy Ciao $$$
Contemporary American **Map** B4
7133 E. Stetson Dr, AZ 85251
Tel *(480) 946-3111*
Inventive dishes, such as duck confit *relleno* and sea scallops crusted with corn nuts, are paired with rare global wines in this sophisticated setting.

SCOTTSDALE: Roaring Fork $$$
Southwestern **Map** B4
4800 N. Scottsdale Rd, AZ 85251
Tel *(480) 947-0795*
Imaginative dishes, including fish tacos and filet mignon with green-chili macaroni, as well as delicious wood-fired pizzas, are served here. There is a daily happy hour.

SCOTTSDALE: Sassi $$$
Italian **Map** B4
10455 E. Pinnacle Peak Pkwy, AZ 85255
Tel *(480) 502-9095*
Designed as a southern Italian villa with an enclosed garden terrace and outdoor patios, Sassi is located at the base of Pinnacle Peak and serves excellent pasta, seafood, and poultry dishes.

TOMBSTONE: Big Nose Kate's Saloon $
American **Map** C5
417 E. Allen St, AZ 85638
Tel *(520) 457-3107*
Large, family-friendly dishes are served at this bustling saloon filled with Western memorabilia, steer heads, and stained glass. There is live country music daily.

TOMBSTONE: OK Café $
American **Map** C5
220 E. Ellen St, AZ 85638
Tel *(520) 457-3980*
Famous for its buffalo burgers, this tiny café also serves exotic charbroiled emu and ostrich burgers. It also offers standard breakfast and lunch fare.

TUCSON: El Charro Café $
Mexican **Map** C5
311 N. Court Ave, AZ 85701
Tel *(520) 622-1922*
In El Presidio historic district, this is one of the oldest family-owned restaurants in the US. Savor the legendary *carne seca* –shredded sun-dried Angus beef –marinated in garlic and lime juice.

Feast's well-stocked bar, Tucson

TUCSON: La Cocina $
International **Map** C5
201 N. Court Ave, AZ 85701
Tel *(520) 622-0351*
Popular, authentic fare is served in the former stables of the 18th-century El Presidio. Dine on the sunny patio or shaded courtyard, or in the colorful cantina filled with sculptures and artwork.

TUCSON: La Parilla Suiza $
Mexican **Map** C5
5602 E. Speedway Blvd, AZ 85712
Tel *(520) 747-4838*
This long-established popular restaurant uses family recipes rooted in Mexico City. Try the tacos overstuffed with diced, charbroiled beef served with refried beans and rice.

TUCSON: Café Poca Cosa $$
Mexican **Map** C5
110 E. Pennington St, AZ 85701
Tel *(520) 622-6400* **Closed** *Sun & Mon*
The chalkboard menu at this casual-chic bistro offers inspired Mexican cuisine with regional flavors. Dishes are listed in both English and Spanish and the menu changes daily.

TUCSON: El Corral $$
Steakhouse **Map** C5
2201 E. River Rd, AZ 85718
Tel *(520) 299-6092*
El Corral is in a welcoming, historic territorial ranch house with fireplaces, flagstone floors, and wood-beamed ceilings. Come here for the house specialty, prime rib. No reservations.

TUCSON: Feast $$
Contemporary American **Map** C5
3719 E. Speedway Blvd, AZ 85712
Tel *(520) 326-9363* **Closed** *Mon*
This sophisticated restaurant has floor-to-ceiling windows facing the Santa Catalina Mountains, and a wine wall filled with boutique labels. The European-influenced menu is continuously evolving.

TUMACACORI: Wisdom's Café $
Mexican **Map** C5
1931 E. Frontage Rd, AZ 85640
Tel *(520) 398-2397* **Closed** *Sun*
This family-run café uses recipes passed from one generation to the next. Try the famous fruit *burro*, a jam-filled tortilla served with a choice of fruit.

Las Vegas

DOWNTOWN: The Buffet $
American **Map** A3
Golden Nugget, 129 E. Fremont St, NV 89101
Tel *(702) 385-7111*
Streams of diners seated in comfy booths enjoy varied food platters and an extensive salad bar here.

DOWNTOWN: Du-Par's Restaurant and Bakery $
American **Map** A3
Golden Gate, 1 Fremont St, NV 89101
Tel *(702) 366-9378*
Du-Par's serves good-value diner fare and is known for its pancakes and pies. It is also the self-billed home of the "original shrimp cocktail." Open 24 hours.

For more information on types of restaurants *see pages 244–5*

Wall menus listing Cap's Specials at Capriotti's sandwich shop, Las Vegas

DOWNTOWN: Hugo's Cellar $$$
International   Map A3
Four Queens, 202 Fremont St, NV 89101
Tel (702) 385-4011
The menu at this romantic subterranean restaurant includes fine dining classics such as lobster or beef Wellington, followed by cherries jubilee.

DOWNTOWN: Top of Binion's Steakhouse $$$
Steakhouse   Map A3
Binion's, 128 E. Fremont St, NV 89101
Tel (702) 382-1600
Enjoy spectacular views of the Strip from Binion's plush interior. Classic dishes include lobster bisque, porterhouse steak, and the signature chicken fried lobster. Live piano music on weekends.

HENDERSON: Sushi + Sake $$$
Japanese   Map A3
Green Valley Ranch, 2300 Paseo Verde Pkwy, NV 89052
Tel (702) 617-7777
An impressive selection of sushi and sakes are served at this ultra-hip restaurant.

OFF STRIP: Capriotti's $
Sandwich shop   Map A3
322 W. Sahara Ave, NV 89102
Tel (702) 474-0229
Capriotti's serves sandwiches measuring up to 20-in (50-cm) long. Special combos come overstuffed: try the "Slaw B. Joe" bursting with house-roasted beef and coleslaw.

OFF STRIP: Egg & I $
American   Map A3
4533 W. Sahara Ave, NV 89102
Tel (702) 364-9686
This family-friendly restaurant offers huge pancakes and renowned eggs Benedict. Giant omelets are served with ranch potatoes and a banana-nut muffin. Burgers, soups, and salads are also on the menu.

OFF STRIP: In-N-Out Burger $
Fast food   Map A3
4888 Dean Martin Dr, NV 89103
Tel (800) 786-1000
High-quality burgers, fries, and shakes can be found at low prices at this wildly popular California-based burger chain.

OFF STRIP: Pink Taco $
Mexican   Map A3
Hard Rock, 4455 Paradise Rd, NV 89109
Tel (702) 693-5525
An ultra-hip, colorful cantina-style restaurant with Mexican craft decor, Pink Taco has classic dishes and an extensive margarita and tequila list.

OFF STRIP: Lotus of Siam $$
Thai   Map A3
953 E. Sahara Ave, 89104
Tel (702) 735-3033
The Thai chef here prepares dishes from northern Thailand from recipes passed down through generations. Choose from a long menu of spicy stews and curries with authentic herbs and spices.

OFF STRIP: Nora's Cuisine $$
Italian   Map A3
6020 W. Flamingo Rd, NV 89103
Tel (702) 873-8990
Savor family recipes with Sicilian accents such as antipasto salad and veal marsala, along with great cocktails and an extensive wine list, at this family-run restaurant.

OFF STRIP: Alizé $$$
European   Map A3
Palms, 4321 W. Flamingo Rd, NV 89103
Tel (702) 951-7000
Gourmet cuisine is served in an elegant, romantic environment with breathtaking views. The seasonally changing menu often includes imported Dover sole or pan-seared Muscovy duck.

OFF STRIP: Morton's The Steakhouse $$$
Steakhouse   Map A3
400 E. Flamingo Rd, NV 89103
Tel (702) 893-0703
Renowned for its fine steaks, Morton's lets diners select their cut. The dining room has a club feel, with dark-wood furniture and photos of famous patrons.

OFF STRIP: Piero's $$$
Italian   Map A3
355 Convention Center Dr, NV 89109
Tel (702) 369-2305
This old-time haunt of the rich and famous, starting with the Rat Pack, is popular with locals for its veal dishes and fresh seafood.

THE STRIP: California Pizza Kitchen $
Pizzeria   Map A3
Mirage, 3400 Las Vegas Blvd S., NV 89109
Tel (702) 791-7111
Wood-fired, crispy pizzas with unusual toppings are served at this chain pizzeria. Try the BBQ chicken pizza with red onions, smoked cheeses, and tangy sauce.

THE STRIP: Grand Lux Café $
International   Map A3
The Venetian, 3355 Las Vegas Blvd S., NV 89109
Tel (702) 414-3888
With a lavish Venetian-style interior, the extensive menu here has global influences and includes Cajun shrimp and Wiener Schnitzel.

THE STRIP: Harley Davidson Café $
American   Map A3
3725 Las Vegas Blvd S., NV 89109
Tel (702) 740-4555
A three-story motorbike heaven, this eatery is instantly recognizable due to the huge Heritage Softail bursting out of the façade. Barbecue favorites include ribs, chicken, and sausages.

Bright casual interior of Egg & I, Las Vegas

THE STRIP: I Love Burgers $
Fast food   Map A3
*The Palazzo, 3327 Las Vegas Blvd S.,
NV 89109*
Tel *(702) 242-2747*
Burgers come in numerous
varieties at this casual eatery –
tuna, buffalo, veggie, and turkey.
There is also an extensive selection
of beer and unique milk shakes.

THE STRIP: Rainforest Café $
American   Map A3
*MGM Grand, 3799 Las Vegas Blvd S.,
NV 89109*
Tel *(702) 891-8580*
Kids will love this jungle-themed
restaurant with faux gorillas,
colorful fish tanks, and simulated
thunder and flashes of lightning.

THE STRIP: Serendipity 3 $
American   Map A3
*Caesars Palace, 3570 Las Vegas
Blvd S., NV 89109*
Tel *(877) 346-4642*
This serves a variety of fare, but it
is the jaw-dropping desserts that
draw the crowds. "Frrrozen" hot
chocolate – a rich icy, concoction
of blended chocolate is a favorite.

THE STRIP: 'Wichcraft $
Sandwich restaurant   Map A3
*MGM Grand, 3799 Las Vegas Blvd S.,
NV 89109*
Tel *(702) 891-1111*
Inventive sandwiches with fillings
such as flank steak with red
pepper pesto and cheddar are
served on freshly-baked bread.

THE STRIP: Cravings Buffet $$
International   Map A3
*Mirage, 3400 Las Vegas Blvd S., NV
89109*
Tel *(702) 791-7111*
This modern restaurant has ten
stations where guests can watch
dishes from a range of cuisines
being cooked.

**THE STRIP: Grand Wok
& Sushi Bar** $$
Asian   Map A3
*MGM Grand, 3799 Las Vegas Blvd S.,
NV 89109*
Tel *(702) 891-8670*
Chefs prepare Thai, Vietnamese,
Korean, Chinese and Japanese
dishes at a bright, open kitchen
and gleaming sushi bar. Tropical
cocktails are on offer.

**THE STRIP: Spice
Market Buffet** $$
International   Map A3
*Planet Hollywood, 3667 Las Vegas
Blvd S., NV 89109*
Tel *(702) 785-5555*
Perfect for groups, an impressive
variety of dishes, including
Mexican, Italian, Asian, Middle

A wine angel selecting a bottle from the
four-story wine tower at Aureole

Eastern, and American, are served
at this restaurant. Leave room for
the decadent desserts.

THE STRIP: Tamba $$
Indian   Map A3
*Hawaiian Marketplace, 3743 Las
Vegas Blvd S., NV 89109*
Tel *(702) 798-7889*
Celebrating India's bold colors
and spices, Tamba is decorated
with giant murals and Hindu
statues. Authentic cuisine is
prepared in clay ovens. Try the
tandoori prawns and chicken
tikka masala.

**THE STRIP: The Buffet
at Bellagio** $$$
International   Map A3
3600 Las Vegas Blvd S., NV 89109
Tel *(702) 693-8111*
This upscale buffet has Tuscan-
inspired decor and serves a wide
range of quality dishes such as
Kobe beef, prime rib, rack of
lamb, smoked salmon, and iced
crab legs, as well as *dim sum*,
sushi, and pasta.

THE STRIP: Aureole $$$
Contemporary American Map A3
*Mandalay Bay, 3950 Las Vegas
Blvd S., NV 89119*
Tel *(702) 632-7401*
Arrive early at Aureole just to
watch the "wine angels" (wine
stewards in harnesses) ascend
the four-story glass tower of
outstanding wines. Dine on the
excellent *prix fixe* tasting menus
in the intimate Swan Court.

THE STRIP: D.O.C.G. $$$
Italian   Map A3
*Cosmopolitan, 3708 Las Vegas
Blvd S., NV 89109*
Tel *(702) 698-7920*
Acclaimed New York City chef
Scott Conant's version of a
relaxed wine-and-food spot, the
menu here ranges from creative
pasta dishes to prime steaks.
Popular dishes include
margherita pizza and
gnocchi with sausage.

**THE STRIP: Emeril's New
Orleans Fish House** $$$
Cajun/Seafood   Map A3
*MGM Grand, 3799 Las Vegas Blvd S.,
NV 89109*
Tel *(702) 891-7374*
Star chef Emeril Lagasse
serves delicious Creole and
Cajun recipes – guests devour
his gumbo and signature
barbecue. The extensive wine
list is embodied by a wine
tower of 2,200 bottles.

THE STRIP: Fin $$$
Chinese   Map A3
*Mirage, 3400 Las Vegas Blvd S., NV
89109*
Tel *(702) 791-7111* **Closed** *Tue, Wed*
Choose from the clay-pot dishes
or select a live fish from the tank
in this elegant restaurant with
emerald-and-gold silk wallpaper.
Guests have a choice of how the
fish is prepared – most can be
braised, wok-fried, or steamed.

THE STRIP: Joe's $$$
Seafood/Steakhouse   Map A3
*Caesars Palace, 3500 Las Vegas
Blvd S., NV 89109*
Tel *(702) 792-9222*
Wooden beams and leather
booths replicate the Miami Beach
institution renowned for preparing
unique stone crabs at your table.

THE STRIP: Lakeside Seafood $$$
Seafood   Map A3
*Wynn, 3131 Las Vegas Blvd S.,
NV 89101*
Tel *(702) 770-3310*
Facing the Lake of Dreams where
a nightly light show takes place,
the specialties here include
swordfish marinated in chipotle
and New Zealand seabass.

THE STRIP: Michael Mina $$$
Contemporary American Map A3
*Bellagio, 3600 Las Vegas Blvd S.,
NV 89109*
Tel *(702) 693-8865*   **Closed** *Wed*
This Michelin-starred chef's
restaurant offers inventive seafood
preparations, and vegetarian and
seasonal dishes. The wine list
features limited productions of
American and European labels.

For more information on types of restaurants *see pages 244–5*

Elegant dining room of the charming Pinot Brasserie inside The Venetian, Las Vegas

THE STRIP: Mizumi $$$
Japanese   **Map** A3
*Caesars Palace, 3131 Las Vegas
Blvd S., NV 89109*
Tel *(702) 248-3463*
Japanese flavors are blended
with French techniques to create
robatayaki and sushi delights,
paired with quality wine and sake.

THE STRIP: Mon Ami Gabi $$$
French   **Map** A3
Paris, 3655 Las Vegas Blvd S., NV 89109
Tel *(702) 944-4224*
Dine on Parisian classics (onion
soup and steak *frites*) on the patio
overlooking Bellagio's fountains.

DK Choice

THE STRIP: Picasso $$$
International   **Map** A3
*Bellagio, 3600 Las Vegas Blvd S.,
NV 89109*
Tel *(702) 693-8865* **Closed** *Tue*
Chef Julian Serrano's creative
dishes are perfect for
celebratory dinners. Tasting
menus explore French-
Mediterranean flavors with
dishes such as sautéed *foie
gras* with honey-roasted figs
and walnuts. Authentic Picasso
artworks adorn the dining area.

THE STRIP: Pinot Brasserie $$$
French   **Map** A3
*The Venetian, 3355 Las Vegas Blvd S.,
NV 89104*
Tel *(702) 414-8888*
Braised pork belly with a ginger
and citrus glaze is one of the
specialties at this brasserie.

**THE STRIP: R. Steak & Seafood
Restaurant** $$$
Seafood/Steakhouse   **Map** A3
*Riviera, 2901 Las Vegas Blvd S.,
NV 89104*
Tel *(702) 794-9233*
An elegant restaurant, the menu
here includes grilled cedar-
planked salmon, scallops, and

fine cuts of steak, all cooked with
the freshest ingredients. The
Snickers pie is a delicious dessert.

**THE STRIP: Restaurant Guy
Savoy** $$$
French   **Map** A3
*Caesars Palace, 3570 Las Vegas
Blvd S., NV 89109*
Tel *(702) 731-7286*   **Closed** *Mon
& Tue*
French chef Guy Savoy prepares
excellent dishes using seasonal
ingredients in an interior that
reflects his famous Paris restaurant.
There is a decadent wine selection.

**THE STRIP: Ruth's
Chris Steakhouse** $$$
Steakhouse   **Map** A3
*Harrah's, 3475 Las Vegas Blvd S.,
NV 89109*
Tel *(702) 693-6000*
Enjoy superb steaks, fine wines,
and great hospitality in a relaxed
atmosphere. Creole appetizers
reflect the chain's Louisiana origins.

THE STRIP: Sinatra $$$
Italian   **Map** A3
*Wynn, 3131 Las Vegas Blvd S.,
NV 89109*
Tel *(702) 248-3463*
This tribute to the crooner displays
iconic pieces from his career. The
varied menu has hearty favorites.

THE STRIP: TAO $$$
Asian   **Map** A3
*The Venetian, 3355 Las Vegas Blvd S.,
NV 89109*
Tel *(702) 388-8338*
Sit under the gaze of a gigantic
bronze Buddha. The menu covers
the entire Pacific Rim.

THE STRIP: Top of the World $$$
Contemporary American   **Map** A3
*Stratosphere, 2000 Las Vegas Blvd S.,
NV 89104*
Tel *(702) 380-7711*
Views stretch for miles and
change slowly from this revolving
restaurant 833 ft (254 m) above

the ground. House specials
include Colorado rack of lamb
and crab-stuffed veal.

THE STRIP: Trattoria del Lupo $$$
Italian   **Map** A3
*Mandalay Bay, 3950 Las Vegas
Blvd S., NV 89119*
Tel *(702) 740-5522*
Diners can watch pizza and pasta
dishes being made in this trattoria-
style restaurant with arched pillars
and wrought-iron fittings.

SUMMERLIN: Hachi $$$
Japanese   **Map** A3
*Red Rock Resort, 11011 W. Charleston
Blvd, NV 89135*
Tel *(702) 797-7576*
A fabulous selection of expertly
prepared dishes is offered at
Hachi. Entrées range from beef
tenderloin medallions in a sake-
soy sauce to chicken *yakisoba*
(fried noodles).

SUMMERLIN: Terra Rossa $$$
Italian   **Map** A3
*Red Rock Resort, 11011 W. Charleston
Blvd, NV 89135*
Tel *(702) 797-7531*
Get a Tuscan country feel with
Terra Rossa's soft beige tones and
elongated lamps. The menu has
classic dishes such as mozzarella-
and-ricotta cheese salad with
sun-dried tomatoes, and lasagna.

Southern Utah

**BOULDER: Hell's
Backbone Grill** $$
Southwestern   **Map** C2
20 N. Hwy 12, UT 84716
Tel *(435) 335-7464*
Jalapeño soup and grilled
chicken tacos with rattlesnake
beans are just two of the
superb regional dishes here,
accompanied by organic wines.

BRYCE CANYON: Foster's $$
Steakhouse   **Map** B2
1150 Hwy 12, UT 84759
Tel *(435) 834-5227*
This family-owned eatery serves
hearty meals through the day. Try
the slow-roasted prime rib.

**BRYCE CANYON: The Lodge at
Bryce Canyon Restaurant** $$
Contemporary American   **Map** B2
Bryce Canyon National Park, UT 84717
Tel *(435) 834-8760*
Stone fireplaces create a relaxing
atmosphere at this rustic, elegant
restaurant nestled among
ponderosa pines. Menu
highlights include chicken
stuffed with brie and apple, and
fudge lava cake for dessert.

For key to prices *see page 248*

CEDAR CITY: Market Grill $
American   Map B2
2290 W. 400 North St, UT 84720
Tel *(435) 586-9325*
A long-running restaurant, Market Grill has a classic Western atmosphere and serves hearty homemade fare. The popular chicken-fried steak comes with mashed potatoes, gravy, and vegetables.

CEDAR CITY: Rusty's Ranch House $$
American   Map B2
2275 E. Hwy 14, UT 84721
Tel *(435) 586-3839*   **Closed** *Sun*
The typical Western decor here has heads of moose, deer, and elk mounted around the dining room. The varied menu includes coconut shrimp, filet mignon, and honey-glazed ribs. There are stunning mountain views.

KANAB: Parry Lodge $
American   Map B2
89 E. Center St, UT 84741
Tel *(435) 644-2601*
Established in 1931, this lodge has been visited by many movie stars, including Tyrone Power and Lana Turner. The daily breakfast buffet is good value.

MOAB: Moab Brewery $
American   Map C2
686 S. Main St, UT 84532
Tel *(435) 259-6333*
A popular microbrewery offering a variety of beers made on site. Food options run the gamut from sandwiches and homemade soups to more substantial fare.

DK Choice

MOAB: Moab Diner $
American   Map D2
189 S. Main St, UT 84532
Tel *(435) 259-4006*
From its all-day and all-night breakfast menu right through to dinner, this simply decorated diner is a hit with locals and visitors alike. Don't miss the signature green-chili cheese burger, and leave room for an ice-cream sundae or shake, available in more than a dozen flavors.

MOAB: Eddie McStiff's $$
American   Map D2
57 S. Main St, UT 84532
Tel *(435) 259-2337*
Choose from a reasonably priced menu of pizzas, pasta dishes, and steaks at this restaurant with a pleasant dining room and a covered garden terrace. A range of micro-brews are served at the bar.

Steel conditioning tanks at the Moab Brewery, the only microbrewery in Moab

MOAB: Slickrock Café $$
American   Map D2
5 N. Main St, UT 84532
Tel *(435) 259-8004*
In an atrium-like space decroated with Saltillo tiles and a funky mix of colors, the menu highlights here include "outlaw" meat loaf and a jalapeño burger with pepper Jack cheese and bacon.

MOAB: Sunset Grill $$
American   Map D2
900 N. Main St, Hwy 191, UT 84532
Tel *(435) 259-7146*   **Closed** *Sun*
Spectacularly located in the hilltop home of uranium prospector Charles Steen, this fine-dining restaurant offers amazing sunset views.

MOAB: Desert Bistro $$$
Southwestern   Map D2
36 S. 100 West, UT 84532
Tel *(435) 259-0756*   **Closed** *Mon*
Savor gourmet cuisine in the town's original dance hall, dating back to 1892. Adventurous offerings include smoked tofu dumplings, and a venison and mushroom burger. There is a lovely outdoor patio.

PANGUITCH: Cowboy's Smokehouse $
Barbecue   Map B2
95 N. Main St, UT 84759
Tel *(435) 676-8030*
Opened by an amateur rodeo bull-rider, this café is decorated with old family and ranch photos, and deer and moose heads. Mesquite-smoked steaks and ribs are served with a homemade barbecue sauce.

SPRINGDALE: Bit and Spur Restaurant & Saloon $
Mexican   Map B2
1212 Zion Park Blvd, UT 84767
Tel *(435) 772-3498*
A family-friendly local favorite with a breezy patio and changing art exhibits. Try the signature dish *bistek asado*, a chili-rubbed rib eye.

SPRINGDALE: Oscars Café $
Southwestern   Map B2
948 Zion Park Blvd, UT 84767
Tel *(435) 772-3232*
This adobe-style café is furnished with mosaics, Mayan masks, and plants. The lovely front patio offers superb views of Zion National Park. The juicy burgers and green-chili *chimichangas* are highlights.

SPRINGDALE: Spotted Dog Restaurant $
American   Map B2
450 Zion Park Blvd, UT 84767
Tel *(435) 772-3244*   **Closed** *lunch*
The art-filled dining room here has a fireplace and tall windows, and the sidewalk tables offer great views of Zion National Park. There is an excellent wine cellar. Open for breakfast and dinner.

Adobe-style entrance of Oscars Café in Springdale

For more information on types of restaurants *see pages 244–5*

Colorful Native American decor at the Capitol Reef Café, Torrey

ST. GEORGE: Bear Paw Café $
American   Map B2
75 N. Main St, UT 84770
Tel *(435) 634-0126*
The extensive menu at Bear Paw features soups, omelets, *frittatas*, waffles, and sandwiches. There is an impressive selection of gourmet coffees and teas.

ST. GEORGE: Pancho and Lefty's $
Mexican   Map B2
1050 S. Bluff St, UT 84770
Tel *(435) 628-4772*
Colorful woven blankets and sombreros add to the traditional Mexican atmosphere here. Choose from freshly made *enchiladas* and *flautas*. Grilled steak, chicken, and shrimp fajitas are served with beans and rice.

ST. GEORGE: Painted Pony $$$
Contemporary American Map B2
2 W. Saint George Blvd 22, UT 84770
Tel *(435) 634-1700*
Moroccan-spiced chicken stuffed with dates and bacon-wrapped duck are popular choices at this modern restaurant with a seasonal menu. Local jazz artists perform occasionally.

TORREY: Capitol Reef Café $$
Seafood   Map C2
360 W. Main St, UT 84775
Tel *(435) 425-3271*
This friendly café offers healthy fare. Select the house specialty: locally farmed trout – grilled, broiled, or smoked – and served with a 10-vegetable salad.

TORREY: Café Diablo $$$
Southwestern   Map C2
599 Main St, UT 84775
Tel *(435) 425-3070*
Sit in the comfortable dining room filled with local art or on the breezy patio. The kitchen uses only local, seasonal ingredients.

For key to prices *see page 248*

ZION NATIONAL PARK: Red Rock Grill $$
Southwestern   Map B2
Springdale, UT 84767
Tel *(435) 772-7760*
Nestled among the cottonwoods, this restaurant boasts splendid views from its open-air terrace. Try the Navajo eggplant with tomatillo cream sauce, and spicy-sweet chipotle tilapia.

The Four Corners

BLUFF: Twin Rocks Café $
American   Map D2
913 E. Navajo Twins Dr, UT 84512
Tel *(435) 672-2341*
A pair of sandstone pillars stands huddled together above the cliffs at this scenic café. The menu offers a range of salads and sandwiches, and a unique "Navajo pizza" made with fry bread.

BLUFF: Cottonwood Steakhouse $$
Steakhouse   Map D2
Main & 4th St E., Hwy 191, UT 84512
Tel *(435) 672-2282*
A giant cottonwood tree provides shade over the picnic tables placed around a barbecue pit at this steakhouse serving generous portions of steak, ribs, chicken, shrimp, and fish with green salad.

CAMERON: Cameron Trading Post $
Southwestern   Map C3
Route 89, AZ 86020
Tel *(928) 679-2231*
Colorful Native American artworks adorn the walls at this restaurant, located at a Four Corners crossroads and overlooking the Little Colorado River gorge. A variety of American, Mexican, and Native American dishes are served.

Signpost for Café Diablo in Torrey, Southern Utah

CHINLE: Sacred Canyon Lodge $
American   Map D3
Navajo Route 7, AZ 86503
Tel *(928) 674-5841*
Located on the Navajo reservation at Canyon de Chelly on the site of an 1896 trading post, this restaurant serves generous portions of classic regional and national dishes.

CHINLE: Garcia's Restaurant $$
Southwestern   Map D3
Navajo Route 7, AZ 86503
Tel *(928) 674-5000*
Right next to the Holiday Inn, Garcia's serves classic regional dishes, plus Native American and Mexican specialties, including fajitas and marinated sirloin steak.

DURANGO: Carver Brewing Co. $
International   Map D2
1022 Main Ave, CO 81301
Tel *(970) 259-2545*
A local institution, Carver has been brewing beer – from light lagers to hardy oatmeal stouts – since 1986. Try the Southwest ravioli made with ancho chili.

DURANGO: Ken and Sue's $$
Contemporary American Map D2
636 Main Ave, CO 81301
Tel *(970) 385-1810*
Enjoy upscale dining in a relaxed atmosphere. Specialties include hoisin-glazed "lollipop" wings with homemade blue cheese dipping sauce, and grilled filet mignon with gorgonzola butter.

DURANGO: Red Snapper $$$
Seafood   Map D2
144 E. 9th St, CO 81301
Tel *(970) 259-3417*
A haven for seafood lovers, Red Snapper flies in fresh fish daily. Diners can enjoy views of the huge illuminated aquarium.

FARMINGTON: Clancy's Pub $
International   Map D2
2703 E. 20th St, NM 87402
Tel *(505) 325-8176*
Housed in an adobe-style building, Clancy's is often referred to as an "Irish cantina." The varied menu includes sushi, massive burgers, and more.

HOPI INDIAN RESERVATION: Hopi Cultural Center $
Native American   Map C3
Route 264, Second Mesa, AZ 86043
Tel *(928) 734-2402*
Traditional Hopi dishes, including mutton stew and blue corn piki bread, are served with hominy and roasted green chilies. Mexican and American options, and a superb salad bar, are also available.

IGNACIO: Rolling Thunder Grill $
American   Map D2
14324 US Hwy 172 N., CO 81137
Tel *(970) 563-7777*
Located in the Sky Ute Casino
resort, Rolling Thunder serves
local favorites such as chicken-
fried steak with mashed potatoes
and gravy, and a cowboy pork
chop with apple chipotle sauce.

KAYENTA: Amigo Café $
Mexican   Map C2
Hwy 163, AZ 86033
Tel *(928) 697-8448*   **Closed** *Sun*
On the Navajo reservation,
Amigo is popular with both
locals and visitors. It serves tacos,
chimichangas, tamales, *tostadas,*
and more. Takeouts are available.

MESA VERDE NATIONAL PARK:
Spruce Tree Terrace Café $
Southwestern   Map D2
Mile Marker 15, Mancos, CO 81328
Tel *1-800-449-2288*
This café is set in a historic stone
building and its expansive menu
offers good value. Dine inside or
on the sunny patio.

MESA VERDE NATIONAL PARK:
Metate Room $$$
Southwestern   Map D2
Mile Marker 15, Mancos, CO 81328
Tel *1-800-449-2288*   **Closed** *mid-
Oct–mid-Apr*
This remote restaurant delights
diners with cuisine based on
sustainable staples used by the
Ancestral Puebloans: cactus dip,
blue-corn trout, and pepper-and-
coriander-crusted elk. This is an
excellent place for local wines.

MONUMENT VALLEY:
Stagecoach Dining Room $$
American   Map C2
Goulding's Lodge, UT 84536
Tel *(435) 727-3231*
High on a hill with panoramic
views, this restaurant caters to
tourists visiting the Monument
Valley. The salad bar, Navajo
tacos, and steaks are highlights.

Patio seating at Spruce Tree Terrace Café in a
historic building, Mesa Verde National Park

Panoramic views from the dining area of The View Hotel Restaurant in Monument Valley

MONUMENT VALLEY: The View
Hotel Restaurant $$
Southwestern   Map C2
*Hwy 163, Monument Valley Tribal
Park, UT 84536*
Tel *(435) 727-5555*
Decorated with Navajo art, this
spacious restaurant has stunning
views of Monument Valley. The
menu features specialties such as
mutton stew with fry bread as
well as steaks and grilled salmon.

OURAY: Backstreet Bistro $
American   Map D2
636 Main St, CO 81427
Tel *(970) 325-0550*
Popular for its sandwiches, soups,
and frozen coffees, this bistro
also serves homemade pastries
and phenomenal cheesecakes.

OURAY: Bon Ton Restaurant $$$
Italian   Map D2
426 Main St, CO 81427
Tel *(970) 325-4951*
This cozy restaurant in a historic
hotel boasts a romantic martini
bar. Enjoy dishes such as grilled
Angus beef wrapped in pastry,
and scampi served in a sherry-
cream sauce over fettuccine.

TELLURIDE: Maggie's
Bakery and Café $
American   Map D2
300 W. Colorado Ave, CO 81435
Tel *(970) 728-3334*
Fresh French roast coffee and
homemade breads and pastries
are served at this small café.
There are also eggs and pancakes
for breakfast, and light sandwiches
and vegetarian options at lunch.

TELLURIDE: Siam $
Thai   Map D2
200 S. Davis St, CO 81435
Tel *(970) 728-6886*
A very popular, casual eatery
(which can mean a long wait for a
table), Siam serves authentically

spiced Asian dishes such as
chicken satay and green curry.
No reservations are taken.

TELLURIDE: 221 South Oak $$$
Contemporary American Map D2
221 South Oak, CO 81435
Tel *(970) 728-9507*
Candlelight and white linen
create an elegant ambience at
this restaurant set in a historic
house. Choose from eclectic
dishes such as sautéed soft-shell
crabs with red peppercorn sauce.

DK Choice

TELLURIDE: Chop House $$$
Contemporary
American   Map D2
231 W. Colorado Ave, CO 81435
Tel *(970) 728-9100*
This upscale restaurant is
committed to sustainable
ingredients and uses only
organic, free-range fowl, non-
threatened fish species, and
local ingredients. Game meat
entrées include pan-seared
elk short loin with sauerkraut
risotto, and 30-day dry-aged
bison rib eye.

TUBA CITY: Hogan Restaurant $
Native American/
Southwestern   Map C3
Main St & Moenave Rd, AZ 86045
Tel *(928) 283-5260*
This eatery is shaped like a Navajo
hogan dwelling and serves
Navajo tacos, as well as Mexican
and American dishes.

WINDOW ROCK: Diné $
American   Map D3
48 W. Hwy 264, AZ 86515
Tel *(928) 871-4108*
Decorated with Navajo art, this
diner offers traditional mutton
stew, fry breads, and tacos, as well
as Mexican and American fare.

For more information on types of restaurants *see pages 244–5*

Santa Fe and Northern New Mexico

CHIMAYÓ: Restaurante Rancho de Chimayó $$
Mexican   Map E3
County Rd 98, NM 87522
Tel *(505) 351-4444*
This old hacienda's adobe walls are decorated with family photos. The fine cuisine is prepared using local ingredients and old Spanish recipes. There is a terrace for alfresco dining in summer and a cozy fireplace during winter.

RANCHOS DE TAOS: Trading Post Café $$
International   Map E3
4179 Hwy 68, NM 87557
Tel *(575) 758-5089*   **Closed** *Sun & Mon*
A historic option near the San Francisco de Asis church, this café is a favorite with celebrities and locals, both for its artworks and its artistically presented meals.

SANTA FE: Bumblebee's Baja Grill $
Mexican   Map E3
301 Jefferson St, NM 87501
Tel *(505) 820-2862*
House favorites at this welcoming restaurant include chargrilled fish tacos served Baja-style with soft corn tortillas, and burritos filled with grilled asparagus, avocado, and Jack and cheddar cheeses.

SANTA FE: Cowgirl $
Southwestern/Barbecue   Map E3
319 S. Guadalupe St, NM 87501
Tel *(505) 982-2565*
Photos, art posters, hides, skulls, and other cowgirl memorabilia cover the walls at this friendly Wild West restaurant where everything is cooked over a mesquite pit. The barbecue dishes are excellent.

SANTA FE: Los Potrillos $
Mexican   Map E3
1947 Cerrillos Rd, NM 87505
Tel *(505) 992-0550*
"The Colts" serves typical, authentic Mexican dishes: from *nopalito* (cactus) leaf to stuffed fish fillets. A colorful horse-themed mural adds to the atmosphere.

SANTA FE: Mu Du Noodles $
Asian   Map E3
1494 Cerrillos Rd, NM 87505
Tel *(505) 983-1411*   **Closed** *Sun & Mon*
Dine on Pacific Rim dishes here, inside or al fresco on the charming patio. The house specialty is beef Jantaboon stir-fry.

SANTA FE: The Shed $
Mexican   Map E3
113½ E. Palace Ave, NM 87051
Tel *(505) 982-9030*
This family-run restaurant is housed in a quaint 17th-century adobe hacienda. Try the chilled raspberry soup laced with rosé wine, followed by a spicy chicken dish, and lemon soufflé for dessert.

SANTA FE: Tia Sophias $
Mexican   Map E3
210 W San Francisco St, 87501
Tel *(505) 983-9880*   **Closed** *dinner*
Popular with locals for its breakfasts and lunches, the highlights on the menu here include homemade chorizo, flaky *sopaipillas*, and huge burritos.

SANTA FE: Tomasita's $
Mexican   Map E3
500 S. Guadalupe St, NM 87501
Tel *(505) 983-5721*   **Closed** *Sun*
Housed in an old brick train station built in 1904, this family-friendly restaurant is a local favorite. No reservations; be prepared to wait.

SANTA FE: Amaya $$
Southwestern   Map E3
1501 Paseo de Peralta, NM 87501
Tel *(505) 955-7805*
In an elegant hotel, Amaya offers indoor dining by the fireplace or outside on the patio. The menu emphasizes regional staples in dishes such as venison marinated in port wine and juniper berries.

SANTA FE: Blue Corn Café $$
Southwestern   Map E3
133 Water St, NM 87501
Tel *(505) 984-1800*
With modern decor and thick wooden beams, this eatery is popular for its draught microbrews and prickly pear iced tea. Tacos made with blue corn, brimming with beef or chicken, are the house specialty.

SANTA FE: La Boca $$
Spanish   Map E3
72 W. Marcy, NM 87051
Tel *(505) 982-3433*
One of the city's most beloved chefs, James Campbell Caruso, prepares a variety of tapas and entrées, blending Spanish and Mediterranean influences, at this cozy bistro with a great wine list.

SANTA FE: Maria's $$
Southwestern   Map E3
555 W. Cordova Rd, NM 87505
Tel *(505) 983-7929*
Chicken, beef, and vegetarian dishes are served here on sizzling platters with *pico de gallo* and guacamole. There are over 100 margaritas to choose from.

SANTA FE: Santa Fe Bar & Grill $$
Southwestern   Map E3
187 Paseo de Peralta, NM 87501
Tel *(505) 982-3033*
Mouthwatering slow-roasted, tamarind-chipotle baby back ribs and sinful adobe mud pie are the popular dishes here. Colorful Mexican furnishings, pottery, and artworks decorate the dining area.

SANTA FE: Anasazi $$$
American   Map E3
113 Washington St, NM 87501
Tel *(505) 988-3236*
This luxurious restaurant offers innovative regional dishes such as chili almond-crusted Atlantic salmon and grilled Rocky Mountain elk short loin. It has a high wood-beamed celing and rustic furniture as well as a patio.

Rustic decor at the upscale Anasazi in Santa Fe

For key to prices *see page 248*

SANTA FE: Café Pasqual's $$$
International   Map E3
121 Don Gaspar, NM 87501
Tel *(505) 983-9340*
In a Pueblo-style adobe house
with murals and Mexican tiles, this
tiny restaurant offers innovative
cuisine using organic ingredients.

DK Choice

**SANTA FE: The Compound
Restaurant** $$$
Contemporary
American   Map E3
635 Canyon Rd, NM 87501
Tel *(505) 982-4353*
In a historic house once known
as the McComb Compound,
this luxurious restaurant's fine
menu is matched by a stylish,
art-filled dining room and
charming patio. Signature
dishes include tuna tartare
topped with Oestra caviar, and
Muscovy duck breast with
rhubarb-ginger compote.

SANTA FE: Coyote Café $$$
Southwestern   Map E3
132 W. Water St, NM 87051
Tel *(505) 983-1615*
Innovative dishes such as papaya
and goat cheese spring rolls, and
mesquite-grilled prime rib chop
with rosemary-horseradish butter
are on the menu here.

SANTA FE: Dinner for Two $$$
Contemporary American Map E3
106 N. Guadalupe St, NM 87501
Tel *(505) 820-2075*   **Closed** *Tue*
Expertly prepared dishes and an
excellent wine list feature at this
romantic restaurant with attentive
service. Live music on weekends.

SANTA FE: El Farol $$$
Spanish   Map E3
808 Canyon Rd, NM 87501
Tel *(505) 983-9912*
"The lantern" has been serving
artists since 1835. It offers tapas
as well as more substantial fare.
Live music in the evenings.

SANTA FE: Geronimo $$$
International   Map E3
724 Canyon Rd, NM 87501
Tel *(505) 982-1500*
Housed in a 1756 building, this
intimate restaurant serves
renowned Southwestern fusion
dishes, such as peppery elk.

SANTA FE: La Casa Sena $$$
Contemporary American Map E3
125 E. Palace Ave, NM 87051
Tel *(505) 988-9232*
In an 1860s territorial-style adobe
building, La Casa Sena is set
around a pretty courtyard perfect

Formal dining room at Geronimo in Santa Fe

for summer dining. Chorizo-
stuffed pork tenderloin with
peach-and-prickly-pear purée is
one of the typically superb dishes.
There is an outstanding wine list.

SANTA FE: Old House $$$
International   Map E3
309 W. San Francisco St, NM 87501
Tel *(505) 988-4455*
Popular with pre-opera diners for
its excellent food and impeccable
service, the seasonal menus here
are based on fine ingredients
such as Maine diver scallops and
Dungeness crab. There is a fine
selection of wines.

SANTA FE: The Pink Adobe $$$
Southwestern   Map E3
406 Old Santa Fe Trail, NM 87051
Tel *(505) 983-7712*   **Closed** *Mon*
Situated in former barracks, the
Pink Adobe has several candlelit
rooms, each with a fireplace,
and one with a tree growing
through the roof. A favorite
with celebrities and locals, it
offers high-end comfort cuisine.

SANTA FE: Santacafé $$$
American   Map E3
231 Washington Ave, NM 87501
Tel *(505) 984-1788*
Set in the adobe hacienda of a
150-year-old building, Santacafé
offers flawless service and
eclectic cuisine based on a
successful blend of Asian and
Southwestern ingredients.

**TAOS: Doc
Martin's Restaurant** $$
Southwestern   Map E3
125 Paseo del Pueblo Norte, NM 87571
Tel *(575) 758-1977*
Named after the county's first
physician, this restaurant offers
superior regional cuisine. Multi-
course *prix fixe* and à la carte
menus are available. Try the red
wine-braised buffalo short ribs.

TAOS: Graham's Grille $$
Southwestern   Map E3
106 Paseo del Pueblo, NM 87571
Tel *(575) 751-1350*
An authentic taste of New Mexico,
ingredients here are sourced
from local farms and ranches.
The chicken is free-range. Sample
the red chili calamari strips
and black bean burgers.

**TAOS: Orlando's New
Mexico Café** $$
Southwestern   Map E3
1114 Don Juan Valdez Ln, NM 87571
Tel *(575) 751-1450*
Local chili aficionados rave about
the regional New Mexican fare
here. The café is colorfully
painted, and large umbrellas
shade the patio. Relax with a beer
by the fire pit on cool evenings.

TAOS: Lambert's of Taos $$$
Contemporary American Map E3
309 Paseo del Pueblo Sur, NM 87571
Tel *(575) 758-1009*
Lambert's serves a variety of
meat, game, and seafood dishes,
from Asian-style shrimp to the
signature pepper-crusted
Colorado lamb. It has an
excellent list of Californian wines.

Buttermilk chicken and cocktails at The
Compound Restaurant, Santa Fe

Albuquerque and Southern New Mexico

ACOMA: Huwaka Restaurant $
Southwestern **Map** D3
*Sky City Casino, I-40 at Exit 102,
NM 87034*
Tel *(505) 552-6017*
In a Native American-themed
casino, this informal eatery
features a buffet with fare such as
green-chili stew and blue corn
enchiladas, as well as a taco bar.

ALAMOGORDO: Peppers Grill $
American **Map** E4
3200 N. White Sands Blvd, NM 88310
Tel *(575) 437-9717*
This family-run restaurant with
efficient service has an extensive
menu offering a choice of hearty
meals – pasta dishes, grilled steaks,
and several vegetarian options.

ALBUQUERQUE: 66 Diner $
American **Map** E3
1405 Central Ave NE., NM 87106
Tel *(505) 247-1421*
Highlights on the menu at this
family-friendly diner with a retro
theme include thick milkshakes,
fried catfish, and green-chili fries.
The jukebox spins 1950s tunes.

DK Choice

ALBUQUERQUE: Church
Street Café $
Southwestern **Map** E3
2111 Church St NW., NM 87104
Tel *(505) 247-8522*
Nestled in the heart of Old Town,
this renowned café is built with
19th-century adobe, and filled
with antique Native American
art and rugs. Dine inside by the
kiva fireplace, or outdoors among
the grapevines. Highly regarded
regional dishes include *carne
adovada al horno* (oven-cooked
pork marinated in red chili).

ALBUQUERQUE: Frontier
Restaurant $
American **Map** E3
2400 Central Ave SE., 87106
Tel *(505) 266-0550*
Good-value breakfasts, burritos,
burgers, and legendary sweet rolls
are served in this memorabilia-
filled restaurant opposite the
University of New Mexico.

ALBUQUERQUE: Garduño's $
Mexican **Map** E3
2100 Louisiana Blvd, NM 87110
Tel *(505) 880-0055*
A popular local chain, the
flavorful dishes here include
guacamole, prepared table-side,

Casual flagstone patio at Church Street Café
in Albuquerque

and burritos and *enchiladas*
smothered with green chilies.
Handshaken margaritas and
mariachis add to the atmosphere.

ALBUQUERQUE: La Placita
Dining Rooms $
Southwestern **Map** E3
208 San Felipe St, NM 87104
Tel *(505) 247-2204*
Housed in a historic hacienda
built in 1706, La Placita has several
dining rooms – one is dominated
by a cottonwood tree. Try fluffy
sopaipillas (quick breads) filled
with cheese, meat, and beans.

ALBUQUERQUE: Lindy's Diner $
American **Map** E3
500 Central Ave SW., NM 87102
Tel *(505) 242-2582*
This friendly eatery has been
serving huge plates of hearty
food since the 1920s. Favorites
include breakfast burritos,
sandwiches, and diner
staples such as meat loaf.

ALBUQUERQUE: Pueblo
Harvest Café $
Southwestern/
Native American **Map** E3
2401 12th St NW., NM 87104
Tel *(505) 724-3510*
Located in the Indian Pueblo
Cultural Center, this restaurant
offers typical Puebloan cuisine
and fusion dishes such as buffalo
tenderloin and grilled salmon.

ALBUQUERQUE: El Pinto $$
Southwestern **Map** E3
10500 4th St NW., NM 87114
Tel *(505) 898-1771*
Decorated with chili *ristras*, El
Pinto has art-filled dining rooms
and mariachis strolling through
the garden patio. It has a varied
menu of New Mexican dishes.

ALBUQUERQUE: Elephant Bar $$
Asian fusion **Map** E3
2240 Louisiana Blvd NE., NM 87110
Tel *(505) 884-2355*
At this safari-themed eatery with
zebra-striped ceilings, wide-
ranging dishes such as Shanghai
cashew shrimp with pineapple
are served in generous portions,
along with flavorful drinks such as
passion fruit *mojitos*.

ALBUQUERQUE: High Finance
Restaurant and Tavern $$
American **Map** E3
40 Tramway Rd NE., NM 87122
Tel *(505) 243-9742*
At the top of the Sandia Peak
Tramway, with mountain views,
this restaurant has paintings of
financiers decorating its wooden
walls. Choose from seafood, steaks,
poultry, and vegetarian dishes.

ALBUQUERQUE: High Noon
Restaurant and Saloon $$
Steakhouse/American **Map** E3
425 San Felipe NW., NM 87104
Tel *(505) 765-1455*
One of Old Town's historic
treasures, High Noon dates back
to 1785 and has numerous dining
rooms, each with a different
theme. Bison rib eye and rack
of lamb are popular options.

ALBUQUERQUE: La Hacienda
Restaurant $$
Southwestern **Map** E3
302 San Felipe NW., NM 87104
Tel *(505) 243-3131*
Carne adovado (red chile pork
stew) is the specialty of this
eatery in an old adobe villa with
a mural depicting early settlers.

ALBUQUERQUE: St. Clair
Winery & Bistro $$
French/American **Map** E3
901 Rio Grande Blvd NW., NM 87104
Tel *(505) 243-9916*
The state's largest winery
operates a tasting room and
bistro serving French-style fare.

Flower-filled planters outside the
popular El Pinto

Many of the entrées, such as Cabernet-braised pot roast and garlic-Chardonnay chicken, are cooked in wine.

ALBUQUERQUE: Yanni's $$
Greek/Mediterranean   Map E3
3109 Central Ave NE., NM 87106
Tel *(505) 268-9250*
Greek crowd-pleasers, such as torched *saganaki* cheese, are served at this local favorite with Aegean blue-and-white decor. There is music on weekends.

ALBUQUERQUE: Artichoke Café $$$
International   Map E3
424 Central Ave SE., NM 87102
Tel *(505) 243-0200*
With a refined, modern look and rotating exhibits of local art, this restaurant's menu features an assortment of contemporary American, Italian, and French dishes, and a varied wine list.

ALBUQUERQUE: Jennifer James 101 $$$
Contemporary American   Map E3
4615 Menaul Blvd NE., NM 87110
Tel *(505) 884-3860*   **Closed** *Sun & Mon*
Acclaimed Chef Jennifer James presents a menu that goes back to the basics, with simple, quality recipes. Seasonal dishes incorporate local, organic produce.

ALBUQUERQUE: Landry's Seafood $$$
Seafood   Map E3
5001 Jefferson St NE., NM 87109
Tel *(505) 875-0101*
This national chain is famous for fresh fish prepared with special seasoning. Seasonal offerings include snapper, halibut, shrimp, and shellfish. There are good vegetarian and meat options too.

ALBUQUERQUE: Seasons Rotisserie & Grill $$$
Steakhouse/American   Map E3
2031 Mountain Rd, San Felipe Plaza, NM 87104
Tel *(505) 766-5100*
Popular dishes at this restaurant with contemporary decor and large floral displays include rotisserie chicken and grilled Colorado lamb.

ALBUQUERQUE: Zinc $$$
Contemporary American   Map E3
3009 Central Ave NE., NM 87106
Tel *(505) 254-9462*
French-inspired bistro classics are served in this classy restaurant with antique mirrors and stained glass. Sit at the zinc bar to watch the chefs in action. For lighter fare and live music, visit the cellar bar.

Bright interior with a Grecian theme at Yanni's in Albuquerque

CARLSBAD: The Flume Room $$
American   Map F5
1829 S. Canal St, NM 88220
Tel *(575) 887-2851*
This casual, family-friendly restaurant is named after the famous Pecos River aqueduct. It offers huge servings of steak, chicken, and seafood.

CLOUDCROFT: Rebecca's $$$
American   Map E4
1 Corona Pl, NM 88317
Tel *(575) 682-2566*
Classic dishes here include escargots and oysters Rockefeller. The restaurant is named for its resident ghost, who some claim can still be found in the elegant Victorian room filled with Queen Anne chairs.

LINCOLN: Isaac's Table $$$
International   Map E4
Mile marker 98, Hwy 380, NM 88338
Tel *(575) 653-4609*
Issac's has gourmet *prix fixe* dinners with seasonal choices such as rack of antelope or venison, and flounder stuffed with crab. Save room for the signature dessert, chocolate whiskey cake.

MESILLA: La Posta de Mesilla $
Mexican/Steakhouse   Map E5
2410 Calle de San Albino, NM 88046
Tel *(575) 524-3524*
Mexican-style favorites are served in this maze of rooms at a historic former hitching post filled with greenery and Mexican tiles and artworks.

MESILLA: Double Eagle $$$
American   Map E5
2355 Calle de Guadalupe, NM 88046
Tel *(575) 523-6700*
Choose from baked brie with pecans and apples, aged steaks, and fresh seafood at this restaurant in an exquisite mid-19th-century building with Baccarat-crystal chandeliers.

RUIDOSO: Café Rio $
International   Map E4
2547 Sudderth Dr, NM 88345
Tel *(575) 257-7746*
The eclectic menu at this family-friendly restaurant includes deep-dish pizzas, calzones, Cajun and Greek dishes, and homemade ice cream.

RUIDOSO: Cattle Baron $$
Steakhouse/Seafood   Map E4
657 Sudderth Dr, NM 88345
Tel *(575) 257-9355*
This local chain is famous for steaks, seafood, and a legendary salad bar. Western-style decor features cowboy saddles, guns, antlers, and wildlife photography. Prime rib is the house specialty.

SILVER CITY: Shevek & Co. Restaurant $$$
International   Map D5
602 N. Bullard St, NM 88061
Tel *(575) 534-9168*   **Closed** *Wed & Thu*
Opt for lighter dining in the form of tapas and meze, or choose from excellent full entrées at this informal, friendly restaurant. It has a good list of wines and beers.

Appetizers and beverages topping the zinc bar at Zinc, Albuquerque

For more information on types of restaurants *see pages 244–5*

SHOPPING IN THE SOUTHWEST

With such an exciting range of Native American, Hispanic, and Anglo-American products, shopping in the Southwest is a cultural adventure. Native crafts, including rugs, jewelry, and pottery, top the list of things that people buy. The Southwest is also a center for the fine arts, with Santa Fe *(see pp196–203)* famous for its many galleries, selling everything from Georgia O'Keeffe-inspired landscapes and the latest contemporary works, to popular bronze sculptures of cowboys or Indians. Across the region, specialty grocery stores and supermarkets stock a range of Southwestern products, from hot chili sauces to blue-corn tortilla chips. In the major cities there is a choice of glamorous fashion districts, usually situated in air-conditioned, landscaped malls. Las Vegas also ranks shopping among its attractions, with its themed malls *(see pp128–9)*.

Shopping Hours and Payment

Most major stores are open from 9 or 10am to between 8 and 10pm, 7 days a week, although some stores may close just after midday on Sunday or Monday. Most stores take MasterCard, Visa, and ATM cards. Other credit cards and out-of-state checks are often not accepted. Added to the price will be a sales tax of 2.9 percent in Colorado, 5.9 percent in Utah, 5.125 percent in New Mexico, 6.6 percent in Arizona, and 6.85 percent in Nevada. Local city and county sales taxes may also be added.

Southwestern Art and Decor

The Southwest has a vibrant artistic heritage, and Santa Fe is the country's second-largest art market after New York. The city's arts district stretches from the downtown Plaza for 2 miles (3 km) along Canyon Road *(see p201)*. More than 200 galleries specialize in locally produced art, with many fine-arts galleries handling leading or up- and-coming Southwestern painters and sculptors. The **Meyer Gallery** specializes in figurative bronze sculpture and features a range of paintings by regional artists. For an evocative souvenir of your time in the area, head to a photographic gallery. The **Andrew Smith Gallery** carries works by Ansel Adams, Edward S. Curtis, and other photographers who captured the landscape and people of the Southwest.

Chimeneas lined up for sale at a local artisan's store in Tubac, Arizona

Native American and Hispanic artists are also well represented, the latter producing carved *santos* and *bultos* depicting saints and other religious figures. Good places to find Hispanic crafts include **Pachamama**, which sells everything from altarpieces and statues to paintings on tin.

Other Southwest cities also have dedicated arts districts. The **Tucson Art District** has more than 40 galleries, while **Old Town Artisans** is a collection of shops in a block of 1850s adobe buildings selling Southwestern art, jewelry, clothing, and crafts. Scottsdale *(see p84)* has the Main Street Arts District, where many galleries are open late on Thursdays for the Scottsdale ArtWalk (7–9pm). **Trailside Galleries** specializes in Western art by leading contemporary artists. More than 25 art galleries can also be found in

Mexican Huichol beaded mask

Albuquerque's Old Town, among them the renowned **Weems Gallery**, featuring high-quality works.

The Southwest's bright colors and traditional designs are an inspiration for home decor. Find original crafts and woven rugs designed by Native Americans, at Albuquerque's **Bien Mur Indian Market Center**.

A good shop in Santa Fe for Mexican-style decor is **Artesanos**, featuring colorful talavera tiles, punched tin mirrors, furniture, and other items. The entire town of Tubac *(see p94)* is an art colony with dozens of galleries and shops selling fine arts. Other shops sell pottery, textiles, gift items from Mexico, and an array of creative Southwestern-style home decor. Some of the best examples are at **Tubac Ironworks**, opposite the art museum.

Native American Arts and Crafts

Discovering the spiritual beliefs that inspire Native arts and crafts can make shopping for these items a rewarding experience, especially when purchasing directly from Native artists – in their homes, at reservation trading posts, or in pueblo or museum stores. The quality of Native crafts can vary greatly, and it is worth knowing a few guidelines. The term "Indian handmade" means that the item has been made solely by Native Americans, while "Indian crafted" means that they have been involved in the production. Buying directly from the artist ensures authenticity and also gives money to the local Native American community.

Many artists display their work at tourist stops such as those at Canyon de Chelly or on reservations. Trading posts, such as the **Hubbell Trading Post** *(see p171)* on the Navajo Reservation, were established to sell Native products to the region's first tourists in the late 1800s. Other sources of good-quality authentic items include the **Cameron Trading Post** 50 miles (80 km) north of Flagstaff, which now holds a gallery displaying historic and modern rugs, pottery, baskets, and carvings. **Fifth Generation Trading Company** in Farmington and **Sewell's Indian Arts** in Scottsdale also offer a wide choice of goods.

The distinctive pottery of the Pueblo Indian communities is highly prized. Pieces by famous artists such as Maria Martínez are collector's items with prices to

match, but you can also buy affordable works by contemporary artists such as Nancy Youngblood. She is represented by **Andrea Fisher Fine Pottery**. Artists in several of the Pueblo communities north of Santa Fe welcome visitors at their home workshops; look for signs outside. The **Indian Pueblo Cultural Center** *(see pp218–19)* in Albuquerque offers Pueblo Indian art at fair prices.

The **Shiprock Trading Company** specializes in vintage and contemporary Native arts, with branches in Farmington and Santa Fe. You can also buy older pieces of Native American art at Santa Fe's **Morning Star Gallery**, set in a lovely old adobe house on Canyon Road. **Nambé Outlets** features the signature metal bowls and other artworks from the Nambé Pueblo north of the city. At **Chief Dodge Indian Jewelry and Fine Arts** in Scottsdale you can watch Native artists at work.

Jewelry

Native American artists are known for their fine jewelry, but cheaply manufactured goods abound in tourist areas, and it can be difficult to tell good-quality natural turquoise from cheaper grades or fakes. If you want a special piece, visit Albuquerque's Turquoise Museum *(see p216)* to learn the difference. High-quality Indian-made jewelry can be expensive. Buy from a reputable dealer who will give you a written guarantee of authenticity.

Examples of fine turquoise jewelry made by the Navajo tribe

The Second Mesa Jewelry Co-operative, on the Hopi Reservation *(see p170)*, is a training facility that offers some of the finest Hopi silverwork. The Native American market under the arcades of the Santa Fe Plaza *(see pp196–7)* is a fun place to buy, with a range of prices and quality. Owned by a Native American artist specializing in turquoise jewelry, **Zachanee** in the Plaza Galeria also sells quality pieces. In Albuquerque, **Native Gold** sells gold jewelry with gem-grade turquoise, coral, and other precious stones.

Museum Shops

Wonderful and authentic Native artworks can also be found in the shops of many museums. In Phoenix, the Heard Museum *(see pp82–3)* has a selection of beautiful Native baskets, paintings, sculpture, and *kachina* dolls, as does Flagstaff's Museum of Northern Arizona *(see p72)*. In Santa Fe, the museum shop at the Palace of the Governors *(see p198)* has fine wood carvings and Hispanic art. The re-created trading post at the Wheelwright Museum of the American Indian *(see p201)* specializes in traditional Navajo jewelry and crafts. Top-quality Spanish Colonial arts, furniture, and weavings can be found at markets organized by the **Museum of Spanish Colonial Art** *(see p201)*.

Native American rugs in the Cameron Trading Post

Typical Southwestern wear

Malls

The searing temperatures of southern Arizona and New Mexico have spawned some of the most stunning malls in the USA. The biggest concentration is in Phoenix, which boasts the enormous **Metrocenter**. Large department stores such as Neiman Marcus can be found at the even larger **Scottsdale Fashion Square**. Phoenix's **Biltmore Fashion Park** sells designer clothing and kitchenware, as well as offering great dining options.

Themed malls are also abundant. **Borgata of Scottsdale** is set in a 14th-century -style village with medieval courtyards. The **Arizona Center** in Phoenix is an oasis of restaurants and shops set among gardens, fountains, and a waterfall.

In Tucson, **La Encantada** is a breath of fresh air, with upscale specialty stores, including Tiffany, Anthropologie, and Crate and Barrel, set around an outdoor plaza. New Mexico's largest mall, the **Coronado Center** in Albuquerque, has 150 stores.

Most major Las Vegas hotels feature designer shopping areas (see pp110–21).

Factory Outlet Malls

If you're looking for bargains, several factory outlet malls offer discounted merchandise and seconds from hundreds of name-brand retailers in apparel, shoes, sportswear, luggage, and homewares. Merchandise is generally of good quality, but check carefully for flaws or damage, and remember that clothing may not be of the current season or latest style.

In the Phoenix suburb of Tempe, **Arizona Mills** has around 175 outlet stores, including the high-end department stores Saks Fifth Avenue and Neiman Marcus. **Outlets at Anthem**, also in Phoenix, has stores selling sporting goods, luggage, and toys. In New Mexico, the **Fashion Outlets of Santa Fe** is located off I-25 and contains around 30 stores.

Western Wear

Among the most popular souvenirs of the Southwest are hand-tooled cowboy boots, cowboy hats, and decorative leather belts. Western wear is made to high standards throughout the region. Phoenix is famous for cowboy clothes, but El Paso (see pp226–7) is also noted for its leather goods.

Az-tex Hats of Phoenix has the largest selection of cowboy hats in the Southwest, while **Saba's Western Store** has been outfitting customers since 1927. **Bacon's Boots and Saddles**, in the historic mining town of Globe (see p87), is owned by craftsman Ed Bacon, who has been making his wares for more than 50 years. For children's Western wear, try **Sheplers** in Mesa, Arizona.

Vintage Western wear can be found at Santa Fe's **Double Take at the Ranch**, which sells everything from boots and embroidered cowboy shirts to jewelry. At **Back at the Ranch** you can design your own cowboy boots or choose from some 1,000 pairs in stock.

Food

Southwesterners are proud of their cuisine, and the grocery stores at most malls sell chile sauces, salsa dips, and blue-corn chips. Specialty shops are good places to discover new Southwestern foods. At the **Santa Cruz Chili and Spice Co.**, along the I-19 frontage road at Tumacacori, you can sample some sauces before you buy. In addition to the usual salsas and hot sauces, **The Chile Shop** in Santa Fe sells chile peanut butter and habanero fudge sauce, as well as chile wreaths, cookbooks, and decorative items. Several companies, such as the **Arizona Pepper Products Co.**, have websites where you can order gourmet regional foods. **New Mexico Chili** ships fresh, frozen, and dried chiles from Hatch (see p222), or you can buy them from small shopkeepers in the town.

Farmers' markets are a good source of local produce, but don't overlook the Arizona supermarket chains. **Food City** caters for the Hispanic market, and most large branches of **Fry's** have dedicated Hispanic foods sections.

Visit **The Pecan Store** for fresh pecans grown in Green Valley, south of Tucson.

Colorful fresh vegetables on sale at a farmers' market

DIRECTORY

Southwestern Art and Decor

Andrew Smith Gallery
122 Grant Ave.,
Santa Fe, NM 87501.
Tel (505) 984-1234.

Artesanos
1414 Maclovia St.,
Santa Fe, NM 87505.
Tel (505) 471-8020.

Bien Mur Indian Market Center
I-25 at Tramway Rd., NE,
Albuquerque, NM 87113.
Tel (505) 821-5400.

Meyer Gallery
225 Canyon Rd.,
Santa Fe, NM 87501.
Tel (505) 983-1434.

Old Town Artisans
201 N. Court Ave.,
Tucson, AZ 85701.
Tel (520) 623-6024.

Pachamama
223 Canyon Rd.,
Santa Fe, NM 87501.
Tel (505) 983-4020.

Trailside Galleries
7330 Scottsdale Mall,
Scottsdale, AZ 85251.
Tel (480) 945-7751.

Tubac Ironworks
217 Plaza Rd., Tubac, AZ
85646. **Tel** (520) 398-2163.

Tucson Art District
Congress and Broadway
streets; Stone and 4th
Aves., Tucson, AZ.
Tel (520) 624-1817.

Weems Gallery
303 Romero St. NW,
Albuquerque, NM 87104.
Tel (505) 764-0302.

Native American Arts and Crafts

Andrea Fisher Fine Pottery
100 W. San Francisco St.,
Santa Fe, NM 87501.
Tel (505) 986-1234.
W andreafisherpottery.com

Cameron Trading Post
Highway 89, Cameron, AZ
86020. **Tel** (928) 679-2231.
W camerontrading post.com

Chief Dodge Indian Jewelry and Fine Arts
1332 N. Scottsdale Rd.,
Scottsdale, AZ 85257.
Tel (480) 970-1133.
W chiefdodge.com

Fifth Generation Trading Company
232 W. Broadway,
Farmington, NM 87401.
Tel (505) 326-3211.
W southwestshowroom.com

Hubbell Trading Post
Highway 264, Ganado, AZ
86505. **Tel** (928) 755-3254.
W nps.gov/hutr

Indian Pueblo Cultural Center
2401 12th St.,
Albuquerque, NM 87104.
Tel (505) 843-7270.
W indianpueblo.org

Morning Star Gallery
513 Canyon Rd., Santa Fe,
NM 87501. **Tel** (505) 982-8187. W morningstar gallery.com

Nambé Outlets
924 Paseo de Peralta;
104 W. San Francisco St.,
Santa Fe, NM 87501.
Tel (505) 988-5528/3574.
W nambe.com

Sewell's Indian Arts
7087 E. Fifth Ave.,
Scottsdale, AZ 85251.
Tel (480) 945-0962.

Shiprock Trading Company
53 Old Santa Fe Trail,
Santa Fe, NM 87501.
Tel (505) 982-8478.

Jewelry

Native Gold
323 Romero St. NW,
Albuquerque, NM 87104.
Tel (800) 444-2242.

Zachanee
66 E. San Francisco St.,
Santa Fe, NM 87501.
Tel (505) 920-2935.

Museum Shops

Museum of Spanish Colonial Art
750 Camino Lejo,
Santa Fe, NM 87505.
Tel (505) 982-2226.

Malls

Arizona Center
400 E. Van Buren St.,
Phoenix, AZ 85004.
Tel (602) 271-4000.
W arizonacenter.com

Biltmore Fashion Park
2502 Camelback Rd.,
Phoenix, AZ 85016.
Tel (602) 955-8400.
W shopbiltmore.com

Borgata of Scottsdale
6166 N. Scottsdale Rd.,
Scottsdale, AZ 85253.
Tel (602) 953-6538.
W borgata.com

Coronado Center
6600 Menaul Blvd. NE,
Albuquerque, NM 87110.
Tel (505) 881-2700.
W coronadocenter.com

La Encantada
2905 E. Skyline Dr.,
Tucson, AZ 85718.
Tel (520) 615-2561.
W laencantada shoppingcenter.com

Metrocenter
9617 N. Metro Parkway,
Phoenix, AZ 85051.
Tel (602) 997-8991.
W metrocenter mall. com

Scottsdale Fashion Square
7014 East Camelback Rd.,
Scottsdale, AZ 85251.
Tel (480) 941-2140.
W fashionsquare.com

Factory Outlet Malls

Arizona Mills
5000 S. Arizona Mills
Circle, Tempe, AZ 85282.
Tel (480) 491-7300.
W simon.com/mall/ arizona-mills

Fashion Outlets of Santa Fe
8380 Cerillos Rd. at I-25,
Santa Fe, NM 87507.
Tel (505) 474-4000.
W fashionoutlets santafe.com

Outlets at Anthem
4250 W. Anthem Way,
Phoenix, AZ 85086.
Tel (623) 465-9500.
W outletsanthem.com

Western Wear

Az-tex Hats of Phoenix
3903 N. Scottsdale Rd.,
Scottsdale, AZ 85251.
Tel (480) 481-9900.
W aztexhats.com

Back at the Ranch
209 E. Marcy St.,
Santa Fe, NM 87501.
Tel (505) 989-8110.

Bacon's Boots and Saddles
290 N. Broad St., Globe,
AZ 85501.
Tel (928) 425-2681.

Double Take at the Ranch
319 S. Guadalupe St.,
Santa Fe, NM 87501.
Tel (505) 989-8886.

Saba's Western Store
W sabaswesternwear. com

Sheplers
829 N Dobson Rd., Mesa,
AZ 85201. **Tel** (480) 668-1211. W sheplers.com

Food

Arizona Pepper Products Co.
P.O. Box 40605, Mesa, AZ
85210. **Tel** (480) 844-0302.
W azgunslinger.com

The Chile Shop
109 E. Water St., Santa
Fe, NM 87501.
Tel (505) 983-6080.
W thechileshop.com

Food City
W myfoodcity.com

Fry's
W frysfood.com

New Mexico Chili
Tel (505) 217-2105.
W nmchili.com

The Pecan Store
1625 E. Sahuarita Rd.,
Sahuarita, AZ 85629.
Tel (800) 327-3326.
W pecanstore.com

Santa Cruz Chili and Spice Co.
1868 East Frontage Rd.,
Tumacacori, AZ 85640.
Tel (520) 398-2591.
W santacruzchili.com

ENTERTAINMENT IN THE SOUTHWEST

The Southwest's blend of cultures has made the region a thriving center for arts and entertainment. The large cities of Phoenix, Santa Fe, Tucson, and Albuquerque have vibrant artistic communities and offer opera, ballet, classical music, and major theatrical productions. The smaller resort towns of Sedona and Taos are famous for their resident painters and sculptors and regularly host noted touring productions, as well as regional theater, dance, and musical events. And almost every city and major town has a lively nightlife that includes country music, jazz, and rock, as well as dinner theater and standup comedy. Sports fans will be happy here with major league and college football, baseball, and basketball teams playing across the region.

Displaying traditional cowboy skills at one of the region's rodeos

Tombstone *(see p96)*, which stages daily mock-gunfights and tours of its Victorian buildings. There are also Western towns built originally as film studios, such as Old Tucson Studios *(see p90)*. Tours of the sets are available. **Rawhide**, north of Scottsdale, has an Old West museum, an old-fashioned ice cream parlor, a famous music venue, and Western theme attractions.

Information

The best source of events information is in the entertainment guides of local newspapers. Phoenix's *The Arizona Republic*, Tucson's *Daily Star*, the *Santa Fe New Mexican*, and *Albuquerque Journal* are the most useful. Most of these newspapers also have websites. There are several regional magazines that review events and nightlife. Most hotels offer magazines, such as *Where* and *Key*, that feature dining, attractions, and entertainment. You can book tickets for most events through **Ticketmaster** outlets, or at www.ticketmaster.com, their online booking service.

Rodeos and Wild West Shows

Since Buffalo Bill's first Wild West shows in the 1880s, the Southwest has been a mecca for Western-style entertainment. Traditional cowboy skills such as roping steers and breaking wild horses have been transformed into categories of rodeo contest, offering winners substantial money prizes. Rodeos owe their name to the Spanish word for round-up, harking back to the 19th century when herds of cattle crossed New Mexico on their way to California. Today's rodeo circuit is highly competitive and dangerous, attracting full-time professionals whose high pay reflects this risky career. Nevertheless, the allure is comparable with the magic of the circus. Among the largest and most popular rodeos are Tucson's **Fiesta de los Vaqueros**, Albuquerque's **New Mexico State Fair and Rodeo** and Prescott's **Frontier Days Rodeo** *(see pp36–9)*. The Southwest offers plenty of opportunities for visitors to sample the atmosphere of the Wild West, either in the many ghost towns or in historic frontier towns such as

Sports

The three most popular spectator sports in the Southwest, as in the rest of the country, are football, baseball, and basketball. The region's largest concentration of major teams is in the Phoenix area. There is only one major league football team in the Southwest, the **Arizona Cardinals** in Phoenix. The Arizona Diamondbacks baseball team joined the majors in 1998 and is based at the $275- million **Chase Field** in Phoenix. Professional basketball is represented by the Phoenix Suns, who share the **US Airways Center** with a football team, the Arizona Rattlers. While tickets may be hard to obtain for league games, it is easy to gain entrance to the many college games in any sport throughout the region. Phoenix's warm

Baseball player

climate also attracts the Cactus League, a series of training games for seven major league baseball teams in February and March.

Classical Music, Ballet, and Opera

In Arizona, the excellent Phoenix Symphony, Arizona Opera, and Ballet Arizona all perform at the **Phoenix Symphony Hall** building. The city's $14-million refurbishment of the Spanish Baroque-style **Orpheum Theater** makes it a stunning addition to more than 20 major venues for arts, sports, and entertainment in and around Phoenix. Arizona Theater Company and Actors'Theater occupies the **Herberger Theater Center**, offering a regular program of performances. With more than 20 theater companies in Phoenix, there is an impressive choice of plays, as well as touring Broadway shows and big-name entertainers.

New Mexico's major cultural activities are based in Santa Fe and Albuquerque. Santa Fe has more than 200 art galleries and is also respected for its performing arts. The **Santa Fe Opera** performs both traditional and contemporary operas in its open-air arena between late June and August. **Santa Fe's Chamber Music Festival**, held at venues throughout the city in July and August, is one of the finest in the US. The **Albuquerque Philharmonic Orchestra** offers free classical concerts by accomplished amateur musicians, and the **El Paso Symphony Orchestra** performs throughout the year in

Dancing couple at the Museum Club in Flagstaff, Arizona

the town's historic 1920s Plaza Theater. **New Mexico Jazz Workshops** stage more than 30 concerts each year.

Nightlife

In almost every town there are restaurants, bars, and nightclubs that offer country music and dancing. Among the most famous country music venues is the Western theme town of Rawhide in Scottsdale, where well-known bands play. The **Museum Club** in Flagstaff is a venerable Route 66 *(see p55)* establishment that hosted such top country music names as Hank Williams in the 1950s and still offers a lively selection of Southwestern bands.

Major cities offer virtually every type of evening entertainment. Jazz bars and cafés are gaining in popularity, and standup comedy and rock music is available in countless venues. Clubs and arenas based in Phoenix, Tucson, Albuquerque, and Santa Fe are regular stops for big stars on US tours. However, the entertainment capital of the region, and some would say the world, is Las Vegas *(see pp130–31)*. The Las Vegas Strip on a single night hosts as much top talent as all the other cities in the Southwest do in a year: everything from Broadway shows and dazzling home-grown productions to a range of free music in the casinos.

Spectacular outdoor setting of the Santa Fe Opera company

SPECIALTY VACATIONS AND ACTIVITIES

With thousands of miles of deep rock canyons, spectacular deserts, and towering, snow-capped mountains, few places in the world offer so many opportunities for outdoor entertainment as the American Southwest. Much of the wilderness here is protected by the Federal Government in national parks, formed during the early 20th century when the region first began to attract tourists. Increasing numbers of visitors are being drawn to the region, and it is now a magnet for climbers, mountain bikers, hikers, and 4WD enthusiasts. The range of organized tours includes whitewater rafting and horseback riding, as well as cultural heritage tours of the many ancient Native American sites. Wildlife enthusiasts, particularly birdwatchers, can spot rare species on the spring and fall migration routes that cross the Southwest. The region is also a center for sports activities, especially for golfers and skiers. For information on the main events in the Southwest's sports calendar see pp266–7.

General Information

The main centers for outdoor activities in the region are Moab (see p145), Durango (see p183), and Sedona (see p75), with their excellent equipment shops and visitor information centers. Advance planning is advisable for activities such as whitewater rafting along the Colorado River in Grand Canyon, or mule trips into the canyon, as these are often booked up to a year ahead (see pp62–67). Hikers and campers exploring the backcountry will also need permits from the National Park Service as well as detailed maps, which can be obtained from either the Bureau of Land Management, the **U.S.D.A. Forest Service**, or the **US Geological Survey**. Both state and local tourist offices can supply the latest advice on trails, permits, and weather conditions at most attractions. Anyone exploring desert or canyon country should be aware of the potential for flash floods and should check weather reports daily, especially during the summer months of July and August.

Golf

With around 275 golf courses in Arizona alone, many of them top-rated, the Southwest is a golfer's paradise. This is particularly true of Southern Arizona with its year-round warm weather. The town of Scottsdale (see pp84–5), is considered by some to be America's premier golf spot and is famous for such resorts as **The Boulders** and the legendary Phoenician, both top-rated championship courses. Tucson is also a well-known golfing area with such offerings as the Jack Nicklaus-designed golf resort **Westin La Paloma**. New Mexico is also known for its courses and affordable greens fees. Albuquerque's Arroyo del Oso is a challenging municipal course with immaculate fairways. Information on the various courses can be found at w **golfarizona.com** or w **golfnewmexico.com**.

Golf course at Phoenix's top-rated Wigwam Resort (see p237)

Hiking

Hiking is the single most popular outdoor activity in the Southwest. Day hikes and longer expeditions draw large numbers of residents and visitors who feel that this is the best way to see the region's stunning scenery. Virtually all of the national parks have excellent well-marked trails as well as fascinating ranger-led hikes that focus on the local flora, fauna, and geology. One of the most famous, and arduous, hikes in the

Whitewater rafting trip on the Colorado River

Mountain biking along one of many red-rock trails near Moab

Southwest is a rim-to-rim hike of Grand Canyon along the Bright Angel and Kaibab trails *(see pp64–67)*. It takes most hikers two to three days to complete. Longer trips into the vast wilderness of Grand Staircase–Escalante National Monument *(see p152)* and the Glen Canyon Recreation Area *(see pp154–5)* are among the highlights of wilderness exploration for hikers.

Organizations that offer guided short and multi-day hiking trips in the region's national parks include the **Grand Canyon Field Institute** and **MNA Ventures**, run by the Museum of Northern Arizona in Flagstaff.

Hikers on the trail to Pueblo Alto at Chaco Canyon *(see pp178–9)*

Rock Climbing

Its dry, sunny climate and extensive mountains, canyons, and sheer rock faces make the Southwest a popular climbing spot. Favored sites include the sheer cliffs of Zion National Park *(see pp158–9)*, the rocky landscape around Moab *(see p146)*, and Utah's Canyonlands National Park *(see p146–7)*. Moab has a good selection of equipment shops, such as **Pagan Mountaineering**. Red Rock Canyon, 15 miles (24 km) west of Las Vegas, is another favorite area, with guided climbs offered by **Jackson Hole Mountain Guides**.

4WD at wetlands near Moab

Mountain Biking and Four-Wheel Driving

All of the region's national parks have trails open to mountain biking, but the centers of this activity are Moab and Durango, Colorado *(see p183)*. The state of Utah has declared itself the mountain bike capital of the world, and the Moab area is something of a pilgrimage site for mountain bikers. Named after a well-known bike trail, **Poison Spider Bicycles** sells and repairs bikes as well as housing Nichols Tours, which leads groups through wilderness

areas. Moab is famous for the Slick Rock Trail, a demanding run across more than 12 miles (19 km) of precipitous rock with stunning views. However, during the summer months the trail can become very crowded.

Around Durango, Colorado, cooler and greener conditions prevail with rides through the pine forests of the Rocky Mountains. Popular bike trails include the level, but scenic, Animas Valley Loop or the more rugged, hilly Animas Mountain Loop. There are also several 4WD trails, leading to remote and beautiful backcountry. Again, Moab is one of the top centers for off-road drivers, with rentals and tours available from **Farabee's Jeep Rentals**. Canyonlands National Park and Canyon de Chelly are also popular. Monument Valley in Arizona *(see pp168–9)* is a prime location for 4WD tours to areas not accessible by a regular car, often led by Navajo guides from **Goulding's Tours** in Monument Valley. Also in Arizona, Sedona's red-rock canyons and Coconino National Forest may be toured by 4WD. **Bikapelli Adventure Tours** and local legend **Pink Jeep Tours** offer a wide variety of tours.

Whitewater Rafting and Kayaking

The Green, San Juan, and Colorado rivers make the Southwest one of the world's top destinations for whitewater rafting. These rivers run fast and deep, offering a thrilling ride, often through breathtaking canyons. Trips ranging from beginner to experienced are offered by most outfitters. Tour companies provide rafts, paddles, and lifejackets, and for multi-day trips that involve camping, food and tents may also be provided. Visitors are advised to check a variety of companies to make sure they get the river experience that suits them best. It is also a good idea to check their safety records and expertise.

One of the most exciting rafting trips in the Southwest is the 12–20 day trip along the Colorado River through Grand Canyon. As numbers for some trips may be limited to eight or fewer people, tours can be booked by as much as a year in advance. Many out fitters offer Grand Canyon raft trips: one of the best known is **Canyon Explorations**.

The confluence of the Green and Colorado rivers lies near Moab, Utah. Just beyond their convergence lies Cataract Canyon, one of the most famous whitewater rapids in the world. Shooting these waters should be undertaken only by experienced rafters. One of the best outfitters to take visitors through the canyon is **Sheri Griffith Expeditions**. The company also offers raft tours of varying degrees of difficulty on the smaller rivers in the area.

Canyon Voyages offers rafting trips ranging from peaceful river journeys to thrilling whitewater adventures. They also offer kayak workshops.

Wild Rivers Expeditions' one-day, gentle drift through the canyons of the Four Corners' San Juan River is led by guides who are also archaeologists and geologists. There are stops at Bluff *(see p176)* and Mexican Hat, as well as at Ancestral Puebloan ruins.

Powerboating near Parker Dam in western Arizona

Water Sports

The dams along the Colorado River have created a chain of artificial lakes starting with Lake Powell *(see pp154–5)* and extending to Lake Mead *(see p124)* and Lake Havasu *(see p74)*. A variety of water sports are available, including powerboating and jetskiing.

Set in the one million-acre (400,000-ha) Glen Canyon Recreation Area, Lake Powell is famous for its houseboat rentals. These offer visitors the chance to experience the many beaches and canyons around the lake. All visitors are shown how to operate the boats and are given an instruction manual. There is also a variety of guided tours available, including cruises to Rainbow Bridge and Antelope Canyon. Gentle raft trips between Glen Canyon Dam and Lees Ferry are offered by **Colorado River Discovery**, the main tour concession for the lake. **Lake Powell Resorts and Marinas** rents out both houseboats and powerboats.

On Lake Havasu all kinds of water-sports equipment, from waterskis to scuba gear, can be rented from Fun Time Boat Rentals. At Lake Mead numerous shops rent fishing boats and jetskis and offer waterskiing lessons. The **Lake Mead Visitor Center** is a useful source of information.

Boaters on all the lakes are provided with information to make water-based vacations safe and pleasurable. Children aged 12 and under must wear lifejackets, and all boats must be driven at wakeless speed within harbor or beach areas.

Fishing

Lakes Mead, Powell, and Havasu are also noted as popular locations for fishing. The lakes are well stocked with game fish such as striped, largemouth, and smallmouth bass during the fishing season, which runs from March to November. River anglers can also fish for salmon and trout. Each state has different regulations and fishing

Fishing in a lake at Cedar Breaks National Monument, Southern Utah *(see p153)*

Mountain views from the Sandia Peak Tramway near Albuquerque

licenses, although catch and release is the rule in many areas. Information about licenses, tournaments, and tours can be obtained from marinas, outdoor equipment stores, local gas stations, and state **Fish and Game Departments**.

Skiing and Winter Sports

In general, the ski season in Southwestern resorts runs from November to April. A range of skiing trips is available, from all-inclusive packages to day-trips from nearby towns. There are plenty of equipment rental outlets, although resort packages usually include skis, lift passes, and lessons if necessary. Other winter sports such as snowboarding, snowmobiling, and cross-country skiing are becoming increasingly popular, with runs and equipment now available in most resorts.

Utah hosted the Winter Olympics in 2002 and offers some of the best skiing in the region. The **Telluride Ski Resort** is set among the 19th-century towns and mountain scenery of southwestern Colorado. The facilities and runs here, with elevations of more than 11,500 ft (3,450 m), attract many visitors during the season, including many of the country's celebrities. **Purgatory-Durango Mountain Resort** is less chic and less pricey, but provides just as much challenge with vertical drops of over 2,000 ft (600 m). New Mexico's **Taos Ski Valley** includes world-class slopes, and the Arizona Snowbowl

near Flagstaff (see p71) is particularly popular with cross-country skiers.

Horseback Riding

Horseback riding is synonymous with the Southwest, and almost every area has stables that rent horses. Some ranches offer guided trail rides as well as the chance to live and work as a cowboy. The range of trips is impressive: from hour-long rides to two-week dude ranch vacations (see p235).

Ranches are dotted across the region, but the best-known are those in southern Arizona, particularly near the town of Wickenburg. The area's pleasant winter climate attracts thousands of visitors, and even large cities such as Phoenix and Tucson have riding stables and offer trails through beautiful desert scenery. Cooler summer locations such as Sedona and Pinetop Lakeside in Arizona are also popular riding centers. Most of the national parks offer trail-riding tours, but the noted mule trip into Grand Canyon (see p66)

needs to be booked well in advance. **Xanterra Parks & Resorts** offers adventurous mule rides that last two days from the South Rim, over-nighting on the canyon floor at Phantom Ranch (see p236).

Air Tours

Air tours are a good option for those time-restricted travelers who wish to see the more remote attractions.

Canyonlands National Park is famous for its vast wildernesses: **Redtail Aviation** offers one-hour flights over all three districts in Canyonlands, as well as over the stunning Dead Horse Point State Park (see p147). The striking red-rock pinnacles formations of Bryce Canyon (see pp156–7) can be seen by both plane and helicopter on tours lasting from 17 minutes to one hour.

The most popular air tours fly over Grand Canyon. Several companies offer day trips from Las Vegas (see p127) – helicopter tours go to the Skywalk, or down to the Colorado River, at Grand Canyon West, while planes can fly all the way to the South Rim of the national park. Both helicopters and planes also fly in fixed circuits from the small airfield in Tusayan, at the park's southern entrance. However, increasing numbers of airborne tourists are raising the issue of noise pollution as a pressing problem throughout the canyon. More and more visitors complain that engine noise diminishes what should be a tranquil experience of the area's beauty.

Horseback riding through the desert near Tuscon, Arizona

International Balloon Fiesta in Albuquerque, New Mexico *(see p38)*

Hot Air Ballooning

Cool, still mornings, dependable sunshine, and steady breezes have made the Southwest the top hot air ballooning destination in America. Balloon trips around Albuquerque are a popular excursion, particularly in October, when the International Balloon Fiesta takes place *(see p38)*. Outfitters such as **Discover Balloons** offer a one-hour flight with champagne brunch. You can also drift over the canyons of Sedona with **Northern Light Balloon Expeditions**, and over the Sonoran Desert with **Hot Air Expeditions**.

Birdwatching

With more than 200 species of bird, including many rare breeds, birdwatching is a popular pastime in the Southwest, particularly in spring, early summer, and fall. These are peak migration seasons for warblers, flycatchers, and shorebirds, while nesting waders and ducks may be seen in New Mexico's **Bosque del Apache Wildlife Refuge**. The refuge also boasts a winter population of more than 17,000 sandhill cranes.

Several habitats across the region suit desert birds such as the roadrunner and elf owl, particularly Saguaro National Park in the Sonoran Desert. Capitol Reef *(see p150)* and Bryce Canyon *(see pp156–7)* national parks attract yellow warblers, northern orioles, and black-chinned hummingbirds.

Southern Utah and southern Arizona are noted for their hummingbird population. Tours devoted to the study of these enchanting creatures are run by **Victor Emmanuel's Nature Tours**. The **Southeastern Arizona Bird Observatory** also offers educational tours in the region.

Broad-billed hummingbird

Many species of hawk may be spotted in the Southwest, and birds of prey such as red-tailed hawks, golden eagles, and peregrine falcons are regular visitors to Bryce Canyon.

Learning Vacations

In the Southwest, some of the most interesting learning vacations focus on Native cultures and ancient civilizations. Two organizations, the **Crow Canyon Archaeological Center** and the **Four Corners School of Outdoor Education**, offer a range of vacation courses on geography, flora and fauna, ancient ruins, and Native arts. Archaeology courses often involve working on digs with professional archaeologists; Native culture courses may study both modern and ancient Native groups, their way of life, religious practices, and arts. Most programs last between four and ten days, and visitors are housed either in college campuses or in motels. **Smithsonian Journeys** offers a popular program on past and present arts of the Hopi, Zuni, and Navajo tribes.

The distinctive cuisine of the region has prompted a number of organizations to offer courses on Southwestern cooking. Good options in New Mexico include the **Santa Fe School of Cooking** and the **Jane Butel Cooking School**, just outside Albuquerque. Arts and crafts courses are also widely available throughout the Southwest. The **Santa Fe Photographic Workshops** offer photography and painting courses for both beginners and professionals, designed to take advantage of the unique light and landscapes of Santa Fe. In Arizona, the **Tubac Center of the Arts**, in the village of Tubac south of Tucson, has a year-round program of sketching, painting, and printmaking classes.

DIRECTORY

Information

U.S.D.A Forest Service
333 Broadway SE., Albuquerque, NM 87102. **Tel** (505) 842-3292.

US Geological Survey
Tel (888) 275-8747.
W usgs.gov

Golf

The Boulders
34631 N. Tom Darlington Drive, Carefree, AZ 85377. **Tel** (480) 488-9028.
W theboulders.com

Westin La Paloma
3800 East Sunrise, Tucson, AZ 85718. **Tel** (520) 742-6000. W westin lapalomaresort.com

Hiking

Grand Canyon Field Institute
P.O. Box 399, Grand Canyon, AZ 86023.
Tel (928) 638-2481.
W grandcanyon.org

MNA Ventures
3101 N. Fort Valley Rd., Flagstaff, AZ 86001.
Tel (928) 774-5211.
W mnaventures.org

Rock Climbing

Jackson Hole Mountain Guides
8221 W. Charleston, Suite 106, Las Vegas, NV 89117. **Tel** (702) 254-0885.
W jhmg.com

Pagan Mountaineering
59 S. Main St., Moab, UT 84532. **Tel** (435) 259-1117.
W climbmoab.com

Mountain Biking and 4WD

Bikapelli Adventure Tours
1695 W. Hwy 89A, Sedona, AZ 86336. **Tel** (928) 282-1312. W mountainbike heaven.com

Farabee's Jeep Rentals
1125 S. Hwy 191, Moab, UT 84532. **Tel** (877) 970-5337. W moabjeep rentals.com

Goulding's Tours
1000 Main St., Monument Valley, UT 84536. **Tel** (435) 727-3231. W gouldings. com/tours

Pink Jeep Tours
204 N. Highway 89A, Sedona, AZ 86336.
Tel (928) 282-5000.
W pinkjeeptours.com

Poison Spider Bicycles
497 N. Main St., Moab, UT 84532. **Tel** (435) 259-7882.
W poisonspider bicycles.com

Whitewater Rafting and Kayaking

Canyon Explorations
675 W. Clay Ave.,, Flagstaff, AZ 86002. **Tel** (928) 774-4559. W canyon explorations.com

Canyon Voyages
211 N. Main St., Moab, UT 84532. **Tel** (435) 259-6007.
W canyonvoyages.com

Sheri Griffith Expeditions
2231 S. Hwy 191, Moab, UT 84532. **Tel** (435) 260-1348. W griffithexp.com

Wild Rivers Expeditions
101 Main St., Bluff, UT 84512. **Tel** (800) 422-7654.
W riversandruins.com

Water Sports

Colorado River Discovery
130 6th Ave., Page, AZ 86040. **Tel** (928) 645-9175.
W raftthecanyon.com

Lake Mead Visitor Center
601 Nevada Way, Boulder City, NV 89005.
Tel (702) 293-8990.
W nps.gov/lake

Lake Powell Marinas
100 Lakeshore Dr., Page, AZ 86040. **Tel** (928) 645-2433. W lakepowell.com

Fishing

Arizona Game and Fish Department
Tel (602) 942-3000.
W azgfd.gov

Colorado Division of Wildlife
Tel (303) 297-1192.
W wildlife.state.co.us

New Mexico Dept. of Game and Fish
Tel (505) 476-8000.
W wildlife.state.nm.us

Utah Division of Wildlife Resources
Tel (801) 538-4700.
W wildlife.utah.gov

Ski Resorts

Purgatory-Durango Mountain Resort
Route 550 Durango, CO 81301. **Tel** (970) 247-9000.
W durangomountain resort.com

Taos Ski Valley
P.O. Box 90, Taos Ski Valley, NM 87525. **Tel** (575) 776-2291. W skitaos.org

Telluride Ski Resort
565 Mountain Village Blvd., Telluride, CO 81435. **Tel** (970) 728-6900.
W tellurideskiresort.com

Horseback Riding

Xanterra Parks & Resorts
Tel (303) 297-2757.

Air Tours

Redtail Aviation
Tel (435) 259-7421.
W redtailaviation.com

Hot Air Ballooning

Discover Balloons
205B San Felipe NW., Albuquerque, NM 87104.
Tel (505) 842-1111.
W discoverballoons.com

Hot Air Expeditions
2243 E. Rose Garden Loop, Suite 1, Phoenix, AZ 85024. **Tel** (480) 502-6999.
W hotairexpeditions. com

Northern Light Balloon Expeditions
455 Dry Creek Rd.,, Sedona, AZ 86336.
Tel (928) 282-2274.
W northernlight balloon.com

Birdwatching

Bosque del Apache Wildlife Refuge
1001 Highway 1, San Antonio, NM 87832.
Tel (575) 835-1828.

Southeastern Arizona Bird Observatory
P.O. Box 5521, Bisbee, AZ 85603. **Tel** (520) 432-1388.
W sabo.org

Victor Emmanuel's Nature Tours
2525 Wallingwood Dr., Suite 1003, Austin, TX 78746. **Tel** (512) 328-5221.
W ventbird.com

Learning Vacations

Crow Canyon Archaeological Center
23390 County Rd. K, Cortez, CO 81321.
Tel (970) 565-8975.
W crowcanyon.org

Four Corners School of Outdoor Education
P.O. Box 1029, Monticello, UT 84535. **Tel** (800) 525-4456. W fourcorners school.org

Jane Butel Cooking School
P.O. Box 2162, Corrales, NM 87048. **Tel** (505) 243-2622.
W janebutelcooking. com

Santa Fe Photographic Workshops
P.O. Box 9916, Santa Fe, NM 87504. **Tel** (505) 983-1400. W santafe workshops.com

Santa Fe School of Cooking
125 N. Guadalupe St., Santa Fe, NM 87501.
Tel (505) 983-4511.
W santafeschoolof cooking.com

Smithsonian Journeys
Tel (855) 330-1542
W smithsonian journeys.org

Tubac Center of Arts
9 Plaza Rd., Tubac AZ 85646. **Tel** (520) 398-2371.
W tubacarts.org

SURVIVAL GUIDE

PRACTICAL INFORMATION

The Southwest US is an area of spectacular natural beauty. Arizona, New Mexico, the Four Corners, and Southern Utah are dotted with dramatic rock formations, canyons, ancient archaeological sites, and wild desert scenery that offer visitors a choice of pleasures, including a wide variety of outdoor activities. The cities here are famous for their combination of laid-back Southern culture and sophisticated urban pursuits with excellent museums and great dining. The unique attractions of Las Vegas, Nevada *(see pp102–135)* also make for an exciting experience, popular with millions across the world. Accommodations are of international standard *(see pp234–43)*, and visitor information centers are plentiful, even in small towns.

The following pages contain useful information for all visitors planning a trip to this region. Personal Security and Health *(see pp280–81)* recommends a number of precautions, while Banking and Communications *(see pp282–3)* answers financial and media queries. There is also information on traveling around the country by both public transportation and car.

When to Go

The Southwest has the advantage of being a year-round destination. Generally speaking, the climate tends to be dictated by the varying elevations in the region. The high-lying areas of northern Arizona and New Mexico, and southern Utah have cold, snowy winters, making them popular destinations for skiing and other winter sports activities. In contrast, the lower elevations of the southern portions of the states are noted for their warm and sunny winter weather, with temperatures averaging a comfortable 70°F (21°C) in the Phoenix area, which receives thousands of winter visitors. Be aware, however, that the summer months of July and August have average temperatures of 100°F (37°C) in Phoenix, making it one of the hottest cities outside the Middle East. Spring and fall are ideal seasons to visit the southwestern United States – there are fewer visitors, and the milder temperatures make outdoor activities, especially hiking, a popular option. However, some services may be closed at these times; the North Rim of Grand Canyon in northern Arizona is open only between May and October, while the mesa tops of the ancient Pueblo site of Mesa Verde in Colorado may be inaccessible because of snow as late as April or May. Whatever the time of year, this is a region known for having a great deal of sun, with northern areas averaging well over 200 days of sunshine each year, and the southern parts famous for having more than 300 sunny days.

Wet weather warning sign in southern Utah

Entry Requirements

Citizens from Australia, New Zealand, and the UK, and many other European countries can visit the US without the need for a visa if they are planning a stay of 90 days or less. Instead they are required to have a passport that is valid for at least six months after they leave the country, and must complete the visa waiver application process online through ESTA, the Electronic System for Travel Authorization (https://esta.cbp.dhs.gov). US embassies have the latest information on which countries are participating in the visa waiver program. As a result of tighter security measures US citizens now require a passport for any border crossings into the US. Canadian citizens must also have a passport when crossing the Canada–US border. Check what documentation is needed before traveling as requirements constantly change.

Visitors from countries who do need a visa must apply to a US consulate or embassy well in advance, and may be asked for evidence of financial solvency, as well as for proof that they are intending to re-turn to their country of origin.

Any visitor wishing to extend their stay beyond the 90-day limit should contact the nearest US Immigration and Naturalization Service (I.N.S.) well in advance of the date stamped on their visa waiver form or visa.

Tourist Information

Visitor information centers in the US are noted for the quality of their information, offering everything from local maps to hotel and B&B bookings. Special tours such as guided history walks, ranger-led archaeological tours, and wildlife watching can often be arranged through these offices. In addition, all the national and state parks have their own visitor centers, which provide hiking maps, safety advice, and special licenses for wilderness hiking and camping. Some of these areas are managed by special Public Land Management Agencies, which can also be contacted for information.

Each state has its own department of tourism, as do all the major towns and cities. All operate websites, which offer comprehensive information, with links to local attractions and activity operators, listings of shops and restaurants, and, in many cases, online booking services for accommodations. Many will also mail out information packs on request. Most states also run large "Welcome Centers" close to the state lines on the major interstate highways, which can be excellent sources of maps, brochures, and discount coupons. In addition, smaller urban communities and sights of special interest run visitor centers, providing local maps and guides.

New Mexico tourist sign

Bear in mind that many of the Southwest's attractions, such as the pueblos of New Mexico and the Navajo Nation in the Four Corners, are located on reservation lands and are managed by different Native American tribal councils. For advice on etiquette, opening times, and admission charges to such sights contact the local Bureau of Indian Affairs or the **Navajo Tourism Department**.

Ranger on a guided tour at Keet Seel, Navajo National Monument

Opening Hours and Admission Charges

Opening times are seasonal. As a rule, most of the major sights are open later through the summer months. Museums and galleries tend to be open through the weekends and closed for one day during the week. Almost all the major outdoor attractions, including all the national parks, remain at least partially open year-round, while many of the cities are even busier and livelier in summer than in winter. In general those places that do close will be shut for such major public holidays as Thanksgiving, Christmas Day, and New Year's Day (see p39).

Most museums, parks, and other attractions in the region charge an admission fee. The amount can vary enormously, and many sights offer discounts for families, children, and senior citizens. Local newspapers may carry discount coupons, while student cards or an I.D. that proves you are over 65 guarantees reduced-cost entry to most major attractions in the Southwest.

Time Zones

There are only two time zones that affect the area covered by this guide – Mountain Standard Time, which covers Arizona, New Mexico, Colorado, and Utah, and Pacific Time in Nevada. Mountain Standard Time is one hour later than Pacific Time. If it is noon in Las Vegas then it will be 1pm across the rest of the region. However, daylight-saving time runs from late spring to early fall, and the clocks are set forward by one hour, except in Arizona, which does not have daylight-saving.

To confuse matters even more, the Navajo Nation (across Arizona and part of New Mexico) does use daylight-saving time, but the Hopi Indian Reservation (in the middle of the Navajo Reservation), does not.

Water fountains in the courtyard of the Heard Museum in Phoenix

Senior Travelers

Although the age when you are considered a senior in the US is 65, a multitude of discounts are also available to people over the age of 50. Reduced rates of up to 50 percent can apply to meals, accommodations, public transportation, and entrance fees, and are often better than those offered to students.

There are several organizations in the US through which discounts can be obtained. The **National Park Service** offers Golden Age Passports that reduce the cost of tours and services in the parks. **Road Scholar** arranges educational trips to various locations for travelers over the age of 55. These include inexpensive accommodations, activities, lectures, and meals. For around $16 senior citizens can join the **American Association of Retired Persons** (AARP), which also offers good travel discounts.

Traveling with Children

The Southwest offers a wide range of attractions, theme parks, and museums suitable for families traveling with young children. However, the age at which a child is eligible for discounts varies greatly from four and under, to under 18 years. Most types of accommodations state whether or not they welcome children, and in many hotels a child can share the parent's room at no extra cost. The more expensive hotels also provide babysitting services and children's clubs offering supervised activities.

Restaurants in the Southwest are generally child-friendly, providing reasonably priced children's menus and high chairs. Although discounted flight tickets are available for children, these can often work out more expensive than an adult Apex fare (see p287). Reduced fares for children on public transportation tend to vary from city to city, and if you are renting a car it is possible to reserve car seats for children in advance.

National Park Service sign

Travelers with Disabilities

The US is famous for having excellent facilities for travelers with physical disabilities. Hotels, restaurants, galleries and museums, and other public buildings are legally required to be wheelchair-accessible and to have suitably designed restrooms. Public transportation also comes under this law, and trains, buses, and taxis are designed to accommodate wheelchairs, while road crossings in busy city centers have introduced dropped curbs to enable easier access. Service animals such as guide dogs for the blind are the only animals allowed on public transportation.

Many national parks and major archaeological sights have paved walkways suitable for wheelchairs. The National Park Service offers free Golden Access passes, which grant free entry to all national parks for one year to those who are disabled or blind.

DisabledTravelers.com and the **Society for Accessible Travel & Hospitality** are two organizations which offer a whole range of advice on traveling for the disabled, from how to rent specially adapted cars to qualifying for parking permits. They also have excellent websites.

Student Travelers

Students from outside the US need to have an identity card, such as the International Student Identity Card (ISIC), to prove their status. This entitles the holder to substantial discounts on admission prices to museums, galleries, and other popular attractions. If you are planning to stay in officially recognized youth hostels you will need to join **Hostelling International/American Youth Hostel (HI/AYH)**.

Wheelchair access

Etiquette and Tipping

The Southwest is noted as one of the US's most relaxed regions. Dress tends to be informal, practical, and dependent on the climate. Jeans may be worn even in upscale restaurants or the theater. In general, people are friendly and polite and, as this is a multicultural country, visitors are expected to be aware of and respect the customs of different peoples.

Some of the region's most famous sights, such as Canyon de Chelly (see pp172–75), and Monument Valley (see pp168–9), are located on reservation land. Visitors are welcome but should be sensitive as to what may cause offense. It is illegal for

Youngsters enjoying the child-friendly environment of the Southwest

alcohol to be brought onto reservations – even a bottle visible in a locked car will land you in trouble. Always ask before photographing anything, especially ceremonial dances or Native homes, and take into consideration that a fee may be requested. Do not go wandering off marked trails as this is forbidden. Try to dress respectfully – for example, the Hopi people request that people do not wear shorts.

Apart from casinos and bars in Las Vegas, most of the Southwest follows the rest of the US in restricting smoking in public places. The majority of hotels are non-smoking, although a few have smoking rooms, or allow customers to smoke in bar areas. However, many restaurants have banned smoking altogether.

Service is not included on restaurant checks, and you should leave 15–20 percent of the total as a tip. Hotel bellhops expect $1–2 per bag, and chamber maids around $1–2 for each day of your stay.

Electricity

Throughout the US the electrical current is 110 volts and 60 Hertz. Visitors from abroad will need an adaptor plug for the two-prong sockets and a voltage converter to operate 220-volt electrical appliances, such as hairdryers and rechargers for cell phones and laptop computers.

Conversion Chart

Bear in mind that one US pint (0.5 liter) is smaller than one UK pint (0.6 liter).

US Standard to Metric
1 inch = 2.54 centimeters
1 foot = 30 centimeters
1 mile = 1.6 kilometers
1 ounce = 28 grams
1 pound = 454 grams
1 US quart = 0.947 liter
1 US gallon = 3.8 liters

Metric to US Standard
1 centimeter = 0.4 inch
1 meter = 3 feet 3 inches
1 kilometer = 0.6 miles
1 gram = 0.04 ounce
1 kilogram = 2.2 pounds
1 liter = 1.1 US quarts

Relaxing in the informal surroundings of a Southwestern restaurant

DIRECTORY

State Offices

Arizona Office of Tourism
1110 W. Washington St.,
Suite 155,
Phoenix, AZ 85007.
Tel (602) 364-3700;
(866) 275-5816.
W arizonaguide.com

Colorado Tourism Office
1625 Broadway,
Denver, CO 80202.
Tel (800) 265-6723.
W colorado.com

Navajo Tourism Department
P.O. Box 663,
Window Rock,
AZ 86515.
Tel (928) 871-6436.
W discovernavajo.com

New Mexico Department of Tourism
491 Old Santa
Fe Trail, Santa Fe,
NM 87501.
Tel (505) 827-7400.
W newmexico.org

Utah Office of Tourism
Council Hall,
Capitol Hill,
Salt Lake City,
UT 84114.
Tel (800) 200-1160.
W visitutah.com

Senior Travelers

American Association of Retired Persons
16165 N. 81st Ave.,
Peoria, AZ 85382.
Tel (866) 389-5649.
W aarp.org

National Park Service
(see also under individual sights).
Intermountain Region,
P.O. Box 25287, Denver,
CO 80225. W nps.gov

Road Scholar
11 Avenue de Lafayette,
Boston, MA 02111.
Tel (800) 454-5768.
W roadscholar.org

Disabled Travelers

DisabledTravelers.com
W disabledtravelers.com

Society for Accessible Travel & Hospitality (SATH)
347 Fifth Ave., Suite 605,
New York, NY 10016.
Tel (212) 447-7284.
W sath.org

Student Travelers

Hostelling International/ American Youth Hostel (HI/AYH)
8401 Colesville Rd.,
Suite 600, Silver Spring,
MD 20910.
Tel (240) 650-2100.
W hiusa.org

US Embassies

Canada
P.O. Box 866,
Station B, Ottawa,
ON K1P 5T1.
W canada.usembassy.gov

England
24/31 Grosvenor Square,
London W1A 1AE.
Tel 020 7499-9000.
W usembassy.org.uk

Personal Security and Health

The Southwest is a relatively safe place to visit as long as some general safety precautions are observed. In contrast to other US cities, the urban centers of the Southwest have lower crime rates, but it is wise to be cautious and to find out which parts of town are unsafe at night. When traveling across remote country roads, take a reliable local map and follow the advice of local rangers and visitor information centers. These sources also offer invaluable information on survival in the wilderness for hikers and on the normal safety procedures that should be followed by anyone engaging in any of the outdoor activities available in the region *(see pp268–73)*. It is also advisable to check the local media such as newspapers, television, and radio for current weather and safety conditions.

Pedal-pushing policeman on duty in Santa Fe, New Mexico

Personal Safety

Most tourist areas in the Southwest are friendly, unthreatening places. However, there is crime here and it is wise to observe a few basic rules. Never carry large amounts of cash, wear obviously expensive jewelry, or keep your wallet in your back pocket, as these are the main temptations for pickpockets. It is also a good idea to wear pocketbooks (handbags) and cameras over one shoulder with the strap across your body. Keep your passport separate from your cash and travelers' checks. Most hotels have safety deposit boxes or safes in which you should store any valuables.

If you are driving, be sure to lock any valuables in the trunk, and to park only in well-lit parking lots. Similarly, when walking at night it is a good idea to stay where there are other people and to be aware of which areas are most likely to be unsafe.

Lost Property

It is unlikely that small items of lost or stolen property will be retrieved, but it is necessary to report all such incidents to the police in order to make an insurance claim. Telephone the **Police Non-Emergency Line** to report the loss or theft, and they will issue you with a police report so that you can make a claim with your insurance company.

If a credit card is missing, call the credit company's toll-free number immediately. Lost or stolen travelers' checks should also be reported to the issuer. If you have kept a record of the checks' numbers, replacing them should be a painless experience, and new ones are usually issued within 24 hours.

If you lose your passport, contact the nearest embassy or consulate. They will be able to issue a temporary replacement as visitors do not generally need a new full passport if they plan to return directly to their home country. However, if you are traveling on to another destination, you will need a full passport. It is also useful to hold photocopies of your driver's license and birth certificate, as well as notarized passport photographs if you are considering an extended visit or need additional identification.

Travel Insurance

The United States has excellent medical services, but they are very expensive. All visitors to the US are strongly advised to make sure they have comprehensive medical and dental coverage for the duration of their stay.

Medical Treatment

For serious emergencies requiring assistance from the medical, police, or fire services call 911. The national organization, **Traveler's Aid Society**, may offer help in a variety of emergencies.

City hospitals with emergency rooms can be found in the Blue Pages of the telephone directory, but they are often overcrowded, particularly in larger cities. Private hospitals offer more personal treatment and are listed in the Yellow Pages of the telephone book. You may be required to provide evidence of your ability to pay before a doctor will agree to treat you, hence the importance of adequate medical insurance.

Hotels will usually call a doctor or recommend a local dentist, and nonprescription painkillers and other medicines can be obtained from drugstores, many of which are open 24 hours. Prescription drugs can be dispensed only from a

Police car

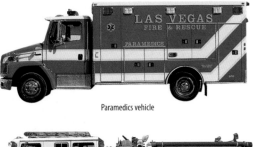

Paramedics vehicle

Fire engine

pharmacy. If you are already taking prescribed medication, be sure to carry extra supplies for your trip.

No specific vaccinations are required before entering the US. However, it is always a good idea to have a tetanus booster

Pharmacy sign

before setting out, particularly if you are planning to engage in adventurous outdoor activities.

Outdoor Hazards

The weather in the Southwest can present visitors with a variety of dangerous situations, especially in Southern Utah's canyon country and parts of

Park Ranger at the Petrified Forest National Park, Arizona

southern Arizona, where sudden summer storms can cause flash floods. Visitors may obtain the latest weather information from the ranger stations in the national parks, as well as by listening to the reports on local radio and television channels. If you are planning a hike in wilderness territory, always tell someone where you are going and when you expect to return.

The dry heat of the region's summers can often be underestimated by visitors, and hikers especially are advised to carry at least a gallon (4 liters) of drinking water per person for each day of walking. It is also extremely important for visitors to guard against the risk of forest fires, which can affect the area with devastating results.

At higher elevations the sun can be surprisingly strong, even on cloudy days. If planning on hiking or engaging in other outdoor activities during the summer, an effective sunscreen and a sunhat should be worn.

While the wilderness of the Southwest is home to certain venomous creatures such as snakes, scorpions, and the Gila monster

Fire Department badge, Sedona

lizard (see p25), these creatures generally avoid humans; it is unlikely you will be bitten if you avoid their habitats. Mostly they hide under rocks and in crevices during the heat of the day. Be careful where you step, and do not turn over rocks. Do not reach up to touch rock ledges with your hands. Insect stings and bites may hurt but are rarely fatal to adults. Always carry a snakebite kit or a first aid kit if you are going into snake or scorpion country. If bitten by a snake or scorpion, seek medical help immediately.

DIRECTORY
Emergency Services

All emergencies
Tel 911 and alert police, fire, or medical services.

Police Non-Emergency Line
Las Vegas
Tel (702) 795-3111.
Phoenix
Tel (602) 262-6151.
Santa Fe
Tel (505) 428-3710.

Traveler's Aid Society
Las Vegas
Tel (702) 369-4357.
Phoenix
Tel (602) 244-1346.

Consulates

The consulates closest to the Southwest are found in California.

Australian Consulate
Century Plaza Tower, 31st Floor, 2029 Century Park East, Los Angeles, CA 90067.
Tel (310) 229-2300.

British Consulate
2029 Century Park E., Suite 1350, Los Angeles, CA 90067.
Tel (310) 789-0031.

Canadian Consulate
550 South Hope St., 9th Floor, Los Angeles, CA 90071-2627.
Tel (213) 346-2700.

New Zealand Consulate
2425 Olympic Blvd., Suite 600 E., Santa Monica, CA 90404.
Tel (310) 566-6555.

Banking and Currency

Aside from the risk of gambling away all of their money in the Vegas casinos, visitors should encounter no problems with financial transactions in the Southwest. Banks and foreign currency exchanges are plentiful throughout the region, although it is wise to check out opening times. There are a great number of automated teller machines (ATMs) in towns and cities that enable visitors to make cash withdrawals 24 hours a day. Credit cards are a more common form of payment than hard currency, especially at hotels or car rental companies, although they can be used to withdraw cash at ATMs.

Automated teller machine (ATM), open 24 hours a day

Banks and Foreign Currency Exchanges

Bank opening times vary throughout the Southwest, but generally they are open between 9 or 10am and 5 or 6pm. Banks in the larger centers will change foreign currency and traveler's checks, but branches in small towns may not provide this service.

Credit, Charge, and Debit Cards

Credit and charge cards are practically essential when traveling in the US. The cards are accepted as a guarantee when renting a car (see p290), and are used to book tickets for most forms of entertainment. The most widely used cards are **VISA**, **American Express**, **MasterCard**, and **Diners Club**.

All credit, charge, and debit cards can be used to withdraw money from an ATM. These are usually found at banks, train and bus stations, airports, and

convenience stores. Withdrawing cash on a debit card costs less than doing it on a credit or charge card. The most common international systems are Cirrus and Plus. Ask both your own bank and credit card company which ATM system your card can access, and how much you will be charged for transactions of differing amounts. Withdrawals from ATMs may provide a better foreign currency exchange rate than cash transactions.

American Express charge cards

Wiring Money

If you need extra cash, have the money wired from your bank at home in minutes using an electronic money service. Cash can be wired to major bank branches or to any Western Union or American Express Moneygram outlet.

Currency

American currency, based on the decimal system, has 100 cents to the dollar. Bills are all the same size and color, so check the number before paying. Smaller denominations are preferred in small towns and remote gas stations.

Large $500–10,000 bills are no longer printed but are still legal tender, usually found in the hands of collectors. The 25-cent piece is useful for public telephones and Las Vegas slot machines. Always carry cash for tips, public transport, and taxis.

Traveler's Checks

Some visitors prefer to carry traveler's checks rather than cash, as they can be replaced if lost or stolen. This is less of a problem now that it is easy to obtain cash from ATMs thus avoiding the need to carry large amounts of cash, but it is not a bad idea to take some traveler's checks. Be sure to have your checks issued in US dollars rather than in the currency of your own country. Foreign currency checks can be cashed at large banks or major hotels, but you are unlikely to get a reasonable exchange rate, while checks in US dollars are accepted as readily as cash in many restaurants, hotels, and stores, so long as you have your passport with you.

Bank of Colorado building in the town of Durango

Coins

American coins come in 50-, 25-, 10-, 5-, and 1-cent pieces. Gold-tone $1 coins, though rarely in use, are in circulation, as are the State quarters, which feature a historical scene on one side. Each value of coin has a popular name: 25-cent pieces are called quarters, 10-cent pieces are called dimes, 5-cent pieces called nickels, and 1-cent pieces called pennies.

25-cent coin
(a quarter)

10-cent coin
(a dime)

5-cent coin
(a nickel)

1-cent coin
(a penny)

Bank Notes (Bills)

Units of currency in the United States are dollars and cents. There are 100 cents to a dollar. Notes come in $1, $5, $10, $20, $50, and $100. The $5, $10, $20, $50, and $100 bills in circulation include security features with subtle color hues and improved color-shifting ink in the lower right hand corner of the face of each note.

1-dollar bill ($1)

5-dollar bill ($5)

10-dollar bill ($10)

20-dollar bill ($20)

50-dollar bill ($50)

100-dollar bill ($100)

Media and Communications

The United States has some of the most sophisticated communications systems in the world. Telephone, mail, and Internet services are all readily available, providing fast and efficient services to destinations both local and worldwide. As most travelers carry their own cell phones these days, it is, however, becoming harder to find public pay phones in the Southwest. Bear in mind that this is a region of remote wildernesses, such as the Four Corners and southern Utah where cell phone reception is often impossible to obtain in the canyons and wide-open spaces.

AT&T phonecards, available from local stores and vending machines

Telephones

All telephone numbers within each local area consist of seven digits. To dial long distance within the US, add a one and the three-digit area code in front of the seven-digit number. Long-distance calls are those made to any number outside the area code you are in and cost less during off-peak times, generally in the evenings and on weekends. International numbers are preceded by 011, then the country code, followed by the city code (dropping the initial 0), and the number.

Toll-free numbers, which start with the digits 800, 866, 877, or 888, are widely used in the US, offering free calls to businesses and services such as hotels and car rental and activity companies. It is seldom possible to call a toll-free number from outside the US; if you do find yourself connected, you will hear a message explaining how you will actually be charged for the call.

AT&T logo

Many hotels include free local calls in their room rates; ask when you check in. Otherwise, be warned that using a hotel telephone, especially for long distance calls, is liable to incur a heavy surcharge over usual rates.

Pay phones can still be found in some public buildings, cafés, bars, gas stations, hotels, and motels, but have the obvious disadvantages of being both expensive and requiring customers to carry and insert a large (especially for international calls) number of coins.

By far the cheapest way to communicate is to use Skype, or a similar program, in order to make free Wi-Fi calls from your phone or laptop. Alternatively, prepaid phone cards – issued both by major telephone companies such as **AT&T** and by all sorts of independent operators – are widely available from gas stations, supermarkets, and other outlets. The cards usually

operate by giving you a series of code numbers to punch into the phone, which accesses your account and tells you how much call time you have left. There are clear instructions on how to use them on each card.

Useful Dialing Codes

- To make a direct-dial call outside the local area code, but within the US or Canada, dial **1** then the area code: Utah **435** (**801** for the Salt Lake City area); Las Vegas **702**; New Mexico (**505** for Albuquerque & Santa Fe area, **575** for rest of state); Arizona (**520** in the south, **928** in the north, **602**, **623** or **480** for the Phoenix area); Colorado **970**.
- To make an international direct-dial call, dial **011** and the appropriate country code. Then dial the area code, omitting the first 0, followed by the local number.
- To make an international call via the operator, dial **01** and then follow the same procedure above.
- For international operator assistance, dial **01**.
- For local operator assistance, dial **0**.
- For international directory inquiries, dial **00**.
- For local directory inquiries, dial **411**.
- For emergency police, fire, or ambulance services, dial **911**.
- **800**, **866**, **877**, and **888** area codes indicate a toll-free number.

Virtually every cell phone functions in Las Vegas

Cell Phones and Internet Access

The most prevalent cell phone service providers are AT&T, Verizon, and Sprint. Any modern cell phone will be able to connect to a local network as long as "roaming" has been activated on your phone. However, it is essential to check with your home provider what charges you may incur in the US, not only for making and receiving calls and texts, but, especially, for browsing the Internet and downloading information.

It is also possible to rent or purchase a cheap cell phone while on vacation in the US; prepaid cell phones can be bought for as little as $10, and 30 minutes of airtime for an additional $10.

Almost every hotel provides Wi-Fi access in its rooms, thus making it possible to use a program such as Skype to make free calls. In Las Vegas the "resort fees" charged by the big hotels, of as much as $25 per day, cover Wi-Fi among other amenities, but elsewhere Wi-Fi is usually free. Most towns hold at least one coffee shop offering a free Wi-Fi connection, while shopping malls, university hangouts, and libraries also provide free or inexpensive Internet access.

Mail Services

Within the US all regular mail is the same "class" and generally takes between one and five days to arrive. The correct zip (postal) code usually ensures a swifter delivery.

International mail sent by air can take between five and ten days to arrive, but parcels that are sent by surface mail may take as long as four to six weeks. There are two special parcel services run by the federal mail: Priority Mail promises faster delivery than regular mail, while the more expensive Express Mail guarantees next day delivery within the US and up to 72 hours delivery for international packages.

Several private international delivery services offer swift, next-day delivery for overseas mail, the best known being **FedEx**, **UPS**, and **DHL**.

All the major cities have a main post office as well as several local offices. In addition, there are post offices in airports, grocery stores, and drugstores.

US mailbox

If you have the correct value of postage stamps, both letters and parcels can be mailed in any one of the many mailboxes dotted around every town. These are generally dark blue and have the collection times posted on them. Any hotel will also be happy to place your mail in their outgoing mailbox. It is also possible to buy postage stamps from convenience stores, vending machines, and in most hotels.

Newspapers, Television, and Radio

The best-selling daily papers country-wide are the *Wall Street Journal*, *New York Times*, *USA Today*, and *Los Angeles Times*, which cover the country as a whole. However, there is a wide selection of local newspapers available at even the smallest town in the region, and these are invaluable for local information. Visitor centers also often carry free papers detailing local news, events, and weather conditions; they may also contain discount vouchers for local attractions.

Various radio stations offer local news bulletins and weather forecasts. National Public Radio is a good source of commercial-free news and entertainment, and is usually located along the FM band.

The US is famous for having a multitude of TV channels, provided by the four networks – ABC, CBS, FOX, and NBC – as well as many cable channels including magazine programs, sitcoms, cartoons, and special Spanish language channels. Most hotel and motel rooms provide at least the network channels (which all have local services), as well as PBS, the public subscription channel (with no commercials), and Cable News Network (CNN). Other popular cable channels include Home Box Office (HBO), which shows movies and entertainment shows. Most daily newspapers provide network program times, and hotel rooms are often equipped with local television schedules.

DIRECTORY

AT&T
Tel (212) 387-5400.

DHL
Tel (800) 225-5345.

FedEx
Tel (800) 463-3339.

UPS
Tel (800) 742-5877.

Reading the paper over coffee in a southwestern café

TRAVEL INFORMATION

Phoenix, Salt Lake City, and Las Vegas are the main gateways for international visitors arriving in the Southwest by air. There are other major airports at Albuquerque and El Paso, Texas, which serve as entry points to the region. Visitors also arrive by car, long-distance bus or, less frequently, by Amtrak train. However, the US is a nation devoted to driving, and the automobile remains the preferred mode of transport for those touring the Southwest. The highways here are well-maintained, gas inexpensive, and the cars air conditioned. Even in the centers of the major cities here, public transportation tends to be the least favored option. The only inter-city train is the Rail Runner *(see p289)*, which runs from Albuquerque to Santa Fe. The city bus networks that do exist are aimed at commuters, and so offer minimal service on evenings and weekends.

Las Vegas's McCarran airport with close-up view of the Luxor *(see p110)*

Arriving by Air

Unlike many other American destinations, there are few non-stop flights into the Southwest from outside the US. Most visitors will have to connect via one of the country's major hubs such as Los Angeles, San Francisco, Chicago, or Dallas airports. Travelers from Pacific countries generally change at Honolulu, Hawaii. Las Vegas, however, is served by an increasing number of direct international flights each year, including services from London on **Virgin Atlantic** and **British Airways**, and several flights from Japan and Southeast Asia. Otherwise, those carriers that fly directly to the Southwest tend to arrive at either Phoenix or Salt Lake City. Major international airlines offering direct flights into those cities include **British Airways**, **Air Canada**, and **Aero Mexico**.

Each state in the Southwest has a major airport, as well as some smaller ones, and a range of airlines here offer connecting flights to and from cities and towns across the country *(see directory box)*. The largest airport in the region is Phoenix's Sky Harbor International, which has three terminals and receives the bulk of domestic arrivals. Phoenix is also a center for major American airlines offering both international and domestic routes, including **American Airlines**, **Delta Airlines**, **Frontier Airlines**, **Grand Canyon Airlines**, **Skywest Airlines**, **Southwest Airlines**, **United Airlines**, and **US Airways**. From Phoenix, US Airways flies to Tucson, Sedona, and Yuma. Albuquerque Sunport International airport is a base for **Southwest**, which is the city's biggest carrier. **New Mexico Airlines** services small cities across New Mexico. Tucson International Airport in southern Arizona flies to Mexico City, but most travelers to and from abroad have to connect at a larger airport. Although there are immigration and customs here, there are no

Skywest Airlines logo

Airport	Information	Distance to City Center	Travel Time by Road
Phoenix	**Tel** (602) 273-3300.  **skyharbor.com**	4 miles (6.4 km)	15 minutes
Las Vegas	**Tel** (702) 261-5211. 🆆 **mccarran.com**	2.5 miles (4 km)	10 minutes
Albuquerque	**Tel** (505) 244-7700. 🆆 **cabq.gov/airport**	5 miles (8 km)	20 minutes
El Paso	**Tel** (915) 780-4749. 🆆 **elpasointernational airport.com**	5 miles (8 km)	20 minutes
Tucson	**Tel** (520) 573-8100. 🆆 **flytucson.com**	8 miles (12.8 km)	30 minutes

money-changing facilities inside the airport. El Paso airport is a base for several Southwestern airlines, including US Airways, and provides links with Tucson, Phoenix, and Albuquerque, among other destinations.

Visitors rarely choose to travel to southern Utah by air, but there is a small airfield near Moab (see p145). In the Four Corners, the largest airport is the Durango-La Plata County Airport serviced by Frontier Airlines, United Airlines, and US Airways. The nearest airport to Mesa Verde National Park (see pp184–5) is the tiny Cortez-Montezuma Airport, served by **Great Lakes Airlines**.

Airport official unloading bags from a tourist flight

International Arrivals

If you are arriving at one of the major Southwestern airports, and you are not a US citizen or resident, you must present your passport and visa to the immigration officials before claiming your baggage. If you are catching a connecting flight, you will have to pick up your baggage at the first point of entry and check it on to your final destination. Completed customs declaration forms are also given to immigration officials on arrival. Adult non-residents are permitted to bring in a limited number of duty-free goods. These include 0.2 gallons (1 liter) of alcohol,

200 cigarettes, 50 cigars (but not Cuban), and up to $100 worth of gifts. Cash amounts over $10,000 must be declared, but there is no legal limit on the amount of money that can be brought into the US.

The major airports offer a good range of services. Car rental, shuttle bus, and taxi services are plentiful, and most terminals offer facilities for the disabled.

Air Fares

There is an array of fare types and prices available for travel to and around the Southwest. If you are traveling from outside the US, research the market well in advance, as the least expensive tickets are booked early, especially for travel during busy seasons, which are between June and September, and around the Christmas and Thanksgiving holidays.

Although there are several websites offering bargains on last-minute bookings, such as telme.com, or lastminute.com, direct flights to the Southwest are more likely to be booked in advance through an airline or travel agent. Agents are a good source of information on the latest bargains and ticket restrictions. They may also offer special deals to those booking rental cars, accommodations, and domestic flights in addition to their international ticket. Fly-drive deals, where the cost of the ticket includes car rental, are generally also a lower-priced option.

It is usually less expensive to book an APEX (Advanced Purchase Excursion) fare, which must be bought no less than seven days in advance. However, these tickets impose such restrictions as a minimum (usually seven days) and a maximum (three to six months) length of stay. It can also be difficult to alter dates of flights after purchase, and you should consider insuring yourself against delays or cancellations.

DIRECTORY

Airline Carriers (US Contact Numbers)

Aero Mexico
Tel (800) 237-6639.
W aeromexico.com

Air Canada
Tel (888) 247-2262.
W aircanada.com

American Airlines
Tel (800) 433-7300.
W aa.com

British Airways
Tel (800) 247-9297.
W britishairways.com

Delta Airlines
Tel (800) 221-1212.
W delta.com

Frontier Airlines
Tel (800) 432-1359.
W flyfrontier.com

Grand Canyon Airlines
Tel (866) 235-9422.
W grandcanyonairlines.com

Great Lakes Airlines
Tel (800) 554-5111.
W flygreatlakes.com

New Mexico Airlines
Tel (888) 564-6119.
W pacificwings.com/nma/nm/

Skywest Airlines
Tel (435) 634-3400.
W skywest.com

Southwest Airlines
Tel (800) 435-9792.
W southwest.com

United Airlines
Tel (800) 241-6522.
W united.com

US Airways
Tel (800) 428-4322.
W usairways.com

Virgin Atlantic
Tel (800) 862-8621.
W virgin-atlantic.com

Baggage Restrictions

International and domestic passengers are usually allowed two bags each with an average weight of 50 lb (23 kg), plus one piece of hand luggage. On smaller domestic or sightseeing flights on light aircraft, only one piece of hand luggage is accepted. Size restrictions also apply on some airlines, so check before you travel.

Traveling by Train and Bus

Although most visitors to the Southwest arrive by plane, and then travel around the region by car, there is also an extensive network of train and bus routes. Long-distance buses connect all the major cities, offering a wider choice of destinations than Amtrak trains, which simply cross the region along three separate east–west corridors. While it is possible to visit most cities using public transport – for example by catching a bus to Phoenix or a train to Albuquerque, and then using those cities' light rail and local bus systems – few of the region's national parks can even be reached by train or bus, let alone explored in depth. Away from the cities, the only real option for visitors who are keen to get out into the wilderness, but not drive themselves, is to book an organized tour, whether as a day's outing from a nearby town, or a multi-day itinerary.

Amtrak booking desk for train tickets in the Southwest

Traveling by Train

The sad decline of railroad travel in the US has left only a few lines, run by **Amtrak**, which cross the Southwest traveling east and west across the country. Visitors can no longer make the epic, non-stop journey from New York in the east to Los Angeles in the west, but the evocatively named *Southwest Chief* runs daily between Chicago and Los Angeles, stopping at the village of Lamy, near Santa Fe, and at Albuquerque, before heading west, via Navajo and Hopi country at Winslow and Gallup, to Flagstaff. From Flagstaff, Amtrak has a connecting bus service to Grand Canyon, and a bus from Lamy takes passengers into Santa Fe. Two other Amtrak services cross the area covered in this book. The *California Zephyr* begins in Chicago and follows a more northerly route to San Francisco, stopping at Green River in southern Utah,

which lies 40 miles (64 km) northwest of Moab and the attractions of Arches and Canyonlands national parks. The *Sunset Limited* service travels from Miami through Texas and along the southern sections of New Mexico and Arizona. Southwest stops on this service include El Paso, Tucson (which has a connecting bus service to Phoenix), and Yuma. All three trains are Amtrak Superliners, which means they have two-tier cars with a choice of accommodations from luxurious cabins with bathrooms to sleeping recliner chairs. The trains also possess full-length domed windows on the upper level for viewing the spectacular scenery, as well as lounge, restaurant, and snack cars.

Specialty Trips

There are three railroad trips on historic rail stock that offer visitors the chance to enjoy some of the region's most delightful scenery. The **Cumbres and Toltec Scenic Railroad**, runs between Chama, New Mexico (*see p207*) and Antonito, Colorado through 64 miles (103 km) of peaks, tunnels, and gorges on a narrow gauge steam locomotive during the summer months. Colorado's **Durango & Silverton Narrow Gauge Railroad** (*see p183*) travels through the foothills of the Rockies past rugged mining country, often including abandoned machinery and wooden shacks, while the **Grand Canyon Railway** offers both diesel and steam rail trips from Williams (*see p74*) to Grand Canyon. The trip takes a little over two hours and offers packages including meals and overnight accommodations at the canyon and features Western entertainments – including a posse of bad guys staging an attack on the train.

Durango & Silverton Narrow Gauge Railroad train

Greyhound bus crossing southwestern desert landscape

Long-Distance Buses

The major bus company in the US is **Greyhound**. Along with a few affiliated companies, it links almost all the major and many of the smaller towns and cities across the Southwest region. Greyhound buses also provide essential links with the major airports and Amtrak services. The Amtrak Thruway is a bus service connecting train stops with the major cities. For example, a bus service takes passengers from the *Southwest Chief* train at Flagstaff on to Phoenix.

Some of the most useful links operate from airports. From Albuquerque, Greyhound provides routes to Durango, Carlsbad, Farmington, and Roswell. From Phoenix's Sky Harbor airport, there are 27 different daily routes throughout Arizona, as well as eight daily trips direct to its second city, Tucson.

Greyhound and a number of other specialist companies, including **Gray Line Tucson** also offer package tours, which can provide a more leisurely way of sightseeing in the area without the need to drive long distances. Everything from national parks such as Grand Canyon to archaeological attractions such as Chaco Canyon can be seen as part of a comfortable tour on luxury, air-conditioned buses, and the package also includes meals and accommodation. Check local papers or the Yellow Pages telephone directory for listings of other bus and coach companies that provide similar services.

Tickets and Bookings

In general, both Amtrak and Greyhound tickets should be booked in advance. Not only does this usually mean less expensive fares but you will also be guaranteed a seat. Through Greyhound you can also get Ameripasses, which are discounted tickets valid for varying lengths of time from 7 to 60 days. Discounts are available for children under 12, students, seniors, military families, and veterans.

Reservations are essential on long-distance Amtrak Superliner services operating in the Southwest, and can be made up to 11 months in advance of the trip. Lower fares are available during off-peak times, between January and mid-May and from mid-September through mid-December.

Public Transportation in Cities

With the exceptions of Santa Fe and Flagstaff, which are best explored on foot, the major cities of the Southwest, such as Phoenix and Albuquerque, cover large areas and are increasingly plagued by traffic problems. In these places you might want to consider using some form of public transport.

Albuquerque's metropolitan bus system, **Sun Tran**, covers most parts of the city, including the airport, Old Town, and University District *(see pp214– 19)*. New Mexico's **Rail Runner Express** connects Albuquerque and Santa Fe, with connections for the Sunport International Airport in Albuquerque. In Phoenix, the **Metro Light Rail** system passes through the heart of Downtown as part of its 20-mile (32-km) run from Camelback Road to the outlying areas of Tempe and Mesa, while Downtown Phoenix also has the convenient and free **Downtown Dash**, which travels between the State Capitol, Arizona Center, and the Civic

Valley Metro bus in Phoenix

Plaza from Monday to Friday. Phoenix, Scottsdale, and the rest of the Valley of the Sun are covered by the **Valley Metro** bus system, and **Ollie the Trolley** is a bus service that runs between Scottsdale's resorts and its many shopping districts.

Traveling by Car and Four-Wheel Drive

When the movie characters Thelma and Louise won a kind of freedom on the open roads of the Southwest, they promoted the pleasures of driving in this visually spectacular region. However, for both residents and visitors, driving is a necessary part of life in the US, particularly in the Southwest, and a car is often the only means of reaching re- mote country areas. Tours of such picturesque regions as central Arizona *(see p75)*, the Enchanted Circle *(see p211)* in New Mexico, or the San Juan Skyway in Colorado *(see p182)* are best made by car. This is possible because the entire region is served by a network of well-maintained roads, from multilane highways to winding, scenic routes.

Spectacular mountain scenery along the San Juan Highway

Renting a Car

Visitors from abroad must have a full driver's license that has been issued for at least a year before the date of travel. International Driving Licenses are not necessary, but they can be helpful if your license is in a script other than Roman. Although it is legal to rent a car to those over the age of 21, some rental companies charge extra to those under 25. It is also essential to have a credit card to pay the rental deposit.

Hertz car-rental logo

There are rental car companies all over the Southwest. Most of the major businesses, such as **Alamo**, **Avis**, and **Hertz**, and some of the budget dealers, such as **Dollar Rent-A-Car**, and **Thrifty**, have outlets at airports and in towns and cities across the region. However, if you are planning to arrive at one of the major hubs such as Las Vegas or Phoenix, the least expensive option is to arrange a fly-drive deal. If you depart from a different airport than the one you arrived at you may be charged a drop-off fee.

Most of the car companies operate a centralized computer booking system, so use the website or toll-free number to find the best rates. Bargains can also be had by booking in advance and for travel during off season. Rates vary from state to state, and there may be deals for business travelers, frequent flyers, or members of the **American Automobile Association** (AAA or Triple A.) Always be aware that the cheapest rates do not always mean the best deal. Check that the price includes unlimited mileage and basic liability insurance, which is a legal requirement and covers any damage to another car. There is also a rental tax of 10 percent. Collision damage waiver saves you from being charged for any visible defects on the car. Choose if possible to return the car with a full tank of gas, and leave plenty of time to complete any formalities.

If you are traveling in summer air conditioning is a necessity. Most rental cars have automatic transmission, although some companies offer a stick shift. Child seats or cars for disabled drivers must be arranged in advance.

Rules of the Road

The major highways in the US are known popularly as either Freeways or Interstates. Highway speed limits are set by each state. In the Southwest the speed limit on the major highways varies between 55 mph (90 km/h) and 75 mph (120 km/h). The Highway Patrol imposes these rules rigorously, and anyone caught speeding will be fined. In cities and in small towns especially, watch for signs indicating the speed limit as it can vary from 45 mph (75 km/h) to as little as 15 mph (35 km/h) in school zones.

Speed limit (in mph)

Rest area indicated off an Interstate

Wildlife warning

Stop at intersection

Traffic flows in a single direction

Traffic signs

A range of different traffic signs offer warnings and instructions to drivers and should be adhered to.

Gas service station on the legendary Route 66 *(see pp54–5)*

(Note that it is illegal to pass a stationary school bus.) Heed road signs, especially in remote areas where they may issue

warnings about local hazards. Heavy penalties are exacted from those who drink and drive, and the alcohol limit is low.

Get information on US traffic rules from your rental company or the AAA. Some rules may seem strange to foreigners. For example, you can turn right on a red light if there is no oncoming traffic, and the first vehicle to reach a Stop sign junction has the right of way. Americans also drive on the right. The AAA provides maps and may offer help to those affiliated with foreign motoring clubs.

Back Country Byway sign

Gas and Service Stations

Gas is relatively cheap in the US, but prices do vary, with service stations in remote areas being more expensive. It is sold not by the liter, as in Europe, but by the US gallon, equivalent to 1.2 UK gallons or 3.8 liters. Service stations are usually self-service, with payment at the pump. If you are using a non-US credit card, you may have to pay inside the station before you fill up. If you are planning a long trip, be aware that gas stations can be less common than many

visitors expect, so fill your tank before driving across remote areas.

Backcountry Driving

For travel in remote parts of the Southwest such as southern Utah's canyon country or the desert regions of Arizona and New Mexico, it is very important to check your route to see if a 4WD-vehicle is required. Although some backcountry areas now have roads able to carry conventional cars, a 4WD is essential in some wild and remote areas. Grand Staircase–Escalante National Monument *(see p152)*, for example, intends to maintain its environment by prohibiting further road building. Motoring organizations and tourist centers can provide information to assess your trip.

There are basic safety points to be observed on any trip of

Unimproved road sign in Utah's Kodachrome Basin *(see p152)*

DIRECTORY

Car Rental Companies

Alamo
Tel (888) 233-8749.
W alamo.com

Avis
Tel (800) 331-1212.
W avis.com

Budget
Tel (800) 527-0700.
W budget.com

Dollar Rent-A-Car
Tel (800) 800-4000.
W dollar.com

Hertz
Tel (800) 654-3131.
W hertz.com

Thrifty
Tel (800) 847-4389.
W thrifty.com

Useful Organizations

American Automobile Association
742 E. Glendale Ave. #182, Phoenix 85027. **Tel** (602) 285-6241. W aaaaz.com

this kind. Plan your route and carry up-to-date maps. When traveling between remote destinations, inform the police or park wardens of your departure and expected arrival times. Check road conditions before you start, and be aware of seasonal dangers such as flash floods in Utah's canyonlands. Carry plenty of food and water, and a cell (mobile) phone as an added precaution. If you run out of gas or break down, stay with your vehicle since it offers protection from the elements. If you fail to arrive at the expected time, a search party will look for you.

Native flora and fauna must not be removed or damaged. Do not drive off-road, unless in a specially designated area and especially not on reservation land. If driving an RV, you must stop overnight in designated campgrounds.

General Index

Acknowledgments

Dorling Kindersley would like to thank the following people whose contributions and assistance have made the preparation of this book possible.

Main Contributors
Donna Dailey is a writer and photographer who has traveled extensively throughout the Southwest and the Rockies. She has written guidebooks to Denver, Los Angeles, the American West, Kenya, Scotland, and Greece.

Paul Franklin is a travel writer and photographer specializing in the United States and Canada. He is the author of several guide books and magazine articles, and is based in Washington.

Michelle de Larrabeiti is a writer and editor who has traveled widely in the United States, Europe, and Asia. Based in London, she has worked on several Dorling Kindersley travel guides.

Philip Lee is a veteran travel writer and is the author of numerous articles and travel books about countries throughout the world. He has traveled widely, particularly in the United States, Canada, and Europe.

Additional Contributors
Randa Bishop, Eric Grossman, Greg Ward.

For Dorling Kindersley
Senior Revisions Editor: Esther Labi
Publishing Manager: Jane Ewart
Senior Designer: Marisa Renzullo
Director of Publishing: Gillian Allan
Revisions Editor: Sherry Collins
Production: Marie Ingledew
Map Co-ordinators: Casper Morris, Dave Pugh

Revisions Team
Claire Baranowski, Bob Barnes, Marta Bescos Sanchez, Tessa Bindloss, Caroline Elliker, Mariana Evmolpidou, Anna Freiberger, Camilla Gersh, Swati Gupta, Sophie Jonathan, Laura Jones, Kathryn Lane, Hayley Maher, Nancy Mikula, Sonal Modha, George Nimmo, Catherine Palmi, Marianne Petrou, Pete Quinlan, Rada Radojicic, Tarini Singh, Ellen Root, Zoë Ross, Sands Publishing Solutions, Brett Steel, Rachel Symons, Roseen Teare, Conrad Van Dyk, Ros Walford.

Additional Picture Research
Rachel Barber, Rhiannon Furbear, Susie Peachey.

Additional Photography
Steve Gorton, Dave King, Andrew McKinney, Neil Mersh, Ian O'Leary, Tim Ridley, Clive Streeter.

Cartography
Ben Bowles, Rob Clynes, Mohammed Hassan, Sam Johnston, James Macdonald (Colourmap Scanning Ltd).

Fact Checking
Eileen Bailey, Alan Chan, Jessica Hughes, Lynn Kidder, Marshall Trimble, Barney Vinson, Greg Ward.

Proof Reader
Sam Merrell

Indexer
Hilary Bird

Special Assistance
Many thanks for the invaluable help of the following individuals: Margaret Archuleta, Heard Museum; Myram Borders, Las Vegas CVA; Jennifer Franklin; Phoenix CVB; Louann C. Jordan, El Rancho de las Golondrinas; Ken Kraus, Utah Travel Council; Joyce Leonsanders, Albuquerque CVB; Steve Lewis, Santa Fe CVB; Jean McKnight, Tucson CVB; Rekha Parthasarathy, Arizona Office of Tourism; Pat Reck, Indian Pueblo Cultural Center; Gary Romero, New Mexico Department of Tourism; Theresa Valles Jepson, Flagstaff CVB; Charles B. Wahler, Grand Canyon National Park; and all the national park staff in the region.

Photography Permissions
Dorling Kindersley would like to thank all the cathedrals, churches, museums, hotels, restaurants, shops, galleries, national and state parks, and other sights for their assistance and kind permission to photograph at their establishments.

Placement Key - a=above; b=below/bottom; c=center; f=far; l=left; r=right; t=top.

Works of art and images have been produced with the permission of the following copyright holders: Capitol Art Foundation, Santa Fe, New Mexico, Capitol Art Collection Holly Hughes *Buffalo* 1992 mixed media sculpture 74" x 50" x 25" 203c;

courtesy of Kit Carson Historic Museum 32c/bl, 208cl/cr, 210t; courtesy of the Frank Lloyd Wright Foundation 27br, 85b; Museum of Indian Arts and Cultures/Laboratory of Anthropology, Museum of New Mexico, 44857/12 Ceramic Figurine, Cochiti Pueblo ca. 1885 201tr.

The publishers would like to thank the following individuals, companies, and picture libraries for their kind permission to reproduce their photographs:

Alamy Images: Tibor Bognar 120tl; Ian G Dagnall 107tr; Danita Delimont/Walter Bibikow 247tl, 262crb; Patrick Eden 109bl; Alan Hanson 262cr; pictures-byrob/fc1 246cl Ben Ramos 203br; **Albuquerque Convention & Visitors Bureau:** Albuquerque Museum of Art & History 217tl; **Arizona Office of Tourism**: Chris Coe 54tr; **Arizona State Library:** Archive+Public Records, Archive Division, Phoenix no.99–0281 40; **Arizona State Parks:** K L Day 97tc; **Associated Press:** 39bl, 100bl, Roy Dabner 266br; Louisa Gauerke 55tl; Mickey Krakowski 37bl; Julia Malakie 49crb; LDouglas C. Pizac 35t; Susan Sterner 37tl; **AT&T Inc.:** 284cb; **AURA/NOAO/National Science Foundation:** 95br; **Aureole:** Charlie Palmer Group 253tc..

George Billingsley: 56br. **Bridgeman Art Library:** Christie's London Walter Ufer (1876–1936) *The Southwest* 8–9; Private Collection/Index Frederic Remington (1861–1909) *The Conversation or Dubious Company* 1902 58bl; Museum of Fine Arts Houston, Texas, USA, Hogg Brothers Collection, Gift of Miss Ima Hogg, Frederic Remington (1861–1909) *Aiding a Comrade* c.1890 58–9; University of Michigan, Museum of Art, USA Charles Ferdinand Wimar (1829–63) *The Attack on the Emigrant Train* 1856 46–7.

Caesars Entertainment: 105tr, 107br; **Cafe Diablo:** 256bc; **Capitol Reef Cafe:** 256tl; **Capriotti's:** 252tl; **El Chorro:** 250bl; **Church Street Cafe:** 260tc; **Compound Restaurant:** 259br; **Corbis:** 29t, 42cr, 45crb, 47tl, 47br, 49tr, 101crb, 140tr, 207tr, James L. Amos 176t; Tom Bean 157br, 165cr, 285br; Patrick Bennett 287cl; Bettmann 43cb/bc, 46cl, 46br, 47t, 48c, 58cb, 100cl, 101tr, 107bl, 140bl, 175bc, 191tr, 229tl, 231br; Jan Butchofsky-Houser 30c; Richard A. Cooke 42cla; Ian Dagnall Commercial Collection 113tr; Tim Fitzharris/Minden Pictures 60; Raymond Gehman 157tc; Blaine Harrington III 274–5; Lindsay Hebberd 232-3; Aaron Horowitz 223t; H. H. HneyLiz 219bc; Hymans 165tl; Dewitt Jones 164tr; Wolfgang Kaehler 210bl; Catherine Karnow 108bl;

Danny Lehman 193br; Buddy Mays 279cl; Joe McDonald 91tr; David Muench 24cr, 157crb, 164–5; Richard T Nowitz 286cla; Pat O'Hara 56bl; Charles E Rotkin 101cla; Phil Schermeister 36bl; Baldwin H Ward + Kathryn C. Ward 190–91; Patrick Ward 141br; Ron Watts 68-9; Nevada Wier 263tr; Adam Woolfitt 266cla. **Cottage Place:** 248bl.

Diana Dicker: 31c, 164b; © Mrs. Anna Marie Houser/The Allan Houser Foundation 33tr; **Discovery Children's Museum:** 123tl; **Dreamstime. com:** Hasan Can Balcioglu 14cla; Archana Bhartia 15br; Cecoffman 13br; Chaitanyo 211cla; Songquan Deng 102; Gelyngfjell 50-1; Enrique Gomez 239tr; Phillip Gray 10cla; Golasza 13tr; Erikamit 224-5; Johnbell 15tc; Lilyling1982 142; Littleny 116-7; Juan Moyano 12bc; Lvphotog1 98-9; Paul Moore 160-1; Nytumbleweeds 78; Photoquest 125br, 240tr; Jennifer Pitiquen 12tr; Beatrice Preve 136-7; Ronalesa Schneider 166; Kenny Tong 2-3; Charles Underwood 10bc; Vacclav 119tc; Volgariver 106tr Minyun Zhou 180-1.

EFX: 130br; **Egg & I:** 252br; **Elote Cafe:** 249tl; **Enchantment Group:** 237tl. **Mary Evans Picture Library:** 46tr.

Feast Restaurant: 251tr; **Paul Franklin:** 67tr.

Geronimo Restaurant: 259tr; **Getty Images:** Philippe Crochet 148-9; David W. Hamilton 18; Photographer's Choice/Gavin Hellier 11clb. **Goulding Lodge:** 169br; **Grand Canyon Caverns:** 54br; **Grand Canyon Railway:** 64br; **Ronald Grant Archive:** MGM 35br; Paramount Pictures 35cr; Universal Pictures 34br; courtesy **Greyhound Lines, Inc:** 289tl; **Greater Phoenix Convention & Visitors Bureau:** 80.

Robert Harding Picture Library: age fotostock 129bc; Geoff Renner 138cl; Nerda Westwater 37tr, 193tr; **Heard Museum:** 82tr, 83b; 83crb; Fred Harvey Collection 83cla; **Heritage Hotels and Resorts:** Hotel Encanto 243tl; **Dave G Houser:** 36cra, 227tl; Ellen Barone 38; Rankin Harvey 39tc; **Hulton Getty Collection:** 190br.

Image Bank, London: Archive Photos 101br; **Impact Photos:** Jacqui Spector 54bl.

Jubilee: 130cra.

Kirvan Doak Communications: 106cl; **Kobal Collection, London:** Hollywood Pictures/Cinergi 35clb; MGM Cinerama 34cra; MGM/PATHE 34crb; Paramount Pictures 59br; RKO 35cla; United Artists 34bl.

Las Vegas Visitors' News Bureau: 100cra, 101clb, 108tr; **Lonely Planet Images:** John Hay 264br.

MGM Mirage: 108ca; **Mining Camp Restaurant:** 249br; **Moab Brewery:** 255tc; **Museum of Church History and Art,** Salt Lake City: American Publishing Co. 141t; © by Intellectual Reserve, Inc CCA Christensen *Handcart Company* 1900 oil on canvas 140–41; **Museum of International Folk Art, a unit of the Museum of New Mexico:** Charles D. Carroll Bequest, Photo Blair Clark *Nuestra Señora de los Dolores/Our Lady of Sorrows* (A.78.93–1) Arroyo Hondo Carver, New Mexico 1830–50 200b; Girard Foundation Collection, Photo Michel Monteaux *Baptism* by the Aguilar family, Octolan de Morelos, Oaxaca, Mexico C.1960 200tr, *Toy Horse* Bangladesh, Indian.C.1960. 201tl; Neutrogena Collection, Photo Pat Pollard *Yogi (Bridal Sleeping Cover)* Probably Kyushu Island, Western Japan. 19th century. 200c; courtesy of the **Museum of New Mexico:** Fray Orci *Portrait of Don Juan Bautista de Anza* 1774 neg. no. 50828 44br(d); **Museum of Spanish Colonial Art:** 1997.10 Jar (Olla), micaceous Clay, 1997, by Jacobo de la Serna, Alcade, New Mexico. 192tr.

NASA: 49br, 191cr; **The New Tropicana Las Vegas:** 112br; **NHPA:** Stephen Dalton 231tl; Stephen Kraseman 25bl; David Middleton 25bc; Rod Planck 24clb; Andy Rouse 25tr; John Shaw 25cr/br, 94br; courtesy of the **National Park Service, Chaco Culture National Historic Park:** 165br; Dave Six 164cb; **Peter Newark Pictures:** 28c, 29cr/br, 43tr, 47cr, 48t/bl, 58cla, 59tl, 140cl, 141cr.

Georgia O'Keeffe Museum: Gift of the Burnett Foundation ©ARS, NY and DACS, London. 2011. Georgia O'Keeffe *Jimson Weed* 1932 198c; **Oscar's Cafe:** 255br.

Papillon Grand Canyon Helicopters: 127br; **Patina Restaurant Group:** Wagstaff Worldwide 254tl; **Phantom Ranch:** 236bl; Courtesy of **Phoenix Art Museum:** Bill Timmerman 81br; **Photoshot:** Art

Foxall 74tr; **El Pinto, Albuquerque:** 260br; **Private Collection:** 28tr, 44crb.

Regional Transportation Commission of Southern Nevada: 126crb; **Branson Reynolds:** 31br, 282bl; **Riviera Hotel & Casino:** 109crb, 120br; **Rosewood Hotels:** Inn of the Anasazi 242bl, 258br; **John Running:** 30crb, 31cla.

Santa Fe Opera: Robert Reck 267bl; **Scottsdale CVB:** Tom Johnson 264tl; **Science Photo Library:** NASA 191tl/b; **Shevek & Co. Restaurant:** 244cla; Courtesy of **Southwest Airlines,** Texas: 287tl; **Spruce Tree Terrace Cafe:** Riester 257; **Starwood Hotels & Resorts:** The Phoenician 235tl; **Stone:** Tom Bean 39cr; Steve Lewis 55tr; Jake Rajs 100crb; Randy Wells 272tl; **Strater Hotel:** Forward Movement 241bl; **SuperStock:** Minden Pictures 186-7; National Geographic 284bl; Piumatti Sergio/Prisma 212; Spaces Images 194.

Tanque Verde Guest Ranch: 238bc; **Tumacacori National Historic Park:** Cal Peters 28br.

University of Nevada, Las Vegas Library: Courtesy of Helen J. Stewart Collection 100tr.

The View Hotel & Restaurant: R.S. Ortega.Two Worlds Photography 257tr.

Wigwam Resort: 268cr.

Yanni's: 261tr; **Yuma Convention and Visitors Bureau:** ©Robert Herko 1999 94tl.

Zinc Restaurant: 261br.

Front Endpaper - Corbis: Tim Fitzharris/Minden Pictures Lclb; **Dreamstime.com:** Songquan Deng Ltl; Paul Moore Rcra; Nytumbleweeds Lbc; Beatrice Preve Rtc; **Superstock:** Spaces Images Rcrb Piumatti Sergio/Prisma Rbc.

Jacket
Front and spine - **Masterfile:** Science Faction.

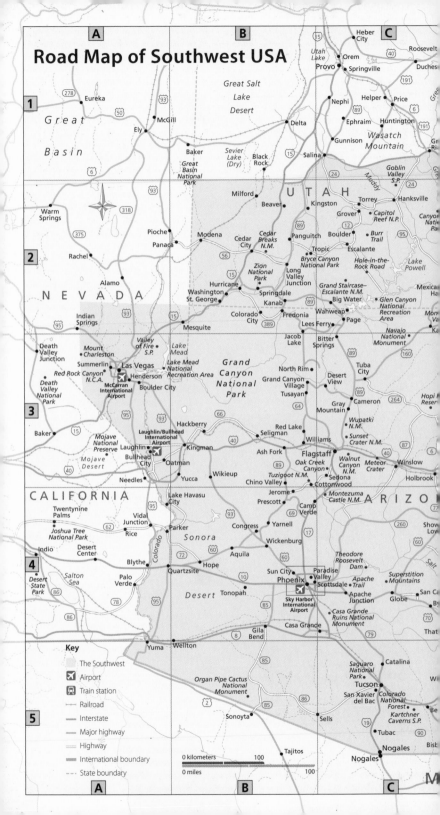